INVESTIGATING
THE PRESIDENT

~ ~ ~

INVESTIGATING THE PRESIDENT

CONGRESSIONAL CHECKS ON PRESIDENTIAL POWER

~~~

Douglas L. Kriner
and
Eric Schickler

PRINCETON UNIVERSITY PRESS
PRINCETON AND OXFORD

In the United Kingdom: Princeton University Press, 6 Oxford Street,
Woodstock, Oxfordshire OX20 1TR

press.princeton.edu

Cover photograph: Scott J. Ferrell / Congressional Quarterly / Alamy

Library of Congress Cataloging-in-Publication Data

Names: Kriner, Douglas L., author. | Schickler, Eric, 1969– author.
Title: Investigating the president : congressional checks on presidential power /
Douglas L. Kriner, Eric Schickler.
Description: Princeton, New Jersey : Princeton University Press, 2016. |
Includes bibliographical references and index.
Identifiers: LCCN 2016010111 | ISBN 9780691171852 (hardback) |
ISBN 9780691171869 (paperback)
Subjects: LCSH: Legislative oversight—United States. | Governmental
investigations—United States. | United States. Congress—Powers and duties. |
Executive power—United States. | BISAC: POLITICAL SCIENCE /
Government / Executive Branch. | POLITICAL SCIENCE /
Government / Legislative Branch.
Classification: LCC JK585 .K76 2016 | DDC 328.73/07456—dc23
LC record available at https://lccn.loc.gov/2016010111

British Library Cataloging-in-Publication Data is available

This book has been composed in Sabon

Printed on acid-free paper. ∞

Printed in the United States of America

1 3 5 7 9 10 8 6 4 2

For Jillian Goldfarb and Terri Bimes

Contents

~ ~

Tables and Figures

~ ~

Chapter 2

Appendix

CHAPTER 3

Appendix

CHAPTER 4

CHAPTER 5

Appendix

CHAPTER 6

CHAPTER 7

Acknowledgments
~ ~

WE ARE GRATEFUL for the thoughtful insights and feedback provided by many individuals who read drafts or responded to queries throughout this project. We would specifically like to thank: Dino Christenson; Linda Fowler; William Howell; Walter Oleszek; Andrew Reeves; Liam Schwartz; Rebecca Thorpe; Robert van Houweling; and our anonymous reviewers. Seminar participants at American University, Boston University, University of Houston, the American Political Science Association, and the Midwest Political Science Association provided still more valuable feedback and suggestions. The excellent research assistance of Margaret Helms, Adrienne Hosek, Ruth Bloch Rubin, Michael Dougal, and Greg Elinson is gratefully acknowledged.

For generous financial support, we thank the Dirksen Center for Congressional Research, Boston University, and the University of California, Berkeley.

Finally, we would also like to thank everyone at Princeton University Press who helped bring this project to fruition. We would specifically like to thank our editor, Eric Crahan, for his guidance throughout the project, as well as Jay Boggis, Nathan Carr, Maria DenBoer, Alexandria Leonard, and Ben Pokross.

INVESTIGATING
THE PRESIDENT

~~~

CHAPTER 1

~ ~

Introduction

IN 1944, MISSOURI senator Harry S Truman, who four years earlier had cast little shadow on the American political stage, joined Franklin Roosevelt atop the Democratic ticket as the vice-presidential candidate. What could account for the meteoric rise of a junior senator once known as a pawn of Kansas City powerbrokers like Tom Pendergast to a figure of national stature, whom the media judged to be "one of the ten most valuable officials in Washington"?[1] Strikingly, Truman built his public reputation not through legislating, but by investigating as chair of the Senate Special Committee to Investigate the National Defense Program. Truman lobbied to create the committee to discover and correct instances of fraud and abuse in government contracting and war procurement programs. While the Roosevelt administration initially resisted any move that would empower congressional snooping into its conduct of the war effort, it eventually relented, and the committee compiled an impressive record of rooting out fraud, abuse, and maladministration during its three-year history.

In a speech to the Senate upon resigning his chairmanship of the committee, Truman extolled investigations as critical to ensuring Congress's place in our separation of powers system: "In my opinion, the power of investigation is one of the most important powers of Congress. The manner in which the power is exercised will largely determine the position and prestige of the Congress in the future."[2] Writing in the immediate aftermath of the Watergate scandal, in which President Richard Nixon orchestrated a massive cover-up of illegalities committed by the Committee to Reelect the President, the historian Arthur Schlesinger Jr. echoed Truman's assessment. Indeed, Truman "could have gone further," Schlesinger argued. "The manner in which Congress exercises the investigative power will largely determine

---

[1] The ranking was by *Look* magazine. See Wilson Miscamble, *The Most Controversial Decision: Truman, the Atomic Bombs, and the Defeat of Japan* (New York: Cambridge University Press, 2011), 23.

[2] *Congressional Record*, August 7, 1944, 6747.

in years to come whether the problem posed in the *51st Federalist* can be satisfactorily answered—whether the constitutional order will in the end oblige the American government to control itself."[3]

The intervening forty years since Schlesinger wrote have produced no shortage of congressional investigations of alleged executive-branch malfeasance. Moreover, as Iran-Contra and the Monica Lewinsky scandal made clear, Richard Nixon would not be the last chief executive to fret over the very future of his presidency in the face of an investigative maelstrom on Capitol Hill. And yet, scholarly assessment of congressional investigations has been limited both in quantity and in scope. A legal literature has traced the evolution of the constitutional and legal authority underlying congressional investigations of the executive branch.[4] Historians have largely focused on the dynamics of individual investigations,[5] or traced the evolution of the investigative power over time.[6] While valuable, these studies tell us comparatively little about the extent to which Congress is able to use the investigative arm of its committees to combat the steady increase in presidential power since World War II. Finally, apart from a handful of isolated studies, political science has paid scant attention to investigations as a potential mechanism for legislative influence.[7]

---

[3] Arthur Schlesinger Jr. and Roger Burns, *Congress Investigates: A Documented History, 1792–1974* (New York: Chelsea House Publishers, 1975), xxvi.

[4] See, e.g., Nelson McGeary, *The Developments of Congressional Investigative Power* (New York: Columbia University Press, 1940); Peter Shane, "Legal Disagreement and Negotiation in a Government of Laws: The Case of Executive Privilege Claims Against Congress," *Minnesota Law Review* 71 (1987): 461–542; John Grabow, *Congressional Investigations: Law and Practice* (Clifton, NJ: Prentiss Hall Law and Business, 1988); Neal Devins, "Congressional-Executive Information Access Disputes: A Modest Proposal—Do Nothing," *Administrative Law Review* 48 (1996): 109–137; Morton Rosenberg, "Investigative Oversight: An Introduction to the Law, Practice, and Procedure of Congressional Inquiry." *CRS Report* (1995): 95–464.

[5] See, e.g., August Raymond Ogden, *The Dies Committee: A Study of the Special House Committee for the Investigation of Un-American Activities, 1938–1944* (Washington, DC: Catholic University of America Press, 1945); Donald Riddle, *The Truman Committee: A Study in Congressional Responsibility* (New Brunswick, NJ: Rutgers University Press, 1964); Arthur Schlesinger Jr. and Roger Burns, *Congress Investigates: A Documented History, 1792–1974* (New York: Chelsea House Publishers, 1975); Keith Olson, *Watergate: The Presidential Scandal that Rocked America* (Lawrence: University of Kansas Press, 2003).

[6] Telford Taylor, *Grand Inquest: The Story of Congressional Investigations* (New York: Simon and Schuster, 1955); James Hamilton, *The Power to Probe: A Study of Congressional Investigations* (New York: Vintage Books, 1976).

[7] See, e.g., David Mayhew, *Divided We Govern: Party Control, Lawmaking, and Investigations, 1946–1990* (New Haven: Yale University Press, 1991); Douglas Kriner and Liam Schwartz, "Divided Government and Congressional Investigations," *Legislative Studies Quarterly* 33 (2008): 295–321; David Parker and Matthew Dull, "Divided We Quarrel: The Politics of Congressional Investigations, 1947–2004," *Legislative Studies Quarterly* 34 (2009): 319–345; David Parker and Matthew Dull, "Rooting Out Waste, Fraud and Abuse: The Politics

Building on Truman's and Schlesinger's insight, we take seriously the idea that investigations offer Congress a valuable tool for constraining an ascendant executive. Investigations do not require the assent of both chambers, the construction of a supermajority to avoid a Senate filibuster, or the president's approval. Critically in an era of intense partisan polarization and seeming institutional dysfunction, Congress can therefore investigate when it cannot legislate. To be sure, investigations cannot, on their own, compel presidential compliance and mandate changes in public policy. Moreover, Congress's investigative zeal waxes and wanes over time depending on the mix of incentives encouraging members to expose or pass over alleged executive-branch misconduct. However, when Congress does investigate, it can focus public scrutiny on the executive branch and bring public pressure to bear on the White House in ways that can materially affect politics and policy.

Of course, investigations are a somewhat blunt instrument of counterattack. Congress does not and cannot investigate every instance of presidential aggrandizement. However, Congress can use the investigative tool to weaken the president politically. And because presidents anticipate Congress's capacity to inflict political damage, the threat of investigations can limit presidential autonomy more broadly, even if the political costs investigations impose may often be fairly general, rather than tied to reversing a specific abuse.

WHY CONGRESS CAN INVESTIGATE WHEN IT CANNOT LEGISLATE

If the constitutional framework of separation of powers sets up an "invitation to struggle" among the branches, the Congress enters the battle at a distinct disadvantage vis-à-vis the executive.[8] Despite the paucity of formal powers enumerated in Article II, presidents have repeatedly stretched the bounds of their authority by shifting policy unilaterally,[9] by tightening their control over the bureaucracy to enhance their influence over the policy

---

of House Committee Investigations, 1847 to 2004," *Political Research Quarterly* 66 (2013): 630–644; Paul Light, *Government by Investigation: Congress, Presidents, and the Search for Answers, 1945–2012* (Washington, DC: Brookings Institution Press, 2014).

[8] The historian Edward Corwin coined this description of the constitutional framework. Edward Corwin. *The President: Office and Powers* (London: H. Milford, Oxford University Press, 1940), 200.

[9] Phillip Cooper, *By Order of the President: The Use and Abuse of Executive Direct Action* (Lawrence, University of Kansas Press, 2002); Kenneth Mayer, *With the Stroke of a Pen: Executive Orders and Presidential Power* (Princeton: Princeton University Press, 2002); William Howell, *Power without Persuasion: The Politics of Direct Presidential Action* (Princeton: Princeton University Press, 2003).

implementation process,[10] and by making broad assertions of wartime power in both the international and domestic arenas.[11] The Constitution grants Congress an array of tools to defend its institutional prerogatives and restore the balance of power. Yet, while the Framers plainly believed that Congress would be the most powerful branch, Congress confronts several institutional limitations on its ability to respond to presidential power grabs.

First, as Terry Moe has stated most forcefully, Congress is beset by collective action problems.[12] Unlike the president, Congress is not a unitary actor. Rather, "Congress is made up of hundreds of members, each a political entrepreneur in his or her own right, each dedicated to his or her own reelection and thus to serving his or her district or state." While members share a stake in the power of Congress vis-à-vis the White House, "this is a collective good that . . . can only weakly motivate their behavior." By contrast, presidents are motivated to defend the power of their institution, since doing so will also directly enhance their power as individuals.[13]

Second, the legislative process is riddled with transaction costs that make it difficult for Congress to respond in a coherent fashion when its interests are threatened. Passing a bill typically requires the coordinated efforts of committees and leaders in two chambers; as a result, a supportive majority coalition is no guarantee of action. Instead, the transaction costs of putting together a coalition to fight the president are simply too great for individual members to bear, given that the benefits are shared by all members, regardless of their contribution to the collective good.

Third, even if Congress succeeds in mustering majorities in both the House and Senate behind legislation to rein in the executive, such efforts will often fail to become law. Presidential co-partisans stand poised to block any legislative initiative that cannot secure the sixty votes required to overcome a filibuster in the contemporary Senate.[14] And even if such a super-majority

[10] Terry Moe, "The Politicized Presidency," in *New Directions in American Politics*, ed. John Chubb and Paul Peterson (Washington, DC: Brookings Institution Press, 1985); David Lewis, *The Politics of Presidential Appointments: Political Control and Bureaucratic Appointments* (Princeton: Princeton University Press, 2008).

[11] Andrew Rudalevige, *The New Imperial Presidency: Renewing Presidential Power After Watergate* (Ann Arbor: University of Michigan Press, 2005); James Pfiffner, *Power Play: The Bush Presidency and the Constitution* (Washington, DC: Brookings Institution Press, 2008); William Howell and David Brent, *Thinking About the Presidency: The Primacy of Power* (Princeton: Princeton University Press, 2013).

[12] Terry Moe, "The Presidency and the Bureaucracy: The Presidential Advantage," in *The Presidency and the Political System*, ed. Michael Nelson (Washington, DC: Congressional Quarterly Press, 1994), 451.

[13] See also Howell 2003.

[14] Gregory Koger, *Filibustering: A Political History of Obstruction in the House and Senate* (Chicago: University of Chicago Press, 2010); Gregory Wawro and Eric Schickler, *Filibuster: Obstruction and Lawmaking in the United States Senate* (Princeton: Princeton University Press, 2006); Thomas Mann and Norman Ornstein, *It's Even Worse than it Looks: How the*

is attained, the president wields a veto pen that requires only thirty-four senators to toe the party line.[15]

While acknowledging Congress's theoretical capacity to check presidential assertions of power, the conventional wisdom rightly notes that in only the rarest of circumstances will Congress actually pass legislation to counter such actions. Even the constitutional power of the purse—mandating that funds can only be spent subject to a lawful appropriation—provides less leverage in practice than is often supposed. Congress has routinely failed to defund programs and initiatives unilaterally instituted by the president. One need only recall congressional Democrats' futile efforts to force the Bush administration to begin a phased withdrawal from Iraq through the appropriations process in 2007 to be reminded that the power of the purse is a remarkably blunt instrument of coercion.[16]

In sum, Congress faces daunting odds when trying to combat the president legislatively. Information asymmetries, steep transaction costs in coalition building, and the looming threat of a filibuster or presidential veto all suggest that legislative efforts to constrain presidents will often fail, even when a strong majority of members opposes the president's action.

We agree with the conventional assessment that Congress is often institutionally hamstrung when trying to use legislation to rein in assertions of presidential power. However, existing scholarship has largely failed to consider how Congress might systematically retain a check on the executive branch through more informal means.[17]

American Constitutional System Collided with the New Politics of Extremism (New York: Basic Books, 2013).

[15] David Brady and Craig Volden, *Revolving Gridlock: Politics and Policy from Carter to Clinton* (Boulder, CO: Westview Press, 1998); Keith Krehbiel, *Pivotal Politics: A Theory of U.S. Lawmaking* (Chicago: University of Chicago Press, 1998); Charles Cameron, *Veto Bargaining: Presidents and the Politics of Negative Power* (New York: Cambridge University Press, 2000).

[16] See Bruce Ackerman and Oona Hathaway, "Limited War and the Constitution: Iraq and the Crisis of Presidential Legality." *Michigan Law Review* 109 (2011): 447–517, for a discussion of the historical evolution of the power of the purse and its waning capacity to constrain the president.

[17] To be sure, past scholarship has occasionally acknowledged this possibility. For example, Moe and Howell warn that should presidents "go too far or too fast, or move into the wrong areas at the wrong time, they would find that there are heavy political costs to be paid—perhaps in being reversed on the specific issue by Congress or the courts, but more generally by creating opposition that could threaten other aspects of the presidential policy agenda or even its broader success." Terry Moe and William Howell, "The Presidential Power of Unilateral Action," *Journal of Law, Economics, and Organization* 15 (1999): 132–179, 138. See also William Howell and Douglas Kriner, "Bending so as Not to Break: What the Bush Presidency Reveals about Unilateral Action," in *The Polarized Presidency of George W. Bush*, ed. George Edwards and Desmond King (Oxford: Oxford University Press, 2007). Nevertheless, having made this nod to the possibility of an alternate, nonlegislative mechanism for constraining the executive, the vast majority of scholarship focuses almost exclusively on the barriers to legislative action.

We focus here on one specific mechanism through which Congress might counter presidential aggrandizement: by using investigative oversight to expose wrongdoing, force executive-branch officials to answer difficult questions, and raise the political costs of noncompliance. These investigations fall within the broad category of congressional "oversight,"[18] but have the particular feature of focusing on allegations of wrongdoing, mismanagement, or abuse of power, rather than simply evaluating the quality of the executive branch's performance in implementing the law.

In an oft-overlooked chapter of his seminal 1991 study, *Divided We Govern*, David Mayhew argues, "Beyond making laws, Congress probably does nothing more consequential than investigate alleged misbehavior in the executive branch."[19] Yet few scholars have followed up on Mayhew's assertion by exploring the dynamics governing investigative activity and its ultimate consequences for politics and policymaking.

We believe this is a mistake. Investigations are a crucial tool precisely because they avoid the most severe problems that plague legislative efforts to check presidential power. Most obviously, veto threats are irrelevant. Rather than requiring supermajority support, investigations can be commenced with only the swing of a chairman's gavel. Moreover, transaction costs are also less likely to pose an important obstacle. Since adoption of the Legislative Reorganization Act of 1946, all Senate committees have had the power to issue subpoenas. On the House side, subpoena power was granted to three committees in 1946 (Appropriations, Government Operations, and Un-American Activities), with the authority extended to the rest of the committees in 1974. Before 1946, committees generally had to receive floor approval for investigations. But even then, the transaction costs were fairly limited. On the House side, the procedure was for the Rules Committee to decide whether to forward proposals for investigations to the floor; given approval from Rules, it required a simple majority vote on the floor to authorize an investigation.[20]

Finally and more subtly, collective action problems may pose a less severe obstacle to investigative oversight activity than to legislation. The key is that the individual members who are most active in spearheading an

[18] See Joel Aberbach, *Keeping a Watchful Eye: The Politics of Congressional Oversight* (Washington, DC: Brookings Institution Press, 1990); Joel Aberbach, "What's Happened to the Watchful Eye?" *Congress and the Presidency* 29 (2002): 3–23; Linda Fowler, *Watchdogs on the Hill: The Decline of Congressional Oversight of U.S. Foreign Relations* (Princeton: Princeton University Press, 2015); Mathew McCubbins and Thomas Schwartz, "Congressional Oversight Overlooked: Police Patrols Versus Fire Alarms," *American Journal of Political Science* 28 (1984): 165–179.

[19] Mayew 1991, 8.

[20] Funding the investigation did, however, require a second resolution in most cases.

investigation are likely to gain publicity that is often an individual benefit—helping boost their reelection and personal power—even as they contribute to the collective good of congressional power. Similarly, under divided party government, investigations can be used by party leaders and committee chairmen as an instrument to serve majority party members' shared interest in tarnishing the brand name of the president's party, even as those inquests simultaneously defend Congress's institutional role. Investigations can thus serve as a "common carrier" for the goals of ambitious members and for all members' shared stake in congressional power.[21]

Attention to members' multiple goals can also help explain the important variation in the volume and intensity of congressional investigations over time. Specifically, we argue that the interplay between legislators' partisan and institutional interests—a struggle the Framers themselves feared—significantly shapes the calculus of when Congress acts. We show that Congress, and particularly the House of Representatives, investigates most aggressively precisely when partisan and policy differences between the legislative and executive branches are maximized. That is, investigations are more likely when there is divided party control of Congress and the White House, particularly when the parties are highly polarized from one another.

HOW INVESTIGATIONS SHAPE AMERICAN POLITICS

Congressional investigations of the executive branch have produced some of the most dramatic moments in American political history: the impeachment and near conviction of President Andrew Johnson; the sensational Credit Mobilier corruption scandal, which targeted both a sitting vice president and future president in the midst of the volatile 1872 election season; the Army-McCarthy hearings; Watergate; Iran-Contra; Whitewater; and Lewinsky. But are investigations mere political theater? Or do they routinely have concrete implications for interbranch politics and policy outcomes?

While the desire for time in the spotlight may have motivated many investigators throughout congressional history, we argue that investigations are more than opportunities for public posturing. Rather, because they can systematically inflict political damage on the president, investigations can influence policy outcomes both in the specific issue area under investigation

---

[21] Eric Schickler, *Disjointed Pluralism: Institutional Innovation and the Development of the U.S. Congress* (Princeton: Princeton University Press, 2001); Eric Schickler, "Entrepreneurial Defenses of Congressional Power," in *Formative Acts: Reckoning with Agency in American Politics*, ed. Stephen Skowronek and Matthew Glassman (Philadelphia: University of Pennsylvania Press, 2007).

and—by informing presidents' anticipatory calculations—more broadly in areas unrelated to the investigation itself.

But how can investigations impose political costs? We argue that one of the most important mechanisms through which investigations raise the costs of noncompliance for the president is by eroding his support among the public. To examine this dynamic, we marshal more than sixty years of public opinion data and couple it with a series of original survey experiments. Taken together, our data convincingly demonstrate that congressional investigations systematically depress presidential job approval ratings, one of the most important and visible metrics on which the president's political capital is judged.

Because investigations can lower presidential approval and change the political landscape, they also can have tangible consequences for policy outcomes. We propose three pathways through which investigations can effect concrete changes in policy. The first two pathways are direct. When Congress investigates the president's actions in a specific policy sphere, it shines a public spotlight on alleged maladministration. By raising the salience of a policy problem and by turning public opinion against the president, an investigation may trigger a legislative response mandating a change in policy. In this way, investigations help Congress overcome collective action dilemmas and other barriers to legislative redress by creating a political environment that incentivizes legislative action. The end result is legislation being written into law that never would have emerged in the absence of the political pressure generated by the investigation.

Even without spurring legislation, however, investigations can lead to direct policy changes by prompting the president to change course on his own initiative. In such cases, the president attempts to preempt further damaging investigative hearings by making policy concessions. We explore these pathways through a series of illustrative case studies that detail how each pathway operates and what conditions must be met for an investigation to influence policymaking (see Chapter 4).

While these direct pathways of influence are important, investigations may be even more consequential to interbranch politics because of their ability to influence presidential behaviors and policy outcomes beyond the immediate focus of ongoing investigations. When deciding what course to chart, presidents anticipate Congress's likely reaction. Most prior scholarship focuses on anticipations of the likelihood that Congress would enact legislation to overturn a presidential action and directly alter policy. However, we argue that the president also surely considers Congress's capacity to impose political costs on the White House through high-profile investigations should the administration stray too far from congressional preferences. Testing for indirect influence through anticipatory calculations is notoriously difficult. However, we marshal substantial evidence that presidents who have experienced heavy investigative oversight are more reluctant to use force in response to international disputes than are presidents who have experienced a relatively quiescent Congress.

Put simply, investigations are far more than a political sideshow. While investigations do not negate the president's many institutional advantages, they offer an important mechanism for increasing the political costs of non-compliance even when legislative coercion is not feasible. By reducing presidential approval and changing the president's anticipatory calculations, investigations can systematically affect policy outcomes both in the area under investigation and more broadly in areas unrelated to the investigation itself.

THE ORIGINS AND EVOLUTION OF CONGRESS'S INVESTIGATIVE POWER

Our main objectives in the chapters that follow are to identify the conditions under which Congress uses its investigative power, and to demonstrate that the real or anticipated exercise of this power significantly constrains the president and produces tangible changes in policy outcomes. As a result, we contend that investigations offer Congress a check on presidential aggrandizement that is often more effective than that provided by its legislative function.

However, Article I of the Constitution makes no mention of Congress's authority to investigate the executive branch. Rather, this power is implied in broader grants of legislative authority, and it has evolved over time in the political give and take that defines our system of separated institutions sharing power.[22] As such, a brief overview of this development provides crucial context before turning to the empirical analyses that form the core of the book.

The first congressional investigation arose in the second Congress and involved a direct challenge to the conduct of a cabinet officer. In August 1791, an army of approximately 1,400 American soldiers under the command of General Arthur St. Clair marched north from Fort Washington (modern day Cincinnati) to construct a series of forts that would become bases of operation against Indian Tribes that were attacking American settlers on the Ohio frontier. At the end of a long day's march on November 3, St. Clair permitted his men to set up camp without first constructing defensive earthworks, a task he thought could wait until the morning. However, before daybreak St. Clair's forces were attacked by Indian fighters. The onslaught took the Americans by surprise, and the ill-trained army was little match for their Indian adversaries. St. Clair soon realized that the only hope was to retreat southward toward Fort Jefferson; after receiving the order to fall

[22] Richard Neustadt, *Presidential Power and the Modern Presidents* (New York: The Free Press, 1990 [1960]).

back, most of his force dropped their kit and ran. More than 650 soldiers, including one of the commanding generals, were killed and 271 more were wounded. The American losses that day far exceeded those of the massacre of Custer and his men at Little Bighorn more than eighty years later.[23] The defeat of St. Clair's army would be one of the greatest Indian victories over American forces in history.

In the midst of a dinner party in Philadelphia on November 9, President Washington received a messenger with news of the fiasco on the Ohio frontier. After suffering through the remainder of the evening in silence, Washington erupted following the departure of the last guest, declaring "Oh God! Oh God! How can he answer to his country?"[24] The news caused a political sensation, with most of the public animus directed toward St. Clair.

On February 2, a motion was made in the House to form a committee to investigate the disaster. However, the motion failed, and the issue slipped from the House's agenda until March 27 when William Giles of Virginia introduced a new motion asking President Washington to conduct an inquest into the St. Clair affair. Opponents countered that the House had a responsibility to conduct its own independent investigation into the episode. Some, like South Carolina's William Smith recoiled against such a plan, noting that it would be the first instance in American history of the House investigating the actions of public officials "immediately under the control of the executive." Invoking separation of powers, Smith argued that the president alone should take the lead in superintending the executive branch.[25] The House was torn by competing considerations. On the one hand, few wanted to offend President Washington; however, on the other, the scale of the disaster and the sizeable appropriations such operations on the frontier required from the Treasury convinced many that an investigation was necessary. Ultimately, the House passed a resolution creating a select committee "to inquire relative to such objects as come properly under the cognizance of this House, particularly respecting the expenditures of public money."[26]

The committee began its investigation by writing the War Department and asking Secretary Henry Knox to deliver to the committee all relevant materials to assist its inquiry into the St. Clair matter. As recorded in the notes of Secretary of State Thomas Jefferson, the request prompted considerable turmoil within Washington's cabinet. Did the House have a right to

[23] Taylor 1955.

[24] George Chalou, "St. Clair's Defeat, 1792," in *Congress Investigates: A Documented History, 1792–1974*, ed. Arthur Schlesinger Jr. and Roger Burns (New York: Chelsea House Publishers, 1975), 8.

[25] Ibid., 9.

[26] Taylor 1955, 22.

request such documents and conduct such an inquiry, and did the executive have a duty to comply? And so began the opening salvo in the centuries-long struggle between the branches over claims of executive privilege versus the right of the legislature to obtain all requisite information to perform its constitutional functions. The cabinet members debated whether earlier parliamentary inquiries of the prime minister in Britain served as a precedent for congressional action.[27] Ultimately, Washington acknowledged the House's right to convene the inquest and the administration's duty to provide information to it. At the same time, the president declared that he had a solemn duty to withhold any information that might endanger the public security. However, in the present case Washington judged that all of the materials requested could be safely released.

As the committee's inquest proceeded, Jeffersonians in the House used it as an opportunity to score political points against key Federalists in the administration. Indeed, the final report exonerated St. Clair himself, and instead reserved most of its criticism for the War Department. The quartermaster general, Samuel Hodgdon, and a War Department contractor, William Duer, friends of Knox and Secretary of the Treasury Alexander Hamilton, were assailed for "gross and various mismanagements" in failing to properly provision the force in a timely fashion. Secretary Knox, himself, also was chastised for failing to spend all of the funds appropriated by Congress for the Indian campaigns.

When the House took up the committee report at the start of the second session, a complicated mix of political battles undermined the investigators. Defenders of Knox successfully reopened the case and thwarted efforts to have the House act on the committee's initial report. However, the inquest did result in several significant policy changes. Spurred on by the report

[27] Parliament had long claimed the power to acquire information essential to perform its constitutional duties, and this capacity to investigate questions of policy and maladministration grew dramatically in the era of Parliamentary Supremacy precipitated by the expulsion of the Stuarts in 1688. Just decades before the American Revolution, Parliament embarked on its most audacious investigation in history: a massive inquest into the alleged abuses of the Walpole regime, which the prime minister's detractors disparaged as "twenty years of treason," after his ouster. The scope of the inquest raised constitutional objections from many parliamentarians, but William Pitt the Elder famously defended the propriety of the Commons' investigative power: "We are called the Grand Inquest of the Nation, and as such it is our duty to inquire into every step of publick management, either Abroad or at Home, in order to see that nothing has been done amiss" (Taylor 1955, 9). Colonial legislatures followed British precedents in embracing investigative powers for themselves. For example, in 1722 the Massachusetts House of Representatives ignored the objections of the crown-appointed governor in demanding that the commanders of the colonial forces in Maine appear before the House to account for their failure to pursue offensive operations called for by the House in the previous session. See C. S. Potts, "Power of Legislative Bodies to Punish for Contempt," *University of Pennsylvania Law Review* 74 (1926): 691–725.

of negligence in the War Department, the Senate authorized Secretary of the Treasury Alexander Hamilton to take charge of military procurement. Under considerable pressure, Knox also relieved his ally, Quartermaster General Hodgdon, of command. Furthermore, the public attack on the War Department and Secretary Knox spearheaded by Jeffersonian legislators embarrassed and politically damaged the Federalists.

The St. Clair affair firmly established Congress's power to investigate the conduct of executive-branch actors, and served as an important precedent for numerous congressional investigations throughout the nineteenth century. Many of these early inquests, like the one into the St. Clair affair, directly involved questions of military policy, a realm in which presidents have consistently claimed considerable prerogative powers.[28] Perhaps most important, congressional critics of the Lincoln administration mobilized early on to investigate the executive's conduct of the Civil War and in so doing to try to maximize Congress's influence over military affairs. After witnessing firsthand the disaster suffered by Union forces at Bull Run in July 1861, Senator Benjamin Wade of Ohio and Senator Zechariah Chandler of Michigan spearheaded the creation of the Joint Committee on the Conduct of the War.[29] Over the next three and a half years, virtually every major decision of the Lincoln administration in prosecuting the war was subjected to congressional scrutiny and second-guessing. So great was their harassment of the administration and its generals, that Confederate Commander Robert E. Lee is alleged to have remarked that the committee was as valuable to his cause as two divisions of Confederate soldiers.[30]

---

[28] For example, Congress investigated General Andrew Jackson's unauthorized invasion of Spanish Florida to attack Seminole Indians in 1818. Congress was also active in the investigative realm outside of military policy. Congress used its investigative powers to launch inquests into the administration of the Treasury Department in 1800 and 1824, the Internal Revenue Bureau in 1828, and the Post Office in 1830. Other investigations focused on specific officials, including hearings targeting the commissioner of Indian affairs in 1849 and the secretary of commerce in 1850 (Taylor 1955, 33–34). After the Civil War, Congress engaged in the most important investigation of governmental corruption of the nineteenth century, the Credit Mobilier scandal, which ultimately ensnared both the sitting and incoming vice president, in addition to multiple members of Congress. Summarizing the scope and tenor of the investigative activity in the antebellum era, James Schouler wrote: "Committees instituted inquiries, ran the eye up and down accounts, pointed out little items, snuffed about dark corners, peeped behind curtains and under beds, and exploited every cupboard of the executive household with a mousing alacrity." *History of the United States Under the Constitution,* vol. 3, *1817–1831* (New York: Dodd, Mead and Company, Publishers 1885), 258.

[29] Ironically, given his future experience at the other end of a congressional investigation that would ultimately result in articles of impeachment, the third senate seat was given to the sole southern Democrat to remain in office after secession, Tennessee Democrat Andrew Johnson.

[30] David McCullough, *Truman* (New York: Simon and Schuster, 1992), 304.

Many of these early investigations proved quite consequential and politically damaging to the incumbent president. In part because of the persistent bludgeoning he received in Congress, Lincoln genuinely believed that he would lose his reelection bid; only General Sherman's seizure of Atlanta reversed Lincoln's political fortunes. The wartime investigative fervor in Congress continued during Reconstruction and provided Radical Republicans with a potent tool to wield against President Andrew Johnson. Johnson, a Democrat and the sole southern senator to remain in his seat after secession, confronted a Congress in which his co-partisans comprised only 20% of both chambers. The resulting investigations of Johnson's alleged abuses in implementing a more lenient Reconstruction policy precipitated the president's impeachment; he survived conviction in the Senate by a single vote. A half century later, a congressional investigation into charges and counter-charges of misconduct in a seemingly minor policy dispute between the conservationist Gifford Pinchot, a Theodore Roosevelt loyalist who was chief of the Forest Service, and President William Howard Taft's secretary of the interior Richard Ballinger, proved so politically damaging to Taft that it split the Republican Party in two, launched Roosevelt's return to politics and third party campaign, and handed the election of 1912 to the Democrat Woodrow Wilson.

Although Congress had investigated alleged executive-branch misconduct for more than a century, it was not until the 1920s that the Supreme Court entered the fray and codified the scope of the legislature's investigative power. The impetus for the Court's action was the most wide-ranging congressional probe into presidential corruption in American history: a multiyear investigation into bribes accepted by high-ranking Harding administration officials to lease the naval oil reserves at Teapot Dome to private corporations. Reversing Wilson administration policy, President Harding transferred authority over the reserves to his secretary of the interior, Albert Fall. In early 1922, Fall concluded a secret agreement with Harry Ford Sinclair and Mammoth Oil Company, a subsidiary created for the express purpose of extracting the oil from Teapot Dome.

When news of the deal leaked, a coalition of opposition party Democrats and progressive Republicans led by Wisconsin senator Robert La Follette called for a formal investigation of alleged misconduct. The Senate unanimously passed La Follette's resolution authorizing an investigation by the Committee on Public Lands and Surveys.[31] Fearing that the committee's chair, the conservative Utah Republican Reed Smoot, had little desire to aggressively investigate the Harding administration, La Follette convinced Montana Democrat Thomas Walsh, the junior Democrat on the panel, to

---

[31] See Senate Resolutions 282 and 294, Sixty-seventh Congress, second session.

lead the inquest.[32] The Teapot Dome investigation is unusual in that the minority Democrats were able to exploit a division within the Republican Party's ranks to become a leading force of the Senate investigation; we explore this dynamic and interchamber differences in the forces driving investigative activity more systematically in the following chapter. As the investigation unfolded, most members of the Republican majority endeavored to thwart Walsh at every turn, even recruiting their own geologists to cast doubt on the investigators' claims. By contrast, Walsh received significant help from Cordell Hull, the chairman of the Democratic National Committee, who provided him with information about additional land deals in New Mexico on which Fall had made considerable sums of money.[33]

The investigators finally broke through in 1924, tracing the money trail to show that Fall had received large kickbacks from Sinclair for the lease at Teapot Dome. The casualties of the investigation ultimately included three cabinet members who resigned in disgrace: the secretary of the interior, Albert Fall; the secretary of the navy, Edwin Penby; and the attorney general, Harry Daugherty.[34]

In addition to generating considerable political fallout, the Teapot Dome scandal also triggered a number of legal challenges concerning the scope of congressional investigative powers that eventually reached the United States Supreme Court. In a pair of landmark decisions, the Supreme Court codified Congress's sweeping power to superintend the executive, and it upheld the constitutionality of two of the most important instruments of investigative practice. In *McGrain v. Daugherty*, 273 U.S. 135 (1927), the Court upheld Congress's power to investigate charges of maladministration concerning the failure of the Justice Department to prosecute violations of the Sherman Anti-Trust and Clayton Acts, as well as the attorney general's failure to arrest and prosecute Secretary of the Interior Fall and the oil company officials who had allegedly conspired to defraud the government. The case involved the attorney general's brother Mally Daugherty who refused to testify before the Senate investigative committee despite being subpoenaed to do so. Daugherty challenged the committee's right to subpoena a private

[32] See Laton McCartney, *The Teapot Dome Scandal: How Big Oil Bought the Harding White House and Tried to Steal the Country* (New York: Random House, 2008), 116. Smoot was the chairman of Public Lands in the 67th Congress, when the resolution authorizing the investigation was passed. The first hearings were held in October of 1923 during the 68th Congress. By that time, Edwin Ladd (R-ND) chaired the committee; though Smoot retained his seat on the committee as well. For Walsh's own account of how he was recruited to lead the charge, see Thomas Walsh, "The True History of Teapot Dome," *The Forum* 72(1) (1924): 1–12.

[33] McCartney 2008, 170–175.

[34] Fall had resigned before the investigation began, but his political reputation was utterly destroyed by committee revelations that he had received $400,000 worth of bribes for his role in leasing the naval reserve.

individual in this matter, as well as the constitutionality of the investigation as a whole on the grounds that it was not legislative in character. A federal district court in Cincinnati ruled in favor of Daugherty. The Supreme Court, however, overturned the lower court's ruling and articulated a broad constitutional interpretation of Congress's investigative power.

Delivering the opinion of the Court, Justice Willis Van Devanter acknowledged that there was no express constitutional provision empowering Congress to initiate investigations and subpoena testimony. The main question at hand, therefore, was whether this power was materially incidental to Article I's general grant of legislative power. The Court concluded: "We are of opinion that the power of inquiry—with process to enforce it—is an essential and appropriate auxiliary to the legislative function."[35]

To reach this conclusion, the Court drew heavily on British precedent and American practice from the St. Clair affair onward. Indeed, the Court noted that as great an authority on the separation of powers as James Madison voted to authorize the St. Clair inquest, strongly suggesting a general and broad grant of investigative power to the legislature. But how directly must an investigation be tied to a legislative purpose? Here, the Court gave Congress considerable latitude.

> It is quite true that the resolution directing the investigation does not in terms avow that it is intended to be in aid of legislation; but it does show that the subject to be investigated was the administration of the Department of Justice—whether its functions were being properly discharged or were being neglected or misdirected, and particularly whether the Attorney General and his assistants were performing or neglecting their duties . . . Plainly the subject was one on which legislation could be had and would be materially aided by the information which the investigation was calculated to elicit. This becomes manifest when it is reflected that the functions of the Department of Justice, the powers and duties of the Attorney General, and the duties of his assistants are all subject to regulation by congressional legislation, and that the department is maintained and its activities are carried on under such appropriations as, in the judgment of Congress, are needed from year to year.[36]

Given that all federal agencies are governed by congressional appropriations, *McGrain* established that virtually any inquest into the affairs of an executive department or agency would meet constitutional muster. Pursuant to exercising this power, the Court also confirmed that Congress

[35] *McGrain* v. *Daugherty*, 273 U. S. 135, 174 (1927).
[36] *McGrain* v. *Daugherty*, 273 U. S. 135, 177, 178 (1927).

possessed wide-ranging subpoena powers to gather the requisite information for the discharge of its responsibilities: "The power of inquiry—with process to enforce it—is an essential and appropriate auxiliary of the legislative function."[37]

In a subsequent case, *Sinclair v. United States*,[38] in which the founder of Sinclair Oil, Harry Ford Sinclair, challenged his conviction for contempt of Congress, the Supreme Court again upheld its articulation of broad congressional investigative powers not directly tied to legislation. Moreover, it affirmed Congress's power to hold in contempt private citizens who as witnesses deliberately withheld information from congressional investigators.[39]

The abuses of the McCarthy era prompted the Court to articulate some limits on Congress's investigative power in an effort to rein in its most egregious excesses. For example, labor organizer John T. Watkins, when called before the House Committee on Un-American Activities (HUAC), dutifully answered its questions about his own affiliation with the Communist Party as well as questions about others whom he still believed to be party members. However, Watkins refused to answer inquiries about people who had left the movement years earlier. Watkins maintained that such questions fell outside of the committee's scope of inquiry and exceeded its constitutional mandate. In *Watkins v. United States*, the Supreme Court agreed. Chief Justice Earl Warren was careful to affirm past precedents granting to Congress broad latitude in exercising its investigative power: "The power of the Congress to conduct investigations is inherent in the legislative process. . . . It comprehends probes into departments of the Federal Government to expose corruption, inefficiency or waste." However, Congress's investigative authority did not extend to inquiries strictly focused on exposing the wrongdoing of private individuals: "But, broad as is this power of inquiry is, it is not unlimited. There is no general authority to expose the private affairs of individuals without justification in terms of the functions of the Congress."[40] Yet, two years later, the Supreme Court in a 5–4 ruling upheld the contempt of Congress conviction of university professor Lloyd Barenblatt for refusing to answer questions about his personal political beliefs

---

[37] *McGrain v. Daugherty*, 273 U. S. 135, 174 (1927).

[38] *Sinclair v. United* States, 279 U. S. 263 (1929)

[39] Rosenberg 1995.

[40] *Watkins v. United States*, 354 U. S. 178, 187 (1957). John Quincy Adams raised similar arguments during the House's investigation into the Second National Bank in 1832. Having returned to the House after his defeat in the election of 1828, Adams sought to amend the resolution authorizing the investigation to limit its focus to the bank's books and proceedings, and to preclude inquiries into the religious and political beliefs of bank officials themselves. See John Macoll, "The Second Bank of the United States, 1832," in *Congress Investigates: A Documented History, 1792–1974*, ed. Arthur Schlesinger Jr. and Roger Burns (New York: Chelsea House Publishers, 1975).

and affiliations. The Court ruled that HUAC did not violate Barenblatt's First Amendment rights and reaffirmed broad congressional investigative powers stating, "the scope of the power of inquiry, in short, is as penetrating and far-reaching as the potential power to enact and appropriate under the Constitution."[41]

* * * * * * *

With these investigative powers formally entrenched in congressional practice and constitutional law, recent decades have produced a dizzying array of investigations that have inflicted significant political damage on presidential administrations. Truman grappled with investigative assaults on multiple fronts from his China policy, to his firing of MacArthur, to allegations of communist infiltration throughout the executive branch. Lyndon Johnson faced off against Senator Fulbright's Foreign Relations Committee over Vietnam. Barack Obama has been besieged by congressional inquests into everything from the Department of Justice's failed "Fast and Furious" operation, to his response to the attacks on the American consulate in Benghazi, to his conduct of immigration policy. Most dramatically, for three presidents—Nixon, Reagan, and Clinton—congressional investigations even provoked concerns about their removal from office. Yet, important questions remain concerning when Congress uses its investigative powers, and when it does so, with what effect. It is to these questions that the remainder of the book turns.

PLAN OF THE BOOK

A *sine qua non* for congressional investigations to play an influential role in rebalancing our separation of powers system is that Congress must actually employ the investigative tools at its disposal to challenge executive-branch actions of which it disapproves. Yet, even a cursory examination of recent history shows that Congress does not use its investigative powers uniformly. Trumped-up charges with little factual basis can provoke a whirlwind of activity in the hearing room, while seemingly clear cases of misconduct can escape sustained congressional scrutiny. Chapter 2 explores the forces driving variation in congressional willingness to use its investigative powers over time. Marshaling an original data set identifying more than 11,900 days of investigative hearings held in the House and Senate from 1898 to 2014, we explore the institutional, partisan, and ideological forces that drive the considerable temporal variation in the frequency with which Congress

[41] *Barenblatt v. United States*, 360 U. S. 109, 111 (1959).

exercises its investigative powers over more than a century of American political history. We find that both partisan forces and policy disagreements drive variation in investigative activity. These effects are most robust in the House of Representatives, where there is a strong, consistent relationship between divided government and investigative activity, and where heightened polarization boosts the impact of divided party control. Because the Senate affords the majority party leadership considerably weaker procedural tools—and accordingly grants much greater prerogatives to individual senators—divided government has little influence on the sheer volume of investigative activity in the aggregate. However, our case studies and additional data analysis show that partisan forces are nonetheless important in shaping aspects of investigative politics in the Senate. By uncovering the dynamics driving variation in investigative activity, we begin to identify the political environments in which presidents are likely to face push-back from congressional investigators, versus those in which they operate relatively insulated from investigative pressures.

But do congressional investigations matter? Can they impose political costs on the president and his administration? Writing in 1885, Woodrow Wilson praised congressional interrogations of the executive branch in the abstract as a valuable tool to inform the public, but expressed considerable skepticism concerning most investigations' substantive reach, and therefore of their efficacy in practice. According to Wilson, "even the special, irksome, ungracious investigations which it from time to time institutes in its spasmodic endeavors to dispel or confirm suspicions of malfeasance or of wanton corruption do not afford it more than a glimpse of the inside of a small province of the administration."[42] Similarly, many modern commentators have concluded that investigations "are more effective at dramatizing than at illuminating issues."[43]

Nevertheless, to sway public opinion and bring popular pressure to bear on the White House, perhaps investigations need not penetrate into every crevice of the federal bureaucracy or illuminate the full complexities of the matter at hand. Indeed, the sensational, headline-grabbing character of many investigations—which led the great journalist Walter Lippmann to decry, "that legalized atrocity, the congressional investigation, where congressmen, starved of their legitimate food for thought, go on a wild, feverish manhunt, and do not stop at cannibalism"—may prove an asset if the primary objective is to move public opinion.[44] Even in the nineteenth century, many investigations appear to have been designed with precisely this goal in

---

[42] Woodrow Wilson *Congressional Government: A Study in American Politics* (Boston: Houghton Mifflin, 1885), 271.

[43] Grabow 1988, 7.

[44] Walter Lippmann, *Public Opinion* (Minneapolis: Filiquarian Publishing, 2007 [1922]), 268.

mind.[45] But the question remains: Do investigations systematically damage the president's public standing?

Chapter 3 explores this question empirically. The analysis begins by examining the relationship between investigative activity and fluctuations in presidential approval for all presidents from Eisenhower to Obama. The chapter then presents the results of several survey experiments that allow us to further isolate the influence of investigations, and various features of each inquest, such as the party leading the hearings, on public support for the president. Through multiple rounds of analysis using both observational and experimental evidence, we find that investigative activity erodes presidential approval.

Finally, we turn to the effects of investigations on public policy. Chapter 4 traces and documents two pathways through which investigations can directly produce concrete policy changes: by prompting legislative action from within Congress, and by encouraging presidents to change course of their own accord to avoid more stringent or costly action from Capitol Hill. A series of case studies explores the operation of these pathways in different policy areas and political environments.

Chapter 5 explores a third pathway of investigative influence: investigations in one policy area may affect presidential actions in unrelated policy areas by raising the threat of new investigative actions should the president stray too far from congressional preferences. In his 1940 analysis of Congress's investigative power, McGeary highlighted the importance of just such an anticipatory mechanism:

> The possible importance of the threat of investigation should not be overlooked. There are no scales with which to measure the unethical and undesirable practices which it may prevent. The fear of publicity through investigation may carry the same restraint as fear of the law.[46]

While the anticipation of future inquests may well affect presidential calculations, we often lack a viable scale on which to assess just how much influence this anticipatory mechanism affords. In Chapter 5, we exploit several important characteristics of military policy making—particularly the plausible assumption that most international crises arise independently of the domestic political environment in the United States—to assess the

---

[45] As Schouler (1885, 258) concluded, more often than not investigators were "not so eager, it would appear, to correct abuses as to collect campaign material for damaging some candidate and playing the detective in preference to the judge." When viewing members' incentives through the lens of Mayhew's electoral connection, this emphasis on publicity seeking is completely consistent with theories of legislative behavior. See David Mayhew, *Congress: The Electoral Connection* (New Haven: Yale University Press, 1974).

[46] McGeary 1940, 24.

concrete impact of even unrelated investigations in the recent past on future policy outcomes. The analysis suggests that the scope of investigative influence may be even greater than it superficially appears. Even when Congress does not investigate, the threat of an investigation and the political costs it generates may well affect the administration's political calculus and its implementation of policy accordingly.

The final empirical chapter uses investigative activity during the Obama administration as a lens for evaluating presidential-congressional relations in the early twenty-first century. Investigative activity declined in intensity in the late 1980s through the first decade of the new century, but Republicans' takeover of the House of Representatives in 2010 sparked a series of high-profile probes. None of these investigations hit their mark and became the next Watergate or provided the impetus for major policy changes. However, collectively they demonstrate the continued vitality of investigations as a mechanism for members of Congress to inflict damage upon the executive branch. In the intensely polarized contemporary era, forcing major direct policy change may have become increasingly difficult, but investigators in divided government have focused their investigative energies on imposing political costs on the president, and they have regularly achieved this goal to considerable effect.

Taken together, our results demonstrate that members of Congress are able to use investigations as an instrument to fight back against the White House, and thus to defend the legislative branch's power even when institutional barriers all but preclude legislative action.

Our approach is rooted in the idea that members are not solely reelection seekers who devote all of their energies to procuring narrow benefits for their districts. Rather, two additional sets of member interests can promote investigative activism that ultimately helps defend their institution's place in the separation of powers system. First, under conditions of divided party government, majority party members' shared interest in undermining the reputation of the opposition party can generate aggressive investigations that target executive power. Second, even under conditions of unified control, individual members can use investigations to promote their own personal power and national prominence. In this way, members' personal interests coincide with the broader goal of institutional maintenance, bolstering the Framers' system of checks and balances even amid the many advantages enjoyed by the modern president.

CHAPTER 2

~ ~

When Congress Investigates

CONGRESSIONAL INVESTIGATIONS HAVE produced some of the most dramatic moments in American political history. With seven words, "I have in my hand a list," junior Wisconsin senator Joseph McCarthy launched the nation on a years-long, televised crusade into alleged communist infiltration of the executive branch. With this inquest, a new word entered into the American political lexicon: "McCarthyism." The Fulbright hearings unearthed the most unsightly skeletons in the deepest closets of the Johnson and Nixon administrations' conduct of the war in Vietnam. The Iran-Contra hearings featured all the elements of a political thriller: clandestine meetings with foreign governments, friend and foe; high stakes arms deals; disappearing documents; and the reemergence of a Nixon era mantra, "what did the president know, and when did he know it?" Similarly, the Republican Revolution of 1994 ushered in more than the Contract with America. It also brought a siege mentality to the Clinton White House, which faced an almost continuous string of allegations—even an inquiry into the potentially improper use of the White House Christmas card list—that culminated in proceedings to impeach the president for personal misconduct and an alleged effort to cover up these indiscretions.

Congressional investigations have brought down a few presidents, and all but politically neutralized several others. More generally, Paul Light shows that investigations have played a pivotal role in reforming wayward bureaucracies, fixing broken policies, enhancing accountability, and shaping the political agenda for future policy makers.[1] Clearly, investigations can be a powerful tool in the legislature's arsenal. Yet, Congress does not employ the investigative arm of its committees uniformly. In some periods, high-profile investigations dominate our national political discourse. In others, investigations flare up and recede with a variable rhythm. And still other periods are marked by relative quiescence on the investigative front.

---

[1] Light 2014.

Scholarly attention to the dynamics governing when Congress investigates is not commensurate with the tool's historical importance. Mayhew undertook the first systematic assessment of the forces driving variation in congressional investigations as part of his larger inquiry into how divided partisan control of the White House and Congress affects legislative behavior.[2] In contrast to congressional oversight more generally, much of which is routine and fails to attract media attention, Mayhew identified a list of "exposure probes" which are defined as "committee-based charge(s) of misbehavior against the executive branch"[3] that received sustained coverage in the mass media. Mayhew found little evidence of significant differences in investigative activity in unified versus divided government; indeed, paralleling the negligible differences he found when analyzing legislative productivity, Mayhew found almost identical rates of high-profile investigations in both unified and divided government.

Subsequent studies have both supported and challenged Mayhew's primary conclusion. Using two different data sets, the first focusing on high-profile investigations and the second employing a broader measure, Kriner and Schwartz and Parker and Dull both found that the frequency and intensity of investigations increase significantly in periods of divided government.[4] However, in a recent analysis, Light compiled a list of the 100 most important investigations between 1945 and 2012 and concluded, "the differences between unified and divided government investigations are more occasional than consistent."[5]

---

[2] Mayhew 1991. As noted in Chapter 1, investigations fall within the broader category of congressional oversight, but with the distinctive feature of focusing on allegations of wrongdoing, mismanagement, or abuse of power, rather than simply evaluating agency performance. In response to the common claim that Congress fails to exercise adequate oversight, see, e.g., James Pearson, "Oversight: A Vital Yet Neglected Congressional Function," *Kansas Law Review* 23 (1975): 277–288; Randall Ripley, *Congress: Process and Policy* (New York: Norton, 1978). McCubbins and Schwartz (1984) articulated a theory of "fire-alarm" oversight: when drafting legislation the enacting coalition in Congress empowers outside groups to monitor compliance with legislative intent by the executive branch. As long as executive agencies are in basic compliance, no active oversight is required; when agencies stray too far from the preferences of the enacting coalition, outside groups pull the fire alarm and Congress springs to action. In one of the first studies to track oversight systematically, Aberbach (1990) shows that Congress has long been more active in exercising oversight than critics had assumed, and that changes in the political environment in the 1970s increased the political payoffs for members to engage in active oversight, producing a dramatic increase in the volume of oversight from 1961 through 1983. Updating the analysis through the 1990s, Aberbach (2002) found that congressional oversight remained vigorous through this period of intense partisan conflict. While trends in oversight have received considerable scrutiny (e.g., Fowler 2015), the forces driving patterns in investigative activity have received less attention.

[3] Mayhew 1991, 9.

[4] Kriner and Schwartz 2008; Parker and Dull 2009.

[5] Light 2014, 50. To construct his list, Light drew on prior research, as well as lists compiled by *Congressional Quarterly,* and Congressional Research Service. From this data, he identified

While the limited prior research on the forces driving temporal variation in investigative activity has focused primarily on divided government, several more nuanced hypotheses have been proposed and tested. For example, Kriner and Schwartz examined the interaction of divided government and majority party cohesion.[6] Consistent with prior work on conditional party government, they found that investigative activity in periods of divided government increased in intensity as the majority party became more internally cohesive and ideologically homogeneous.[7] Parker and Dull also argue that divided government became an even more important driver of investigative activity after Watergate.[8]

However, the ability of past research to test these more nuanced hypotheses is hindered by the studies' limited time horizon–the post–World War II era. For example, during this period majority party cohesion is very highly correlated with time, which limits our ability to identify what causal forces are in play. Similarly, Parker and Dull place great emphasis on the transformation of the political environment after Watergate; yet, the reforms emphasized in their account took effect as the parties were polarizing ideologically. Disentangling which factor is truly moderating the effect of divided government on investigative activity is all but impossible.

INCENTIVES TO INVESTIGATE

In this chapter, we seek to explain the significant variation over time in Congress's use of its investigative powers against the executive branch. We explore the incentives that might lead members of Congress to engage in investigative oversight, and we use these incentives to derive predictions about what temporal patterns we should observe. We test these predictions using the largest empirical database of investigative activity constructed, encompassing more

---

a list of 100 as being the most significant. Light (2014, 6) acknowledges that narrowing the list to the 100 most significant involved "a mix of subjective and objective questions."

[6] Kriner and Schwartz 2008.

[7] For such prior work, see, e.g., John Aldrich, *Why Parties? The Origin and Transformation of Political Parties in America* (Chicago: University of Chicago Press, 1995); John Aldrich and David Rohde, "Theories of the Party in Legislature and the Transition to Republican Rule in the House," Paper Presented at annual meeting of the American Science Association, Chicago, 1995; C. Lawrence Evans and Daniel Lipinski, "Obstruction and Leadership in the U.S. Senate," in *Congress Reconsidered*, 8th ed., ed. Lawrence C. Dodd and Bruce I. Oppenheimer (Washington, DC: CQ Press, 2005); David Rohde, *Parties and Leaders in the Postreform House* (Chicago: University of Chicago Press, 1991); Barbara Sinclair, *Party Wars: Polarization and the Politics of National Policy Making* (Norman: University of Oklahoma Press, 2006).

[8] Parker and Dull (2009) find some evidence consistent with this hypothesis in the differences in means presented in Table 3 (334); however, they do not include a test of the hypothesis (i.e., an interaction between the divided government variable and the post-1975 dummy variable) in the multivariate analyses in Table 2 (332).

than 4,500 hearings conducted over more than 11,900 days spanning more than a century of American political history from 1898 to 2014. We find that divided party control has a strong impact on investigative activism in the House, particularly in periods when the two parties are ideologically polarized. Indeed, in the contemporary highly polarized House, investigations have become almost exclusively a feature of divided government. By contrast, echoing a long literature documenting significant differences across the chambers, divided government does not increase the quantity of Senate investigations. Individual entrepreneurship, coupled with systematic responses to conditions such as the health of the economy and the onset of major wars, appears to be more central to understanding Senate investigative activity over time. Nonetheless, while the volume of Senate investigations is unaffected by partisan control, the case studies with which the chapter concludes suggest that which party wields the gavel can indeed affect the scope and ferocity of individual investigations in the upper chamber.

Institutional

The checks and balances system erected by the Framers depended on Congress instinctively contesting any presidential attempt to transgress on congressional prerogatives. It also anticipated that presidents would reflexively contest any efforts of legislative overreach through all means at their disposal. In this way, power would never be concentrated in only a few hands, and in the words of *Federalist 51* "the private interest of every individual may be a sentinel over the public rights."

If dominant, this institutional incentive predicts that whenever presidents or executive-branch officials push on the boundaries of their power, members of Congress will push back through whatever tools are available, including investigations. Instances of possible executive misconduct are therefore opportunities for legislative attacks in the great interbranch struggle for power. If institutional incentives provide the most important impetus behind congressional investigative activity, then patterns in investigations should not be strongly correlated with political factors, such as the partisan balance of power across the branches.[9] Instead, one might expect investigative activity to be fairly constant—with legislators consistently seeking to shine a light on and punish possible instances of executive misconduct. Or, alternatively, one might expect investigative activity to increase following episodes of presidential aggrandizement, such as during (and immediately following) times of major war. Crucially, however, this variation would be

---

[9] We consider the possibility below that the likelihood of presidential aggrandizement might differ under unified as compared to divided government.

in response to shifts in the institutional power balance rather than patterns of party control.

Partisan

While playing the role of constitutional architects, before they began the more mundane struggle of actually organizing and running a government, many of the Founding Fathers were acutely distrustful of political parties.[10] Madison, for instance, used the words "party" and the more pejorative term "faction" interchangeably. Capturing the majority view of eighteenth-century Anglo-American political thought, Bolingbroke wrote: "Faction is to party what the superlative is to the positive: party is a political evil, and faction is the worst of all parties."[11] Parties were vehicles through which individuals pursued their own more narrow interests over that of the public good.

Despite the Framers' protestations, political parties quickly emerged, in part as a means to bridge the formal constitutional division of power across branches.[12] The party system that eventually developed—two broad-based mass political parties that both represented a wide range of economic and geographic interests—has largely avoided the Framers' fear that many small parties or factions would pursue narrow interests, seeking to impose them on the larger body politic. However the Framers' concern that loyalty to party might trump other, higher forms of loyalty was in many respects realized. Most consequential for the health of our system of checks and balances, partisan loyalties often eclipse institutional loyalties. This, in turn, threatens the very bedrock of checks and balances articulated in *Federalist 51*: that "the interests of the man be connected with the constitutional rights of the place."

The emergence of political parties potentially changed the strategic calculations of legislators. Rather than instinctively protecting their institution's power vis-à-vis the executive, members may also consider the broader ramifications of investigations for all office seekers running under the president's partisan banner. In a two-party system, it is simply no longer clear that a legislator's political interests are best served by always and everywhere aggressively defending Congress against executive-branch incursions. When a co-partisan president acts to pursue the party's goals, even at the expense of

[10] Richard Hofstadter, *The Idea of a Party System: The Rise of Legitimate Opposition in the United States, 1780–1840* (Berkeley: University of California Press, 1969).

[11] Henry St. John, Lord Bolingbroke, "The Idea of a Patriot King," in *Bolingbroke: Political Writings*, ed. David Armitage (New York: Cambridge University Press 1997 [1738]), 257.

[12] James Q. Wilson, "Political Parties and the Separation of Powers," in *Separation of Powers—Does it Still Work?* ed. Robert Goldwin and Art Kaufman (Washington, DC: American Enterprise Institute, 1986); Steven Calabresi, "Political Parties as Mediating Institutions," *University of Chicago Law Review* 61 (1994): 1479–1533.

Congress's institutional prerogatives, same-party legislators may judge their interests better served by supporting the president, rather than investigating any usurpations of power. These conflicting loyalties to both party and institution, with the former often proving stronger than the latter, fundamentally disrupt the Framers' carefully poised, Newtonian system of checks and balances.

Prior scholarship has explored how interbranch relations often differ significantly in periods of unified versus divided partisan control. Several studies have shown that divided government is associated with reduced legislative productivity as it becomes harder to reach a cross-branch consensus on major policy change.[13] The very nature of legislation itself changes, as Congress delegates significantly less discretion to the executive branch when it is controlled by a president of the opposition party,[14] often at the cost of significant losses in efficiency.[15] Even in foreign policy, long held to be a bailiwick of presidential discretion, the commander-in-chief is significantly more constrained and the legislature consistently more aggressive in periods of divided rather than unified government.[16] A similar dynamic could also drive fluctuations in investigative activity.

If partisan incentives primarily shape investigative behavior, then we would expect to see significantly more investigative activity in periods of divided government when partisan and institutional incentives align. Would-be investigators can seek to expose damaging evidence of wrongdoing, secure in the knowledge that any revelations will bolster both their institutional power and their partisan political prospects. While nominally defending the institutional prerogatives of Congress, the president's partisan opponents can use high-profile investigations in an orchestrated attempt to sour public perception of the president's party.[17]

[13] See, e.g., James Coleman, "Unified Government, Divided Government, and Party Responsiveness," *American Political Science Review* 93 (1999): 821–835; William Howell, E. Scott Adler, Charles Cameron, and Charles Riemann, "Divided Government and the Legislative Productivity of Congress, 1945–94," *Legislative Studies Quarterly* 25 (2000): 285–312. But see Mayhew 1991.

[14] David Epstein and Sharyn O'Halloran, *Delegating Powers: A Transaction Cost Politics Approach to Policy Making under Separate Powers* (New York: Cambridge University Press, 1999).

[15] McCubbins, Noll, and Weingast 1987, 1989; Moe 2012.

[16] William Howell and Jon Pevehouse, *While Dangers Gather: Congressional Checks on Presidential War Powers* (Princeton: Princeton University Press, 2007); Douglas Kriner, *After the Rubicon: Congress, Presidents, and the Politics of Waging War* (Chicago: University of Chicago Press, 2010).

[17] Gary Cox and Mathew McCubbins, *Legislative Leviathan: Party Government in the House* (Berkeley: University of California Press, 1993); Gary Cox and Mathew McCubbins, *Setting the Agenda: Responsible Party Government in the U.S. House of Representatives* (New York: Cambridge University Press, 2005); D. Roderick Kiewiet and Mathew McCubbins, *The Logic of Delegation: Congressional Parties and the Appropriations Process* (Chicago: University of Chicago Press, 1991); Aldrich 1995; Frances Lee, *Beyond Ideology: Politics, Principle and Partisanship in the U.S. Senate* (Chicago: University of Chicago Press, 2009).

By contrast, in periods of unified government the majority party in Congress has strong partisan incentives not to investigate the executive branch, for undermining the party's leader in the White House may damage its collective fortunes in the next electoral cycle.[18] Even in cases of clear misconduct, the political calculations for presidential co-partisans are complicated. Investigating and criticizing failures in the executive branch could help insulate members from the administration's deeds. However, further weakening their party leader in the White House can be devastating to the partisan brand name at the next election. As a result, we would expect significantly less investigative activity in unified government.

One caveat to this prediction is that presidents may anticipate lax investigative oversight under unified government and, as a result, could be more likely to take the sort of aggressive actions that spark a backlash in Congress. This dynamic would, in principle, depress the difference observed in investigative activism between unified and divided party control, as presidents would take fewer provocative actions under divided control. Since our results reveal a substantial increase in investigative activity in the House but not in the Senate when there is divided control, it does not appear that anticipated reactions are driving our findings.

Ideological

If partisan incentives, alone, are the decisive drivers of variation in investigative activity, then we should see a consistent relationship between partisan control and investigations; divided government should always increase investigative activity. However, if other incentives also spur investigative activity, then the strength of the relationship between divided government and investigations may be stronger in some political environments than in others. In particular, members may also use investigations as a tool to wage ideological battles with the executive branch.[19] For example, the Republican-controlled House Committee on Oversight and Government Reform has held a myriad of hearings investigating various elements of the Obama

[18] Gary Jacobson, *The Politics of Congressional Elections* (New York: Pearson Longman, 2004); James Campbell, "The Presidential Surge and its Midterm Decline, 1868–1988," *Journal of Politics* 53 (1991): 477–487; Gregory Flemming, "Presidential Coattails in Open-seat Elections," *Legislative Studies Quarterly* 20 (1995): 197–211; Jeffery Mondak and Carl McCurley, "Cognitive Efficiency and the Congressional Vote: The Psychology of Coattail Voting," *Political Research Quarterly* 47 (1994): 151–175.

[19] Another possibility is that partisan incentives will be more salient when majority status is seen to be at risk. See Frances Lee, "Presidents and Party Teams: The Politics of Debt Limits and Executive Oversight, 2001–2013," *Presidential Studies Quarterly* 43 (2013): 775–791. We assessed this by examining whether the effect of party is greater when the majority party has only a slim majority (e.g. 55% or fewer seats, 60% or fewer seats), but there was no evidence that the divided government / unified government split is sharper under such conditions.

administration's implementation of the Affordable Care Act (ACA), from whether the administration overstepped its authority in selectively granting waivers and delaying the implementation of requirements in specific cases, to whether the president lied when he promised Americans that they could keep their current coverage under the new law if they wished to do so. Partisan motives to damage the president and the Democratic Party likely fueled this flurry of investigative activity. However, ideological incentives and sharply divergent policy preferences may also have spurred Oversight chair Darrell Issa (R-CA) and colleagues into action. After all, no Obama administration policy has aroused greater anger from conservatives, who have denounced the ACA as socialized medicine that threatens the very fabric of the American health care system.[20]

Disentangling the relative influence of partisan and policy motives in such cases is difficult. However, we can clearly see the importance of ideological conflict in driving a number of high-profile investigations begun during periods of unified government when partisan incentives should encourage presidential co-partisans to dampen investigative challenges to their party leader in the White House. For example, when Democrats were divided ideologically between conservative southerners and liberal northerners in the late 1930s through the 1950s, southern-led committees were often aggressive investigators of alleged abuses by the Roosevelt and Truman administrations despite the presence of unified government. Some of the most prominent investigations were led by Virginia Democrat Howard Smith's Committee to Investigate Acts of Executive Agencies Beyond the Scope of Their Authority. Created in 1943 with the unanimous support of minority party Republicans, along with the overwhelming backing of southern Democrats, the Smith Committee conducted several damaging investigations, particularly of the Office of Price Administration, which conservatives disliked because it limited profits and was unsympathetic to rural interests.[21]

---

[20] Existing scholarship offers mixed findings on the role of ideology. Parker and Dull find little evidence that committee investigative oversight increases as the ideological gap between the committee chair and the president widens. See David Parker and Matthew Dull, "Rooting Out Waste, Fraud, and Abuse: The Politics of Congressional Investigations, 1947–2004," *Political Research Quarterly* 66 (2013): 630–644. By contrast, McGrath shows that committee oversight increases as the ideological divergence between the committee's median member and the president's ideal point increases, but only during periods of divided government. See Robert McGrath, "Congressional Oversight Hearings and Policy Control," *Legislative Studies Quarterly* 38 (2013): 349–376. Rather than focusing on variation in ideological distances between individual committees and the president, we take a different approach and examine whether the strength of the relationship between divided government and investigative activity varies across periods of high and low polarization.

[21] Schickler 2007. Similarly, the importance of ideological forces and preference congruence between the president and key congressional players also helps explain forgone potential

If both partisan interests and policy preferences affect members' willingness to use the investigative powers at their disposal, then the influence of divided government on investigative activity in the aggregate should be conditional on the degree of partisan polarization in Congress.

When the parties overlap with one another, policy disagreements with the administration could encourage congressional investigations in both unified and divided government, depending on the disposition of the relevant committee chair and his or her colleagues. In such periods of low polarization, policy and partisan forces may frequently push committee chairs in opposing directions. Presidential co-partisans may strongly disagree with actions in the executive branch and desire to investigate alleged misbehavior; by contrast, some opposition party chairmen may well agree with the president's policy course and therefore be reluctant to investigate executive actions. If policy incentives temper and in some cases surpass partisan ones, then we would expect the differences in investigative activity between unified and divided government to attenuate in periods of low polarization.

By contrast, in periods of intense polarization, partisan and policy incentives reinforce each other. As the gap between the president's and the congressional majority's preferences widens under divided government, efforts by the president to move policy at the implementation stage in his preferred direction are more likely to prompt cries of abuse of power.[22] Furthermore, amid heightened polarization, the presidential veto becomes a more potent tool to thwart the legislative ambitions of the congressional majority in divided government.[23] Blocked from pursuing their agenda legislatively, members of Congress may be particularly eager to continue the policy battle in a new venue, the committee hearing room. In this way, investigations can serve both partisan and policy goals. Finally, conditional party government theory suggests that high polarization is associated with stronger party leadership and less independent committee leaders.[24] This makes it more likely

---

investigations in periods of divided government. For example, whereas Democrats aggressively investigated a range of Bush administration unilateral actions from the firing of a number of U.S. Attorneys to charges that the administration had violated the Foreign Intelligence and Surveillance Act of 1978, congressional Democrats said little about unilateral directives that fit with Democrats' policy priorities. For example, even though Executive Order 13423, which required the federal government to cut its use of oil-derived fuels by 2% and to increase its use of renewable fuels by 10% per year, went far beyond the goals established by the Energy Policy Act of 2005, congressional Democrats held no hearings on this assertion of unilateral presidential power as it accorded with their environmental policy preferences.

[22] This is also consistent with the delegation literature (e.g., Epstein and O'Halloran 1999), which argues that delegation should decrease as the ideological distance between the president and congressional majority grows.

[23] See, e.g., Cameron 2000.

[24] Rohde 1991; Aldrich and Rohde 1995.

that the majority party will effectively harness the energies of committee investigators to pursue the party's shared interest in greater investigative scrutiny of presidents under divided government. In unified government, by contrast, the president's co-partisans in Congress have strong partisan and policy incentives to use their powers of negative agenda control to block potentially damaging investigations of the executive branch. As a result, when polarization is high, we expect to observe larger differences in aggregate investigative activity across periods of unified and divided government.[25]

Many prior studies of polarization's impact on legislative and interbranch politics have struggled with a major barrier to inference: since 1945, when many time series begin, the increase in partisan polarization in Congress has been almost perfectly collinear with time.[26] As a result, it is difficult to ascribe changes in legislative-executive relations to increasing polarization versus other possible explanations that have also unfolded over the decades. Our solution is to examine the dynamics driving variation in investigative activity over more than a century of American history. This longer time span allows us to examine the politics driving investigative activity during a period of relatively high polarization in the late nineteenth and early twentieth centuries; then during a period of low polarization in the middle of the twentieth century; and again as the polity has polarized significantly in recent decades. If partisan forces trump policy considerations, then divided government should always spur more aggressive investigative activity, regardless of whether the policy gap between the president and opposition partisans in Congress is wide or narrow. However, if policy differences are also important drivers of investigations, then the interaction of partisan and ideological incentives suggests that divided government will produce even more investigations as the level of partisan polarization within Congress increases.[27]

---

[25] As described shortly, we test the hypothesis by examining aggregate investigative activity in the House and Senate. Because our focus is on investigative activity writ large, we cannot test hypotheses concerning variation in oversight and/or investigative activity across committees (see Parker and Dull 2013; McGrath 2013; Fowler 2015).

[26] The correlation coefficient between one of the most prevalent measures of polarization in the House—the difference in the mean first dimension NOMINATE score of Democratic versus Republican members—and a year time trend variable from 1946 through 2014 is .93.

[27] In examining the extent to which polarization moderates the relationship between divided government and investigative activity, we also contribute to a long-standing debate in the legislative politics literature over the relative importance of ideology versus partisanship in driving legislative behavior. The bulk of this scholarship has looked to roll call voting data in search of an answer. Some argue for the preeminence of policy views. See, e.g., Keith Krehbiel, "Where's the Party?" *British Journal of Political Science* 23 (1993): 235–266. Others contend that party remains a highly influential force, along with preferences, in affecting members' voting behavior. See, e.g., James Snyder Jr. and Tim Groseclose "Estimating Party Influence in Congressional Roll-Call Voting," *American Journal of Political* Science 44 (2000): 193–211;

Interchamber Differences

Finally, it is possible that institutional differences across the two chambers will moderate the influence of partisan and ideological incentives on patterns in investigative activity.[28] Structurally, there are important reasons to believe that divided government will have less influence on the intensity of investigative activity in the Senate.[29] Most fundamentally, the Senate's rules have long afforded members of the minority with extensive prerogatives that cut against strict majority party agenda control. Individual senators have the "right to be recognized" when they seek to speak on the floor. Once recognized, the senator can (generally) speak for as long as he or she desires. Individual senators can also propose amendments that are unrelated to the legislation under consideration. These nongermane amendments, alongside the recognition and unlimited debate practices, give individual senators wide latitude to use the Senate floor as a venue to bring attention to issues that the majority party would prefer to ignore. By contrast, the House majority party is able to use the Rules Committee and the Speaker's discretion over recognition to greatly limit the subjects that come up for active debate

Stephen Ansolabehere, James Snyder Jr, and Charles Stewart III, "Candidate Positioning in U.S. House Elections," *American Journal of Political Science* 45 (2001): 136–159; Lee 2009. Other scholarship has looked for insight into the party versus preferences debate in areas ranging from fights over House rules (Eric Schickler, "Institutional Change in the House of Representatives, 1867–1998: A Test of Partisan and Ideological Power Balance Models," *American Political Science Review* 94 (2000): 269–288), to signatures on discharge petitions (Sarah Binder, Eric Lawrence, and Forrest Maltzman, "Uncovering the Hidden Effect of Party," *Journal of Politics* 61 (1999): 815–831), to roll call voting in the Congress of the Confederate States of America (Jeffery Jenkins, "Examining the Robustness of Ideological Voting: Evidence from the Confederate House of Representatives," *American Journal of Political Science* 44 (2000): 811–822). We seek fresh insight into this debate by examining the forces driving patterns in congressional investigative activity over time.

[28] In an empirical assessment of levels of House and Senate oversight of the Federal Reserve, Taylor found no evidence of systematic differences in the factors driving temporal variation in oversight across chambers. See Andrew Taylor, "Congress as Principal: Exploring Bicameral Differences in Agent Oversight," *Congress & the Presidency* 28 (2001): 141–159. In a later study of seventy-two instances of congressional "assertion" against the executive, however, Taylor finds that divided government increases the likelihood of legislative assertion, but only in the House. Andrew Taylor, "When Congress Asserts Itself: Examining Legislative Challenges to Executive Power," *The Forum* 10 (2012): Article 2.

[29] Kriner and Schwartz 2008; Parker and Dull 2009. Indeed, even though Mayhew's main emphasis is on the *lack* of a significant difference in the incidence of investigations across periods of unified and divided government, Mayhew (1991, 31) also notes a potential interchamber difference. "Perhaps the House leaned toward shooting or holding fire according to partisan criteria. Eight out of eleven, or 73 percent, of the House probes occurred when the other party held the presidency—the state of affairs 59 percent of the time. But these numbers are too small to tell much. The Senate, which attracted much more media coverage, ran twenty-two probes without showing any such partiality."

on the floor. Where a charge of executive wrongdoing can be lodged at virtually any time in the Senate, sidetracking discussion of pending legislation,
minority party members are much more constrained in their ability to force
issues onto the House agenda.

The committee process largely reproduces and reinforces this interchamber-
ber difference. The Senate has long guaranteed minority committee members greater procedural rights, in addition to more equal resources, than the
minority receives in the House.[30] For example, the right of extended debate
applies in committee as well as on the floor.[31] Senate committees themselves
have often enjoyed greater autonomy to pursue investigations without the
approval of top party leaders or the chamber as a whole: thus, the Legislative Reorganization Act of 1946 granted subpoena power to all Senate
committees, but to just three House committees. Prior to the passage of further reforms in 1974, most House committees required chamber approval—
which in turn generally required the help of the Rules Committee—in order
to launch investigations that could compel testimony.

More subtly, the Senate has long granted individual entrepreneurs freer
rein to set their own agendas and priorities. Senate committee chairmen
are likely to see themselves as relatively independent operators, cultivating
their own national reputation and audience that may be at least partly
independent of a president of their own party. Given the multifaceted and
idiosyncratic goals that motivate individual chairmen, this creates a potential alternative source of variation: individual entrepreneurs who desire a higher national profile and perhaps even the presidency itself may
seize upon investigations as a tailor-made way to attract media attention
and boost their political standing. The greater individualism that has long
marked the Senate likely means that senators are better positioned to seize
upon the personal power and publicity benefits that investigations potentially offer. Such individual-level forces can cause investigative activity to
ebb and flow in both unified and divided government alike. By contrast,
in the House, patterns of committee investigative activity are heavily influenced by party leaders and partisan concerns, particularly in periods of
intense polarization.[32]

[30] Rosenberg 1995, Sinclair 2006.

[31] Rosenberg 1995, 44. Each committee decides for itself whether or not to create its own
rule by which it can limit or end debate. Judy Schneider "Minority Rights and Senate Procedure," *CRS Report*, August 22, 2005. Judiciary and Finance are the only committees that
have rules to shut down committee filibusters (personal communication, Walter Oleszek of the
Congressional Research Service, October 27, 2015). Individual senators also are accorded the
right to hire a staff representative on committees; this prerogative is generally available only to
chairs and ranking members on House committees.

[32] Rohde 1991; Aldrich 1995.

The Role of Scandal Itself

Superficially, it may seem strange that an analysis of the factors driving investigative activity does not focus first and foremost on variation in wrongdoing by the executive branch. After all, it is logical to surmise that there must be some actual wrongdoing or abuse of power for Congress to investigate in the first place. Such a view conceptualizes congressional investigations as primarily reactive in nature. Some actor in the executive branch transgresses a boundary. The abuse or potential infraction is detected. Congress springs into action.[33] To be sure, applying this paradigm to investigations makes some sense. There would have been no Watergate if the Committee to Re-elect the President had not authorized the burglary of the Democratic National Committee headquarters and if the "plumbers" had not been caught.

However, recent research has shown that more often than not scandals are not exogenous events that emerge of their own accord and rock the political system. Rather, many scandals are politically constructed. Brendan Nyhan has argued that one of the most important problems with past research on scandal is that it wrongly conceptualizes scandal as the result of the disclosure of some act of wrongdoing.[34] However, even a superficial reading of recent political history makes clear that some allegations of abuse of power or wrongdoing elicit a firestorm, while others pass all but unnoticed by the media and the vast majority of Americans.[35] As Robert Entman notes, both Dan Quayle and George W. Bush joined the National Guard and thereby avoided service in Vietnam.[36] Whereas the former erupted into a furious and damaging political scandal, the latter brought down not George W. Bush, but Dan Rather, the journalist who pursued the allegations most aggressively. Similarly, whereas Bill and Hillary Clinton's prepresidential financial dealings in Whitewater provoked years of vituperative inquests and a media firestorm, George W. Bush's financial dealings with Harken Energy failed to attract sustained scrutiny.

The data suggest that scandals do not simply emerge; rather they are constructed. For example, Entman emphasizes the critical role that

---

[33] See McCubbins and Schwartz (1984) for a model of oversight along these lines.

[34] Brendan Nyhan, "Scandal Potential: How Political Context and News Congestion Affect the President's Vulnerability to Media Scandal," *British Journal of Political Science* 45 (2015): 435–466.

[35] Nyhan also shows evidence of this at the state level. See Brendan Nyhan, "Governors and the Politics of Scandal: How Contextual Factors Affect Coverage of Alleged Wrongdoing," Paper Presented at the Annual Meeting of the American Political Science Association, Washington, DC, August 28–31, 2014. For additional discussion of the role of the media in producing presidential scandals, see Brandon Rottinghaus, *The Institutional Effects of Presidential Scandal* (New York: Cambridge University Press, 2015).

[36] Robert Entman, *Scandal and Silence: Media Response to Presidential Misconduct* (Cambridge: Polity Press, 2012).

opposition political elites play in triggering—or that supportive elites play in blocking—a cascade of media coverage transmitting the scandal frame to the public.[37] Similarly, while acknowledging that the precipitating circumstances and strength of the evidence can influence the likelihood of a scandal taking root, Nyhan argues that political factors are often equally or more important: "When the political and news environment is unfavorable [to the target], scandals may erupt in the press despite thin evidentiary support. By contrast, under more favorable conditions, even well-supported allegations can languish."[38]

Theories of media scandal emergence place considerable emphasis on the role of opposition political elites in generating scandal. For example, in Nyhan's account the level of support for the president among members of the opposition party in the mass public determines the level of political demand for scandal coverage and investigations of alleged misconduct and abuse.[39] Finally, research by Berinsky further speaks to the possibility of elite-generated rumors and media feeding frenzies taking hold in the public imagination, regardless of the underlying facts substantiating a claim.[40]

Taken together, this new wave of scholarship underscores the decidedly political dimension of scandal politics. As such, we proceed in this chapter to investigate how congressional investigative activity varies as a function of political factors, primarily partisanship and polarization. While the supply of potential misconduct investigations may vary somewhat over time, we argue that the scope of the executive branch insures sufficient opportunities for Congress to lodge and investigate charges of misconduct and abuse if it so chooses.

MEASURING CONGRESSIONAL INVESTIGATIVE ACTIVITY, 1898 TO 2014

When launching scholarly efforts to understand temporal patterns in Congress's use of its investigative powers, Mayhew narrowed his focus to high-profile "exposure probes."[41] To do this, he identified every congressional

---

[37] Entman 2012.

[38] Nyhan 2015, 436.

[39] The second pillar of Nyhan's approach focuses on how otherwise crowded the media's agenda is. During slow news periods, the media will pounce on opportunities to cover presidential scandal; when the media's agenda is already full, coverage of scandal incurs greater opportunity costs.

[40] Adam Berinsky, "Rumors, Truths, and Reality: A Study of Political Misinformation," typescript, MIT, 2012.

[41] Mayhew 1991.

inquest into the actions of the executive branch that received twenty or more days of front-page coverage in the *New York Times*. Some subsequent studies have continued to use Mayhew's list, but disaggregated it to account for the varying intensity of the investigations in question.[42] Others have cast a wider net, identifying a broader range of investigations than those captured by Mayhew's criteria.[43]

We build on this recent work and use Congressional Information Service (CIS) abstracts to create the most comprehensive catalogue to date of committee hearings investigating alleged misconduct by some entity within the executive branch. Examining the content of congressional hearings directly rather than media coverage offers several important advantages. First, it eliminates concerns about changing patterns of media attention and coverage skewing our measure of congressional activity. Second, examining the descriptions of congressional hearings themselves allows us to construct a more direct and comprehensive measure of investigative activity over a longer time span. Some investigations attract considerable media coverage, while others fail to generate sustained media attention. Nyhan has shown that the process by which media scandals emerge is a function of factors endemic to politics and from within the media itself.[44] A more direct measure of investigative activity independent of the media's reaction to such actions thus provides a better test of our hypotheses concerning the forces driving variation in Congress's willingness to use its investigative powers over time.

Full details of our coding procedures are provided in the Appendix to Chapter 2. In brief, to identify relevant committee hearings we engaged in a two-step process. First, we ran a basic textual search on the CIS database to identify all hearings that involved some official or entity within the executive branch, as well as at least one key word that could imply some allegation of misconduct or abuse.

Following the initial textual search, a team of coders then examined the summary and testimony descriptors of each returned hit and identified those hearings that contained specific allegations of possible abuse or misconduct by some entity within the executive branch. Hearings that involved oversight of the executive branch—even explicit criticism of its actions—but that did not contain a specific allegation of abuse or misconduct were not coded as investigations. We thus aim to identify hearings that go beyond the routine evaluation of agency performance and instead are settings for accusations of wrongdoing by actors in the executive branch.

[42] Kriner and Schwartz 2008.
[43] Parker and Dull 2009.
[44] Nyhan 2015.

Employing this process, we identified 4,522 hearings from the CIS abstracts that constituted committee investigations of alleged misconduct by the executive branch from 1898 through 2014.[45] While published as a single document with a unique identification number, a single investigative "hearing," as coded by CIS with a unique identification number, could stretch over multiple days, even months. However, because CIS also reported the specific dates on which hearings were held, we were able to construct measures of the number of days of investigative hearings held by congressional committees in each month. The investigations in our data set took place over more than 11,900 days of hearings during this period.[46]

We focus on days of investigative activity—in this chapter as our dependent variable, and in later chapters as our independent variable of interest—for both theoretical and practical reasons. From a practical perspective, trying to devise a list of discrete "investigations" by grouping related hearings together would require a process that necessarily involves considerable subjectivity. For example, during the Clinton administration should "Filegate," "Troopergate," the investigation into the suicide of Vince Foster, Whitewater, and others each be treated as a separate investigation? Should all or some of them be lumped together? Different analysts can reach different, completely defensible, assessments. The number of "investigations" that Clinton faced could thus vary widely based on the criteria used.[47] Our focus on days of investigative activity is not affected by such subjective assessments. From a theoretical perspective, we believe that the volume of investigative activity is more politically consequential than the number of issues on which

[45] Our measure of investigative activity is broader than the one devised by Parker and Dull (2009). Through their method, Parker and Dull identified 1,015 investigative hearings from 1947 to 2004. Our coding procedure identified 2,566 misconduct hearings during this period. In addition to the hearing tallies mentioned in the text, our search criteria returned 161 additional hits containing appendices and other document collections that accompanied committee testimony; 51 of these items involved investigations, and 110 accompanied oversight hearings. These hits were not included in the analysis.

[46] Changing reporting norms by CIS over time led us to rely on days of hearings rather than the number of hearing documents. Before 1990, approximately 40% of investigative hearings (identified with a unique CIS number) were held over two or more days. More than 15% were held over five or more days. By contrast, from 2001 through 2006, more than 85% of hearings identified with a unique number by CIS were held on a single day. Using days of hearings rather than the number of hearing documents alleviates problems with comparability across the almost 120-year span of our data.

[47] For example, Mayhew identified three major investigations during the Clinton era (Whitewater—both in the 103rd and 104th Congresses; campaign finance scandals; Lewinsky). David Mayhew, *Divided We Govern: Party Control, Lawmaking, and Investigations, 1946–2002*, 2nd ed. (New Haven, CT: Yale University Press 2005), 224–225. Alternative coding criteria could yield a vastly greater number. The number of days of investigative hearings, however, remains constant and is insensitive to such judgment calls.

the president is being investigated. We contend that the number of days in which congressional actors are investigating alleged misconduct within the executive branch in the public eye is the most politically relevant indicator.

Figure 2.1 summarizes the trend in investigative activity, measured as days of investigative hearings held in each year, from the William McKinley to Barack Obama administrations.[48] The dark bars from 1898 through 2006 indicate data obtained from searches of the CIS hearings database conducted via Lexis Nexis. The lighter-shaded bars extend the time series from 2007 through 2014 through identical searches of the CIS hearings database conducted after the data migrated to ProQuest.[49] The first evident burst in investigations occurs early in the Progressive Era, which featured probes of alleged wrongdoing in the General Land Office (the Ballinger-Pinchot affair), the United States Department of Agriculture (Everglades reclamation investigation), and the Office of Indian Affairs (regarding its administration and spending). The government's handling of World War I sparked more investigations in 1918–19, followed by a flurry of investigations of executive-branch corruption under Warren Harding (including the famous Teapot Dome scandal, which was a target of Senate investigators).[50]

---

[48] Before the adoption of the twentieth amendment, which moved the expiration date of each Congress from March 4 to January 3, some hearings were held by the outgoing Congress early in the calendar year before the new Congress elected in November took office. To ensure that investigative activity was matched to the congressional data of the Congress holding them, such hearings were re-assigned to the election year in our data. For example, hearings held by the 68th Congress between January 1, 1925, and March 3, 1925, were reassigned to 1924 in our data to match them with data from the 68th Congress and not the 69th Congress, which took office on March 4, 1925. The number of affected hearings is quite small, just over 200. Moreover, replicating all of the analyses in Tables 2.1–2.4 using the number of days of investigations by Congress, instead of by year, yields virtually identical results.

[49] When we began creating the investigations data set in 2008, we performed our initial text searches of the Congressional Information Service hearings database using Lexis Nexis Congressional Universe for 1898–2006. In 2010, the CIS hearings database was acquired by ProQuest. To update the data set through 2014, we executed the same text searches on the CIS hearings using ProQuest (and the resulting hearings were then hand coded using the same procedures described above). Because the underlying data base is constant, we believe that the data should be comparable before and after the migration of the CIS data from Lexis Nexis to ProQuest. It is, however, possible that Lexis Nexis and ProQuest employ different search algorithms. If so, the same sequence of search terms might return different hits using the two engines. We use the entire investigations time series from 1898 through 2014; however, all of our results are virtually identical if we limit the analysis to 1898 through 2006.

[50] These early spikes help alleviate a potential concern about the comparability of this measure of investigative activity over such a large time span. The length and detail of hearing abstracts varied over the more than century under examination (with the abstracts tending to be shorter in the first part of the twentieth century). However, even in the early twentieth century, our coding process yielded significant numbers of investigations, with some of the highest tallies occurring in the early 1910s and then later in the decade during and immediately after World War I.

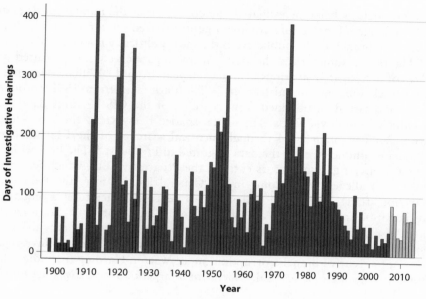

FIGURE 2.1. Days of Investigative Activity by Year, 1898–2014.
Note: Updated series from 2007–2014 constructed from ProQuest indicated by different shading.

A smaller clutch of investigations occurs in the late 1930s as congressional conservatives began to target the National Labor Relations Board and other New Deal agencies for their alleged radicalism. This wave crests by the early 1950s, as investigations into alleged communist infiltration into various parts of the executive branch reached their peak. Investigative activity again surged in the early 1970s with inquests into the Nixon administration's conduct of the Vietnam War and Watergate; the intensity of congressional investigative activity remained high through most of the decade. Finally, the pace of investigative activity increased again during the Reagan years, fueled in part by the Iran-Contra scandal, but then slackened off, in raw terms, in the 1990s and 2000s. The latter years of the Obama administration have witnessed a modest resurgence of investigative activity, but one that falls short of (at least in terms of the raw number of days of hearings) earlier bursts in the 1950s, 1970s, and 1980s.[51]

[51] A potential reason for the decline in investigative activity since the 1980s is the concomitant decrease in committee hearing activity overall (e.g., Fowler 2015, 27–30). An alternative way to examine changing patterns of investigative activity is to examine how the percentage of all days of hearing activity devoted to investigations has changed over time. Appendix

This downward trend, particularly the relatively small tallies of days of investigations during the Clinton years, is surprising at first glance. After seizing control of Congress for the first time since the 1950s, congressional Republicans expended considerable effort investigating an array of Clinton administration alleged scandals.[52] Yet the total number of hearing days under Clinton was lower than in the 1950s or 1970s. The relatively low level of investigative activity over the past two decades is consistent with concerns raised by some scholars and observers that today's Congress is failing to live up to its oversight responsibilities.[53] While this chapter focuses on the broad sweep of over a century of investigative activity, Chapter 6 explores investigative politics in recent years, and examines directly whether the decline in the raw number of days of hearings represents a troublesome decline in congressional scrutiny of the executive branch.

Armed with this comprehensive data set of congressional investigative activity, we explore the factors driving variation in Congress's willingness

---

Figure 2.1 plots the total number of days of hearings held in Congress from 1946 through 2012. The data was obtained from the Policy Agendas Project. In the top panel of Appendix Figure 2.2 we graph the percentage of all hearing days each year that involved investigations (i.e., the total number of days of investigative hearings divided by the total number of days of all hearings). The bottom panel again plots only the number of days of investigative activity per year, the same as Figure 2.1 but only for this shorter time period. The two series track each other very closely. Indeed, they are highly correlated with one another, $r = .89$. As such, changing patterns in investigative activity are plainly not merely a function of a general decline in overall hearing activity. Replicating the analyses below using the percentage of all hearings that involved investigations of alleged misconduct in the executive branch yields substantively similar results. Finally, we note that when examining recent investigative activity as a percentage of total hearing activity, the burst of investigative activity following the return of divided government in 2007 and 2008, and again in 2011 and 2012 is much more comparable to earlier bursts of investigative activity in the 1980s and 1990s.

[52] The Whitewater hearings do contribute significantly to the final spike in the time series in 1995.

[53] Thomas Mann and Norman Ornstein, *The Broken Branch: How Congress Is Failing America and How to Get It Back on Track* (New York: Oxford University Press, 2006); Louis Fisher, *Congressional Abdication on War and Spending* (College Station: Texas A&M University Press, 2000); Jasmine Farrier, *Congressional Ambivalence: The Political Burdens of Constitutional Authority* (Lexington: University of Kentucky Press, 2010); Fowler 2015). Fowler (2015, 5) similarly observes a significant decline in foreign relations oversight in both chambers since the mid-1990s. One potential concern with our reliance on CIS publications to identify a comprehensive set of investigations is that changes in CIS reporting over time, and particularly the shift to more detailed abstracts beginning in 1971, might lead to temporal inconsistencies in the data. Fortunately, Figure 2.1 shows no evidence of a major shift in the number of investigations identified by our search process before and after this change in format. The event count models presented in Table 2.2 are also robust to the inclusion of period dummies that indicate the timing of this coverage shift. The coefficient for this dummy is substantively small and statistically insignificant.

to use this tool to challenge the executive over time. We begin by providing the most comprehensive assessment yet of the hypothesis that divided government increases investigative activity. The analysis then proceeds to a more nuanced analysis to test whether the influence of divided government is constant, or whether it varies over time with the level of partisan polarization.

DIVIDED GOVERNMENT AND INVESTIGATIVE ACTIVITY

As an initial test of the influence of divided government on investigative activity, we first compare the average number of days of investigative activity per year during periods of unified versus divided government for the full 1898–2014 period. The data, summarized in the first column of Table 2.1, shows that investigative activity is greater under divided control. When the same party controls both chambers of Congress and the presidency, Congress held, on average, just over eighty-seven days of hearings investigating some allegation of misconduct by the executive branch in a typical year. However, when at least one chamber of Congress is held by the opposition party the average level of investigative activity increases dramatically.[54] In divided government, the average Congress held over 123 days of investigative hearings in a typical year, a 41% increase. Thus, when employing a more comprehensive measure of investigative activity over a time series almost twice as long as that examined in previous studies, we find strong evidence that divided government significantly fuels the intensity with which Congress investigates the executive branch.

As noted above, there are strong reasons to suspect that divided government may be a greater driver of investigative activity in the House than in the Senate. To examine this possibility, we disaggregate our data by chamber. As shown in the final two columns of Table 2.1, divided government only increases investigative activity in the House. Across the 116-year period, the House averaged nearly three times as much investigative activity under divided government: eighty-nine days of investigative hearings, as compared to a mere thirty-one days in unified government.

By contrast, we find no evidence of a significant difference in the average volume of Senate investigative activity in unified versus divided government. In fact, over the full period examined, the average level of

---

[54] In the initial comparison of investigative activity conducted by Congress as a whole, we define divided government as occurring whenever the presidency and at least one chamber of Congress are controlled by opposing political parties. In the chamber-specific analyses that follow, the divided government measure is solely determined by the partisanship of the specific chamber under examination.

TABLE 2.1: Differences in Mean Investigative Activity in
Unified vs. Divided Government, 1898–2014

	All	House	Senate
Unified	87.7	31.0	52.1
Divided	123.2	88.6	42.9

Note: The differences in italicized means across periods of unified
and divided government are statistically significant, p < .05, two-
tailed test.

investigative activity is actually somewhat higher (52.1 days) in unified
government than that observed in a typical year in divided government
(42.9 days); the difference, however, is not statistically significant. This
stark interchamber difference is consistent with past research suggesting
that different motives govern many behaviors across the lower and upper
chambers.

The contrast between the strong divided government effect in the House
and the null results in the Senate also helps us rule out a potential alternative
to our argument that partisan incentives are driving the increased investigative activity in the House observed in divided party control. Specifically,
one might worry that presidents, frustrated legislatively in Congress, are
more likely to push on the bounds of their authority in periods of divided
government. If so, presidential aggrandizement could drive any increase
in investigative activity rather than the partisan calculations of members
of Congress.[55] However, if presidents are creating more opportunities for
investigations in divided government, both chambers should launch more
investigative hearings in divided than in unified government. However, investigative activity only increases in the House. This supports our argument
about the importance of partisan forces in the lower chamber, and is inconsistent with the alternate hypothesis that presidents create more opportunities for investigations in divided government.

[55] There is little empirical evidence that presidents are more brazen in periods of divided
government. To be sure, some divided government presidents, like Richard Nixon, chafed at
congressional strictures and aggressively sought to expand presidential power—many would
say abusing it in the process. However other presidents accused of being "imperial," such as
Lyndon Johnson and George W. Bush (Schlesinger 1973; Rudalevige 2005), governed during
periods of unified government. In one of the most comprehensive empirical studies of presidential unilateral power, Howell (2003, 69–75, 90–93) finds that presidents actually issue
fewer significant executive orders on average in periods of divided government than in unified
government. Thus, the presidential aggrandizement alternative is unlikely to be driving our
result.

MODELING INVESTIGATIVE ACTIVITY IN THE HOUSE

A simple comparison of average levels of investigative activity in the House
during periods of unified and divided government suggests that partisan
forces drive variation in investigative activity. However, other factors undoubtedly also influence the intensity with which Congress investigates the
executive branch. To gain a more complete picture, we estimate a statistical count model.[56] We model the number of days of investigative hearings
that the House holds in each year as a function of several explanatory
variables.

Our main explanatory variable is a simple indicator identifying periods
of divided government. We expect there to be a strong positive relationship
between divided government and investigative activity.

The model also includes several additional variables that control for other
factors that may also influence Congress's eagerness to investigate the executive branch. As recent research has shown, we should not think of scandals
as exogenous events that emerge suddenly on the political stage, but rather
as politically constructed.[57] Different political environments should therefore present varying levels of demand for scandal. For instance, research has
long shown that presidential administrations grow increasingly vulnerable
as the economy worsens.[58] A poor economy may render the president an
attractive target for congressional opponents and make the public receptive to investigations of alleged executive misconduct. By contrast, when the
economy is robust, the president's political position is likely to be stronger,
the public less receptive to attacks on the executive branch, and the demand
for scandal may be lower. Consider, for example, the changing fortunes of
President Clinton. Elected in the midst of a sharp economic downturn, President Clinton's first term began in a challenging fiscal and economic climate.
While the economy ultimately rebounded, it did so slowly. As Zaller shows,
Clinton's first term ranks well below average when comparing presidential
first terms on the metric of average four-year growth in real disposable income.[59] In this parlous economic and political environment, President Clinton was battered by investigations ranging from Whitewater to his conduct

[56] Because there is evidence of overdispersion (i.e., the standard deviation is greater than the
mean) in our dependent variable—days of House investigative hearings in each year—we use a
negative binomial model. A poisson model yields virtually identical results.

[57] Nyhan 2015.

[58] Douglas Hibbs, "Bread and Peace Voting in U.S. Presidential Elections," *Public Choice*
104 (2000): 149–180; Michael MacKuen, Robert Erikson, and James Stimson, "Peasants or
Bankers? The American Electorate and the U.S. Economy," *American Political Science Review*
86 (1992): 597–611.

[59] John Zaller, "Monica Lewinsky's Contribution to Political Science," *PS: Political Science
& Politics* 31 (1998): 182–189, esp. 185.

of military action in Somalia. However, the economic upturn toward the end of Clinton's first term matured into what the president repeatedly reminded Americans was "the longest peacetime economic expansion in our history."[60] Amidst this backdrop, Clinton's approval rating became largely immune to the media feeding frenzy that accompanied the release of every salacious detail of the Lewinsky scandal. The public demand for investigations in this environment was strikingly low, and the investigations congressional Republicans and independent counsel Kenneth Starr did launch, failed to resonate with the American public.[61]

Accordingly, our model includes measures of the health of the economy as one factor contributing to the demand for scandal. Perhaps the greatest barrier to overcome in this regard is finding a consistent measure of economic strength that is available from 1898 to 2014. Many commonly used metrics, such as the unemployment rate, are not available for the entire period. However, we are able to include two measures of economic health in our model: the annualized inflation rate and the percentage change in GDP per capita. As inflation rises, the demand for investigations may also rise. Conversely, as per capita GDP increases, the demand for investigative activity may fall.

Another factor that may drive variation in the intensity of congressional investigative activity is whether the country is at war or at peace. James Madison wrote that "war is in fact the true nurse of aggrandizement."[62] As Madison predicted, many American wars have led to dramatic expansions of presidential power, often at the expense of the legislature.[63] Investigations of executive misconduct may be one way for Congress to try to claw back some power seized by an aggrandizing executive. To control for the influence of war on temporal fluctuations in investigative activity, we include an indicator variable identifying years in which the United States was involved

[60] William Jefferson Clinton, "Address Before a Joint Session of Congress on the State of the Union," *Public Papers of the President,* January 19, 1999.

[61] In an interesting analysis of the public reaction to the Lewinsky scandal, Zaller (1998) emphasizes Clinton's broader record of accomplishment (e.g., the federal budget was on the verge of balance for the first time in two decades; crime was falling; the country was at peace), as well as his championing of ideologically moderate policy initiatives, such as using the budget surplus to shore up Social Security, and increase investment in infrastructure and public education, in addition to the roaring economy, in helping to transform Clinton into a teflon president. Sustained support for Clinton in the wake of the Lewinsky mess was, for Zaller, a triumph of "political substance" over media sensationalism as a driver of public opinion.

[62] James Madison, Helvidius No. 4, *The Writings of James Madison,* vol. 6, *1790–1802,* ed. Gaillard Hunt (New York: G.P. Putnam's Sons, 1906), 174.

[63] Schlesinger 1973; Schickler 2001; William Howell, Saul Jackman, and Jon Rogowski, *The Wartime President: Executive Influence and the Nationalizing Politics of Threat* (Chicago: University of Chicago Press, 2013).

in a war that resulted in the deaths of more than 10,000 American soldiers: World War I, World War II, Korea, and Vietnam.[64]

Finally, the model includes two variables to determine whether investigative activity varies systematically with the electoral cycle. To do this, the model includes indicator variables identifying presidential and midterm election years.

RESULTS

Table 2.2 shows that divided government remains one of the most substantively important (and statistically significant) predictors of investigative activity in the House even after controlling for a range of additional factors. Model 1 presents the results for the entire time span from 1898 through 2014. To illustrate the substantive size of the effect, we estimate a series of first differences holding all other variables constant at their means or medians. This shows that a switch in partisan control of Congress from the president's party to the opposition significantly increases the expected amount of investigative activity, from a predicted thirty-one days in unified government to eighty-three days in divided government. Clearly, partisan politics play a critically important role in driving the House's willingness to use its investigative powers.

The model also finds some evidence consistent with the hypothesis that Congress will investigate an administration more doggedly when the president faces a struggling economy. The coefficient for the inflation variable is positive and statistically significant. First differences reveal that a standard deviation increase in the inflation rate is associated with a roughly 30% increase in the predicted level of investigative activity, if all other factors are held constant. The coefficient for the percentage change in GDP per capita, however, is statistically indistinguishable from zero.[65]

---

[64] Defining what constitutes a "war" is an intrinsically difficult proposition. Also occurring during our long time series is the Spanish-American War; the Philippine-American War; the 1990–1991 Persian Gulf War; wars in Afghanistan and Iraq; as well as a myriad of smaller conflicts from the invasions of Grenada and Panama to extended peacekeeping missions in Bosnia and Kosovo. We have re-estimated the statistical model with a number of alternative operationalizations of the war variable that use different cut-offs for the level of hostilities required for a year to be coded as one during which the country was at war. Across operationalizations, we find very little evidence that House investigative activity significantly increased in times of war.

[65] We use the percentage change in per capita GDP over the preceding year. However, replicating the model in Table 1 with GDP per capita or change in GDP per capita in the current year yields null findings for the GDP variable and significant effects for divided government and inflation.

TABLE 2.2: Factors Influencing Intensity of House Investigative Activity

	1898–2014	1947–2014	1900–2014
Divided government	0.99***	0.65***	0.97***
	(0.20)	(0.18)	(0.20)
Inflation	0.06***	0.10***	0.05**
	(0.02)	(0.03)	(0.02)
% Change in GDP per capita	1.24	4.01	1.82
	(2.07)	(3.65)	(2.04)
Unemployment		0.09*	0.00
		(0.05)	(0.03)
War	0.22	0.46*	0.18
	(0.28)	(0.28)	(0.30)
Presidential election year	0.12	−0.35*	0.09
	(0.25)	(0.19)	(0.24)
Congressional election year	0.23	0.08	0.24
	(0.22)	(0.19)	(0.21)
Constant	3.03***	2.59***	3.03***
	(0.20)	(0.44)	(0.31)
Observations	117	68	115

Note: Models are negative binomial event count regressions of the factors influencing the number of days of investigative hearings held by the House of Representatives in a given year. Column 2 includes annualized unemployment rate data from the Bureau of Labor Statistics. Column 3 includes BLS unemployment data from 1947 through 2014, and estimated unemployment rate data from the National Bureau of Economic Research for 1900 through 1946. Robust standard errors are reported in parentheses. All significance tests are two-tailed.

*p < .10   **p < .05   ***p < .01

To probe the relationship between investigative activity and economic conditions further, we estimated a pair of additional models. The first model in Table 2.2 did not include unemployment because the Bureau of Labor Statistics did not begin reporting unemployment data until 1947. Model 2 of Table 2.2 limits the time span to the 1947–2014 period, which allows us to account for the average annual unemployment rate. Consistent with expectations, this statistical model finds a positive relationship between unemployment and investigative activity. Congress investigated the president more aggressively in periods of high unemployment than in more robust economic climates, all else equal. The impact of divided government is unaffected by the inclusion of unemployment.[66] The final model in Table 2.2 expands the analysis to include estimated unemployment rates for 1900 through 1946 obtained from the National Bureau of Economic Research. In this specification, we continue to find strong evidence that Congress investigates the executive branch more intensely in periods of divided government and high inflation. However, the relationship between unemployment and investigative activity is no longer statistically significant. This null finding is almost certainly driven by the very high unemployment rates observed during the Great Depression, which coincided with an era of relatively low investigative activity in the aggregate.

Although there are several well-known examples of important wartime investigations, when examined broadly there is little evidence that major wars consistently increase investigative activity in the House. When examining the entire time period from 1898 through 2014 (model 1) the relevant coefficient in the model is positive; however, the standard error for the estimate is large, and the relationship is not statistically significant. When limiting the analysis to only the post–World War II era (model 2), we find modest evidence that the Korean and Vietnam Wars increased investigative activity. However, if we broaden the definition of major war to include recent wars in Iraq and Afghanistan, the relationship between war and investigative activity disappears.[67]

[66] As a robustness check, we re-estimated model 2 in Table 2.2 while also controlling for the number of days the House was in session in a given year for 1953–2014. While investigative activity is positively correlated with the number of days the House was in session ($r = .21$), the coefficient for days in session is not statistically significant in the event count model. All other results remain substantively similar. Most important, we continue to find a strong and statistically significant relationship between the presence of divided government and the level of investigative activity. We will further explore the relationship between monthly variation in investigative activity and days in session in the following chapter.

[67] The effect of major wars on investigative activity may linger, and perhaps even intensify, in the aftermath of a major conflict. For example, after the conclusion of both World War I and World War II, Congress investigated the administration's war policies. The Nye Committee aggressively investigated whether the munitions industry and financial concerns exerted undue influence over the Wilson administration and American foreign policy in the lead up to WWI. See Mariah Zeisberg, *War Powers: The Politics of Constitutional Authority* (Princeton: Princeton University Press, 2013). After WWII, Congress created a joint committee to investigate alleged failures of the Roosevelt administration to prevent the Pearl Harbor attacks that occurred four years prior. See Wayne Thompson, "The Pearl Harbor Inquiry, 1945," in *Congress Investigates: A Documented History, 1792–1974*, ed. Arthur Schlesinger Jr. and Roger Burns (New York: Chelsea House Publishers, 1975). As a result, we re-estimated the models in Table 2.2 with additional operationalizations of the war variable. When looking at the entire time period, we consistently fail to find evidence of a significant relationship between war and investigative activity. When examining only 1947 through 2014, we find evidence that the Vietnam and Korean Wars (and their aftermaths) were associated with increased investigative activity; however, the Iraq and Afghan Wars were not. Including Iraq and Afghanistan in the war variable yields a substantively small, statistically insignificant coefficient across multiple operationalizations.

Finally, the model finds modest evidence that investigative activity in the House fluctuates systematically with the electoral calendar. Across the entire time series, election years, be they presidential or midterm, do not appear to generate higher or lower levels of investigative activity, all else being equal, than non-election years. Since World War II, however, there is some evidence that investigative activity may lag in the lead-up to presidential contests as the focus shifts from Capitol Hill to the impending general election.[68]

Polarization, Divided Government, and Investigative Activity

The House investigates allegations of executive misconduct with greater gusto in periods of divided government than when the president's partisan allies wield the committee gavels on Capitol Hill. This appears to be clear evidence for the critical importance of partisan factors in driving investigative activity. When the majority can score partisan political points by attacking an opposition party president and bringing public scrutiny to bear on alleged misconduct, it embraces the opportunity wholeheartedly.

However, ideological forces could also play an important role. In contemporary politics, partisan and ideological incentives are so reinforcing that disentangling their influence is all but impossible. However, in other periods of our century-spanning time series, ideological orientations and partisanship were not so closely aligned.

There are many ways to measure the degree of ideological polarization between the two parties. One of the simplest methods is to plot the gap in ideal points between the average Democrat and Republican in Congress over time.[69] To do this, we use the difference in the first dimension NOMINATE scores of the average member of each party in Congress; NOMINATE is a scaling metric that uses information about each member's roll call voting behavior to put all members on a common scale. The scale is bounded between −1 and 1. In contemporary politics (i.e., post–New Deal), the more liberal a member of Congress, the further left she is on the scale (i.e., closer to −1).

---

[68] One potential concern with the event count models presented in Table 2.2 is serial correlation in the dependent variable. See, e.g., Patrick Brandt and John Williams, "A Linear Poisson Autoregressive Model: The Poisson AR(p)," *Political Analysis* 9 (2001): 164–184. To alleviate these concerns, we re-estimated an identical specification to model 1 using an autoregressive poisson model. (Alternatively, estimating the negative binomial model presented in Table 2.1 with a lagged dependent variable also yields virtually identical results.) Results are presented in Appendix Table 2.1. The autoregressive poisson model does show evidence of an AR(1) process; however, even after accounting for this, the results are virtually identical to those presented in Table 2.2. Most important, the coefficient for divided government remains positive, substantively large, and statistically significant.

[69] See, e.g., Nolan McCarty, Keith Poole, and Howard Rosenthal, *Polarized America: The Dance of Political Ideology and Unequal Riches* (Cambridge: MIT Press, 2006); Sean Theriault, *Party Polarization in Congress* (New York: Cambridge University Press, 2008).

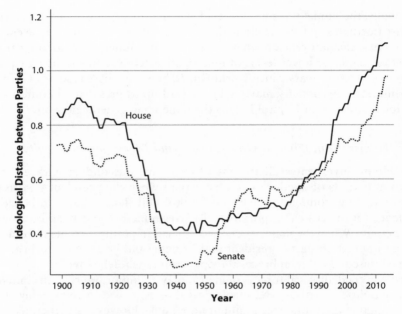

FIGURE 2.2. Partisan Polarization in the U.S. Congress, 1898–2014.

Moderates sit at the center of the scale (i.e., near 0), and more conservative members cluster to the right of the scale (i.e., closer to 1).[70]

Figure 2.2 illustrates the well-known dramatic shifts in partisan polarization in the House of Representatives over the course of the twentieth century. Polarization began a steep decline from its previously high levels in the 1920s, bottoming out by about 1940 and remaining low through the 1950s; polarization began to increase again, albeit slowly in the 1960s and 1970s, and then accelerating sharply in the 1980s through the 2000s.

If partisan incentives are the dominant force driving greater investigative activity during divided government, then we would expect the divided government gap to be roughly the same size, regardless of the level of polarization.

[70] Prior to the New Deal, it is less clear whether the labels "liberal" and "conservative" can be applied to the scale without risk of anachronism. See Devin Caughey and Eric Schickler, "Substance and Change in Congressional Ideology: NOMINATE and Its Alternatives," *Studies in American Political Development* (Fall 2016). One way to think about the scale over a long span of time is that it measures the behavioral difference in roll call voting patterns between Republicans and Democrats. From this perspective, a high polarization score indicates that the two parties' typical members behaved very differently in their roll call votes, though the gap could reflect a complex mix of factors.

Table 2.3: Differences in Mean House Investigative Activity Across
Three Periods of Congressional History

	1898–1936	1937–1980	1981–2014
Unified	21.3	47.1	18.0
Divided	195.5	81.5	66.7

Note: All differences in means across periods of unified and divided government
are statistically significant, p < .05, two-tailed test.

The opposition party will always stand to gain more politically from launching potentially damaging investigations against the president than will the president's co-partisans, regardless of where they stand ideologically. If, however, ideological incentives also drive investigative activity, we would expect the divided-unified government gap in investigative activity to be greater in periods of high polarization than in periods of low polarization. In the former, partisan and policy incentives reinforce one another. In the latter, they are more likely to pull would-be legislators in opposing directions.

As an initial exploration into how the influence of divided government on House investigations varies over time, we examine the difference in means in investigative activity during unified and divided government in three periods: 1898 to 1936 was a period of generally high partisan polarization; 1937 to 1980, which roughly corresponds to the era in which the conservative coalition was prominent and partisan polarization was relatively low; then from 1981 through 2014, as partisan polarization in the House increased steadily and reached new heights.[71] Table 2.3 presents the average number of days of investigative hearings held in a given year during unified and divided government in each era.

In all three periods, we observe a statistically significant difference between House investigative activity in unified and divided government, with investigations always being significantly more prominent in the latter. However, the gap in average investigative activity between unified and divided government is significantly greater in the two periods of high partisan polarization book-ending our time series than in the middle era of much greater ideological heterogeneity within the parties.

From 1898 to 1936, investigations were rare in unified government, averaging about twenty-one days of hearings per year. By contrast, in divided government the average level of investigative activity in the House soared to almost 200 days per year. In this era of sharp party divisions in roll call

[71] The average difference in first dimension NOMINATE scores from 1898 through 1936 was .75; from 1936 through 1980 it was .46; and from 1981 through 2014 it was .82.

voting, presidential co-partisans all but snuffed out investigative activity aimed at the executive branch when they controlled the committee apparatus. By contrast, on those rare occasions when the opposition party ruled the House, they fully exploited the legislature's institutional capacity to cause trouble for the executive through investigations.

Partisan polarization waned significantly in the 1930s, and by the 1950s and 1960s there was considerable ideological heterogeneity within both major parties. Despite being an era of nominal Democratic control of Congress, a conservative coalition of Republicans and southern Democrats wielded considerable influence over the legislative agenda. On many issues, conservative southern Democrats found more common ground with Republicans than they did with their liberal northern co-partisan brethren. In this era when partisan and ideological incentives often pulled many members in competing directions, divided government continued to produce greater investigative activity, on average, than unified government. However, the increase under divided government pales in comparison to the earlier era of high polarization: in contrast to the 900% increase in investigations under divided partisan control in the early period, the volume of investigations is less than twice as high under divided government than in unified government in the low-polarization era.

As partisan polarization began to accelerate in the 1980s, the gap between investigative activity in unified versus divided government again widened significantly. Over the last thirty-five years, the average Congress in divided government has held almost four times as many days of investigations of the executive branch as has the average Congress in unified government, all else being equal. While the overall level of investigative activity has dampened somewhat in recent decades, divided government has become a much stronger predictor of the intensity of investigative activity in our polarized polity.

While the preceding periodization allows us to examine the effect of divided government on investigative activity in periods of relatively high and low levels of polarization, this periodization is admittedly coarse. As a further test of our argument that polarization heightens the influence of divided government on House investigative activity, we re-estimated our event count analysis for the entire time series with two new variables: the continuous measure of partisan polarization within the House summarized in Figure 2.2 and its interaction with the divided government variable. Table 2.4 presents the results.

Strongly consistent with our argument, the coefficient on the interaction variable is positive and statistically significant. Figure 2.3 illustrates the effect of increasing levels of polarization on the predicted amount of House investigative activity in periods of unified and divided government. Across all levels of polarization, our model finds more investigative activity when the president's partisan opponents control the House than when the

TABLE 2.4: Divided Government, Polarization, and House Investigative
Activity, 1898–2014

Divided government	−0.58
	(0.52)
Divided government * Polarization	2.39***
	(0.79)
Polarization	−2.02***
	(0.57)
Inflation	0.05***
	(0.02)
% Change in GDP per capita	−0.49
	(2.22)
War	−0.05
	(0.25)
Presidential election year	0.13
	(0.25)
Congressional election year	0.30
	(0.20)
Constant	4.38***
	(0.44)
Observations	117

Note: Model is a negative binomial count regression of the factors influencing
the number of days of investigative hearings held by the House of Representatives in a given year. The variable *Polarization* is the difference in the first
dimension NOMINATE score between the average Democrat and average
Republican within the chamber. Robust standard errors are reported in parentheses. All significance tests are two-tailed.

*$p < .10$ **$p < .05$ ***$p < .01$

president's partisan allies wield the committee gavels. However, this gap
widens significantly as partisan polarization increases. A polarized House
in divided government investigates the executive branch more aggressively
than a less polarized House. By contrast, during unified government as
the level of partisan polarization increases, the investigative machinery of
the House all but grinds to a standstill. At very high levels of polarization,
our model predicts fewer than twenty days of investigative hearings. In the
contemporary period where partisan and ideological forces again routinely

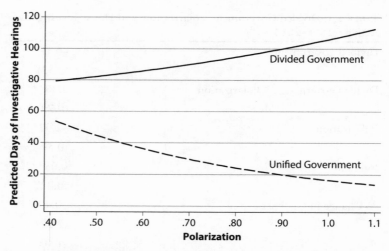

FIGURE 2.3. Effect of Polarization on House Investigative Activity in Unified and Divided Government.

reinforce one another, investigations in the House have become almost exclusively a phenomenon observed in divided government.

MODELING INVESTIGATIVE ACTIVITY IN THE SENATE

Whereas divided government significantly increases investigative activity in the House, the initial difference in means analysis presented in Table 2.1 offered no evidence that it does so in the Senate. To explore the very different dynamics driving variation in investigative activity over time in the Senate, we estimated a series of event count models parallel to those constructed for the House. Table 2.5 presents the results.

The first model examines Senate investigative activity over the entire time series from 1898 through 2014.[72] Consistent with the difference in means results, we find no evidence that Senate investigative activity systematically varies across periods of unified and divided government. The coefficient for the divided government variable is negative and statistically insignificant. This suggests that in the Senate other incentives aside from partisanship—for example, the desire of individual policy entrepreneurs to use investigations

---

[72] As a robustness check to address concerns about possible serial correlation in the dependent variable, we re-estimate this specification using an autoregressive poisson model. The results presented in Appendix Table 2.2 are substantively similar.

TABLE 2.5: Factors Influencing Intensity of Senate Investigative Activity

	1898–2014	1947–2014	1900–2014
Divided government	−0.22	−0.40*	−0.22
	(0.21)	(0.22)	(0.21)
Inflation	0.01	0.04	0.01
	(0.01)	(0.03)	(0.02)
% Change in GDP per capita	−4.01**	−2.79	−3.68**
	(1.77)	(5.21)	(1.81)
Unemployment		−0.03	0.01
		(0.07)	(0.02)
War	0.62***	0.74***	0.62***
	(0.21)	(0.28)	(0.22)
Presidential election year	−0.33	−0.27	−0.35
	(0.27)	(0.33)	(0.27)
Congressional election year	0.36*	0.05	0.37*
	(0.21)	(0.32)	(0.21)
Constant	3.76***	3.98***	3.69***
	(0.15)	(0.57)	(0.22)
Observations	117	68	115

Note: Models are negative binomial event count regressions of the factors influencing the number of days of investigative hearings held by the Senate in a given year. Column 2 includes annualized unemployment rate data from the Bureau of Labor Statistics. Column 3 includes BLS unemployment data from 1947 through 2014, and estimated unemployment rate data from the National Bureau of Economic Research for 1900 through 1946. Robust standard errors are reported in parentheses. All significance tests are two-tailed.

*p < .10   **p < .05   ***p < .01

to raise their national stature and reputation—drive variation in investigative activity over time.

We do find some evidence that senators are less aggressive in investigating the executive branch in times of economic prosperity. While inflation is uncorrelated with investigative activity, the coefficient for the change in per capita GDP variable is negative and statistically significant. This is consistent with the hypothesis that economic growth may insulate the president somewhat from aggressive investigations on Capitol Hill.

Consistent with the Senate's greater formal powers in the area of foreign policy, wars evidently have a clearer impact on investigative activity in the Senate than the House. World War I, World War II, and Vietnam each prompted major Senate investigations into the executive branch's conduct.

These and other war-related inquests produced dramatic wartime surges in Senate investigative activity. Simulations reveal that an ongoing major war almost doubled the predicted number of investigative days in the Senate, all else equal. Modifying the war variable to include a year or two after the conclusion of World War I, World War II, Korea, and Vietnam only intensifies the effect. This suggests that once the fighting has stopped investigations have historically been an important tool through which the Senate has endeavored to win back some of the power it lost to the executive branch in wartime.

Finally, there is at least suggestive evidence that Senate investigative activity varies with the electoral calendar. As in the House, the model reveals that Senate investigative activity is somewhat lower, on average, in presidential election years. However, the coefficient, while negative, fails to reach conventional levels of statistical significance. The coefficient for congressional election years, by contrast, is positive and marginally significant. This suggests that Senate investigative activity is moderately higher, on average, in midterm election years, all else being equal.

The final pair of models in Table 2.5 probe further whether Senate investigative activity responds to economic conditions by including measures of unemployment. In the post–World War II period (model 2), we see no evidence that Senate investigative activity varies with the state of the economy.[73] Neither inflation nor unemployment predicts investigative activity. The coefficient for changes in GDP per capita, while still negative, is no longer statistically significant when limiting the temporal scope of analysis to 1947 through 2014. In the post-1946 period, the models also find no evidence that Senate investigative activity varies with the electoral calendar.

In both of the final models, war continues to be associated with significant increases in Senate investigative activity, but with an important caveat: as with the House, the Senate data unequivocally shows that wars in Iraq and Afghanistan did not have the same influence as earlier wars. If Afghanistan and Iraq are added to the war variable, the effect becomes both substantively and statistically insignificant across all model specifications. Finally, in neither model do we find any evidence of divided government increasing investigative activity in the Senate.

Polarization, Divided Government, and Senate Investigative Activity

In the House, we saw that the effect of divided government on investigative activity was greatly intensified in periods of high partisan polarization. To this point, we have found little evidence that divided government increases

---

[73] As a further robustness check, we also re-estimated model 2 of Table 2.5 controlling for the number of days that the Senate was in session in a given year. This yields a positive and statistically significant coefficient for the days-in-session variable. In this specification, no other variable is a significant predictor of Senate investigative activity.

TABLE 2.6: Differences in Mean Senate Investigative Activity Across
Three Periods of Congressional History

	1898–1936	1937–1980	1981–2014
Unified	51.4	72.6	21.8
Divided	66.0	61.3	21.8

Note: None of the differences in means across periods of unified and divided
government are statistically significant, p < .10, two-tailed test.

investigative activity in the Senate. However, as a final assessment we rep-
licate our earlier analyses examining the interaction of divided government
and partisan polarization with Senate investigative activity data.

Table 2.6 again divides the data into three periods: a period of higher
than average polarization from 1898 through 1936; a period of lower than
average polarization from 1937 to 1980; and the contemporary period of
high and increasing partisan polarization from 1981 to 2014 (see Figure
2.2). In the first period of high polarization, the Senate did average more
days of investigations in divided government (sixty-six), than in unified
government (fifty-one). However, the difference is not statistically significant. During the conservative coalition era, the relationship is roughly
reversed. The Senate averaged seventy-two days of investigative hearings
in unified government versus only sixty-one in divided government. However, this difference, too, is not statistically significant. Finally, in the highly
polarized era that has emerged since 1981, the Senate has averaged just
under twenty-two days of investigative hearings in both unified and divided government.

Finally, replicating the regression analysis using the continuous measure
of partisan polarization and its interaction with divided government for the
Senate yields similarly null results. As shown in Appendix Table 2.3, the
coefficient on the interaction term is substantively small and statistically
insignificant. Divided government does not increase the volume of Senate
investigative activity in either periods of high or low partisan polarization.

CASE STUDIES OF INVESTIGATIONS THAT SPAN UNIFIED
AND DIVIDED GOVERNMENT

The preceding analyses only examine differences in the *frequency* of investigations in unified versus divided government. While important, such raw
data tell us little about how the substance of investigations differs across the
partisan control divide. One way to gain insight into how investigations of
the executive may be qualitatively different in unified versus divided government is to examine closely investigations that spanned periods of both

configurations of partisan control. This approach holds constant the nature of the investigation itself and the administration behavior that precipitated it, allowing only the partisan composition of the legislature to vary.

Each of our three most recent presidents have held the White House during stretches of both unified and divided government. In the case studies that follow, we examine first the investigation into the Clintons' prepresidency involvement in the Whitewater Development Corporation and then inquests into the Bush administration's prosecution of the war in Iraq, with an eye toward differences in how Congress investigated the associated scandals in unified and divided government. We return to explore investigative activity in the Obama era more fully in Chapter 6.

Whitewater

In 1978, the Governor of Arkansas, Bill Clinton, and his wife Hillary joined a land venture with James and Susan McDougal called the Whitewater Development Corporation to sell vacation homes in Arkansas. The deal went belly-up, and in 1992 the Clintons reported a loss of over $40,000 on their investment. Hillary Clinton also provided legal services for McDougal's Madison Guaranty Savings and Loan, which like many other Savings and Loan banks across the country collapsed in the late 1980s.

In November of 1993, the Democratically controlled House Banking Committee announced that, pursuant to a request from the committee's Republicans, it would "collect information" about the Clintons' ties to the Madison Savings and Loan and whether money from the bank was improperly funneled into Clinton's 1984 gubernatorial campaign.[74] The president, however, was not initially a target of the committee's inquiry. Questions about the Savings and Loan and the Whitewater land deal received increasing media scrutiny as 1993 drew to a close, to the point that in January of 1994 the administration announced that it welcomed the appointment of a special counsel to probe the matter.[75] However, congressional Republicans were unsatisfied. The Senate Minority Leader Robert Dole (R-KS) and the ranking Republican on the House Banking Committee James Leach (R-IA) led the charge for a parallel congressional investigation, either in the Banking Committee or by a newly created select committee. Dole argued that "the appointment of a special counsel doesn't take away our responsibility

[74] Andrew Taylor, "Thrift Industry: Banking Panel Plans Probe of Failed Arkansas Thrift," *CQ Weekly*, November 13, 1993, 3109.

[75] The 1978 Independent Counsel statute had lapsed; hence this was originally a "special counsel." The Whitewater furor proved an important impetus for Congress renewing the statute. When the independent counsel statute was renewed, Kenneth Starr replaced Fiske as prosecutor, because the latter had been appointed by Attorney General Janet Reno.

in the Congress" and urged action by the Banking Committee: "If the Banking Committee would proceed, that would probably take care of any concerns that I have. It's almost unprecedented to have so many serious questions without even one congressional committee looking into the matter."[76] The Democratic chair of the House Banking Committee, Henry Gonzalez of Texas, resisted, calling the Republican accusations a "witch hunt" and "an array of half-truths, old rumors, half-baked conspiracy theories and outright lies."[77] Similarly, Senate Banking chair Don Riegle (D-MI) rebuffed the minority's initial call for hearings.

Republican leaders also called for Attorney General Janet Reno to appoint a special counsel to investigate the allegations. Reno, however, refused, arguing that anyone she appointed would not be viewed as impartial, *ipso facto.* The Clinton administration countered by calling on Congress to renew the provision of the 1978 Ethics in Government Act allowing for the appointment of an independent counsel by the Special Division of the D.C. Circuit. The independent counsel statute had lapsed in 1992, in large part because of Republican anger over the Walsh investigation into Iran-Contra.[78]

Ultimately, Clinton directed Reno to appoint a special prosecutor. The attorney general selected Robert Fiske, Jr., a Republican former U.S. Attorney appointed by President Ford who had also served as chairman of the American Bar Association's Committee on the Federal Judiciary. The appointment was praised by Senator Alphonse D'Amato (R-NY), the ranking minority member on the Senate Banking Committee: "I will tell you this about the integrity of Bob Fiske. It is second to none. I would have every confidence in any investigation undertaken by Bob Fiske."[79]

The appointment of Fiske, however, did little to quell calls for congressional hearings. Minority Leader Dole railed against Senate Democrats' refusal to hold hearings and threatened to use it against them in the midterm election campaign. "If the Democrats don't want to have a hearing, they're going to suffer the consequences."[80] Eventually, congressional Democrats in both chambers bowed to political pressure. Seeking to defuse the political issue looming over the upcoming midterms, Democratic chairmen of both the House and Senate Banking Committees agreed to hold hearings.

[76] Andrew Taylor, "Special Counsel May Not Quiet Clamor Over Whitewater," *CQ Weekly,* January 15, 1994, 61.

[77] Andrew Taylor, "Banking: Gonzalez's Reluctance Complicates Whitewater Hearings Picture," *CQ Weekly,* April 9, 1994, 842.

[78] Neil Lewis, "Special Counsel in Clinton Deals Depends on Congress, Reno Says," *New York Times,* January 7, 2014, A1.

[79] Stephen Labaton, "Special Counsel Picked by Reno," *New York Times,* January 20, 1994, A1.

[80] Richard Berke, "G.O.P. Challenges Clinton Agenda: Promises Fight on Most Issues— Dole Issues Warning on Whitewater Hearing," *New York Times,* January 23, 1994, 14.

However, they battled intensely with Republicans over the scope of the inquests and the powers that the committee investigators would wield.

Republicans demanded a wide-ranging investigation of all aspects of the Whitewater deal, as well as the power to hold their own hearings and issue subpoenas. Democrats, by contrast, argued that the committees should focus exclusively on the "Washington phase"—the death of Vince Foster, and any other Whitewater-related activities that took place during the Clinton presidency—leaving to the special counsel all prepresidency matters. The tensions escalated to the point that Senate Republicans filibustered an airport improvements bill to try to force the Democrats' hands, but ultimately they relented and the narrower approach was adopted.[81]

The House Banking Committee began its hearings on July 26 with a series of witnesses from the administration. Democrats were buoyed by the initial report of special counsel Fiske confirming the official designation of Foster's death as a suicide and finding no evidence that any administration official had broken the law or obstructed an ongoing investigation.[82] Moreover, while Republicans tried their best to land political punches, they were seriously hampered by the narrow scope of the investigations, which did not probe into events from the 1980s before Clinton became president. Once the hearings began, Gonzalez seized on the Fiske report to limit the investigation's scope further still. Given that Fiske had ruled Foster's death a suicide that was completely unconnected to Whitewater, Gonzalez ruled that the circumstances of Foster's death and its aftermath were off limits. Republicans cried foul. Ranking minority member James Leach lamented that the House hearings would deal with only "1 percent" of the Whitewater scandal.[83]

Aside from limiting the scope of the investigations, Democrats used their agenda powers in other ways to blunt GOP attacks. For example, as *Congressional Quarterly* observed: "Republicans complained that many of the White House staff aides they were particularly interested in questioning were relegated to a 10-person panel that testified July 28. On the other hand, White House counsel Lloyd N. Cutler and former White House counsel Bernard Nussbaum, both sophisticated attorneys, were solo witnesses."[84] Even the *New York Times,* in an editorial entitled

---

[81] In the assessment of Republican senator William Cohen (R-ME), the leadership caved because it was unable to generate any public pressure to force the Democrats' hand. "No one is paying attention" to the GOP filibuster, Cohen noted. "Executive Branch: Whitewater Hearings to be Held on Democrats' Terms," *CQ Weekly,* June 18, 1994, 1588.

[82] Douglas Jehl, "First Whitewater Report Pleases Clinton Advisers," *New York Times,* July 1, 1994, A10.

[83] Stephen Labaton, "House Committee Told of Contacts Over Whitewater," *New York Times,* July 27, 1994, A1.

[84] Andrew Taylor, "Witnesses Fend Off GOP's Jabs as Whitewater Hearings Open," *CQ Weekly,* July 30, 1994, 2112.

"Censorship, Gonzalez Style," criticized the Democratic chairman's efforts to eviscerate the investigation procedurally: "The irascible Texan has twisted the already stringent rules to make it virtually impossible for members to develop a continuous, productive line of inquiry into even the narrow matter at hand."[85] Thanks in large part to the iron fist of chairman Gonzalez, the House hearings on Whitewater in the 103rd Congress ended not with a bang, but a whimper. In the concluding assessment of the *Times*: "Last week's Whitewater hearings before the House Banking Committee numbed the senses. That was the way committee Democrats and the White House planned it."[86]

Although the Senate hearings on Whitewater were more aggressive and damaging than those in the House, they nonetheless were much more circumscribed than key Republicans had hoped. Dole and D'Amato initially demanded a wide-ranging inquiry into all facets of the Whitewater scandal. Indeed, for nearly three weeks in June Dole rallied his troops and exploited the procedural rights given to the minority to hold up virtually all Senate business as they battled Majority Leader Mitchell over the scope of Whitewater hearings.[87] After an initial wave of defeats, Dole offered a compromise: that the hearings only focus on Whitewater developments that occurred after Clinton became president. However, Mitchell and Senate Democrats refused.[88]

Ultimately, Mitchell succeeded in limiting the scope of inquiry even further. However, the authorized scope of the investigation did allow Republicans to probe the circumstances surrounding Vince Foster's death. This concession was likely the result of the widely held expectation that the special prosecutor's report would present forensic evidence leaving little doubt that Foster's death was indeed a suicide.[89] By allowing Republicans to pursue their quixotic and increasingly bizarre investigation into Foster's suicide—in protest of the House Banking Committee's reluctance to hold hearings, Congressman Dan Burton (R-IN) famously "recreated" Foster's death by personally shooting a pumpkin to determine the distance at which the sound could be heard—Democrats hoped to discredit larger, less fanciful charges of wrongdoing.

[85] "Censorship, Gonzales Style," *New York Times*, July 28, 1994, A22.
[86] "More White House Damage Control," *New York Times*, July 31, 1994, C14.
[87] David Hess, "Limited Whitewater Hearings Backed," *Philadelphia Inquirer*, June 22, 1994, A2.
[88] Helen Dewar, "GOP Offers Concessions on Whitewater Inquiry," *Washington Post*, June 17, 1994, A10.
[89] David Rosenbaum, "Senate Will Hold Hearings on Whitewater," *New York Times*, June 15, 1994, A22. Undeterred by Fiske's report and conclusion, Republicans did investigate Foster's death, both in 1994 and again more aggressively in 1995 after they gained control of both chambers of Congress.

During the hearings, Democrats also allowed Republicans to concentrate their fire on Deputy Treasury Secretary Roger C. Altman, a longtime friend of President Clinton. Republicans were even joined by several Senate Democrats in their condemnation of the deputy treasury secretary.[90] The crux of the controversy centered on whether Altman, while acting head of the Resolution Trust Corporation (RTC), the regulatory agency managing the Savings and Loan bailout, improperly shared information with the White House concerning the RTC's criminal investigation against Madison Guaranty Savings and Loan. The independent Office of Governmental Ethics headed by Stephen Potts, a Bush appointee, concluded that, while Altman may have shown poor judgment in having such conversations, no laws or ethics rules were broken. The special prosecutor concurred. Yet, committee Republicans, joined by a few Democrats, pounced on inconsistencies in Altman's testimony. Ultimately, Altman, along with the Treasury Department's general counsel Jean Hanson, resigned in the face of congressional criticism.

However, aside from these casualties, the Senate hearings ended in early August with relatively few political fireworks. The focus on Altman gave the hearings the appearance of something of a sideshow. As reporter and critic Walter Goodman wryly noted, "Meantime, the true objects of attention—everybody knows who—remain offstage, which is always a problem for a play."[91] The conduct of President Clinton and the First Lady received virtually no scrutiny.[92] On balance, the unified party government phase of the Whitewater investigation suggests that while the minority did enjoy greater leverage in pressuring the Senate to take on the president, even the upper chamber's investigation was limited by the majority party's influence over the committee system. In many cases where the attack on the president as an individual is less direct, the minority may well be able to use its leverage to compel a vigorous Senate investigation. However, in cases like Whitewater where the proposed investigation is a direct assault on the president himself and the political stakes are highest, the Senate majority has strong incentives to use its influence over agenda-setting to limit the political damage.

When Republicans gained control of the committee gavels following the 1994 midterms, the investigative fury over Whitewater intensified

[90] Andrew Taylor, "Stories Conflict, Tempers Flare in Marathon Week of Hearings," CQ Weekly, August 6, 1994, 2225–2228.

[91] Walter Goodman, "Mining Some Drama from Whitewater at Last," New York Times, August 4, 1994, C16.

[92] The hearings also failed to resonate with the American public. Isabel Wilkerson, "Outside the Beltway, Whitewater Hearing Looks Like a Dud: As Scandals Go, This is No O.J.," New York Times, August 8, 1994, A8.

significantly. While the House Banking Committee held its own hearings in August of 1995, most of the action took place in the Senate. The Republican leadership quickly created a Senate special committee solely to investigate Whitewater and the scope of its inquiry expanded dramatically to include all aspects of the alleged scandal. Whereas Democrats had used the investigation of special prosecutor Fiske to declare most of the key events of the scandal—which took place a decade earlier in Arkansas—off limits when they wielded the committee gavels, Republican investigators imposed no such limits, despite the ongoing investigation of the new independent counsel, Kenneth Starr. The entire complicated history of the Clinton's relations and actions in Arkansas in the 1980s were explored in laborious detail. Perhaps even more important, whereas the main target of the 103rd Congress's Senate investigation ultimately proved to be the deputy secretary of the treasury, the Republican-led special committee's inquest quickly focused on a much more high-profile target: the first lady, Hillary Rodham Clinton.

Thirteen months after the hearings began, Senate Republicans issued a 769-page report denouncing various aspects of the administration's conduct. The GOP-led Whitewater investigations would also spawn separate investigations into the White House's use of FBI files, which along with the president's personal improprieties would also be taken up by the Whitewater independent counsel, Kenneth Starr.

Considered as a whole, the three-year congressional investigation of Whitewater both illustrates and slightly deviates from the larger patterns observed in the analysis of aggregate data of all investigative activity from 1898 to 2014. Perhaps most important, the Whitewater case illustrates the power of co-partisan committee chairs, particularly in the House, to blunt the force of investigations into an allied White House. While House Democrats could not rebuff calls for an investigation altogether, they were able to use their control over the machinery of the institution to insure that it would yield little ammunition to their partisan adversaries.

The Senate's investigation, by contrast, was in certain respects more robust than that conducted in the House, even in unified government. The minority Republicans succeeded in gaining more leeway for their questioning, and their criticism of Treasury Department officials' handling of Whitewater was even joined by some Democrats. The political pressure generated by this inquest directly led to Deputy Secretary Altman's resignation. However, in terms of its scope and content, the Senate investigation conducted in the 103rd Congress under unified government paled in comparison to that embarked upon by the newly minted Republican Senate majority in the 104th Congress.

Over more than a century of congressional history, divided government had little impact on Senate investigative activity in the aggregate. However, the Whitewater case—one of the few investigations to span periods of unified and divided partisan control—suggests that on major investigations with the potential to directly damage the president, partisan incentives can significantly shape the scale, scope, and duration of an investigation, even in the Senate.

The Iraq War

The war in Iraq also affords an opportunity to examine the nature of congressional investigations of the same issue in periods of unified and divided government. In the lead-up to the war, Bush administration officials routinely declared that it would be simple, relatively cost-free, and short. Indeed, the initial plans for the Office of Reconstruction and Humanitarian Assistance envisioned the United States completing its work in Iraq by August of 2003 and leaving behind only a small residual force by September. However, the eruption of looting and civil unrest following the fall of Baghdad and the kindling of an insurgency quickly mired the American military in what would become its bloodiest war since Vietnam. As the years dragged on, the situation in Iraq posed innumerable opportunities for congressional investigators: the failure to find weapons of mass destruction; the abuse of Iraqi prisoners at Abu Ghraib; the failure to provide adequate body armor and armored vehicles to protect American soldiers; the Haditha massacre; the poor treatment of disabled war veterans at Walter Reed. Yet, the record makes plain that the partisan control of Congress was the single most important factor driving both the number and intensity of congressional investigations into the war.

Figure 2.4 presents the trend in Iraq-related investigative activity in Congress from March 2003 through the end of the 110th Congress in December 2008. According to our search criteria, congressional Republicans did not allow a single day of investigative hearings of the Iraq War in 2003.[93] The strength of this negative agenda control is remarkable given how quickly the situation in Iraq deteriorated after the toppling of Saddam Hussein's statue in Firdos Square. Despite the looting, widespread civil disorder, and escalating attacks on American troops throughout the country, the president's allies in Congress toed the party line. In 2004, public revelations of the systematic abuse of prisoners at Abu Ghraib all but compelled Congress to hold investigative hearings. However, the horrors of Abu Ghraib were virtually the

[93] Other studies have cast a broader net and examined all critical oversight activity by Congress. See Howell and Kriner 2009; Douglas Kriner, "Can Enhanced Oversight Repair the 'Broken Branch'?" *Boston University Law Review* 89 (2009): 765–793.

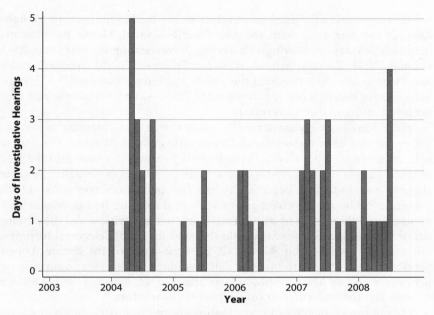

FIGURE 2.4. Days of Investigations of the War in Iraq, 2003–2008.

only wartime development that could compel congressional Republicans to investigate their partisan leader in the White House and his conduct of the war. Of the twenty-five days of investigative hearings held when Republicans controlled the committee gavels, all but seven focused almost exclusively on Abu Ghraib.[94] Every other potential area of war-related inquiry received virtually no attention from congressional investigators during the conflict's first four years.

Investigative activity increased dramatically when the opposition Democrats gained control of Congress following the 2006 midterm elections. Indeed, the average number of investigative days per year almost doubled from an average of 6.5 days of investigative hearings on the Iraq War per year during unified government to 12.5 days per year during divided government. However, as in our analysis of all investigative activity above, the return of divided government mainly fueled investigative activity in the House. When Republicans controlled the House, they quashed most calls

[94] And of these remaining seven, the only charge of abuse levied in one hearing was via the minority's report of allegations of fraud and abuse in contracting.

for investigations of alleged misconduct in the Bush administration's handling of the war. Even with the Abu Ghraib scandal, House Republicans held only 3.4 days of hearings, on average, investigating the war from 2003 through 2006. By contrast, when Nancy Pelosi sat in the Speaker's chair and Democratic chairmen held the gavels, the House averaged 9.5 days of investigative hearings per year from 2007–2008—almost triple the rate that occurred under unified government.

In the Senate, by contrast, there is no evidence of an increase in investigative activity with the return of Democratic control. Whereas the Senate held an average of 3.1 days of investigative hearings per year into the war in unified government, investigative activity continued at virtually the same sluggish rate (3.0 days per year) in the Democratically controlled 110th Congress.[95] The sparse investigative activity during unified government is almost certainly a result of widespread fears that any criticism of the administration's conduct of the war would threaten the GOP's electoral fortunes. For example, when John Warner (R-VA), the chair of the Senate Armed Services Committee, dared to schedule two days of hearings to investigate prisoner abuse at Abu Ghraib, he was attacked vociferously by his House counterpart for undermining support for the war effort.[96]

The continued paucity of investigations of the war after the Democratic takeover, while consistent with the absence of divided government effects in our aggregate analysis, is nonetheless surprising. However, Senate criticism of the Iraq War and the administration's conduct of it did increase, even if this critical oversight did not produce investigations of alleged misconduct. Indeed, in the first year of the Democratically controlled 110th Congress, Senate committees held more days of critical oversight hearings of the war than the chamber had in the preceding four years combined.[97] These oversight hearings focused on criticism of the administration's policy performance but did not reach the point of alleging executive abuses of power or malfeasance. As such, they are not counted as "investigations" by our coding criteria. Thus, the Iraq War case suggests one potential explanation for the somewhat surprising result that divided government does not increase Senate investigative activity in the aggregate. Divided government may increase criticism of the president and his administration's policies; however, unlike House members, senators' hearings in divided

---

[95] While the tally of investigative hearings even in divided government is modest, critical oversight of the Iraq War—that is hearings that criticized and challenged the Bush administration's conduct of the war, but that did not explicitly allege misconduct or abuse—surged after the Democrats' regained control of Congress (Kriner 2009).

[96] Fowler 2015, 21.

[97] Figures calculated from data on congressional oversight of the Iraq War reported in Kriner 2009, 776–778.

government, even if more critical, are not more likely to allege executive malfeasance.[98]

Finally, the scope of the investigations also increased dramatically. Congressional Democrats—primarily in the House—launched additional probes into the torture of detainees and abuses by contractors. House Democrats also began new inquests into the "outing" of covert operative Valerie Plame in retaliation for her husband Ambassador Joe Wilson's questioning of the administration's claim that Saddam Hussein was acquiring yellowcake uranium; abuses of executive power in misleading the nation into war;[99] and an investigation into the deplorable conditions facing returning wounded veterans at Walter Reed Army Medical Center. Even as conditions improved on the ground in Iraq in late 2007 and early 2008, Democratic investigators consistently used the committee room to offer a counter-narrative to that advanced by the administration. Contrasting the flurry of investigative oversight under the Democrats with the more lethargic pace of the preceding two Congresses, Illinois Democrat Rahm Emanuel perhaps put it best: "What a difference a year makes."[100]

CONCLUSION

Investigations offer a potential tool through which members of Congress might combat the expansion of presidential power when they cannot overcome the barriers to acting legislatively. However, even a cursory review of

[98] Indeed, we find additional evidence of this in our larger data set. As described above, many hearings returned by our initial search terms did not contain an allegation of executive-branch misconduct. Those that involved oversight of the executive branch, even if very critical of administration actions and policies, but that did not contain explicit allegations of executive-branch wrongdoing were coded as "critical oversight" but not "investigations." As shown in Appendix Table 2.4, in both the House and Senate divided government significantly increased the number of days of critical oversight; however, divided government only increased *investigative* oversight in the House. The analysis in Appendix Table 2.4 ends in 2006; after the migration of the CIS data to ProQuest, we did not endeavor to update the oversight measure from 2007 to 2014. We do not emphasize the oversight findings in our larger quantitative analysis, however, because our search terms were initially designed to identify investigations, not oversight; as such, we worry that our "critical oversight" measure is incomplete (i.e., it likely misses some critical oversight hearings that did not include any reference to the search terms we had used in our effort to hone in on the narrower set of investigative hearings).

[99] This House Judiciary Committee investigation even raised the word "impeachment" in order to heighten the political heft of the attack.

[100] Peter Baker, "Libby Verdict Brings Moment of Accountability," *Washington Post*, March 7, 2007, A1. Critical oversight hearings—such as those focusing on the Iraq government's failures—are not included in our count of hearing days unless a charge of misconduct, wrongdoing, or abuse of power is made against the administration.

the data makes clear that investigative activity has been far from uniform throughout congressional history. Under what conditions have members of Congress used investigative oversight to challenge the executive branch's conduct and contest assertions of presidential power? To answer this question, we constructed the most comprehensive database of congressional investigations yet compiled, one that spans more than a hundred years of congressional history from 1898 through 2014. Armed with this data, we then analyzed the dynamics driving the considerable variation in investigative oversight over time, and exploited this variation to test hypotheses about the fundamental incentives that drive members to take on the executive.

We find that for more than a century the House of Representatives has investigated the president more aggressively when the partisan opposition controls the committee gavels than when the president's co-partisans wield them. The volume of investigative activity writ large in the Senate, by contrast, seems unrelated to partisan control of the chamber. This strong interchamber difference is striking, and it suggests an interesting and more subtle dynamic between partisanship and investigative activity in the Senate. The motivations of individual members and other idiosyncrasies drive the ebb and flow in Senate investigative activity.[101] This is in accordance with a long literature arguing that the Senate leadership has never developed institutional resources and procedural powers on par with their counterparts in the House.[102] However, the Whitewater case study suggests that, at least on the most high-profile investigations, those conducted in divided government may be broader in scope and more aggressive in tone than those conducted in unified government.[103] Moreover, the Iraq War case study shows that the return of divided government in the Senate did prompt a significant surge in critical oversight of the Iraq War; however, most of this critical oversight stopped short of alleging outright misconduct or abuse of power by executive-branch actors.

[101] McGeary 1940.

[102] Steven Smith, *Party Influence in Congress* (New York: Cambridge University Press, 2007); Barbara Sinclair, *Unorthodox Lawmaking: New Legislative Processes in the United States Congress*, 2nd ed. (Washington, DC: Congressional Quarterly Press, 2000).

[103] For recent accounts suggesting that despite their more limited arsenal of formal prerogatives, Senate parties nonetheless exert a degree of agenda control, see Andrea Campbell, Gary Cox, and Mathew McCubbins, "Agenda Power in the US Senate, 1877–1986," in *Party, Process and Political Change in Congress*, ed. David Brady and Mathew McCuibbins (Stanford: Stanford University Press, 2002); Sean Gailmard and Jeffery Jenkins, "Negative Agenda Control in the Senate and House: Fingerprints of Majority Power," *Journal of Politics* 69 (2007): 689–700; Chris Den Hartog and Nathan Monroe, *Agenda Setting in the United States Senate: Costly Consideration and Majority Party Advantage* (New York: Cambridge University Press, 2011); Chris Den Hartog and Nathan Monroe, "Home Field Advantage: An Asymmetric-Costs Theory of Legislative Agenda Influence in the U.S. Senate," paper presented at the Conference on Party Effects in the United States Senate, Duke University, 2006.

While divided government is the single biggest predictor of investigative activity in the House, the degree to which divided partisan control of the chamber and the White House drives fluctuations in investigative oversight has changed significantly over time. Majority party members of the House use the investigative powers of the committees most actively when the president is of the other party and when partisan polarization is high. In these conditions, majority party members possess both strong partisan and ideological incentives to challenge the executive branch. By contrast, in unified government during an era of high polarization, overlapping partisan and policy goals between the congressional majority and White House mutes Congress's aggressiveness.[104]

The persistence of a divided government effect even in periods where ideological alliances cross-cut the parties—such as the conservative coalition era—indicates that partisan incentives are an important consideration. But the impact of divided government is weaker when polarization is lower. Thus, the data also makes clear that Congress engaged in a considerable number of investigations in periods of unified government during the conservative coalition era. From the Dies Committee's investigation of communist influence in the New Deal to Howard Smith's aggressive probes of the National Labor Relations Board and Office of Price Administration, many of these investigations were fueled by strong policy disagreements between committee chairs and a co-partisan president. This suggests a significant role for individual entrepreneurship in an era of relatively weaker partisan control. When parties in Congress are internally divided and interpartisan polarization is low, such an environment affords space for individual, entrepreneurial members to promote investigations that simultaneously promote their policy agenda and challenge executive dominance.[105]

Ultimately, our analysis demonstrates that Congress has often used the investigative arm of its committees to expose instances of executive malfeasance and to counter efforts to expand presidential power at the expense of the legislature. Moreover, for decades, this was a power that Congress used with considerable frequency even in periods of unified government. However, as partisan polarization has increased, investigations have become more and more exclusively a feature of divided government. Today's investigations are more likely to be coordinated by party leaders than to bubble

---

[104] Moreover, in the contemporary era of high polarization between the parties and considerable intrapartisan ideological homogeneity, conditional party government theory (Rohde 1991; Aldrich 1995) suggests that strengthened leadership structures further diminish the prospects of individual entrepreneurs initiating successful investigations that are not part of their party's program.

[105] See, e.g., Eric Schickler and Katherine Pearson, "Agenda Control, Majority Party Power, and the House Committee on Rules, 1937–52," *Legislative Studies Quarterly* 34 (2009): 455–491; Schickler 2007.

up from the entrepreneurial actions of individual members. This makes it possible to develop a coordinated response to presidential actions, but only under conditions of divided control. As a result, this dependence on partisan structures and leaders is likely to generate oscillation between periods of congressional assertion and abdication. The deepest challenge to congressional efforts to use its investigative powers to superintend the executive today appears rooted not in collective action dilemmas, but instead in the close alignment between the congressional majority party and the White House when ideological homogeneity, a centralized party leadership apparatus, and unified government coincide.

APPENDIX

To identify all congressional investigative hearings from 1898–2006, we adopted a two-stage coding procedure. First, we conducted a series of full text searches using the Lexis Nexis database of CIS abstracts to identify hearings that potentially included a charge of executive misconduct or abuse of power. Because we are only interested in hearings that alleged misconduct within the executive branch, we required that the hearing include at least one of the following words: president; administration; executive; department;

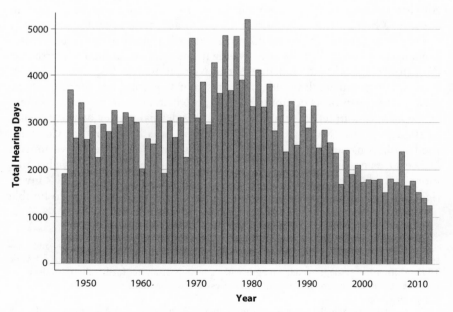

APPENDIX Figure 2.1. Total Days of Congressional Hearings, 1946–2012.

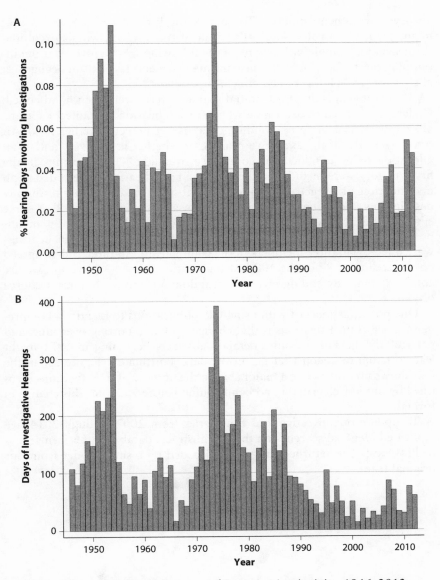

APPENDIX Figure 2.2. Two Measures of Investigative Activity, 1946–2012.
A. As a Percentage of Total Hearing Activity. B. Days of Investigative Activity.
Note: The two time series are strongly correlated, $r = .89$.

agency; government; military. To narrow the list further to hearings that might plausibly involve some allegation of misconduct, we also required the hearing to contain at least one of the following words: investigation; inquiry; inquest; abuse; malfeasance; mismanagement; favoritism; negligence; alleg*; corrupt*; impropriety; ethic*; superintend*.

All hearings meeting these initial search criteria were then hand coded. Coders were asked to determine whether each hearing contained a specific allegation of executive misconduct or abuse of power, whether it constituted oversight of the executive branch, or whether it involved neither an allegation of misconduct nor committee oversight. Only hearings in the first category were included in the analysis. For a hearing to be coded as an investigation of alleged misconduct, the abstract or individual testimony descriptions had to contain a specific accusation or suggestion that some entity within the executive branch had acted illegally, unethically, or improperly.[106] To insure intercoder reliability, a random sample of 100 hearings was coded by all three members of the coding team. All three coders agreed on the coding of 97 of the 100 hearings in the sample. As a result, we are confident that any coding errors are random and not a significant source of bias.

One potential concern with using CIS publications to identify a comprehensive set of investigations is that changes in CIS reporting over time, and particularly the shift to more detailed abstracts beginning in 1971 might lead to temporal inconsistencies in the data. Fortunately, Figure 2.1 in the text shows no evidence of a major shift in the number of investigations identified by our search criteria and hand coding before and after this change in format.

To update our investigations time series from 2007 through 2014, we replicated identical searches on the CIS abstracts database after it migrated to ProQuest. The returned hits were all coded by a single coder from our original team.

---

[106] Additional details, including examples of coded hearings, are available at: http://people .bu.edu/dkriner/Kriner%20and%20Schickler%20JOP%202014%20SI.pdf, accessed February 28, 2016.

APPENDIX TABLE 2.1: Autoregressive Poisson Model of
House Investigative Activity, 1898–2014

Divided government	1.04***
	(0.19)
Inflation	0.06***
	(0.02)
% Change in GDP per capita	1.67
	(2.12)
War	-0.10
	(0.25)
Presidential election year	–0.06
	(0.24)
Congressional election year	0.22
	(0.22)
AR(1)	0.32***
	(0.10)
Constant	3.08***
	(0.20)
Observations	116
R-squared	0.36

Note: Model is an autoregressive poisson count regression of the
factors influencing the number of days of investigative hearings
held by the House of Representatives in a given year. Robust
standard errors are reported in parentheses. All significance tests
are two-tailed.

*$p < .10$ **$p < .05$ ***$p < .01$

APPENDIX TABLE 2.2: Autoregressive Poisson Model of
Senate Investigative Activity, 1898–2014

Divided government	−0.24
	(0.19)
Inflation	0.01
	(0.02)
% Change in GDP per capita	−4.13***
	(1.56)
War	0.55***
	(0.20)
Presidential election year	−0.38*
	(0.21)
Congressional election year	0.41**
	(0.18)
AR(1)	0.48***
	(0.09)
Constant	3.77***
	(0.14)
Observations	116
R-squared	0.30

Note: Model is an autoregressive poisson count regression of the
factors influencing the number of days of investigative hearings
held by the Senate in a given year. Robust standard errors are
reported in parentheses. All significance tests are two-tailed.

*p < .10   **p < .05   ***p < .01

APPENDIX TABLE 2.3: Divided Government, Polarization, and Senate
Investigative Activity, 1898–2014

Divided government	−0.50
	(0.78)
Divided government * Polarization	0.66
	(1.28)
Polarization	−2.39***
	(0.57)
Inflation	0.01
	(0.02)
% Change in GDP per capita	−4.01**
	(1.92)
War	0.36
	(0.24)
Presidential election year	−0.37
	(0.27)
Congressional election year	0.40**
	(0.19)
Constant	5.08***
	(0.33)
Observations	117

Note: Model is a negative binomial count regression of the factors influencing the
number of days of investigative hearings held by the Senate in a given year. The
variable *Polarization* is the difference in the first dimension NOMINATE score between the average Democrat and average Republican within the chamber. Robust
standard errors are reported in parentheses. All significance tests are two-tailed.

*$p < .10$ **$p < .05$ ***$p < .01$

APPENDIX TABLE 2.4: Differences in Mean Oversight Activity in Unified
vs. Divided Government, 1898–2006

	All	House	Senate
Unified	143.6	87.2	59.6
Divided	329.9	219.5	132.4

Note: Each difference in means across periods of unified and divided government
is statistically significant, $p < .01$, two-tailed test.

CHAPTER 3

~ ~

Investigations and Public Opinion

BETWEEN 1953 AND 2014, Congress held more than 6,200 days of hearings investigating alleged misconduct or abuse of power by some actor within the executive branch. As the previous chapter showed, legislators' eagerness to use the investigative powers at their disposal has varied significantly over time. In some political environments, Congress has aggressively challenged presidents. In other periods, congressional investigators have been reluctant to engage in interbranch battles in the hearing room. Nevertheless, when Congress does exercise its investigative powers, do the resulting probes produce any tangible results? Do investigations serve as a viable tool for Congress to constrain an executive branch that, particularly since the outbreak of World War II, has persistently accrued more and more power at the expense of the legislature? Or are investigations just another example of congressional "position-taking": are they simply instances of posturing designed to aid the career ambitions of restless legislators, and do they consequently have little concrete influence on the course of politics and public policy?[1]

As we argued in Chapter 1, investigations avoid some of the problems that generally plague legislative efforts to check presidential power. Transaction costs can be much lower; collective action problems may be overcome more easily; and supermajoritarian requirements, such as the Senate filibuster and the two-thirds requirement to override a veto, are inoperative. Thus, when presidents push too far on the bounds of their power and provoke concern in Congress, legislators may well be able to investigate, even when they cannot enact legislation.

An obvious limitation of investigations, however, is that unlike legislation, committee probes, in and of themselves, cannot directly compel the

[1] The observational analysis and first experiment in this chapter draw heavily on previously published work: Douglas Kriner and Eric Schickler, "Investigating the President: Committee Probes and Presidential Approval, 1953–2006," *Journal of Politics* 76 (2014): 521–534. © Southern Political Science Association, 2014. In this chapter, we have updated the analysis of the capacity of investigations to erode presidential approval through 2014.

president to change course. But investigations can nonetheless constrain the president by bringing political pressure to bear on the White House.

In this chapter, rather than focusing on the direct impact of any single investigation, we propose and empirically test a general mechanism through which congressional investigative activity could affect presidential behavior and policy making more broadly: by influencing the president's well of support among the American people. More than 125 years ago, Woodrow Wilson emphasized the informative function of congressional investigations. In some cases, investigations can provide valuable information to Congress itself as it seeks to redress problems legislatively. More often than not, however, the primary intended audience for an investigation is the American public. As Mayhew has shown, a common feature of most investigations is the desire for *publicity*.[2] As such, the concerns of prior analysts that investigations have routinely proved more successful at highlighting problems than at solving them comes into a different focus. Shining the light of public scrutiny on alleged misconduct in the executive branch may be an end in and of itself. By using the investigative arm of its committees, we argue, the president's opponents in Congress can often weaken the president's support among the public, reduce his political leverage, and thereby provide at least a partial counterweight to presidential power, even when Congress is institutionally unable to constrain the president formally through legislative sanction.

The chapter proceeds in four parts. The following section describes two mechanisms through which committee investigations of executive misconduct are well positioned to shape levels of public support for the president. Congressional investigations can both bring charges of executive misconduct firmly onto the public agenda, and they can imbue such charges with institutional legitimacy. The empirical analysis then begins by asking a basic, but essential pre-cursor question: does the public generally support Congress employing its investigative powers to uncover and pursue allegations of abuse of power by the executive branch? Having answered this question in the affirmative, the analysis continues by merging the database of congressional investigative activity described in the previous chapter with more than sixty years of public opinion data measuring support for the president. The statistical analysis shows a strong, consistent negative relationship between investigative activity and presidential approval. The chapter then presents the results of several original survey experiments that isolate the influence of congressional investigations on public opinion independent of potential confounding factors. The experiments also afford a direct test of the credibility mechanism, which cannot be tested directly in the statistical analysis using observational data.

[2] Mayhew 1991.

Two Mechanisms of Investigative Influence on Public Opinion

At first blush, there are good reasons to be skeptical that congressional investigations can shape public opinion. After all, more than three decades of opinion polls have consistently shown that Congress is the least popular of the three branches of government. Since 1974, Gallup has measured the percentage of Americans approving of Congress's job performance. More often than not, the judgment has not been positive. From 1978 through 1997, not a single poll registered a majority of Americans approving of Congress's job performance. The soaring economy of the late 1990s allowed congressional approval to exceed the 50/50 benchmark in a few polls, and the terrorist attacks of 9/11 buoyed popular confidence in governing institutions across the board. However, this era of good feelings would not last long. Congress's approval rating fell to 50% in June of 2003, and it has never flirted with the breakeven point since. Congress's approval rating last surpassed 40% in February of 2005, and in November of 2013 during the dark days of the budget shutdown it plummeted to a new, single-digit low of 9%.[3] Given such long-standing and wide-spread distrust of Congress as an institution, can the positions expressed in Congress really sway public opinion?

Nonetheless, a substantial body of public opinion scholarship suggests that the actions taken and the positions articulated by members of Congress do indeed have major implications for public opinion formation. Because most Americans are relatively inattentive to politics and lack sophisticated information on which to base their political judgments,[4] most look to cues from political elites when forming their political assessments.[5] To be sure, presidents who command the institution's proverbial bully pulpit are important cue-givers. However, they are far from the only cue-givers. In fact, while much is often made of the president's ability to "go public" and take his case directly to the American people,[6] empirical scholarship has found surprisingly limited evidence that presidents can actively change public opinion.[7] Rather levels of public support for the president and his policies appear in large part to be a function of the reaction of other political elites.

---

[3] http://www.gallup.com/poll/1600/congress-public.aspx#1, accessed February 28, 2016.

[4] Lippman 1992 [1922]; Michael Delli Carpini and Scott Keeter, *What Americans Know about Politics and Why It Matters* (New Haven: Yale University Press, 1997).

[5] Samuel Popkin, *The Reasoning Voter: Communication and Persuasion in Presidential Campaigns* (Chicago: University of Chicago Press, 1991); Arthur Lupia, "Shortcuts Versus Encyclopedias: Information and Voting Behavior in California Insurance Reform Elections," *American Political Science Review* 88 (1994): 63–76.

[6] See, e.g., Samuel Kernell, *Going Public: New Strategies of Presidential Leadership* (Washington, DC: CQ Press, 1997).

[7] See, e.g., George Edwards, *On Deaf Ears: The Limits of the Bully Pulpit* (New Haven: Yale University Press, 2006).

Bipartisan consensus bolsters support for the president, while dissension among political elites provides a counter-narrative to that offered by the White House and decreases public support.[8] Much of the evidence for this dynamic, somewhat ironically, has focused on public opinion in foreign policy—a realm where presidents are commonly thought to enjoy particular advantages over Congress. For example, Groeling and Baum show that the level of media coverage showing congressional criticism of the president's policies is one of the single largest predictors of the size of the rally effect in approval that the president enjoys in the wake of a military action.[9] Similarly, Berinsky argues that a broad bipartisan elite consensus allowed Roosevelt to maintain strikingly robust levels of support both for the war effort and for himself personally, despite the early military setbacks and massive casualties sustained in World War II.[10] As "the chief institutional locus of elite opposition,"[11] Congress plays a pivotal role in providing cues to a low information electorate.

Engaging policy debates in what Mayhew termed "the public sphere" is thus one of the most important ways in which Congress can retain a check on the president, even when it is unable to constrain him legislatively.[12] Formal committee investigations, we argue, are one of the most important tools at Congress's disposal through which its members can publicly challenge the administration and seek to influence public opinion.

There is considerable research showing that low approval ratings make it more difficult for presidents to pursue their policy and political agendas.[13] Perhaps most important, presidents with high approval ratings enjoy significant advantages in legislative battles with Congress. For example, Canes-Wrone and DeMarchi find that strong approval ratings significantly bolster the president's probability of winning many of the most important roll call

[8] Richard Brody, *Assessing the President: The Media, Elite Opinion, and Public Support* (Stanford: Stanford University Press, 1991); John Zaller, *The Nature and Origins of Mass Opinion* (New York: Cambridge University Press, 1992).

[9] Timothy Groeling and Matthew Baum, "Crossing the Water's Edge: Elite Rhetoric, Media Coverage, and the Rally-Round-the-Flag Phenomenon," *Journal of Politics* 70 (2008): 1065–1085.

[10] Adam Berinsky, *In Time of War: Understanding American Public Opinion from World War II to Iraq* (Chicago: University of Chicago Press, 2009).

[11] Scott Althaus, Jill Edy, Robert Entman, and Patricia Phalen, "Revising the Indexing Hypothesis: Officials, Media, and the Libya Crisis," *Political Communication* 13 (1996): 407–421.

[12] David Mayhew, *America's Congress: Actions in the Public Sphere, James Madison through Newt Gingrich* (New Haven: Yale University Press, 2000).

[13] See, e.g., Douglas Rivers and Nancy Rose, "Passing the President's Program: Public Opinion and Presidential Influence in Congress," *American Journal of Political Science* 29 (1984): 183–196; Bryan Marshall and Brandon Prins, "Strategic Position Taking and Presidential Influence in Congress," *Legislative Studies Quarterly* 32 (2007): 257–284; Andrew Barrett and Matthew Eshbaugh-Soha, "Presidential Success on the Substance of Legislation," *Political Research Quarterly* 60 (2007): 100–112.

votes in Congress—votes on issues that are complex and highly salient.[14] Taking a slightly different approach, Beckmann finds that bills passed in Congress are significantly more likely to move policy in the president's preferred direction when he enjoys strong support among the public than when his level of political capital is lower.[15] Moreover, the tangible benefits of high public approval extend far beyond the legislative arena. For example, even in the judicial sphere, where presidential approval ratings normatively should be irrelevant, Howell finds that popular presidents are significantly more likely to defeat legal challenges to their unilateral orders.[16]

But precisely how do investigations affect levels of public support for the president? We posit two mechanisms. First, investigative activity can play an important agenda-setting role. As Mayhew noted, most committee investigations are consciously designed to attract media attention. As recent research on political scandal has emphasized, scandals are not exogenous events that simply appear like magic on the nation's political radar out of nowhere. Rather, most scandals are politically constructed events.[17] For example, in March 2006 a car bombing near the American consulate in Karachi, Pakistan killed American diplomat David Foy, along with three Pakistanis. While the loss of an American diplomat was mourned, Congress did not hold a single hearing into the security arrangements at the consulate, which failed to prevent the deadly attack. By contrast, the 2012 attack on the American consulate in Benghazi, Libya, that resulted in the tragic death of Ambassador Christopher Stevens and three other Americans quickly became a cause célèbre among congressional Republicans that captured months of sustained media attention thanks in large part to an onslaught of congressional hearings investigating a string of alleged Obama administration failures surrounding the disaster. Alternatively, when President Bush fired a cadre of U.S. Attorneys on December 7, 2006, the move barely registered a blip in the media. However, once newly empowered Democrats began holding hearings into allegations that the firings were politically motivated, a full-fledged political scandal ensued, complete with a catchy title: "the Pearl Harbor Day Massacre."[18]

[14] Brandice Canes-Wrone and Scott De Marchi, "Presidential Approval and Legislative Success," *Journal of Politics* 64 (2002): 491–509.
[15] Matthew Beckmann, *Pushing the Agenda: Presidential Leadership in US Lawmaking, 1953–2004* (New York: Cambridge University Press, 2010), 141–142.
[16] Howell 2003, 158–160.
[17] Howell 2003, 158–160.
[18] "The Pearl Harbor Day Massacre." *ABC News*, March 6, 2007, http://blogs.abcnews.com/politicalradar/2007/03/the_pearl_harbo.html accessed March 3, 2016; Adam Zagorin. "Why Were the U.S. Attorneys Fired?" *Time*, March 7, 2007. http://content.time.com/time/nation/article/0,8599,1597085,00.html, accessed February 28, 2016. Prior to the House Judiciary Committee hearings, the *New York Times* ran only one article, a January 15th editorial, mentioning the firings; and this article reported allegations by a number of high-ranking Democrats alleging misconduct by the White House in the case.

In trying to put charges of administration misconduct at the forefront of the public's agenda, the media is a strong ally. Media norms emphasize conflict,[19] particularly conflict from official Washington sources.[20] As a result, what committees investigate inherently becomes newsworthy. Through their very nature, investigative committee hearings, which can span many days or even months, also provide a public forum through which congressional investigators can endeavor to secure *sustained* coverage of their proceedings over time. This may be particularly critical, as repeated media coverage of a political challenge to a president over an extended period is much more likely to reach and inform an inattentive public than a story that grabs headlines for a single day, but then vanishes.

Yet, investigations hold the potential to do more than merely set the agenda by bringing certain facts, disputes, and allegations to light and then keeping them in the public eye. A second key mechanism is that formal committee inquiries imbue such challenges with institutional legitimacy. Past scholarship has shown that the credibility of a source can be just as important as the substance of the cue itself in determining its influence on public opinion.[21] Charges of misconduct or abuse of power formally investigated by a congressional committee may be more credible than identical charges that are not taken up by actors within the legislature. And while past research has shown that even criticism by individual legislators may be influential, formal committee hearings represent a genuine institutional challenge to the executive branch, one that may resonate more with reporters and citizens alike.

The Benghazi case is illustrative. Immediately after the September 11, 2012, attacks on the Benghazi consulate, conservative pundits were quick to charge the Obama administration with an alleged cover-up of its mishandling of the security situation at the consulate. For example, just nine days after the attack on September 20, 2012, Sean Hannity minced few words declaring, "We are witnessing a widespread cover-up based on flat-out lies."[22] For most

[19] Doris Graber, *Mass Media and American Politics* (Washington, DC: CQ Press, 1997); Timothy Groeling, *When Politicians Attack: Party Cohesion in the Media* (New York, Cambridge University Press, 2010).

[20] W. Lance Bennett, "Toward a Theory of Press-State Relations in the United States," *Journal of Communication* 40 (1990): 103–125; Jonathan Mermin, *Debating War and Peace: Media Coverage of U.S. Intervention in the Post-Vietnam Era* (Princeton: Princeton University Press, 1999).

[21] See, e.g., Jeffrey Mondak, "Source Cues and Policy Approval," *American Journal of Political Science* 37 (1993): 186–212; James Kuklinski and Norman Hurley, "On Hearing and Interpreting Political Messages: A Cautionary Tale of Citizen Cue-Taking," *Journal of Politics* 56 (1994): 729–751; Arthur Lupia and Mathew McCubbins, *The Democratic Dilemma: Can Citizens Learn What They Need to Know?* (Cambridge: Cambridge University Press, 1998); James Druckman, "On the Limits of Framing Effects: Who Can Frame?" *Journal of Politics* 63 (2001): 1041–1066.

[22] Eric Boehlert, "Under Bush, Hannity Denounced 'Politicizing' National Security, With Benghazi, Hannity Can't Stop," *Huffington Post*, October 24, 2012, http://www.huffingtonpost.com/eric-boehlert/under-bush-hannity-denoun_b_2008967.html, accessed February 28, 2016.

Americans, charges levied by Sean Hannity alone have little influence. By contrast, when the same charges are investigated by a congressional committee, they gain a significant measure of legitimacy and are therefore poised to have greater weight in shaping public opinion.

As a result, because of their agenda-setting capacity and the institutional credibility they lend to charges of executive misconduct, we hypothesize that committee investigations are well positioned to depress presidential job approval ratings.

PUBLIC SUPPORT FOR CONGRESS'S INVESTIGATIVE FUNCTION

If congressional investigations are to erode public support for the president, it stands to reason that Americans should generally approve of Congress using its powers of investigation to raise and pursue allegations of misconduct within the executive branch. However, the public's long-standing disapproval of Congress's job performance gives reason to question Americans' receptivity to congressional investigations. Will the public view investigations as offering legitimate criticisms of the executive branch and reconsider their approval of the sitting president accordingly? Or will Americans dismiss congressional investigations as blatant grandstanding by a dysfunctional legislature?

On the eve of the 2014 midterm elections, with Congress's job performance hovering at near-historic lows,[23] we implemented a simple survey experiment to assess the level of public support for Congress using its investigative powers. The experiment was included in the 2014 Cooperative Congressional Election Study (CCES), a nationally representative public opinion survey. Our goal was to examine support for congressional investigations in the abstract, as well as to examine whether support for investigations remains robust when subjects are reminded of major recent congressional investigations of alleged abuses in both the Obama and George W. Bush administrations. Given Congress's abysmal approval ratings, we are confident that if the public supports congressional investigations of the executive branch in this environment, it almost certainly backed congressional use of its investigative powers in earlier contexts where Congress as an institution enjoyed greater support.

We randomly assigned subjects in our 900-respondent sample to one of three experimental groups.[24] All subjects received a simple prompt informing

[23] Rebecca Rifkin, "2014 U.S. Approval of Congress Remains Near All-Time Low," December 15, 2014, *Gallup.com*, http://www.gallup.com/poll/180113/2014-approval-congress-remains-near-time-low.aspx, accessed February 28, 2016.

[24] This question was included on the postelection survey; because of drop-off between the two waves of the CCES our final sample size for this question was just under 900 (the first wave had 1000 respondents).

them that "Congress has the power to investigate alleged abuses of power by the executive branch." Subjects in the control group were provided with no additional contextual information.

After receiving the basic prompt, subjects in our first treatment group read several examples of major investigations in the Obama era: "In recent years, Congress has investigated: President Obama's implementation of the Affordable Care Act; whether the IRS singled out conservative groups for special scrutiny; the Obama administration's decisions and activities surrounding the 2012 terrorist attacks on the U.S. consulate in Benghazi, Libya; as well as the exchange of five Taliban prisoners for the release of a U.S. Army prisoner of war and the Obama administration's failure to consult with Congress about the exchange."

Finally, subjects in the second treatment group instead received contextual information about investigations of both the Bush and Obama administrations, with examples of Bush era investigations receiving greater prominence by being presented first: "In recent years, Congress has investigated: the Bush administration's firing of U.S. Attorneys pursuing corruption charges against Republican politicians; the abuse of prisoners during the Bush administration at Abu Ghraib in Iraq; President Obama's implementation of the Affordable Care Act; and the Obama administration's decisions and activities surrounding the 2012 terrorist attacks on the U.S. consulate in Benghazi, Libya."

All subjects were then asked the same question: "Do you support or oppose congressional efforts to investigate abuses of power by the executive branch?"[25] Table 3.1 presents the percentage of respondents supporting congressional investigations across the three treatment groups. Because subjects were randomly assigned to one of the three groups, the resulting differences in means are unbiased.

As shown in column 1, across all three treatment groups, supermajorities of Americans supported congressional efforts to investigate alleged abuses of power by the executive branch. In the control group, more than 83% of subjects supported Congress's exercise of its investigative power to superintend the executive. In the abstract, at least, support for investigations as a component of checks and balances is overwhelming.

Perhaps even more important support for Congress using its investigative power remained very strong when subjects were reminded of recent partisan-fueled investigations of both the Obama and Bush administrations. Among subjects primed to consider recent Republican-led investigations of

[25] We measured support for investigations on a four-point likert scale ranging from strongly support to strongly oppose. To ease interpretation, in Table 3.1 we collapse the strongly support and somewhat support categories into a percentage supporting measure. Ordered logit analysis using the full four-point scale of the dependent variable yields very similar results to those presented in the text. This alternate analysis is presented in Appendix Table 3.1.

TABLE 3.1: Support for Congressional Investigations

	All	Democrats	Non-Democrats
Control group	83.3%	73.0%	92.9%
Obama treatment	69.1%	47.7%	87.3%
Bush and Obama treatment	79.6%	72.0%	86.5%

Note: For all respondents and for Democrats, the mean in the Obama investigations treatment is significantly lower than in the other two experimental groups (p < .01, two-tailed test). For non-Democrats, none of the differences in means are statistically significant (p < .05, two-tailed test).

the Obama administration, ranging from Benghazi to the implementation of Obamacare, support for Congress's use of its investigative power stood at 69%. This is significantly lower than the 83% level of support observed in the control group.[26] However, even in this treatment only a small minority of respondents opposed Congress's use of its investigative powers.

In the treatment informing subjects of major investigations during both the Bush and Obama presidencies, support for Congress's investigative power was almost 80%—a figure indistinguishable from that observed in the control. Thus, across all three experimental conditions we observed overwhelming public support for congressional investigations of alleged executive-branch abuse.

Finally, we examine how political partisanship moderates the influence of our two experimental treatments on support for investigations. Logically, Democrats might be the most sensitive to the first experimental treatment reminding subjects only of a host of recent Republican-led investigations of alleged wrongdoing by the Obama administration. To examine this dynamics, the final two columns of Table 3.1 disaggregate our sample into Democrats and non-Democrats.[27]

Nearly three-quarters of Democrats supported congressional investigations of the executive branch in the control group baseline. This strong level of baseline support is significant as many Democrats undoubtedly viewed the question through the lens of the incumbent Democratic president confronting Republican majorities in both chambers of Congress. As expected, in the first treatment group exposed to information only about a series of Republican-led investigations of the Obama administration, support for

[26] A t-test shows that the difference in means across the control and Obama treatments is statistically significant, p < .01, two-tailed test.

[27] We include those who "lean" toward the Democratic Party as Democrats. Just under 50% of our sample identified as Democrats. Thirty-three percent of our sample identified as Republicans. The remaining respondents did not affiliate with either party.

Congress's investigative power among Democrats was significantly lower than in the control group; nevertheless, in this treatment group just under a majority backed Congress's use of its investigative power. By contrast, among Democrats reminded of major investigations of both the Bush and Obama administrations, support for congressional investigations was again very high and statistically indistinguishable from the level observed in the control group. Among non-Democrats, levels of support for congressional investigations were very high across all three groups, and neither experimental treatment had a statistically significant impact on support for investigations.[28]

The experimental survey evidence thus presents a strong *prima facie* case consistent with our argument that congressional investigations have the potential to erode public support for the president. Despite the low esteem in which most Americans hold the contemporary Congress, overwhelming majorities of Americans support Congress's use of its investigative powers to pursue allegations of executive-branch abuse and misconduct. Moreover, support for congressional investigations remains robust across informational contexts concerning recent investigations and across partisan political divides.

Investigations and Presidential Approval, 1953–2014

To assess whether congressional investigations systematically erode the president's standing among the public, we integrate our original database of investigative activity with more than sixty years of public opinion data from 1953 through 2014.[29] We then create a statistical model that allows us

[28] None of the mean levels of support are significantly different from each other, p < .05, two-tailed test. Disaggregating the non-Democratic category into Republicans and independents yields similar results. Among Republicans, there were no statistically significant differences in support for investigations across the three experimental groups. Among independents, the only statistically significant difference is that the control group has slightly greater support for investigations than does the second treatment group describing investigations of both the Bush and Obama administrations. However, the sample sizes with pure independents are very small, and even in the Bush-Obama treatment group, more than two-thirds of independents supported congressional investigations of executive-branch wrongdoing.

[29] While presidential approval has long been one of the most queried political commodities, we did encounter several gaps in constructing a monthly time series for 1953 through 2014, particularly in the early years. For example, Gallup did not conduct approval polls for eight of Eisenhower's ninety-six months in office; similarly Gallup did not ask the approval question in the months leading up to the 1956, 1964, 1972, and 1976 general elections. To construct a complete time series, we first used simple linear interpolation to fill gaps in the series. However, as a robustness check, we also used kalman filtering to fill any gaps and smooth the entire series. The first series using linear interpolation and the kalman smoothed series are almost

to assess the effect of investigative activity on presidential approval while controlling for the most important factors known from past research to influence public support for the president.

The biggest hurdle to overcome in determining the extent to which investigative activity erodes public support for the president is that these political dynamics are almost certainly mutually reinforcing. Because investigations attract significant media attention, shine a spotlight on alleged executive-branch wrongdoing, and lend institutional credibility to such charges, they are well-positioned to affect public opinion. However, as shown in the preceding chapter, the frequency with which members of Congress use the legislature's investigative powers varies substantially over time. While the previous chapter focused on the influence of partisanship, ideological polarization, and war, another factor that might logically drive some of this variation is the president's standing among the public. Put simply, chief executives with lower approval ratings may be more attractive investigative targets.

Even a Congress dominated by the opposition party may be reticent to challenge a popular president in the hearing room, as such inquests could backfire and damage the investigators as much as the executive. By contrast, it may be easier for committee chairs to quash an investigation of their own party's president under unified party government if the president is popular, while blunting calls for an investigation will be harder when the president's public standing is low. Saddled with an unpopular incumbent of their own party, some chairs may even be eager to hold hearings to distance themselves from an administration that is out of favor with the public.[30] Past research has found evidence of greater investigative activity when presidents are unpopular, although it has not sorted out the direction of causation.[31]

Accordingly, we model the relationship between approval and investigative activity using a system of simultaneous equations. This approach allows us to recover estimates of the influence of investigative activity on presidential approval, and of approval on investigative activity in Congress, while accounting for the reciprocal nature of the relationship between the two. To estimate a system of simultaneous equations requires instrumental variables to identify each equation—variables that are strong predictors of

---

perfectly correlated at $r = .99$. For the analyses reported in the chapter, we use the series completed via linear interpolation. However, replicating all of the analyses in the text and appendices with the kalman filtered series yields virtually identical results.

[30] As we move to consider the effects of investigative activity on policy, it is important to recognize a second source of endogeneity: presidents who anticipate an aggressive investigative response from Congress may have an incentive to adapt their behavior in an effort to forestall potentially costly public inquests. We examine this dynamic directly in Chapter 5.

[31] Kriner and Schwartz 2008; Parker and Dull 2009.

investigative hearings and approval, respectively, but that have no independent influence on the other endogenous variable. The first instrument is the number of days that Congress was in session in a given month. This is a strong predictor of investigative activity, but has no independent influence on presidential approval. The congressional calendar should be correlated with a number of factors, including the level of pressing business before each chamber and the electoral cycle; however, there is no theoretical reason drawn from existing literatures to expect the calendar to be independently correlated with presidential approval. The second instrument is the Index of Consumer Sentiment (ICS), a survey-based measure that incorporates both Americans' prospective and retrospective evaluations of the economy. The stronger the ICS, the more optimistic Americans are about the state of the economy, and the more likely they should be to approve of the president's job performance. A long literature has shown that this indicator is a strong predictor of presidential approval; however, there is no reason to expect the ICS to have any effect on the level of investigative activity in Congress, except through its influence on the president's approval rating.[32]

With this approach we can now assess the independent effect of investigative activity on presidential approval. To complete the model, we also include a number of standard control variables culled from decades of research on the forces driving public support for the president. In addition to consumer sentiment, the model accounts for the role of major international and domestic events by including the number of positive and negative rally events that occurred in each month.[33] Positive events, which may bolster presidential approval ratings, include American military actions, threats to American security, and major administration accomplishments. Negative events, such as major protests, domestic conflict, and other controversies,

[32] Erikson, MacKuen, and Stimson have shown that after controlling for public perceptions of the state of the economy, objective indicators such as unemployment and inflation have little additional explanatory power. Over the past three decades, scholars have debated the relative influence of prospective versus retrospective economic evaluations of the economy. See, e.g., Robert Erikson, Michael MacKuen, and James Stimson, "Bankers or Peasants Revisited: Economic Expectations and Presidential Approval," *Electoral Studies* 19 (2000): 295–312; Harold Clarke and Marianne Stewart, "Prospections, Restrospections, and Rationality: The "Bankers" Model of Presidential Approval Reconsidered," *American Journal of Political Science* 38 (1994): 1104–1123. However, following a number of recent studies we employ the undifferentiated index as a control. See Barry Burden and Anthony Mughan, "International Economy and Presidential Approval," *Public Opinion Quarterly* 67 (2003): 555–578; Douglas Kriner and Liam Schwartz, "Partisan Dynamics and the Volatility of Presidential Approval," *British Journal of Political Science* 39 (2009): 609–631. When monthly data is not available, quarterly data is used.

[33] These two measures are drawn from Paul Brace and Barbara Hinckley, *Follow the Leader* (New York: Basic Books, 1992) and updated by Paul Gronke and John Brehm, "History, Heterogeneity, and Presidential Aproval: A Modified ARCH Approach," *Electoral Studies* 21 (2002): 425–452; and Kriner and Schwartz 2009.

may hurt the president's standing among the public. To further account for the influence of war on popular support for the president, we also include the number of American casualties in both the Vietnam and Iraq wars in the preceding six months.[34] To allow for different base levels of support due to personal and environmental factors not captured in the model, all specifications also include unreported fixed effects for each administration. Finally, presidential approval tends to move slowly over time. Presidential approval in a given month is strongly related to what it was in the preceding month, with new information moving it above or below this baseline. To account for this dynamic, the model includes the level of presidential approval in the preceding month as a final control variable.[35]

Main Results

Table 3.2 presents the results of our analysis for the entire time period from 1953 through 2014. The top half of the table presents the results from the *Approval Model*, which estimates the influence of investigative activity and the other factors included in the model on presidential approval. Consistent with our argument, we find strong evidence that investigative activity significantly erodes the president's standing among the public. Figure 3.1 graphically illustrates the influence of increasing levels of investigative activity on presidential approval. The solid line plots the predicted level of public support for the president at each level of investigative activity; dotted lines represent the 95%

---

[34] On the effect of Vietnam and Iraq War casualties on presidential approval, see John Mueller, *War, Presidents, and Public Opinion* (New York: Wiley, 1973); Eric Larson, *Casualties and Consensus: The Historical Role of Casualties in Domestic Support for U.S. Military Operations* (Santa Monica, CA: RAND, 1996); Scott Gartner and Gary Segura, "War, Casualties and Public Opinion," *Journal of Conflict Resolution* 42 (1998): 278–300; Christopher Gelpi, Peter Feaver, and Jason Reifler, "Success Matters: Casualty Sensitivity and the War in Iraq," *International Security* 30 (2005/2006): 7–46; Richard Eichenberg, Richard Stoll, and Matthew Lebo, "War President: The Approval Ratings of George W. Bush," *Journal of Conflict Resolution* 50 (2006):783–808; Erik Voeten and Paul Brewer, "Public Opinion, the War in Iraq, and Presidential Accountability," *Journal of Conflict Resolution* 50 (2006): 809–830; Kriner and Schwartz 2009.

[35] Failing to include lagged approval leads to autocorrelation in the residuals. However, after including the lagged dependent variable on the right-hand side of the equation, the Breusch-Godfrey LM test shows no evidence of autocorrelation. For a review of the use of lagged dependent variables in time series models, see Luke Keele and Nathan Kelly, "Dynamic Models for Dynamic Theories: The Ins and Outs of Lagged Dependent Variables," *Political Analysis* 14 (1996): 186–205. Because we include lagged approval, the models exclude the first month of each presidency (and the first two for Eisenhower as his first approval rating appeared in February 1953). As a further robustness check, we re-estimated all of the models in Tables 3.2, 3.3, and 3.4 excluding the first two months of every new administration. Results are virtually identical.

TABLE 3.2: Effect of Investigative Activity on Presidential Approval, 1953–2014

Approval Model	
Days of investigative hearings	−0.12***
	(0.04)
Index of consumer sentiment	0.06***
	(0.02)
Positive events	3.07***
	(0.40)
Negative events	−0.56
	(0.34)
Vietnam casualties in last 6 months (100s)	−0.03**
	(0.01)
Iraq casualties in last 6 months (100s)	−0.00
	(0.00)
Honeymoon	1.70***
	(0.36)
Lagged approval	0.87***
	(0.02)
Investigations Model	
Approval	−0.14***
	(0.03)
Days in session	0.27***
	(0.02)
Positive events	0.52
	(0.92)
Negative events	0.90
	(0.76)
Vietnam casualties in last 6 months (100s)	−0.16***
	(0.03)
Iraq casualties in last 6 months (100s)	−0.00
	(0.00)
Honeymoon	−0.24
	(0.81)
Observations	732

Note: Results of a simultaneous equations analysis. Both the *Approval* and *Investigations Models* include unreported presidential fixed effects. Standard errors are reported in parentheses. All significance tests are two-tailed.

* $p < .10$ ** $p < .05$ *** $p < .01$

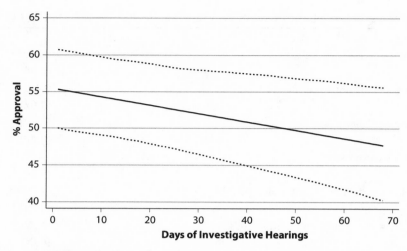

FIGURE 3.1 Effect of Misconduct Hearings on Presidential Approval.
Note: Estimates derived from model in Table 3.2. Dotted lines delineate the
95% confidence interval, obtained from simulations, about the predicted
values. The x-axis of the figure stretches to seventy days, since when multiple
committees are holding hearings there can be more than thirty hearing days
per month. The highest monthly total is sixty-eight hearing days, which occurred in May of 1974, when Congress was investigating not only the Watergate scandal, but also allegations of abusive domestic wiretapping programs,
the solicitation of improper presidential campaign contributions, and corruption or misconduct at the Department of Health, Education and Welfare, Small
Business Administration, and Internal Revenue Service, among others. The
average number of days of investigative hearings in a month in 1953–2014 is 9
(the median is 5), and the standard deviation is almost 10.

confidence interval, obtained from simulations, around the point estimates.
For example, increasing the number of days of investigative hearings in a
month from 0 to 20, slightly less than a two standard deviation shift, decreases presidential approval by approximately 2.5%.[36] The implications for
presidents are clear. Sustained investigative activity over a period of months
has a significant potential to diminish their well of public support.[37]

---

[36] This is the point estimate obtained from the model in Table 3.1. The 95% confidence
interval around this point estimate suggests that a twenty-day increase in investigative hearings
should produce a decrease in approval ranging from .8% to 4.0%.

[37] The x-axis of Figure 3.1 stretches to 70 days, since when multiple committees are holding
hearings there can be more than thirty hearing days per month. The highest monthly total is 68

It is important to note that our model shows strong evidence that investigative activity lowers presidential approval, even after controlling for a range of other factors that also influence public support for the president. The results for all of these control variables accord with expectations. Consistent with past research, we find that as Americans' assessments of the economy improve, so too does presidential approval. Similarly, the president's approval rating responds to major events, increasing in the wake of military actions and major positive developments, and dropping in the aftermath of negative events. During both the Vietnam and Iraq wars, presidential approval fell during periods of high casualties. And finally, consistent with both past research and conventional wisdom, we find that presidential approval tends to be higher during the honeymoon period than in later years, all else being equal.

The bottom half of Table 3.2 presents the results from the second equation estimating the influence of presidential approval on the intensity of investigative activity in a month. We label this the *Investigations Model*. Two results are of note. First, consistent with our suspicion that the amount of investigative activity both affects presidential approval and is affected by it, we find strong evidence of a reciprocal relationship. The coefficient for presidential approval in the *Investigations Model* is negative and statistically significant. This shows that high presidential approval ratings significantly decrease Congress's willingness to aggressively investigate the executive branch. Such presidents are not attractive targets, and investigations entail greater political risks. Second, as discussed previously, the key to being able to estimate the influence of investigative activity on approval, given that the relationship is reciprocal and each affects the other, was to identify an instrumental variable that predicts investigative activity, but otherwise exerts no independent influence on presidential approval. The instrument we proposed was the number of days that Congress was in session in a given month. Consistent with our hypothesis, the *Investigations Model* confirms that this is indeed a strong and statistically significant predictor of investigative activity.[38] Moreover, standard diagnostic tests confirm the strength of

---

hearing days, which occurred in May of 1974, when Congress was investigating not only the Watergate scandal, but also allegations of abusive domestic wiretapping programs, the solicitation of improper presidential campaign contributions, and misconduct at the Department of Health, Education and Welfare, Small Business Administration, and Internal Revenue Service, among others. The average number of days of investigative hearings in a month in 1953–2014 is just under 9 (the median is 5), and the standard deviation is just over 10.

[38] In her analysis of oversight patterns in the House Foreign Affairs and Senate Foreign Relations Committees, Fowler (2015) found strong evidence of quarterly effects in oversight activity. The days-in-session variable in our model already accounts for much of this variation. However, as a robustness check, we also re-estimated the analysis in Table 3.2 with quarterly fixed effects in the Investigations Model. This robustness check confirms that investigative activity is less

the instrument.[39] As a result, we are confident that investigative activity does indeed significantly erode public support for the president.

House vs. Senate

In the previous chapter, we showed that different dynamics drive the variation in House and Senate investigative activity over time. However, we have little reason to suspect that the chamber leading an investigation of alleged executive-branch misconduct will affect the investigation's capacity to influence public opinion. The media is unlikely to give substantially greater coverage to investigative hearings held by one chamber than to those held by the other. Similarly, both House and Senate investigations represent a serious and credible institutional challenge to the executive branch. As a result, we have no reason to expect that charges levied by one house will be more influential with the public than charges by the other, all else being equal.

To test our hypothesis that both House and Senate investigations decreased presidential approval, we re-estimated the model presented in Table 3.2, first for House investigations (using the number of days the House was in session in a given month as the relevant instrument) and then for Senate investigations (using the number of days the Senate was in session in each month as the relevant instrument). The results presented in Table 3.3 confirm that both House and Senate investigations decrease presidential approval. Both of the relevant coefficients are negative, of almost exactly the same magnitude, and statistically significant.[40] Both chambers have the potential to weaken the president politically by investigating allegations of misconduct.

Partisan Control and Watergate

Analyzing more than sixty years of data from 1953 through 2014, we find unambiguous evidence that when Congress aggressively investigates the president, it can damage his reservoir of support among the public. This is

---

intense in the fourth quarter (which routinely contains election and Christmas recesses) than in other quarters, all else being equal. All of the other results remain virtually unchanged.

[39] The Anderson canonical correlation statistic allows us to reject the null of model under-identification, $p < .01$; and the Anderson-Rubin test statistic, which is robust to weak instruments, allows us to reject the null hypothesis of no relationship between investigative activity and presidential approval, $p < .01$.

[40] The larger coefficients on the investigations variables (compared to those observed in Table 3.2) are a result of the number of investigative hearings held by a single chamber being considerably smaller than when both chambers are considered together. For example, a one standard deviation increase in House hearings is roughly six days of hearings, versus being ten days when considering both chambers together.

TABLE 3.3: Effect of House and Senate Investigations on Presidential Approval

Approval Model	House	Senate
Days of investigative hearings in relevant chamber	−0.23***	−0.26***
	(0.07)	(0.10)
Index of consumer sentiment	0.06***	0.06***
	(0.02)	(0.02)
Positive events	3.13***	2.99***
	(0.41)	(0.42)
Negative events	−0.55	−0.58
	(0.35)	(0.36)
Vietnam casualties in last 6 months (100s)	−0.02*	−0.04**
	(0.01)	(0.02)
Iraq casualties in last 6 months (100s)	−0.00	−0.00
	(0.00)	(0.00)
Honeymoon	1.84***	1.53***
	(0.37)	(0.38)
Lagged approval	0.87***	0.88***
	(0.02)	(0.02)
Investigations Model		
Approval	−0.10***	−0.03
	(0.02)	(0.02)
Days in session in relevant chamber	0.31***	0.22***
	(0.03)	(0.03)
Positive events	0.57	−0.09
	(0.63)	(0.61)
Negative events	0.51	0.43
	(0.52)	(0.51)
Vietnam casualties in last 6 months (100s)	−0.06***	−0.11***
	(0.02)	(0.02)
Iraq casualties in last 6 months (100s)	0.00	−0.00
	(0.00)	(0.00)
Honeymoon	0.36	−0.69
	(0.56)	(0.54)
Observations	732	732

Note: Results of a simultaneous equations analysis. Both the *Approval* and *Investigations Models* include unreported presidential fixed effects. Standard errors are reported in parentheses. All significance tests are two-tailed.

* p < .10   ** p < .05   *** p < .01

an important mechanism through which investigations may bring substantial political pressure to bear on the president to change course and accord more closely with congressional preferences. However, it is possible that investigations may not affect presidential approval ratings in all contexts and political environments.

One important question is whether investigations in unified government have the same effect on presidential approval as those undertaken when a member of the partisan opposition wields the gavel. Competing hypotheses suggest themselves. On the one hand, the incentives governing the committee majority holding an investigation in unified government are significantly different from those guiding the majority in divided government.[41] In divided government, the opposition party may use committee investigations in an effort to score political points against the president in the hopes of bolstering its party's prospects in the next election. By contrast, in unified government, committee chairs and majority members, who typically set the ground rules for committee inquests in the contemporary Congress, generally do not stand to gain electorally by aggressively pursuing and bringing to light evidence of executive-branch misconduct. As a result, the character of the investigative hearings themselves may be qualitatively different in unified versus divided government, with the latter being more likely to attract press and public scrutiny and generate a popular response. Indeed, we saw evidence of such a dynamic in Chapter 2's discussion of the Whitewater investigations. The Republican-led probe in the 104th Congress was significantly more wide-ranging and combative than the Democratic investigation in the 103rd Congress. As a result, it is possible that the more contentious Republican-led inquest would have a greater impact on public opinion than the more muted investigation allowed under the Democrats.

However, media scholars have long noted that while the press emphasizes conflict in Washington in general, it accords greater prominence to congressional criticism of a president levied by members of his own political party.[42] For example, while Democratic criticism of the Bush administration's alleged mishandling of the Iraq War was certainly covered in the press, media attention spiked when Republicans like North Carolina representative Walter Jones or Nebraska senator Chuck Hagel criticized the administration. Moreover, opinion scholars have argued that same-party criticism of the president is particularly influential in swaying public opinion.[43] While most Democrats and many Independents may simply shrug

[41] Kriner 2009.

[42] See, e.g., Groeling 2010; Groeling and Baum 2008.

[43] Matthew Baum and Timothy Groeling, "Shot by the Messenger: Partisan Cues and Public Opinion Regarding National Security and War," *Political Behavior* 31 (2009): 157–186; Kriner 2010.

off Republican criticism of the Obama administration's conduct of foreign policy, even ordinary Democrats may question the president's actions when prominent congressional Democrats, such as Senate Foreign Relations Committee chair Diane Feinstein, join in the sharp criticism of administration policy. Thus, even if members of the president's own party try to blunt the force of investigations while they control the committees, the mere presence of same-party criticism may threaten the president's standing among the public.

To test between these competing possibilities, we disaggregated our data and estimated two models, one for periods of unified government and the other for years of divided government. Table 3.4 presents the results. The results are clear; investigative activity negatively affects presidential ratings in both unified and divided government, and to roughly the same degree. The relevant regression coefficients are negative, statistically significant, and roughly similar in magnitude. Regardless of who controls Congress, investigations pack a powerful political punch.[44]

An additional question is whether investigations have always significantly undermined the president's standing among the public, or whether this relationship is a distinctly post-Watergate phenomenon. Political scientists and historians alike have long documented the changes dating to Watergate, from the rise of new media norms of combative journalism to the growing ideological polarization between the parties. It is possible that only investigations in the post-Watergate era are able to generate the requisite attention to effect major changes in public support for the president.

To examine whether investigations have always had the potential to erode presidential approval, or whether it is exclusively a pre- or post-Watergate phenomenon, we again disaggregated our data and estimated two separate models, one for the period from 1953 through 1973, and the other for 1974 through 2014. Table 3.5 presents the results. This additional cut of the data yields convincing evidence that investigative activity has undermined presidential support among the public throughout the entire sixty-two-year period. Both before and after Watergate, the coefficients for investigative activity are negative, statistically significant, and virtually identical in terms

---

[44] An additional interesting finding is that in unified government there is no evidence that approval ratings have any influence on investigative activity. This suggests that the political incentives governing investigations are different in unified versus divided government. Under unified government, low presidential approval does not appear to drive decisions to investigate. By contrast, in divided government, the majority carefully assesses whether investigations are likely to yield its party political advantages, and it looks to the president's political standing accordingly. Investigations targeted against a popular president may backfire, as Republicans learned in the impeachment fiasco of the late 1990s. However, inquests into the affairs of a less popular president may be more likely to pay political dividends.

TABLE 3.4: Effect of Investigative Activity on Presidential Approval in Unified and Divided Government

	DG	UG
Approval Model		
Days of investigative hearings	−0.12***	−0.16**
	(0.04)	(0.08)
Index of consumer sentiment	0.07***	0.07*
	(0.02)	(0.05)
Positive events	3.18***	3.17***
	(0.50)	(0.66)
Negative events	−0.08	−1.33**
	(0.40)	(0.66)
Vietnam casualties in last 6 months (100s)	0.01	−0.06***
	(0.02)	(0.02)
Iraq casualties in last 6 months (100s)	−0.01***	0.02
	(0.00)	(0.03)
Honeymoon	1.43***	2.11***
	(0.56)	(0.52)
Lagged approval	0.85***	0.81***
	(0.02)	(0.03)
Investigations Model		
Approval	−0.19***	0.08
	(0.04)	(0.07)
Days in session	0.28***	0.24***
	(0.03)	(0.04)
Positive events	0.49	−0.24
	(1.15)	(1.31)
Negative events	1.82**	−1.65
	(0.87)	(1.27)
Vietnam casualties in last 6 months (100s)	−0.22***	−0.02
	(0.04)	(0.04)
Iraq casualties in last 6 months (100s)	−0.01	−0.00
	(0.01)	(0.06)
Honeymoon	−2.07*	−0.47
	(1.23)	(1.07)
Observations	471	261

Note: Results of a simultaneous equations analysis. Both the *Approval* and *Investigations Models* include unreported presidential fixed effects. Standard errors are reported in parentheses. All significance tests are two-tailed.

* p < .10   ** p < .05   *** p < .01

TABLE 3.5: Effect of Investigative Activity on Presidential Approval Before and After Watergate

	1953–1973	*1974–2014*
Approval Model		
Days of investigative hearings	–0.13**	–0.12**
	(0.06)	(0.05)
Index of consumer sentiment	0.10**	0.05**
	(0.05)	(0.02)
Positive events	4.04***	2.76***
	(0.90)	(0.46)
Negative events	–1.27**	–0.25
	(0.62)	(0.41)
Vietnam casualties in last 6 months (100s)	–0.03**	
	(0.01)	
Iraq casualties in last 6 months (100s)		–0.00
		(0.00)
Honeymoon	2.25***	1.40***
	(0.62)	(0.44)
Lagged approval	0.83***	0.89***
	(0.03)	(0.02)
Investigations Model		
Approval	–0.13	–0.01
	(0.09)	(0.03)
Days in session	0.25***	0.28***
	(0.04)	(0.03)
Positive events	3.46	–0.90
	(2.30)	(0.83)
Negative events	1.26	0.67
	(1.66)	(0.73)
Vietnam casualties in last 6 months (100s)	–0.12***	
	(0.03)	
Iraq casualties in last 6 months (100s)		0.00
		(0.00)
Honeymoon	1.26	–1.49*
	(1.68)	(0.78)
Observations	247	485

Note: Results of a simultaneous equations analysis. Both the *Approval* and *Investigations Models* include unreported presidential fixed effects. Standard errors are reported in parentheses. All significance tests are two-tailed.

* $p < .10$ ** $p < .05$ *** $p < .01$

of substantive size.[45] In short, there is no evidence that Congress's ability to use committee investigations to reduce the president's support among the public is exclusively a post-Watergate phenomenon.

Robustness Checks

In the Appendix to Chapter 3, we report the results from a series of additional robustness checks. Perhaps most important, we consider a potential methodological concern with our data: whether presidential approval is a stationary series. We addressed this concern in two ways. First, we re-estimated our models using a fractionally differenced approval series.[46] Second, we re-estimated all of our preceding analyses with the change in approval as the dependent variable. In both rounds of additional analysis, we find strong evidence that investigative activity significantly decreases presidential approval and that our results are not an artifact of a time series complication with the data.

TESTING THE CREDIBILITY MECHANISM: AN EXPERIMENTAL APPROACH

The preceding analyses drawing on more than six decades worth of public opinion data showed strong statistical evidence that congressional investigations can significantly undermine the president's standing among the public. Even after accounting for the complicated and reciprocal nature of the relationship, we found considerable evidence that investigative activity systematically erodes public support for the president.

However, one important lingering question is whether congressional investigations themselves depressed the president's approval rating, or whether the scandal or alleged improprieties that precipitated the committee probes would have produced similar drops in support independent of

---

[45] An additional interesting result concerns whether high approval ratings dissuaded investigators to the same extent before and after Watergate. In the 1953–1973 model, the coefficient is negative, of almost the same magnitude as the coefficient observed in the entire time series in Table 3.2, and only narrowly fails to reach conventional thresholds of statistical significance. By contrast, after Watergate the coefficient decreases in magnitude to almost zero. This may suggest that congressional investigators are less reluctant to investigate a popular president in the post-Watergate era. While an interesting possibility, given data limitations we are reluctant to place too much emphasis on this result.

[46] See, e.g., Janet Box-Steffensmeier and Renee Smith, "Investigating Political Dynamics Using Fractional Integration Methods," *American Journal of Political Science* 42 (1998): 661–689; Matthew Lebo and Daniel Cassino, "The Aggregated Consequences of Motivated Reasoning and the Dynamics of Presidential Approval," *Political Psychology* 28 (2007): 719–746.

congressional action. This concern may be particularly acute in periods of unified government. Given that the president's co-partisans have little incentive to seize upon relatively minor infractions that might lead to more politically costly revelations, it is possible that Congress only investigates when all but compelled to do so by circumstances. Thus, the nature of the charge or misconduct, not the investigation per se, may be causing the observed drops in approval.

While both factors undoubtedly matter, there are strong reasons to believe that whether Congress formally investigates a scandal or charge of misconduct has significant ramifications for the size of its impact on public opinion. First, the media will give greater credence and attention to allegations that are made by a congressional committee than to those that lack such institutional backing. Indeed, some media scholars have argued that the media relies so heavily on official Washington sources that it marginalizes criticism that is not also expressed by government sources.[47]

Second, congressional committees and their chairs have considerable discretion in what they choose to investigate and how intensely they decide to do so. Consider, for example, the myriad allegations of abuse of power, government waste, and gross mismanagement that arose during the Iraq War and American occupation. To be sure, many such instances received some coverage in the mainstream media. However, few allegations—despite their severity—became full-fledged political scandals, in large part because Republican committee chairmen repudiated virtually every call by congressional Democrats to hold formal inquests backed with subpoena power. Some scandals, such as the furor over prisoner abuse at Abu Ghraib fueled by irrefutable proof in the form of leaked photographs, were so egregious that even Republican committee chairs could not turn completely deaf ears to calls for hearings. However, as Rep. Henry Waxman (D-CA) ruefully noted, the Republican-controlled Armed Services Committee held only 5 hours of testimony on Abu Ghraib, compared to 140 hours of House testimony on whether Bill Clinton improperly used the White House Christmas card list.[48] Supporting such claims, recent research by Nyhan analyzing the emergence of presidential scandals over a more than thirty year period suggests that political factors, not events themselves, often determine when scandals take hold.[49] For example, Nyhan argues that when presidents enjoy little support among opposition-party identifiers in the mass public, they may find themselves besieged by allegations of misconduct despite a dearth of factual

[47] W. Lance Bennett, Regina Lawrence, and Steven Livingstone, *When the Press Fails: Political Power and the News Media from Iraq to Katrina* (Chicago: University of Chicago Press, 2007); Mermin 1999.

[48] Henry Waxman, *Congressional Record*, June 21, 2005, H4829, Vol. 151, No. 83.

[49] Nyhan 2015.

evidence; by contrast, when presidents maintain a moderate level of support among opposition party identifiers, they may escape sustained congressional scrutiny despite clear signs of misconduct.

As a result, because sustained media attention is needed for charges of wrongdoing to seep into the consciousness and political evaluations of a relatively inattentive public, we argue that formal congressional investigations and the coverage they generate play a substantial role in shaping popular attitudes toward the president. However, testing this hypothesis with observational data alone is exceedingly difficult. Except in the rare cases of a completely manufactured claim of abuse, it is almost impossible to examine the influence of congressional investigation independent of the triggering scandal or misconduct itself.

An experimental approach, however, can afford such a test. By creating a realistic, but hypothetical charge of executive misconduct and varying the identity of the source alleging the impropriety, we can isolate the influence of the investigation itself on public support for the president. In so doing, the experiment also offers a direct test of the credibility mechanism posited previously. In addition to bringing charges of executive malfeasance to an otherwise inattentive public, investigations may be particularly influential because they lend institutional credibility to charges of misconduct. This increased credibility may allow a charge of executive misconduct levied by Congress to hold more sway over public opinion than an identical charge not attributed to a congressional source. Finally, by exploiting the presence of split partisan control of the House and Senate in the 112th Congress, our experiment also allows us to examine whether the influence of the investigation is conditional on which party controls the committee holding the investigative hearings.

EPA Experiment

In April of 2011, we embedded an experiment within an online survey of 1,167 adult Americans recruited via Mechanical Turk. While not nationally representative, our sample shows considerable diversity. Subjects hailed from 49 states; 23% were nonwhite; and 43% possessed a bachelor's degree. Younger Americans are over-represented in the sample (median age 28), and Republicans are somewhat under-represented (16%, 28% including "leaners"); however, the sample is considerably more diverse than undergraduate samples routinely used in many studies of public opinion.[50]

---

[50] See, e.g., Scott Gartner, "The Multiple Effects of Casualties on Popular Support for War: An Experimental Approach," *American Political Science Review* 102 (2008): 95–106; Brendan Nyhan and Jason Reifler, "When Corrections Fail: The Persistence of Political Misperceptions," *Political Behavior* 32 (2010): 303–330.

Moreover, recent research by Berinsky, Huber, and Lenz demonstrates that replicating experiments on samples recruited in this way yields very similar results to previously published studies with nationally representative samples.[51] Thus, while the nature of our sample provides some barriers to generalizability, we believe that the observed results are reflective of how a large segment of the American public would respond to the experimental stimuli. Summary statistics for the sample's demographics are presented in Appendix Table 3.8.

The treatments consist of a series of mock newspaper stories. All subjects received the following prompt at the beginning of the article: "Under President Obama, the Environmental Protection Agency (EPA) has prepared new regulations to curb the emission of greenhouse gasses." Subjects were then randomly assigned to one of four groups. Those in the control group received no additional information. Subjects in the first treatment group were told in the course of the article that the Democratically controlled Senate Energy and Natural Resources Committee "is investigating allegations that the Obama administration has abused its regulatory powers to dramatically expand the power of the EPA." These subjects were further told that "The committee's Democratic chairman and other Democrats on the committee warn that the new proposed regulations of greenhouse gasses could increase the price of energy and slow economic growth." We deliberately chose to examine the potential of a fairly mundane allegation of executive misconduct to shape public opinion; more politically explosive allegations of corruption or abuse of power should have even larger effects on presidential approval.

Subjects in the second treatment group were given an identically worded experimental cue. However, the sources for the allegations in this treatment were the Republican-controlled House Natural Resources Committee, its chairman, and Republican members.

Finally, to test whether a charge of presidential misconduct has more influence over public opinion when made by a congressional committee than an identical charge made by a source that lacks such institutional legitimacy, we included a third treatment. Subjects in this group received an almost identically worded experimental cue, except that "some political observers" were the source for the charge that the Obama administration was abusing its regulatory powers and for the claim that the proposed regulations of greenhouse gasses could increase energy prices and slow economic growth. All respondents were then asked whether they approved or disapproved of

[51] Adam Berinsky, Greg Huber, and Gabriel Lenz, "Evaluating Online Labor Markets for Experimental Research: Amazon.com's Mechanical Turk," *Political Analysis* 20 (2012): 351–368.

the way Barack Obama is handling his job as president on a five-point scale, ranging from strongly approve to strongly disapprove.

Results

Because subjects were randomly assigned to one of the three treatments or to the control, the resulting differences in means are unbiased. In the control group baseline, informed only that under Obama the EPA was preparing new greenhouse gas regulations, 48% of respondents either strongly approved or approved of Barack Obama's performance in office. For comparison, the realclearpolitics.com presidential approval poll average for April 18, 2011, the last day our survey was in the field, stood at 49.2%.

Learning of a congressional investigation into potential abuse of power by the administration significantly decreased levels of popular support for the president. The president's approval rating plummeted by 8% among subjects told that the Democratic Senate was investigating the administration's regulatory actions. Similarly, the president's approval rating among subjects told that the Republican House Natural Resources Committee was investigating the administration fell by a smaller, but still significant 5.5%.

The experiment also strongly suggests that congressional investigations play an important role in shaping public opinion beyond simply raising policy critiques that might not otherwise enter the public sphere. Rather, the institutional legitimacy that a formal congressional investigation affords increases the influence that a charge of misconduct has on public support for the president. Subjects in the final treatment group received the same charge of administration misconduct and an identical policy critique that the administration's actions could raise energy costs and stunt economic growth. However, in the final treatment these positions were attributed only to "some political observers." And in this group, 47% of subjects replied that they approved of President Obama's job performance; this figure is statistically indistinguishable from that observed in the control group.

As an addditional test for the relative influence of the various experimental cues, we employ a statistical model that allows us to estimate the effect of each experimental treatment on the probability of a subject approving of Obama while also controlling for each subject's demographic characteristics, including their partisanship, gender, age, race, and education.[52] Results

---

[52] The job approval question asked subjects to rate Obama's job performance on a five-point likert scale ranging from strongly approve to strongly disapprove. Table 3.6 presents results from an ordered logit model that uses the full five-point scale as the dependent variable.

TABLE 3.6: Effect of EPA Investigations on Presidential Approval

Democratic investigation	−0.54***
	(0.15)
Republican investigation	−0.34**
	(0.15)
Generic criticism	−0.12
	(0.15)
Democrat	1.68***
	(0.14)
Republican	−1.81***
	(0.16)
Male	−0.10
	(0.11)
Age	−0.01**
	(0.01)
White	−0.67***
	(0.15)
Education	0.15***
	(0.04)
Observations	1,167

Note: Model is an ordered logit regression. Robust standard errors are reported in parentheses. All significance tests are two-tailed.

* p < .10   ** p < .05   *** p < .01

are presented in Table 3.6. Consistent with the simple differences in means, the coefficients for both of the investigation treatment variables are negative and statistically significant. Learning of a congressional investigation into President Obama's regulatory powers significantly decreased a respondent's approval for his job performance—regardless of whether the Republican-controlled House or Democratically controlled Senate led the inquest. However, the model suggests that the Democratic investigation was even more damaging than the Republican investigation.[53] While presidents stand to

[53] The coefficient for the Republican-led investigation is smaller than that for the Democratic investigation, and a Wald test suggests that the difference is borderline statistically significant (p < .10).

lose political capital in the form of public support from congressional investigations in general, the EPA experiment suggests that they risk losing the most when their co-partisans lead the investigative charge. This is consistent with a considerable literature on the importance of "costly" signals.[54] Political arguments that conflict with a political actor's predispositions and self-interest—such as Democratic congressional criticism of a Democratic president—may be more influential with the public than the same criticism levied by political actors who also stand to benefit from making the charge of misconduct.

In the statistical model, we continue to find strong support for the credibility mechanism suggesting that a charge of misconduct made by a congressional actor will be more persuasive and have a greater influence on public opinion than an identical charge not made by Congress. The estimated effect of the generic "some political observers" treatment in Table 3.6 is negative, but substantively small and statistically insignificant.[55] This strongly suggests that the institutional legitimacy lent to a charge of misconduct by a formal congressional investigation plays an important role in driving the negative influence of investigative activity on presidential approval.

The control variables included in the model performed as expected. Democrats were significantly more likely to support Obama than were Independents, and Republicans were less so. Whites and older respondents were less supportive of the president than nonwhites and younger respondents. And support for the president's job performance also rose with educational attainment.

Finally, we also considered the possibility that respondent partisanship would condition the response to the experimental stimuli. To assess this possibility, we examined whether the influence of each experimental treatment differed for members of each partisan group—Republicans, Democrats, and Independents. The full model is presented in Appendix Table 3.7. We find that when Democrats are identified as doing the investigating, all three partisan groups respond to the costly signal of members taking on a president of their own party, and roughly to the same degree.[56] The Republican-

---

[54] See, e.g., Randall Calvert, "The Value of Biased Information: A Rational Choice Model of Political Advice," *Journal of Politics* 47 (1985): 530–555; Groeling and Baum 2008.

[55] A Wald test shows that the Democratic investigation effect is greater than the generic political observers treatment, p < .01 (one-tailed, given our directional expectation). For Republicans, the difference falls just short of statistical significance (p = .08; one-tailed test).

[56] Wald tests cannot reject the null that all three coefficients are statistically indistinguishable from one another. The negative coefficient for the Republican interaction, while roughly equivalent to the other two partisan groups in magnitude, narrowly fails to meet conventional levels of statistical significance.

led investigation had a significant negative effect on support for President Obama among Independents (58% of our sample using a three-point party ID measure); the coefficient for this treatment's influence on Republican respondents is also negative and substantively large, though it narrowly fails to meet conventional levels of statistical significance. By contrast, Democrats did not respond at all to charges of executive misconduct levied by congressional Republicans. Finally, no partisan group responded to the identical, but generic criticism of the Obama administration that was not attributed to a congressional actor.[57]

To illustrate the substantive size of the effect of each treatment variable for the median Independent respondent, Figure 3.2 presents a series of predicted probabilities of approving or strongly approving of the president's job performance. Error bars indicate plus or minus one standard error around each point estimate. In the control group, the predicted probability of the median Independent respondent approving of Obama's job performance is .45. Hearing of a Democratic-led congressional investigation decreases that figure sharply to just over .30; the Republican-led investigation treatment also significantly decreased the probability of a respondent approving of Obama, but not to the same degree as the co-partisan investigation. In the generic opposition treatment, the median Independent respondent has a predicted probability of approving of Obama that is statistically indistinguishable from that in the control group.[58]

ABUSE OF POWER VS. POLICY CRITICISM

In the EPA experiment, we found strong evidence that allegations of executive wrongdoing made by Congress in the context of a formal committee investigation are more influential with the public than identical charges of wrongdoing not attributed to an institutional actor. This strongly suggests that congressional investigations imbue charges of executive-branch wrongdoing with credibility.

[57] We also used a nonparametric rank sum test to ensure that our conclusions were not driven by particular modeling choices. The test offers similar results; among all respondents the Democratic investigation is statistically different from the control (p < .01; two-tailed test); the Republican investigation is borderline statistically different from the control (p < .10; two-tailed test); and the generic criticism treatment is not statistically distinguishable from the control (p = .52; two-tailed test). If we look only at Independent respondents, both the Democratic and Republican investigation treatments were statistically different from the control (p < .01; two-tailed test); again, the generic criticism had no effect (p = .84).

[58] The estimates in Figure 3.2 are derived from simulations of the model presented in Appendix Table 3.7.

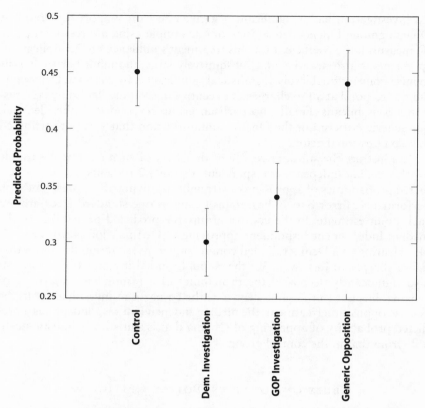

FIGURE 3.2. Effect of Charges of EPA Abuse of Power on Presidential Approval.
Note: The figure plots predicted probabilities for the median Independent
respondent approving of President Obama's job performance in each treatment
group. First differences derived from interaction model in Appendix Table 3.7.
Error bars indicate one standard error above and below each point estimate.

Throughout this book, we define investigations as committee-led inquiries into allegations of abuse of power or misconduct by some official within
the executive branch. Implicit in this focus on investigations of misconduct
is a supposition that high-visibility congressional probes into alleged wrongdoing by the executive branch are qualitatively different and more influential than more routine criticisms of presidential policy decisions that are
ubiquitous features of our politics. For example, we suggest that it was more
politically consequential when members of Congress alleged that the Bush
administration manipulated intelligence and consciously misled the country into the Iraq War than when opponents of the war limited themselves

to critiques of the policy itself—such as cost overruns and high American casualties—that did not involve allegations of wrongdoing or abuse of power. Are misconduct investigations a particularly potent weapon in Congress's strategic arsenal?

Investigations vs. Oversight

As an initial answer to this question, we return to our analysis of observational presidential approval data to examine whether congressional oversight—which, while it can be critical of the administration's policies, does not explicitly allege wrongdoing or abuse of power by the executive branch—also damages the president's standing among the public. Investigations of alleged executive misconduct represent only a small fraction of congressional actions in the committee hearing room. Because investigations of misconduct are generally designed to attract media attention and focus public scrutiny on executive behavior, we believe investigative hearings should be most likely to negatively affect the president's standing among the public. Yet this still leaves open the question of whether investigations of alleged executive misconduct have a uniquely powerful effect on presidential approval, or whether there is a negative relationship between other forms of general oversight activity and approval ratings.

As described in the Appendix to Chapter 2, the search procedures that we used as an initial cut to identify investigations resulted in more than 13,000 hits when applied to the CIS hearings database in Lexis Nexis for the 1953–2006 period. These hearings were then hand coded to identify which ones explicitly mentioned an allegation of misconduct or abuse within the executive branch. Many of the hearings returned by our search did not meet our criteria to be coded as an investigation. During this period, we identified 3,507 hearings from the CIS abstracts that involved committee investigations of alleged wrongdoing by the executive branch. Almost three times as many hearings, 9,761, were identified by coders not as investigations but as oversight hearings that did not explicitly allege misconduct in the summary or testimony descriptors. The oversight hearings identified in this way do not constitute a comprehensive measure of all congressional oversight.[59] Our text search required that the hearing summary and descriptors have at least one word that might imply criticism of the executive branch's actions (e.g., inquiry, misconduct, abuse, corruption, ethics, mismanagement) in order for the hearing to be subject to the additional hand-coding. Thus, it

---

[59] Because of concerns about comparability of the search algorithms in Lexis-Nexis and ProQuest, we did not ask coders to record information on hearings that were oversight, but not investigations of alleged misconduct or abuse when we updated the series from 2007 through 2014.

is perhaps better to think of this as a measure of "critical" oversight, though many of the oversight hearings captured by the search parameters were relatively routine.[60]

To examine the relative influence of oversight and investigative activity on presidential approval, we re-estimate the statistical model from Table 3.2 with one additional variable: the number of days of critical oversight hearings conducted in each month. Table 3.7 presents the results. As in Table 3.2, we continue to find a strong, negative effect for investigative activity. The more aggressively Congress investigates the president, the greater the hit his approval rating takes among the American public. By contrast, the model finds no evidence that oversight hearings systematically decrease presidential approval. The relevant coefficient in the statistical model is substantively very small, positive, and not statistically significant. Thus, the models strongly suggest that committee investigations of alleged misconduct are quite distinct in their capacity to influence public opinion as compared to the other oversight activities in which committees routinely engage. Trends in general oversight had no systematic effect on public opinion. Investigations of alleged executive misconduct, by contrast, have a significant downward effect on presidential approval ratings.[61]

Libya Experiment

As a final assessment of whether allegations of misconduct or abuse of power carry more weight than strong policy criticisms that do not allege wrongdoing, we again employ an experimental design. We seek to isolate the influence of charges of abuse of power versus policy critiques in the same political context, in this case President Obama's response to the 2011 Libyan Civil War.

In February of 2011, the winds of change ushered in by the Arab Spring blew over Libya, a country ruled by the dictator Moammar Gadhafi for more than forty years. Demonstrations in Tripoli and Benghazi were met with brutal force from the Gadhafi regime. By the beginning of March, anti-Gadhafi forces had made considerable gains and appeared to threaten the capital city of Tripoli itself. The Libyan regime launched a major counteroffensive and

[60] In other words, while the hearing summary and descriptors had at least one word that might imply criticism, reading the summary and descriptor revealed there was no explicit charge of abuse of power or wrongdoing.

[61] If one enters the general oversight measure without the investigations measure, general oversight does appear to have a statistically significant impact on approval ratings. The two measures are correlated at $r = .47$. However, after controlling for investigative activity, as shown in Table 3.7 we find no relationship between oversight and approval. It is thus reasonable to conclude that the general oversight measure captures some of what we mean by critical investigative activity, but that it is a rougher measure as it also evidently incorporates a substantial amount of other, more generic oversight activity.

TABLE 3.7: Effect of Investigations vs. Oversight on Presidential Approval, 1953–2006

Approval Model	
Days of investigative hearings	−0.15**
	(0.06)
Days of oversight hearings	0.01
	(0.01)
Index of consumer sentiment	0.08***
	(0.02)
Positive events	3.56***
	(0.46)
Negative events	−0.63
	(0.40)
Vietnam casualties in last 6 months	−0.03**
	(0.01)
Iraq casualties in last 6 months (100s)	−0.78***
	(0.24)
Honeymoon	1.65***
	(0.39)
Lagged approval	0.85***
	(0.02)
Investigations Model	
Days of oversight hearings	0.09***
	(0.01)
Approval	−0.13***
	(0.04)
Days in session	0.20***
	(0.03)
Positive events	0.81
	(1.00)
Negative events	0.71
	(0.86)
Vietnam casualties in last 6 months (100s)	−0.12***
	(0.03)
Iraq casualties in last 6 months (100s)	−0.31
	(0.52)
Honeymoon	−0.70
	(0.85)
Observations	637

Note: Results of a simultaneous equations analysis. Both the *Approval* and *Investigations Models* include unreported presidential fixed effects. Standard errors are reported in parentheses. All significance tests are two-tailed.

* $p < .10$ ** $p < .05$ *** $p < .01$

with lightning speed began to push the rebels back across the desert toward the eastern city of Benghazi. On March 10, 2011, the Director of Central Intelligence James Clapper testified before the Senate that the intelligence community believed that, because of his superior military resources, Gadhafi and the regime would ultimately prevail. By March 17, Gadhafi took to the airwaves with a chilling message for the retreating rebels: "The moment of truth has come. There will be no mercy. Our troops will be coming to Benghazi tonight."[62] Hours later, the United Nations Security Council passed Resolution 1973, which called for a cessation of hostilities; authorized the establishment of a no-fly zone; and empowered member states to take "all necessary measures" to protect civilians. Two days later, a coalition of countries including the United States began to attack Libyan military targets.

President Obama did not seek congressional authorization for the use of force in Libya. As the mission continued, Obama faced growing calls that the War Powers Resolution required him to go to Congress or to stop the military action within sixty days. The administration and its lawyers denied that the president needed congressional authorization to continue the policy, arguing that it constituted a "kinetic military action," rather than a war. Congressional opponents attacked Obama's claim to have the authority to act on his own, while also criticizing what they saw as an aimless mission with shifting goals that had failed to produce immediate results in shifting the balance of power on the ground.[63]

In April of 2011, we embedded an experiment in an online survey with a convenience sample recruited through Mechanical Turk to examine the relative influence of congressional policy critiques versus allegations of abuse of power on the public's support for President Obama's handling of the situation in Libya. Summary statistics for the sample's demographics are presented in Appendix Table 3.8. Subjects were randomly assigned to one of six treatment groups. All subjects read the following prompt about the situation in Libya: "President Obama has ordered U.S. forces to participate in a multinational mission establishing a 'No-Fly Zone' over Libya. The mission was authorized by the United Nations to prevent government attacks on civilians in the civil war-torn country." Subjects in the control group received no further information.

Subjects in the first treatment group learned of a Democratic-led investigation into allegations that President Obama had abused his power as

[62] Ian Black, "Gaddafi Threatens Retaliation in Mediterranean as UN Passes Resolution," *The Guardian*, March 17, 2011, http://www.theguardian.com/world/2011/mar/17/gaddafi-retaliation-mediterranean-libya-no-fly-zone, accessed February 28, 2016.

[63] For an overview of the political reaction, see Michael Lewis, "Obama's Way," *Vanity Fair*, October 2012, http://www.vanityfair.com/politics/2012/10/michael-lewis-profile-barack-obama, accessed February 28, 2016.

commander-in-chief in the Libya case. "The Democratic-controlled Senate Foreign Relations Committee is investigating President Obama's conduct of the military operation. The committee's Democratic chairman and several other committee Democrats charge that the president's failure to consult with Congress about the mission violates the War Powers Resolution of 1973. These Foreign Relations Committee Democrats argue that the president's decision to use force unilaterally is a serious abuse of presidential power."

Subjects in the second group instead received a prompt concerning Democratic criticism of the administration's strategy in Libya. "The Democratic-controlled Senate Foreign Relations Committee is investigating President Obama's conduct of the military operation. The committee's Democratic chairman and several other committee Democrats charge that the president has failed to provide a clear set of goals for the mission and to specify a strategy for bringing it to a successful conclusion. These Foreign Relations Committee Democrats argue that the president's decision to use force was a mistake."

Subjects in the third and fourth treatment groups received identically worded prompts; however the charges of abuse of power and policy criticisms were attributed instead to the Republican-controlled House Foreign Affairs Committee. Finally, subjects in the fifth treatment group received an identical charge that Obama had failed to consult with Congress, violated the War Powers Resolution, and abused his power. However, in this treatment group the charge was attributed to the more generic "some political observers" rather than to a congressional committee. All subjects were then asked the same question: "Do you approve or disapprove of the way Barack Obama is handling the situation in Libya?"

The statistical model presented in Table 3.8 allows us to estimate the influence of each experimental treatment on public support for Obama's actions in Libya, controlling for subjects' demographic characteristics, including partisanship, gender, age, race and educational attainment.[64] To visualize the substantive effect of each treatment, Figure 3.3 plots the predicted probability of the median respondent in each group approving of President Obama's handling of the Libya crisis.

Both the Democratic and Republican investigations into allegations that President Obama had abused his power by unilaterally initiating military action in Libya significantly decreased the probability of a subject approving

[64] As in the EPA experiment, the dependent variable was measured on a five-point likert scale ranging from strongly approve to strongly disapprove. As a result, Table 3.8 presents the results of an ordered logit model. In Figure 3.3, we present the predicted probability of the median Independent respondent in each treatment strongly approving or approving of Obama's handling of the situation in Libya.

TABLE 3.8: Effect of Investigation vs. Policy Criticism on
Support for Administration's Handling of Libya

Democratic abuse charge	-0.74***
	(0.22)
Democratic policy criticism	-0.51**
	(0.23)
Republican abuse charge	-0.69***
	(0.21)
Republican policy criticism	-0.37
	(0.24)
Generic abuse charge	-0.22
	(0.23)
Democrat	1.09***
	(0.15)
Republican	-1.13***
	(0.19)
Male	-0.00
	(0.14)
Age	-0.02***
	(0.01)
White	-0.26
	(0.19)
Education	-0.07
	(0.05)
Observations	798

Note: Model is an ordered logit regression. Robust standard errors
are reported in parentheses. All significance tests are two-tailed.

* p < .10   ** p < .05   *** p < .01

of Obama's handling of the situation. As shown in Figure 3.3, whereas the
probability of this median subject supporting Obama was about .42 in the
control group, this plummeted precipitously in the Democratic and Republican misconduct investigations treatments to .26 and .27, respectively.[65]

[65] Unlike in the EPA experiment, Wald tests show that the Democratic and Republican investigation coefficients are not significantly different from one another in the Libya experiment.

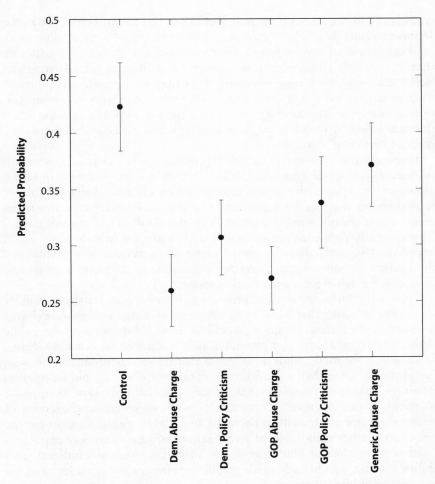

FIGURE 3.3 Effect of Charges of Abuse of Power and Policy Criticism on Support for Obama's Handling of Libya Crisis.

Note: The figure plots predicted probabilities for the median Independent respondent approving of President Obama's handling of the crisis in Libya in each treatment group. First differences derived from model in Table 3.8. Error bars indicate one standard error above and below each point estimate.

Table 3.8 shows that the Democratic policy criticism treatment also had a statistically significant negative effect on presidential approval. The estimated effect is smaller than that found for the Democratic investigation into abuse of power. As shown in Figure 3.3, for the median subject the predicted probability of supporting the president's handling of the Libyan crisis is .31 in the Democratic policy criticism treatment, versus .26 in the Democratic charge of abuse treatment. However, the uncertainty surrounding both estimates make it impossible to say with a high degree of certainty that Democratic charges of abuse are more influential than Democratic policy criticism; the greater observed effect may be a product of chance.[66] Even policy critiques that do not rise to the level of charges of administration wrongdoing may have a significant influence on public opinion when they are levied by members of the president's own party and therefore are deemed particularly credible.

Our model also suggests that the Republican policy criticism treatment decreased support for President Obama's handling of the situation in Libya. However, the relationship is not statistically significant. Moreover, further testing shows that the estimated effect of the GOP policy criticism treatment is statistically smaller than that of the GOP abuse investigation.[67] Thus, when Republicans are the actors challenging the president, the Libya experiment suggests that charges of abuse of power are more influential than policy critiques, even strong ones questioning the policy's goals and prospects for achieving a successful outcome.

Finally, the Libya experiment provides further support for the credibility mechanism positing that when a congressional investigation makes a charge of executive-branch wrongdoing, it will be more influential with the public than an identical charge not attributed to a congressional actor. As shown in Table 3.8, the model finds no evidence that the charge of Obama abusing his power in Libya had a statistically significant effect on public opinion when the charge was made by unidentified political observers, as opposed to members of Congress.[68] These results again suggest that allegations of abuse alone are insufficient to decrease significantly public support for the president. Rather, congressional investigations of such charges of executive-branch misconduct or abuse imbue the allegations with institutional credibility and can significantly erode public support for the president and his conduct of public policy.

[66] A Wald test cannot confirm that the Democratic abuse coefficient is significantly greater in magnitude than the Democratic policy criticism coefficient ($p = .16$).

[67] A Wald test confirms that the Republican abuse coefficient is significantly greater in magnitude than the Republican policy criticism coefficient, $p < .10$. The point estimate for the effect of the Democratic policy criticism ($-.11$) is larger than that estimated effect for Republican policy criticism ($-.08$). However, Wald tests cannot confirm that this difference is statistically significant.

[68] The regression coefficient is negative and statistically insignificant. Moreover, Wald tests confirm that it is significantly smaller in magnitude than the negative effect for both the Democratic and Republican committee abuse investigation treatments ($p = .01$).

CONCLUSION

We find that committee-based investigations are an important tool that members of Congress can use to impose political costs on the president. The combination of observational and experimental data strongly suggest that congressional investigations are more than mere publicity stunts designed to allow members of Congress to grandstand before the cameras in search of personal glory. Rather, investigations systematically impose political costs on the president by diminishing his support among the public. This suggests an informal mechanism of congressional influence over an ascendant executive. Even when it cannot legislatively compel the president to change course, Congress can raise the political costs of certain executive actions by alleging abuses of power and battling the president in the public sphere.

Two cautionary notes about this potential source of congressional leverage over the executive branch merit discussion. First, the media is undoubtedly a critical player in this interbranch dynamic. If investigators are unable to secure media coverage of their charges, committee probes are unlikely to materially affect the president's standing among the public. Indeed, as we will see in Chapters 4 and 7, some investigations, such as the GOP probe of the Obama administration's loan to soon-to-be bankrupt solar manufacturer Solyndra, fail to attract sustained coverage in major media outlets. The scant national news coverage of the Solyndra scandal from major media outlets—aside from Fox News—severely limited the investigation's ability to inflict political damage on the president. Congressional investigations will not automatically attract sustained media scrutiny, resonate with the public, and impose political costs on the president. Rather, members of Congress must exploit windows of opportunity or actively seek to generate them to force their charges of wrongdoing into the public eye.

Second, Congress must actually use its investigative powers in order to shape public opinion. The preceding chapter suggested that Congress spent considerably less time, on average, investigating the executive branch from 1988 through 2006 than it did in earlier decades. The reemergence of divided government first in 2007 and 2008, and then again in 2011 triggered a significant increase in investigative activity; however, in terms of the raw number of hearing days, these more recent tallies are smaller than those observed in earlier periods of high investigative intensity. Perhaps more important, in the contemporary era of highly polarized parties, investigations have increasingly become a phenomenon limited to periods of divided government, particularly in the House. Nevertheless, when the contemporary Congress does investigate alleged executive misconduct—witness, for example, the flurry of Democratic inquests into the Bush administration's failings in Iraq during the 110th Congress—it imposes serious political costs on the president, a blow that is only compounded in an era of lower base levels of public support for the president.[69]

Despite these caveats, our results showing the systematic impact of investigative activity on the president's support among the public offers a partial corrective to game-theoretic approaches that emphasize the institutional barriers and political incentives that hinder congressional efforts to counter presidential aggrandizement.

Notwithstanding the supermajoritarian requirements and transaction costs that beset legislative action, Congress may retain a measure of influence over the executive through informal means. In sharp contrast to legislative remedies, launching an investigation does not require complex procedures and the assemblage of large, cross-partisan coalitions. Similarly, investigative efforts can often overcome collective action dilemmas by serving as common carriers to further both the individual goals of members and broader institutional or partisan interests. To be sure, investigations may rarely formally compel presidents to adjust their behavior. Yet, our results show that they do consistently weaken the president by undermining his reservoir of public support.

Thus, strategic presidents must anticipate more than simply whether a proposal will be filibustered or a veto overridden, as most separation of powers models emphasize.[70] They must also anticipate how members of Congress, particularly committee chairs, will react to various maneuverings within the executive branch, for congressional investigations—even if they fail to result in new legislation or legal charges of wrongdoing—may undermine public confidence in the White House and jeopardize presidents' ability to move on other key items of their programmatic agendas.

In the two chapters that follow, we examine more directly how investigations affect the strategic calculations of both presidents and members of Congress. We draw upon multiple sources of evidence to specify conditions under which congressional investigations can produce significant changes in policy outcomes.

APPENDIX

CCES Experiment on Support for Investigations

As a robustness check on the difference in means analysis presented in Table 3.1, Appendix Table 3.1 estimates an ordered logit analysis of the effect

---

[69] See, e.g., Kriner 2009.
[70] See, e.g., Krehbiel 1998; Cameron 2000.

APPENDIX TABLE 3.1: Effect of Experimental Treatments and Demographics on Support for Investigations

	(1)	(2)
Obama investigations treatment	−0.55***	−0.17
	(0.17)	(0.25)
Obama investigations treatment * Democrat		−0.78**
		(0.34)
Obama and Bush investigations treatment	−0.16	−0.51**
	(0.16)	(0.24)
Bush and Obama investigations treatment * Democrat		0.64**
		(0.32)
Republican	1.54***	1.56***
	(0.20)	(0.20)
Democrat	−0.76***	−0.75***
	(0.17)	(0.26)
Male	0.30**	0.31**
	(0.14)	(0.14)
Education	−0.05	−0.06
	(0.05)	(0.05)
Age	0.00	0.01
	(0.00)	(0.00)
White	0.18	0.21
	(0.16)	(0.16)
Observations	886	886

Note: Models are ordered logit regressions. Robust standard errors are reported in parentheses. All significance tests are two-tailed.

* p < 0.10   ** p < .05   *** p < .01

of the two experimental treatments on support for congressional investigations, controlling for subjects' demographic characteristics including partisanship, age, gender, race, and educational attainment. The dependent variable is support for congressional investigations on a four-point likert scale from strongly support to strongly oppose. Results are presented in model 1 of Appendix Table 3.1. Consistent with the differences in means presented in Table 3.1, the Obama treatment significantly decreased support for congressional investigations. By contrast, the Bush and Obama treatment had no effect on support for investigations.

APPENDIX TABLE 3.2: Demographic Characteristics of 2014 CCES Survey Sample

	2014 CCES
Republican	22%
Republican (including leaners)	32%
Democrat	37%
Democrat (including leaners)	47%
Male	47%
Education	Some college
Age	50
White	73%
Black	13%
Latino	7%
Income	$60,000 to $69,999
Observations	1,000

Note: Each cell presents averages, except for education and income, which report medians.

Finally, to assess whether partisanship moderates the influence of the experimental treatments, we interact the two treatment indicator variables with the indicator variable identifying Democratic respondents. Results are presented in model 2. Consistent with the differences in means presented in Table 3.1, an ordered logit model confirms that the negative effect of the Obama treatment is statistically significant only for Democrats. The ordered logit model also shows that the Bush and Obama treatment negatively influenced support for investigations among non-Democrats, but had no effect on the opinions of Democratic subjects.

The demographic characteristics of the CCES sample are summarized in Appendix Table 3.2.

INVESTIGATIONS AND PRESIDENTIAL APPROVAL

We begin by considering a potential methodological concern with our data: whether presidential approval is a stationary series. Augmented Dickey-Fuller tests and Phillips-Perron tests both reject the null hypothesis of a unit root, p < .01. However, recent research warns that the approval series may be near-integrated or fractionally integrated.[71] One method of dealing with fractional integration is to use Robinson's semiparametric estimator to calculate an estimate of d, the degree of fractional integration in the approval series.[72] We then used this estimate to construct a fractionally differenced version of the approval series. As shown in Appendix Tables 3.3 and 3.4, re-estimating all of the models presented in the text with this new operationalization of the dependent variable again yields virtually identical results.

An alternative method of dealing with the stationarity issue is to use the change in approval, which is stationary. To test the robustness of our findings, we re-estimated all of our preceding analyses with the change in approval as the dependent variable. These models also include the level of presidential approval in the preceding month as an additional control, because when approval levels are very high, further increases are unlikely and vice versa when approval levels are very low.[73]

Appendix Tables 3.5 and 3.6 presents the results. As in the models presented in the text, in each model the coefficient for the days of committee investigations variable is negative and statistically significant. The coefficients for the interactions are substantively small and statistically insignificant; this strongly suggests that investigative activity depresses presidential approval across time periods and political environments.

EPA EXPERIMENT

In the text we reference a model interacting each experimental treatment with partisan dummy variables to examine whether the influence of our investigation treatments is conditional on the partisanship of the recipient. The full results for this model are presented in Appendix Table 3.7. Figure

---

[71] Box-Steffensmeier and Smith 1998; DeBoef and Granato 1997; Lebo and Clark 2000.

[72] Matthew Lebo, Robert Walker, and Harold Clarke, "You Must Remember This: Dealing with Long Memory in Political Analyses," *Electoral Studies* 19 (2000): 31–48; Harold Clarke and Matthew Lebo, "Fractional (Co) Integration and Governing Party Support in Britain," *British Journal of Political Science* 33 (2003): 283–301; Brian Lai and Dan Reiter, "Rally 'Round the Union Jack? Public Opinion and the Use of Force in the United Kingdom, 1948–2001," *International Studies Quarterly* 49 (2005): 255–272; Luke Keele, "Social Capital and the Dynamics of Trust in Government," *American Journal of Political Science* 51 (2007): 241–254.

[73] Including the lagged approval measure as an independent variable significantly improves model fit in both equations. However, omitting this variable from the models yields virtually identical results across specifications; most important, in each case the coefficient for the investigations variable is negative and statistically significant.

APPENDIX TABLE 3.3: Robustness Checks Using Fractionally Differenced Series

	All	DG	UG	1953–1973	1974–2014
Approval Model					
Investigations (days)	–0.13***	–0.10**	–0.27***	–0.16**	–0.11*
	(0.05)	(0.05)	(0.10)	(0.07)	(0.06)
ICS	0.04**	0.06***	–0.05	0.03	0.05***
	(0.02)	(0.02)	(0.03)	(0.05)	(0.02)
Positive events	3.06***	3.10***	3.18***	4.01***	2.85***
	(0.46)	(0.54)	(0.80)	(0.94)	(0.53)
Negative events	–0.82**	–0.62	–1.45*	–1.36**	–0.62
	(0.39)	(0.43)	(0.79)	(0.63)	(0.48)
Vietnam casualties	–0.01	0.00	–0.02	–0.01	
	(0.01)	(0.02)	(0.02)	(0.01)	
Iraq casualties	0.00	–0.00	0.14***		0.00
	(0.00)	(0.00)	(0.04)		(0.00)
Honeymoon	2.63***	1.59**	3.27***	2.70***	2.75***
	(0.42)	(0.62)	(0.63)	(0.68)	(0.52)
Logged approval	0.05*	0.08**	–0.03	–0.01	0.05
	(0.03)	(0.04)	(0.06)	(0.02)	(0.04)
Investigations Model					
Approval	–0.90	–0.82	–1.27	–3.70	0.84
	(0.69)	(0.53)	(1.53)	(2.26)	(0.69)
Days in session	0.24***	0.26***	0.15	0.10	0.31***
	(0.04)	(0.04)	(0.10)	(0.12)	(0.04)
Positive events	2.32	2.01	3.97	15.70	–3.49
	(2.41)	(2.16)	(5.29)	(9.63)	(2.28)
Negative events	0.36	1.31	–2.69	–4.55	1.22
	(1.08)	(1.05)	(2.19)	(4.76)	(0.95)
Vietnam casualties	–0.13***	–0.24***	–0.06*	–0.08	
	(0.03)	(0.05)	(0.04)	(0.05)	
Iraq casualties	0.01	0.00	0.19		0.00
	(0.01)	(0.01)	(0.22)		(0.00)
Honeymoon	0.63	–0.73	3.68	9.08	–4.03*
	(2.27)	(1.74)	(5.16)	(7.68)	(2.22)
Observations	720	471	249	235	485

Note: Results of a simultaneous equations analysis. Both the *Approval* and *Investigations* *Models* include unreported presidential fixed effects. Standard errors are reported in parentheses. All significance tests are two-tailed.

* p < .10   ** p < 0.05   *** p < 0.01

APPENDIX TABLE 3.4: Robustness Checks Using Fractionally Differenced Series, House vs. Senate

	House	Senate
Change in Approval Model		
Days of investigative hearings in relevant chamber	–0.23***	–0.30***
	(0.08)	(0.11)
Index of consumer sentiment	0.04**	0.04**
	(0.02)	(0.02)
Positive events	3.09***	3.00***
	(0.46)	(0.48)
Negative events	–0.80**	–0.84**
	(0.39)	(0.41)
Vietnam casualties	–0.00	–0.02
	(0.01)	(0.02)
Iraq casualties	0.00	0.00
	(0.00)	(0.00)
Honeymoon	2.70***	2.52***
	(0.42)	(0.44)
Lagged approval	0.05	0.05*
	(0.03)	(0.03)
Investigations Model		
Approval	–0.21	–0.60
	(0.44)	(0.46)
Days in session	0.14***	0.10***
	(0.02)	(0.02)
Positive events	0.53	1.50
	(1.53)	(1.63)
Negative events	0.57	–0.11
	(0.69)	(0.73)
Vietnam casualties	–0.04**	–0.10***
	(0.02)	(0.02)
Iraq casualties	0.01	0.00
	(0.00)	(0.00)
Honeymoon	–0.22	0.54
	(1.44)	(1.53)
Observations	720	720

Note: Results of a simultaneous equations analysis. Both the *Approval* and *Investigations Models* include unreported presidential fixed effects. Standard errors are reported in parentheses. All significance tests are two-tailed.

* p < .10   ** p < .05   *** p < .01

APPENDIX TABLE 3.5: Robustness Checks Using Change in Presidential Approval

	All	DG	UG	1953–1973	1974–2014
Change in Approval Model					
Investigations (days)	−0.12***	−0.12***	−0.16**	−0.13**	−0.12**
	(0.04)	(0.04)	(0.08)	(0.06)	(0.05)
ICS	0.06***	0.08***	0.10**	0.05	0.06***
	(0.02)	(0.02)	(0.05)	(0.05)	(0.02)
Positive events	3.07***	3.18***	3.21***	4.15***	2.76***
	(0.40)	(0.50)	(0.66)	(0.90)	(0.46)
Negative events	−0.56*	−0.08	−1.29**	−1.33**	−0.26
	(0.34)	(0.40)	(0.66)	(0.62)	(0.41)
Vietnam casualties	−0.03**	0.01	−0.06***	−0.03**	
	(0.01)	(0.02)	(0.02)	(0.01)	
Iraq casualties	−0.00	−0.01***	0.02		−0.00
	(0.00)	(0.00)	(0.03)		(0.00)
Honeymoon	1.71***	1.44***	2.15***	2.20***	1.44***
	(0.36)	(0.56)	(0.52)	(0.62)	(0.44)
Lagged approval	−0.13***	−0.16***	−0.20***	−0.15***	−0.12***
	(0.02)	(0.02)	(0.03)	(0.03)	(0.02)
Investigations Model					
Change in approval	0.05	0.44	4.12	−3.87**	1.90*
	(0.64)	(0.62)	(2.98)	(1.87)	(1.02)
Lagged approval	−0.12*	−0.13*	0.77	−0.57**	0.16
	(0.07)	(0.07)	(0.53)	(0.26)	(0.10)
Days in session	0.28***	0.30***	0.39***	0.12	0.35***
	(0.03)	(0.04)	(0.14)	(0.10)	(0.05)
Positive events	−0.05	−1.54	−12.61	17.89**	−6.38**
	(2.17)	(2.29)	(9.60)	(8.16)	(3.17)
Negative events	1.03	2.04**	2.96	−4.64	1.26
	(0.88)	(0.92)	(4.48)	(4.05)	(1.11)
Vietnam casualties	−0.16***	−0.24***	0.18	−0.18***	
	(0.03)	(0.05)	(0.18)	(0.07)	
Iraq casualties	0.00	−0.00	−0.01		0.01
	(0.01)	(0.01)	(0.13)		(0.01)
Honeymoon	−0.54	−3.10*	−8.80	8.85*	−4.16**
	(1.30)	(1.61)	(6.62)	(4.72)	(1.82)
Observations	732	471	261	247	485

Note: Results of a simultaneous equations analysis. Both the *Change in Approval* and *Investigations Models* include unreported presidential fixed effects. Standard errors are reported in parentheses. All significance tests are two-tailed.

* $p < .10$ ** $p < .05$ *** $p < .01$

APPENDIX TABLE 3.6: Robustness Check Using Change in Approval, House vs. Senate

	House	Senate
Change in Approval Model		
Days of investigative hearings in relevant chamber	−0.21***	−0.30***
	(0.07)	(0.10)
Index of consumer sentiment	0.06***	0.05***
	(0.02)	(0.02)
Positive events	3.12***	2.99***
	(0.41)	(0.43)
Negative events	−0.57	−0.55
	(0.35)	(0.37)
Vietnam casualties in last 6 months (100s)	−0.02	−0.04**
	(0.01)	(0.02)
Iraq casualties in last 6 months (100s)	−0.00	−0.00
	(0.00)	(0.00)
Honeymoon	1.85***	1.49***
	(0.36)	(0.39)
Lagged approval	−0.14***	−0.12***
	(0.02)	(0.02)
Investigations Model		
Change in approval	0.51	−0.41
	(0.47)	(0.44)
Lagged approval	−0.05	−0.07
	(0.05)	(0.05)
Days in session in relevant chamber	0.18***	0.10***
	(0.02)	(0.02)
Positive events	−1.27	1.03
	(1.58)	(1.49)
Negative events	0.93	0.16
	(0.64)	(0.61)
Vietnam casualties in last 6 months (100s)	−0.05***	−0.11***
	(0.02)	(0.02)
Iraq casualties in last 6 months (100s)	0.00	−0.00
	(0.00)	(0.00)
Honeymoon	−0.49	−0.19
	(0.95)	(0.89)
Constant	1.73	1.39
	(2.48)	(2.33)
Observations	732	732

Note: Results of a simultaneous equations analysis. Both the *Change in Approval* and *Investigations Models* include unreported presidential fixed effects. Standard errors are reported in parentheses. All significance tests are two-tailed.

* $p < .10$ ** $p < .05$ *** $p < .01$

APPENDIX TABLE 3.7: Effect of EPA Experimental Cues by Partisanship of
Respondent

Democratic investigation X Democrat	−0.49*
	(0.29)
Democratic investigation X Republican	−0.47
	(0.33)
Democratic investigation X Independent	−0.58***
	(0.21)
Republican investigation X Democrat	0.11
	(0.31)
Republican investigation X Republican	−0.54
	(0.37)
Republican investigation X Independent	−0.48**
	(0.19)
Generic criticism X Democrat	−0.03
	(0.30)
Generic criticism X Republican	−0.49
	(0.36)
Generic criticism X Independent	−0.05
	(0.20)
Democrat	1.51***
	(0.26)
Republican	−1.73***
	(0.27)
Male	−0.09
	(0.11)
Age (in 10s)	−0.15***
	(0.05)
White	−0.67***
	(0.15)
Education	0.15***
	(0.04)
Observations	1,167

Note: Model is an ordered logit regression. Robust standard errors are reported in parentheses. All significance tests are two-tailed.

* p < .10   ** p < .05   *** p < .01

APPENDIX TABLE 3.8: Summary Statistics for Experimental Samples

	EPA	Libya
Democrat	26.6%	30.1%
Republican	15.5%	16.7%
Male	43.0%	40.5%
Age	32.1	33.6
White	77.3%	83.1%
Education	some college	some college
Income	$20,000–$39,999	$20,000–$39,999
Observations	1,167	798

Note: Each cell presents averages, except for education and income, which report medians.

3.2 in the text presents the effect of each treatment, derived from simulations, on the median Independent respondent.

SURVEY DEMOGRAPHICS

In April of 2011, we embedded a pair of experiments on two online surveys of adult Americans recruited via Mechanical Turk. The demographic characteristics of the two samples are summarized in Appendix Table 3.8.

CHAPTER 4

The Direct Influence of Congressional Investigations on Policy Outcomes

OVER THE PAST century, members of Congress have held almost 12,000 days of investigative hearings highlighting alleged misconduct and abuses of power within the executive branch. Moreover, when Congress investigates, even the relatively inattentive American public listens. Drawing on a wealth of observational and experimental data, the preceding chapter shows that congressional investigations can significantly erode the president's standing among the public. But do investigations have any tangible impact on policy outcomes?

Over the course of the next two chapters, we will explore three pathways through which investigations have the potential to influence public policy. In this chapter, we focus on two direct pathways through which investigations can produce concrete changes in the specific policy area targeted by the investigation. First, investigations may provide the impetus for new legislation that otherwise would not have passed in its absence. Investigative hearings can spur congressional action and generate political pressure on the president and members of his party to vote for and sign legislation that they may have otherwise resisted through the filibuster or veto. Second, even when investigations are not followed by legislative action compelling the administration to change its behavior, high-profile committee inquiries into executive-branch actions may bring enough political pressure to bear on the White House that it opts to make concessions rather than continue a bruising public fight with the legislature.

SPURRING LEGISLATION

Senator Gerald Nye, who chaired an eponymous committee investigating the alleged role played by the munitions industries in precipitating American involvement in World War I, argued that investigations yield great benefit by serving as an impetus to new legislation. "Out of practically every investigation there comes legislation improving the security of the Government and the people against selfishness and greed."[1] Plainly, Nye overstated investigations' efficacy in routinely producing legislative remedies. Not every investigation culminates in new bills that navigate the multiple hazards of the legislative process to become law. However, investigations may under some conditions help overcome the barriers to effective legislative response to abuses of power in the executive branch.

Many skeptics of Congress's institutional capacity to combat executive-branch excesses begin by noting that its 535 members face a severe collective action dilemma. Protecting Congress's institutional power stakes is in the institutional interests of all legislators. However, this is a collective good that all members will enjoy whether they contribute to the costs of providing it or not. As a result, whenever aggressively defending the legislature from executive-branch incursions is costly—whether due to partisan incentives, constituency pressures, or even simply other demands on their time and energies—members will rationally give short shrift to efforts at institutional defense.

However, as we argued previously, investigations to combat executive-branch abuses can act as a common carrier for multiple member interests, not just institutional ones. For example, members may pursue investigative committee leadership for personal political gain, perhaps to raise their national profile in anticipation of a run for higher office. The Church Committee investigating intelligence abuses, which we examine shortly, is a clear example of such a dynamic. The committee's chair, Frank Church, sought to boost his campaign for the 1976 Democratic presidential nomination by aggressively battling the executive branch.

The linking of institutional and other political incentives in the form of an investigation as a common carrier can generate greater impetus for action in the legislative realm as an investigation concludes. Having invested so much in the investigation and staked his national political reputation on its success, Church had an incentive to see the investigation produce concrete changes in law that would both bolster Congress's institutional position against the executive, and also serve his own political interests. Church was thus incentivized to subsidize the costs of collective action by doing much of the legislative groundwork and public advocacy needed to make legislation possible.

Aside from the collective action dilemma, the legislative process itself is an arduous one replete with veto points. Perhaps most important, any legislation must either secure the president's signature—a particularly difficult proposition for legislation spurred by alleged executive-branch abuse—or

---

[1] Quoted in McGeary 1940, 7.

amass two-thirds majorities in both chambers to override a presidential veto. In most cases, legislation curbing presidential power, limiting executive discretion more broadly, or even just adjusting policy so that it better reflects congressional rather than presidential preferences is unlikely to overcome these hurdles. However, as the preceding chapter demonstrated, investigations may change the political dynamic and calculations in play by building and sustaining public demand for remedial action. When investigations succeed in generating significant media attention and in provoking popular calls for action, more members may perceive their own electoral interests as being best served by supporting legislative efforts at reform. As internal support for legislation within Congress broadens, so too does the possibility of legislative vehicles surviving the gauntlet of congressional procedure. Moreover, public demand for action may encourage presidents to sign legislation that they might have preferred to veto in the absence of popular support for reform.

This logic suggests that the capacity of an investigation to attract sustained media attention and to build public awareness of a problem and a desire for reform are important factors shaping the likelihood that an investigation will ultimately produce new legislation that materially affects public policy.

PROMPTING PREEMPTIVE PRESIDENTIAL ACTION

Investigations need not result in new legislation in order to shape policy outcomes. Indeed, presidents may at times choose to make concessions through executive action in the hopes of forestalling a congressional move for a more dramatic legislative shift.

The logic here is similar to that articulated in William Howell's *Power Without Persuasion*. Howell's book is most often remembered for the argument that presidents can unilaterally move policy within the "gridlock interval" toward their preferences, secure in the knowledge that Congress will be unable (because of supermajoritarian requirements, such as the veto) to undo the administration's policy shift through new legislation. Yet Howell also argued that presidents may occasionally use their unilateral powers to shift the status quo *away* from their preferences and toward those of the congressional majority in an effort to preempt even less favorable (from the standpoint of the executive) legislative action. Howell gives the example of President Reagan's actions toward South Africa in 1985. With Congress poised to enact legislation imposing strong sanctions on the apartheid regime that would undermine the administration's proclaimed strategy of "constructive engagement," Reagan gave ground unilaterally. Executive Order 12532 borrowed heavily from the legislative language pending in

Congress, but substantially weakened the scope and intensity of the sanctions. Liberal Republicans, who previously preferred strong sanctions to no sanctions, now preferred the new status quo established by the limited sanctions regime of the executive order to the more stringent requirements of the bills pending in Congress. They switched their position and opposed the legislation.[2]

Investigations may spur similar instances of presidential preemption. Following the logic of the previous section, investigations that attract media attention and public scrutiny may mobilize public opinion and build political pressure on legislators to act. As legislative vehicles take shape and slowly work their way through the congressional process, presidents have ample opportunity to assess the situation and craft more moderate unilateral policy responses designed to sap support for the legislative initiatives on offer.

Moreover, presidents may feel pressure to act even when a legislative response from Capitol Hill is not imminent. Investigations of executive-branch abuse, either explicitly or implicitly, cast the administration in a bad light. If the allegations of misconduct resonate with the American public, then presidents may feel political pressure to change course in the hopes of minimizing the political fallout from the inquest, even when a legislative response is at best a remote threat. This implies that the ability to generate favorable media coverage and to arouse and sustain public desire for reform are also key conditions influencing the capacity of an investigation to spur policy change through this preemptive pathway.

THE DIRECT POLICY IMPACT OF INVESTIGATIONS

Assessing the policy effects of any intervention is challenging. Investigations are no exception; some investigations surely leave little mark on policy, while others have had major impacts. Accordingly, our analysis proceeds in two steps. First, we conduct a series of case studies that allow us to trace in detail how each congressional investigation succeeded—or failed—to trigger the legislative or preemptive pathway of influence. To address concerns about generalizability, the chapter concludes with a broader assessment of the extent to which each of David Mayhew's significant investigations from 1947 through 2002 prompted a legislative or preemptive response.[3]

To construct our case study analysis, we consider a diverse set of cases spanning more than fifty years of American political history. In each case,

[2] See Howell 2003.
[3] Mayhew's last update to his investigations data set extended the original time series through 2002. In Chapter 6, we examine the policy impact of major investigations during the Obama presidency.

we chart the history of the investigation of alleged executive-branch misconduct as it unfolds. To assess the first pathway, we simply examine whether Congress, at the conclusion of an investigation, enacts legislation designed to redress some of the misconduct or adverse policy consequences unveiled during the course of the investigation. To examine presidential preemption, we look for the presence or absence of a shift in White House actions during or in the wake of committee hearings. If a policy shift is detected, we then engage in careful process tracing to assess whether the evidence indicates that actions in Congress's committee rooms really did affect the political calculations of administration officials and help precipitate the observed shift in policy.

The first three case studies endeavor to trace how a disparate set of investigations—the Truman Committee's inquest into administration of the war effort on the home front during World War II; the Church Committee's probe of abuses by the intelligence agencies in the mid 1970s; and the 1982–1984 investigation into alleged abuse of power in the Environmental Protection Agency (EPA)—produced tangible impacts on public policy outcomes.

Case selection is always a delicate issue. How can we be sure that any causal pathways we observe at work in the chosen investigations are generalizable to the larger universe of congressional inquiries from which these have been selected?[4] Several features of our case selection choices were designed to alleviate concerns about generalizability. First, we consciously eschewed focusing on the most high-profile investigations, such as Watergate, that shook the very political foundations of the country to its core. Demonstrating that Watergate directly led to sweeping legislative changes with major implications for public policy is easy; however, generalizing from this case to other much less intensive and wide-ranging investigations would be fraught with peril.[5] As a result, although all of the investigations we examine were important and attracted considerable attention both within Washington and outside of it, none are clear outliers in terms of their importance and salience. Rather, each is typical of a broader set of major investigations, such as the lists identified in previous research by Mayhew and Light.[6] Smaller

[4] For a nice overview of the general problem and various case selection strategies to overcome the challenges it poses, see John Gerring "Case Selection for Case-Study Analysis: Qualitative and Quantitative Techniques," in *The Oxford Handbook of Political Methodology*, ed. Janet Box-Steffensmeier, Henry Brady, and David Collier (New York: Oxford University Press, 2008, 645–684).

[5] For example, Watergate was instrumental in producing the 1974 amendments to the Federal Election Campaign Act, the 1974 Freedom of Information Act, and the Ethics in Government Act of 1978.

[6] Mayhew 1991 and Light 2014. Between 1947 and 2002, Mayhew identified thirty-five high-profile investigations that secured twenty or more days of front page coverage in the *New York Times*. See David Mayhew, *Divided We Govern: Party Control, Lawmaking, and*

scale investigations that attracted far less media and public scrutiny are unlikely to have similar effects; however, because these cases are fairly typical
of a large number of significant investigations, they should offer insight into
a broad universe of cases.

Second, each of these cases represents, in some respects, a difficult test
case for our arguments about investigative influence on policy. Two of the
cases, the Truman Committee and the EPA investigation, involved congressional inquests into popular presidents with extensive electoral mandates,
with the former being conducted in a wartime environment when legislators
are often assumed to grant considerable deference to the president.[7] The
Church Committee and EPA investigations involved agencies—the first, the
CIA, FBI, and other intelligence agencies; the second, the EPA—which have
long enjoyed considerable bureaucratic autonomy.[8] As such, these agencies
may be even less responsive to congressional pressures to change course than
other entities within the executive branch. Second, both the Church and EPA
cases involved presidents with significant ideological stakes in the matter at
hand. Although President Ford entered office in a greatly weakened position
following President Nixon's resignation under threat of impeachment, he
believed that defending the presidency from institutional incursions from a
resurgent Congress was of paramount importance. Similarly, President Reagan, who also enjoyed a much stronger political position than Ford, entered
office committed to reducing the regulatory scope of government—including
in the environmental realm—and reducing burdensome regulations that he
believed were hampering economic growth. As a result, evidence of policy
concessions in the wake of these investigations would show that policy can
shift in response to investigations not only in areas where the president is in-
different, but even on ideologically charged policy questions of considerable
importance to the president and his administration.

The final case study discusses an investigation that failed to produce significant policy change, either from Congress or the president: the investigation into the Obama administration's massive stimulus loan to solar panel
manufacturer Solyndra, which defaulted on the loan and filed for bankruptcy in 2011. Given the idiosyncrasies of any investigation, and political

---

Investigations, 1946–2002, 2nd ed. (New Haven: Yale University Press, 2005).The Church
Committee investigation was one of the more high-profile probes on Mayhew's list. Its sixty-
nine days of front page New York Times coverage exceeded the average of fifty-three days;
however, this total pales in comparison to the most high-profile investigations, such as the
Army-McCarthy hearings, Watergate, and Iran-Contra. The Reagan EPA probe received
twenty-eight days of front-page coverage, placing it below the median across all thirty-five
high-profile probes.

[7] See, e.g., Howell, Jackman, and Rogowski 2013.

[8] See, e.g., B. Dan Wood, "Principals, Bureaucrats, and Responsiveness in Clean Air Enforcements," American Political Science Review 82 (1988): 214.

moment more generally, many differences separate this case from the other three. However, consistent with our theoretical emphasis on media scrutiny and public opinion, we show that in comparison to the other three cases, the Solyndra investigation failed to generate the same levels of media attention and public political pressure for change.

THE TRUMAN COMMITTEE AND WAR PRODUCTION

In the spring of 1940, the Nazi blitzkrieg began its sweep across Western Europe. Almost overnight, Denmark and Norway fell before the German armed forces in March. On May 10, German tanks roared into the Netherlands. An allied force predominantly of French and British troops moved into Belgium to meet the German advance. However, four days later on May 14, the Wehrmacht broke through the Ardennes and into northern France itself, outflanking the allied force. Two days later on May 16, amidst what he termed a "hurricane of events," President Roosevelt appeared on Capitol Hill before a joint session to beat the drums of war.[9] "These are ominous days," Roosevelt began, "days whose swift and shocking developments force every neutral nation to look to its defenses in the light of new factors." Roosevelt described for the nation the new reality of modern war; mechanized units could tear through enemy territories at lightning speed covering up to two hundred miles a day. The Atlantic and Pacific oceans no longer provided all but impenetrable protection from hostile air and naval forces. Confronted with this threat, America must place itself on a war footing. While the administration had already taken action to strengthen the army and naval forces, Roosevelt argued that much more must be done. "This means military implements—not on paper—which are ready and available to meet any lightning offensive against our American interest. It means also that facilities for production must be ready to turn out munitions and equipment at top speed." Toward this end, Roosevelt set a mind-boggling goal of producing at least 50,000 war planes a year and asked Congress for more than one billion dollars in new appropriations and authorizations to sustain a massive military buildup.[10]

Days before FDR's request, Senate Republicans led by Henry Cabot Lodge (R-MA) and 1940 presidential hopeful Arthur Vandenberg (R-MI) called for an investigation into the nation's defense program. Lodge and

[9] James MacGregor Burns, *Roosevelt: The Lion and the Fox, 1882–1940* (New York: Harcourt Brace Jovanovich, 1956), 419.
[10] Franklin D. Roosevelt, "Message to Congress on Appropriations for National Defense," in Gerhard Peters and John T. Woolley, The American Presidency Project, http://www.presidency.ucsb.edu/ws/?pid=15954, accessed February 28, 2016.

Vandenberg demanded a thorough accounting of how past appropriations had been spent, and they called for more vigorous oversight of the administration's response to the emergency in Europe, both in terms of domestic preparedness and strategic questions of foreign policy.[11] Many conservative Democrats, such as Missouri's Bennett Champ Clark, shared the Republicans' concerns and supported an inquest. Clark asked his colleagues whether they were "willing, before we are called on to vote vast sums of money again, to find out what has become of the $7,000,000,000 we have spent in the last six years, if it is true as we are now told, that we are pitiably unprepared?" Clark favored an investigation "before we again pour a billion dollars down the same rat hole."[12] The Democratic leadership, however, rallied behind the White House and squashed efforts to create an investigative committee.

Even before the American public could come to grips with the full implications of Roosevelt's speech, the situation in Europe deteriorated from bad to worse. By the end of May, amidst the dark days of the British evacuation at Dunkirk, Roosevelt returned to Congress and asked for more than a billion dollars in additional funds to further expedite arms production and military preparedness.[13] Roosevelt had long walked a political tightrope, trying to awaken public consciousness of the dangers posed by Nazi Germany, and to aid the allies, while not advancing too far out in front of domestic public opinion. The allied fiasco in Belgium and the fall of France, however, pushed the administration past the point of no return, and the American military buildup began in earnest. During the last six months of 1940, FDR secured authorization from Congress for $10.5 billion in defense spending—an astronomical figure that exceeded the total budget of the United States for any of the Depression years of the 1930s.[14] So great was this peacetime military expansion that by the time America formally entered the war following the Japanese surprise attack on Pearl Harbor, Congress had already appropriated more funds for army procurement alone than it had for the army and navy during all of World War I.[15]

Inevitably, this exponential growth in defense spending raised concerns about waste, fraud, and abuse. On February 10, 1941, another Missouri

---

[11] *Congressional Record*, May 15, 1940, 6162.

[12] *Congressional Record*, May 15, 1940, 6163.

[13] Franklin D. Roosevelt: "Message to Congress on Appropriations for National Defense," May 31, 1940, in Gerhard Peters and John T. Woolley, The American Presidency Project, http://www.presidency.ucsb.edu/ws/?pid=15961, accessed February 28, 2016.

[14] Alonzo Hamby, *Man of the People: A Life of Harry S. Truman* (New York: Oxford University Press, 1995), 248.

[15] *Mobilization: The U.S. Army in World War II*. CMH-Publication 72–32, http://www.history.army.mil/documents/mobpam.htm, accessed February 28, 2016.

senator, Harry S Truman, took to the floor and called for the creation of a new investigative committee to oversee the defense production establishment. Truman was motivated, in part, by a desire to insure that smaller producers in rural areas received their fair share of war contracts. Lamenting the concentration of procurement contracts in a small number of industrial centers, Truman argued that "the little manufacturer, the little contractor, and the little machine shop have been left entirely out in the cold. The policy seems to be to make the big man bigger and to put the little man completely out of business."[16] However, Truman also raised the specter of cronyism, political favoritism, and mismanagement. After giving examples of each, Truman concluded, "I consider public funds to be sacred funds, and I think they ought to have every safeguard possible to prevent their being misused and mishandled."[17]

The Roosevelt administration was no more eager for a congressional investigation into war production contracts and management in early 1941 than they had been in summer 1940. However, while the administration had corralled the Democratic leadership into beating back earlier efforts, calls for an investigation had only intensified in recent months. Both Eugene Cox, an antilabor Democrat from Georgia, and Henry Cabot Lodge had agitated for investigations, with Lodge seeking a wide-ranging inquest that would "formulate and develop a consistent and complete defense policy for the United States."[18] Sensing that an investigation of some sort was all but inevitable, administration officials decided to back Truman's request in the hopes of sapping energy for a more aggressive investigative effort. When Cox's resolution requesting the establishment of a new investigative committee was discussed in the White House, James Byrnes replied, "I can fix that by putting the investigation into friendly hands."[19]

The Truman Committee held its first hearings in April 1941. The scope of the inquest was wide-ranging, with initial hearings ranging from camp construction to a pending strike by the United Mine Workers. The committee intensely investigated flaws in the mobilization process. For example, in the summer of 1941, it turned its attention to aluminum shortages, which threatened to wreak havoc on aircraft production. This began a lengthy battle between the investigative committee and the Office of Production Management. What particularly provoked the committee's ire in this case was the presence of a large number of "dollar-a-year" men, business leaders who

[16] *Congressional Record*, February 10, 1941, A671.
[17] *Congressional Record*, February 10, 1941, 837.
[18] Theodore Wilson. 1975. "The Truman Committee, 1941," in *Congress Investigates: A Documented History, 1792–1974*, ed. Arthur Schlesinger Jr. and Roger Burns (New York: Chelsea House Publishers), 3122.
[19] Ibid.

agreed to enter government service essentially for free to help manage the war effort, many of whom maintained their regular salaries. The Truman Committee argued that aside from patriotism, many of these individuals were motivated by a desire to advance the interests of their companies from their new positions within the bureaucracy. The committee charged that Alcoa had discouraged growth in the industry to protect its dominant position, and the committee later took aim at government subsidies awarded to Alcoa to expand production, calling the contract one "which makes the government a party to this monopoly's historic low production, high price policy."[20] Under pressure, the administration would later recant and renegotiate the Alcoa subsidies.[21]

More broadly, the revelations of waste, failures of planning, and lack of coordination across agencies raised deeper questions about the Roosevelt administration's management of the war effort. Lamenting the administration's failures to coordinate across agencies charged with war production, Republican senator and committee member Owen Brewster of Maine charged, "the biggest bottleneck in our preparedness effort is on the president's desk."[22] Although he insisted that the committee investigation maintain its nonpartisan credentials and focus single-mindedly on encouraging steps that must be taken to speed victory, Truman largely agreed. When delivering the committee's first report to the Senate in August of 1941, Truman was asked by another committee member, Republican Arthur Vandenberg of Michigan, "in other words, the senator is now saying that the chief bottleneck which the defense program confronts is the lack of adequate organization and coordination in the administration of defense . . . who is responsible for that situation?" Truman frankly replied, "There is only one place where the responsibility can be put." Vandenberg pressed, "Where is that—the White House?" Truman answered simply, "Yes, sir."[23]

Sensing that public support and pressure would be critical to shaking up the executive branch's management of the war effort, the committee went to great lengths to build public awareness of and support for their undertaking.[24] In addition to issuing its own news releases, committee members aggressively pursued opportunities to make their case directly to reporters

[20] "Assail Contract for Alcoa Plants," *New York Times*, November 1, 1941, 9.
[21] Hamby 1995, 251.
[22] Chesly Manly, "Senate Report Brings Dispute Over Aluminum," *Chicago Daily Tribune*, June 27, 1941, 29.
[23] *Congressional Record*, August 14, 1941, 7117–7118.
[24] A letter from U.S. District Judge Lewis Schwellenbach to Truman on January 23, 1942 made precisely this point: "Senatorial investigating committees have to be particularly careful to keep building up a body of public sentiment in their favor at the same time as they are carrying on their work of investigation." Letter reproduced in Wilson 1975, 3179.

and the American people. For example, in July 1941 Truman and fellow committee member Styles Bridges (R-NH) appeared on CBS Radio to discuss the investigation's work, its preliminary findings, and its importance to the war effort.[25]

The entry of the United States into the war following the Japanese surprise attack on Pearl Harbor cast the committee's future in doubt. On December 10, 1941, Truman pledged on the Senate floor that the committee would refrain from any second-guessing of military strategy or tactics and would redouble its focus and efforts on maximizing the efficiency of the war production effort.[26] Undersecretary of War Robert Patterson, instead, publicly called on Congress to scrap the investigative committee. While presidents, of course, have no formal role in determining whether an investigation is continued or concluded, Roosevelt's overwhelming popularity in the aftermath of Pearl Harbor almost certainly insured that the president could have sapped the committee of all momentum and support if he had publicly opposed it. Truman met with FDR early in 1942 to plead his case to continue the investigation. Roosevelt acquiesced.[27]

In early January 1942, the Truman Committee submitted its first complete report to the Roosevelt administration in anticipation of its public unveiling to the full Senate and public. While refraining from blaming the president himself, the report presented a scathing critique of the Office of Production Management. Summarizing the critique, Truman declared on the Senate floor: "Its record has not been impressive; its mistakes of commission have been legion, and its mistakes of omission have been even greater." The report lamented the "ineptitude" of many OPM officials and cited case after case of maladministration. The report also lambasted the appearance of naked cronyism as almost 1,000 men in OPM and other government agencies working for a dollar a year or without any compensation at all leveraged their new positions to secure contracts for industries in whose employ they remained.[28]

Press reaction to the report was overwhelmingly positive and underscores the immediate attention commanded by the committee's call for action. The *New York Times* led its front page with "waste, inefficiency, self-interest, and failures in the national defense program were charged today in a report by the Senate's special investigating committee."[29] Under the banner front

---

[25] Transcript of C.B.S. Radio Program, "The Congressional Mailbag," July 22, 1941. Reproduced in Wilson 1975, 3154–3162.

[26] *Congressional Record*, December 10, 1941, 9600–9601.

[27] Hamby 1995, 253.

[28] *Congressional Record*, 77th Congress, 2nd session, January 15, 1942, 380–391.

[29] C.P. Trussell, "Defense Bungling Charged by Senate's Investigators," *New York Times*, January 16, 1942, 1.

page headline, "Seek to Jail Arms Bunglers," the *Chicago Daily Tribune* opened, "Demands for courts martial and criminal prosecutions were made by Sen. Harry S. Truman (D, MO) today when he gave the senate a report of a special investigation committee exposing grave inefficiencies in the national defense armament program and severely indicted its conduct by the Roosevelt administration."[30]

Roosevelt had long resisted calls for a significant shakeup in government administration of the war effort. As early as June 1940, the president's supporters blocked an amendment introduced by Senator Robert Taft (R-OH) to put the war effort under a new agency with a single head. Another measure introduced by Vermont Republican Warren Austin was also voted down by the Senate after FDR wrote to the Senate in opposition. Taft reintroduced his measure in April 1941, but it was again stymied by Roosevelt's Senate allies.[31] However, with the Truman Committee indictment of OPM about to be made public, Roosevelt could no longer resist the pressure for change. On January 13, 1942, he preempted congressional action by announcing an executive order creating a new super-agency, the War Production Board (WPB), with a single head, as called for by the Truman Committee, former Sears Roebuck executive Donald Nelson.[32] Executive Order 9024 creating the WPB was officially signed on January 16, one day after the public release of the Truman Committee's report calling for a dramatic restructuring of the war production effort. The Truman Committee was widely credited with precipitating the administration's sharp reversal.[33]

On the heels of its well-received report, the Truman Committee was reauthorized by Congress with a significantly expanded budget. One of its first inquiries in 1942 focused on a serious rubber shortage. The committee once again levied devastating criticisms of the now-defunct Office of Production Management for allowing an "orgy of consumption" as the clouds of war thickened. However, more important, the investigative committee formulated policies offering a way forward, including a massive conservation program, gasoline rationing, a national speed limit, and restrictions on how many tires individual Americans could own. Ultimately, the Roosevelt administration adopted the committee's policy prescriptions.[34]

[30] Chesly Manly, "Seek to Jail Arms Bunglers: Senate Report Assails Waste by U.S. Units," *Chicago Daily Tribune*, January 16, 1942, 1.

[31] *Congressional Record*, January 15, 1942, 379.

[32] Roosevelt's unilateral move appears to have maximized his flexibility by preempting legislative action. For example, even after the announcement of the WPB's creation by executive order, Senator Taft argued that the office should also be authorized by statute to firm up its authority. However, sapped of energy by FDR's unilateral announcement, the proposal went nowhere. *Congressional Record*, January 15, 1942, 380.

[33] Wilson 1975, 3131.

[34] Hamby 1995, 255.

While the committee enjoyed these and other successes, it continued to be highly critical of the administration's management of the war effort. The creation of the War Production Board had largely failed to provide the overarching coordination and accountability that the investigators insisted was necessary. The committee assiduously backed WPB chair Nelson, but repeatedly urged him to use the power given him to tighten the reins over the wartime procurement process and end the waste and abuse permeating the system. Dissatisfied with Nelson's and the administration's efforts, in November 1942 Truman penned a provocative call to action in *American Magazine*, "We Can Lose the War in Washington." Truman argued that the WPB had merely replicated many of the failings of the old OPM.[35] "The reasons for the waste and confusion, the committee found, were everywhere the same: the lack of courageous, unified leadership and centralized direction at the top." To rectify the situation, Truman again urged the president to consider a dramatic reorganization of the wartime administration effort. "With the world going up in flames about us, we owe it to ourselves to insist that the president act promptly to halt the selfish fights for power, the endless bickering and dissension, which have so far blocked the complete utilization of our productive energies."[36]

By February 1943, against a growing din of unhappiness on Capitol Hill, President Roosevelt relieved Nelson of his duties and replaced him with the former World War I mobilization czar Bernard Baruch. The Truman Committee, however, was not mollified and continued to insist on a more dramatic reorganization of the executive branch's management of the war effort. The committee wryly noted that while the chairman of the War Production Board was nominally in charge, his authority was undercut repeatedly by the administration creating other officials such as a Rubber Director and an administrator of petroleum programs who answered directly to the president. Such arrangements satisfied Roosevelt's desire for personal control. But they made a mockery of the clear lines of authority and accountability demanded by the committee.[37]

The public scrutiny generated by the Truman Committee's investigation provided the impetus for legislative action to compel the administration to change course. A group of leaders including Truman, fellow committee member Senator Harley Kilgore (D-WV), and Representative John Tolan (D-CA)

---

[35] For example, in December 1942, the committee recommended a formal censure for WPB officials responsible for lumber shortages. "Acute Shortage in Lumber Seen," *New York Times*, December 16, 1942, 16.

[36] Harry Truman, "We Can Lose the War in Washington," *American Magazine*, November 1942. Reproduced in Wilson 1975, 3202–3203.

[37] Truman Committee Report on Conflicting War Programs, May 6, 1943. Reproduced in Wilson 1975, 3231.

drafted legislative language that would create a single Office of War Mobilization, uniting "under one civilian roof" control over the entire nonmilitary economy. Another effort spearheaded by Senators Maloney and Taft would instead establish an independent Civilian Supply Administration that would essentially strip power away from the oft-criticized War Production Board. While the Truman Committee itself opposed the latter bill, expressing concern that it would further fragment authority, its relentless unmasking of the WPB's many failures created the climate that made such legislative assertions possible.[38] The Maloney-Taft measure actually passed the Senate on May 10. In response, FDR again acted unilaterally to preempt more drastic congressional action. Roosevelt created a new organization, the Office of War Mobilization, to run the war effort and tapped James Byrnes as its head. The executive order was firmly built on the foundations of the Truman-Kilgore and Tolan proposals.[39]

The Truman Committee backed the move and claimed FDR's latest abrupt reversal was caused by its political pressure.[40] The *New York Times'* Arthur Krock agreed. "The fact is that [these changes] have been urged on the president ever since the emergency became obvious. . . . He chose, however, to try almost every other solution except real centralization of authority and policy-making just under himself."[41] Only under tremendous political pressure and the threat of legislative action, which never would have materialized without the revelations uncovered and the political pressure generated by the Truman Committee investigation, did Roosevelt change course.

In 1943, Harry Truman graced the cover of *Time* magazine for its feature article titled "Billion-Dollar Watchdog." The article began by summarizing some of the investigation's most impressive accomplishments.

They had prodded Commerce Secretary Jesse Jones into building synthetic-rubber plants, bludgeoned the president into killing off doddering old SPAB and setting up WPB. They had called the turn on raw-materials shortages, had laid down the facts of the rubber famine. . . . [O]ne single investigation, of graft and waste in Army camp building had saved the U.S. $250,000 . . . their total savings ran into billions, partly because of what their agents had ferreted out in the sprawling war program, partly because their hooting curiosity was a great deterrent to waste.

[38] "Senate Votes Bill for Civilian 'Czar,'" *New York Times*, May 11, 1943, 14.
[39] Arthur Krock, "'War Cabinet' Creation Follows Wilson's Plan," *New York Times*, May 30, 1943, E3.
[40] Wilson 1975, 3133.
[41] Arthur Krock, "'War Cabinet' Creation Follows Wilson's Plan," *New York Times*, May 30, 1943, E3.

Within weeks of the article's publication, the investigation would score perhaps its greatest victory, the replacement of the WPB with the new Office of War Mobilization, built largely according to Truman and Kilgore's design. How did it exert so much tangible influence on the conduct and course of American war mobilization policy? As *Time* noted, the committee "had no power to act or order." Instead, they had used "Congress's old prerogative to look, criticize, and recommend, they had focused the strength of public opinion on the men who had the power."[42]

THE CHURCH COMMITTEE AND THE
INTELLIGENCE COMMUNITY

The National Security Act of 1947 established the fundamental basis of the national security state that governed the nation throughout the Cold War era. The bill sought to modernize the nation's security apparatus by creating the National Security Council, reorganizing the armed forces under the control of a new secretary of defense, and creating an independent air force. The act also sought to bolster the nation's intelligence capabilities by creating a new Central Intelligence Agency (CIA). The precise mandate of the CIA, however, was shrouded in statutory ambiguity. Plainly the CIA was empowered to interpret intelligence, but it was not explicitly authorized to collect it. Representing perhaps a somewhat extreme view, Idaho Democrat Frank Church, who in 1975 would be tapped to head a select committee investigating the CIA, argued, "The CIA's role was to marshal covert intelligence that was conducted by others [e.g., other departmental intelligence units] so it could be analyzed and assessed."[43] Others accepted that the CIA was implicitly empowered to collect "foreign intelligence." However, what measures the agency could employ to collect such intelligence was a matter of considerable debate. For example, could the CIA engage in domestic clandestine operations that aim to gather foreign intelligence? The legislative language was no more illuminating regarding the legal authority for the CIA to engage in covert operations. Such actions were never explicitly authorized by statute; however, they could be implied by a loophole allowing the agency "to perform such other functions and duties related to intelligence affecting the national security as the National Security Council may from time to time direct."[44]

---

[42] "Billion-Dollar Watchdog." *Time*, March 8, 1943.
[43] *CQ Almanac*, 1975, 389.
[44] National Security Act of 1947, Section 102, (d)(5). The relevant section of the U.S. Code (50 U.S.C. §3036) has since been amended after 9/11.

Vague legislative provisions opened the door to expansive exercises of power by the intelligence community and the executive branch. However, rather than aggressively superintend the intelligence services, Congress largely ceded the field to the executive branch. Oversight responsibilities were entrusted to the House and Senate Armed Services and Appropriations Committees, whose memberships were packed with senior legislators with close ties to the military establishment.[45] Neither committee provided vigorous oversight, and Congress defeated almost 200 proposals to strengthen its oversight of the CIA in the quarter century following the agency's creation. Most notably, in 1955 future senate majority Leader Mike Mansfield proposed the creation of a Joint Committee on Intelligence modeled on the highly successful Joint Committee on Atomic Energy. Mansfield's proposed reform was even backed by the Second Hoover Commission on Executive Branch Organization. By the time S. Con. Res. 2 made it to the floor in 1956, however, twelve of Mansfield's original co-sponsors had reconsidered their positions and the initiative failed miserably on a 27–59 vote.[46]

While 1974 may be best remembered for the culmination of the Watergate scandal and the resignation of President Richard Nixon, several sensational leaks rekindled old debates about limits on the CIA and other intelligence agencies. On September 8, 1974, papers across the country exploded with banner headlines revealing that the Nixon administration had authorized more than $8 million for CIA covert activities to destabilize and overthrow the Chilean regime of Salvador Allende.[47] The details were leaked to the press by Massachusetts Democrat Michael Harrington. Harrington learned of the CIA's machinations in Chile in April of 1974 during the secret executive session testimony of CIA Director William Colby before the House Armed Services Committee. Harrington leaked the testimony to the press (in the form of a letter to House Foreign Affairs Committee chairman Thomas Morgan) in the hopes of building public pressure for a more thorough investigation into the CIA's activities, particularly any involvement in the September 11, 1973, coup that killed Allende and toppled his government.[48]

On December 22, 1974, the clamor for an investigation intensified exponentially following the publication in the *New York Times* of Seymour

<hr/>

[45] Patrick McGarvey, *CIA: The Myth and the Madness* (Baltimore: Penguin, 1975).

[46] Frederick Kaiser, "Legislative History of the Senate Select Committee on Intelligence," *CRS Report*, August 16, 1978.

[47] Seymour Hersh, "C.I.A. Chief Tells House of $8 million Campaign Against Allende in '70–'73," *New York Times*, September 8, 1974, 1. Laurence Stern, "CIA Role in Chile Revealed: Anti-Allende Funding Put at $11 million," *Washington Post*, September 8, 1974, A1.

[48] L. Britt Snyder, *The Agency and the Hill: CIA's Relationship with Congress, 1947–2004* (Washington, DC: Center for the Study of Intelligence, 2008).

Hersh's column unveiling widespread abuse at the CIA under the Nixon administration, including many instances of the agency turning its clandestine powers against domestic enemies of the administration. [49] Hersh had managed to obtain many materials from a report—referred to within the agency as the "family jewels," which CIA Director James Schlesinger had commissioned a year earlier in the hopes of starting with a clean slate after Watergate. The *Times* published a laundry list replete with some of the agency's most egregious abuses of power. Hersh reported that the CIA had endeavored to infiltrate the antiwar movement, as well as other domestic groups opposed to the Nixon administration and its policies. More broadly, the CIA engaged in widespread acts of domestic espionage including break-ins and mail openings in the course of maintaining files on more than 10,000 American citizens.

Seeking to avoid a politically damaging congressional investigation of the intelligence community and the executive branch, the Ford administration sprung into action in early 1975. On January 5, President Ford announced the creation of a blue ribbon commission chaired by Vice President Rockefeller to determine "whether the CIA has exceeded its statutory authority," and if so to propose recommendations for reform. As CIA Director William Colby remembers, the administration hoped that the commission would "still the outcry and thus prevent a full investigation of intelligence from getting started." [50] However, Ford's gambit failed to stem the calls for an independent investigation on Capitol Hill and in the press. For example, in an op-ed appearing in the *Los Angeles Times*, Walter Pincus argued that to correct abuses, provide new safeguards, and defend legitimate intelligence-gathering capacity, "far more is needed than a narrow blue-ribbon commission studying a narrow set of allegations." [51]

On January 27, 1975, the Senate voted 82–4 to create a Select Committee to Study Government Operations With Respect to Intelligence Activities. Idaho Democrat Frank Church, who would announce his own bid for the Democratic presidential nomination in August, was tapped to head the

[49] Seymour Hersh, "Huge C.I.A. Operation Reported in U.S. Against Antiwar Forces, Other Dissidents in Nixon Years," *New York Times*, December 22, 1974, 1.

[50] William Colby and Peter Forbath, *Honorable Men: My Life in the CIA* (New York: Simon and Shuster, 1978), 398. There was precedent for such a maneuver working. In 1967, President Johnson succeeded in squelching pressure for a full-scale congressional investigation of ties between the CIA and the National Student Association by appointing a presidential commission chaired by Undersecretary of State Nicholas Katzenbach. Loch Johnson, *A Season of Inquiry: The Senate Intelligence Investigation* (Lexington: University of Kentucky Press, 1985), 10–11. See also, Robert Donovan, "Johnson Orders Investigation as CIA Controversy Widens," *Los Angeles Times*, February 17, 1967, 1.

[51] Walter Pincus, "For Full CIA Probe: President Will Have to Help," *Los Angeles Times*, January 26, 1975, F3.

bipartisan panel that would henceforth be widely known as the Church Committee.[52]

The early months of the Church Committee were spent in a protracted dance with the executive branch over access to administration and intelligence officials and, more important, to reams of sensitive documents. Ford and his aides feared that blanket claims of executive privilege would inevitably evoke Nixonian comparisons. As a result, rather than being summarily denied, requests for information were often met with stonewalling and side stepping. Committee member Walter Mondale (D-MN) worried openly that the White House delays were part of a larger strategic goal of simply waiting out the committee and running out the clock on its mandate. Philip Hart (D-MI) summarized the conundrum: "[The administration] had given us two go-to-hells. What is our response going to be?"[53]

Much of the committee's early work was done behind closed doors in executive session. However, by the fall of 1975 the committee was ready to make its case in televised hearings. The undertaking was always politically risky. From the very outset CIA officials had warned that the investigation risked jeopardizing national security and even putting American lives in danger. For example, Director Colby admonished investigators in February, even before the first hearing had been held, "these exaggerations and misrepresentations of CIA activities can do irreparable harm to our national intelligence apparatus and if carried to the extreme could blindfold our country as it looks abroad."[54] President Ford upped the ante on August 19 when he declared in a nationally televised address: "Intelligence in today's world is absolutely essential to our national security—even our survival. It may be even more important in peace than in war. Any reckless

---

[52] The House formed its own investigative panel chaired by Lucien Nedzi (D-MI) on February 19, 1975. However, the House investigation was quickly derailed when it was revealed that Nedzi had received secret briefings on intelligence activities in 1974 as chairman of the Armed Services Special Subcommittee on Intelligence. This poisoned Nedzi in the eyes of many liberals keen on major reform. As a result, the Nedzi Committee was disbanded, and on July 17, 1975, the House formed a new select Committee chaired by Otis Pike (D-NY). The Pike Committee operated in parallel with the Church Committee and also provided an impetus for many of the reforms to intelligence that would occur throughout the late 1970s. However, the Pike Committee failed to achieve the level of consensus in the House that the Church Committee succeeded in marshaling in the Senate; indeed, the Pike Committee's final report was never officially published because of heightened opposition. As a result, we focus on the Church Committee, while acknowledging that both investigations played an important role in precipitating the major policy changes in intelligence that occurred throughout the late 1970s.

[53] Johnson 1985, 39.

[54] Robert Jackson, "CIA Critics Hinder Work, Colby Warns," Los Angeles Times, February 21, 1975, A1.

congressional action to cripple the effectiveness of our intelligence services in legitimate operations would be catastrophic."[55]

Nevertheless, the investigators persevered, and the public hearings commenced with an inquiry that cut straight to the heart of accountability within the CIA: the agency's failure to comply with a 1970 presidential order to cease production of and destroy existing stockpiles of biological weapons. These initial hearings presented to the public a scene seemingly ripped from the latest James Bond movie. The committee revealed that the CIA had maintained a secret store of deadly poisons, enough to kill the entire population of a small city. For dramatic effect, at the hearing Senator Church held aloft an actual dart gun designed to deliver an almost imperceptibly small poisoned dart into an unsuspecting target from more than 300 feet away. The carefully planned visual procured the desired effect from the media. The front page of the *Chicago Tribune* blared, "CIA bares poison arsenal," and right under the headline was a large picture of the bespectacled Senator Barry Goldwater aiming the dart gun itself and staring down its telescopic sight.[56] While critics charged that Church was "dazzled by the klieg lights" and more interested in playing to the cameras than conducting a reasoned and fair investigation, the chairman did take the opportunity to remind the media of the larger issue: how the CIA command and control structure had permitted this stockpile to persist (apparently it was the product of actions taken by a mid-level official with little oversight from the top) despite the president's order to eliminate it. "The real question here," Church reminded reporters, "is how presidential orders can be disobeyed on a matter of such importance."[57]

As the fall progressed, the Church Committee turned its attention to allegations of abuses of power in domestic spying and surveillance. They investigated the "Huston Plan," named after a Nixon aide who sought to enlist the FBI, CIA, and NSA in an elaborate effort to intensify surveillance on domestic dissenters. They probed Operation CHAOS, a clandestine CIA operation that spied on student protesters. Inquiries into mail-opening programs revealed an operation that had been conducted on a much larger scale than previously suspected.

The Church Committee clashed most publicly and vehemently with the Ford administration when it finally set its sights on the activities of the National Security Agency (NSA) in late October 1975. The president insisted that any disclosure of the ultrasecretive NSA's activities, past or present,

---

[55] Gerald R. Ford, "Address in Minneapolis Before the Annual Convention of the American Legion." August 19, 1975 in Gerhard Peters and John T. Woolley, The American Presidency Project, http://www.presidency.ucsb.edu/ws/?pid=5174, accessed February 28, 2016.

[56] Harry Kelly, "CIA Bares Poison Arsenal: Dart Gun Can Kill Without Any Clues," *Chicago Tribune*, September 17, 1975, 1.

[57] Johnson 1985, 74.

could adversely affect national security. Ranking committee Republican John Tower backed the administration, arguing that in this case, "I do believe the people's right to know should be subordinated to the people's right to be secure."[58] However, Church pushed on, undeterred, arguing that the investigation was essential to examine activities of "questionable propriety and legality," and to insure that the NSA never again violated the "inalienable rights guaranteed Americans by the Constitution."[59]

The Church Committee then delved headlong into the clandestine world of Operation SHAMROCK and Project MINARET. The former had its origins in World War II–era censorship programs. Through a secret agreement with three major private international telegraph companies, the government obtained daily copies of all international cables transmitted on the wires, including private communications of American citizens. The NSA then identified communications involving Americans on a "watch list" created and continually updated by agencies across the executive branch and transmitted those communications to the requesting agency. The program operated for decades without any judicial oversight, and it seized private communications without warrants. Church and other committee Democrats charged that the operation violated both the Federal Communications Act and the Fourth Amendment.[60]

By late November of 1975 after considerable debate and unease in the Senate, the Church Committee finally released its interim report on the CIA's assassination programs. The report, which gripped and divided the nation, traced the evolution of various plots to assassinate Cuba's Fidel Castro and Congo's Patrice Lumumba. Poisoned cigars, exploding seashells, and even mafia hits were among the plans considered by the CIA—and revealed by the Church Committee. The report also uncovered mountains of evidence that various officials from across the executive branch had discussed diverse plots against a number of other leaders including our ostensible ally Ngo Dinh Diem of South Vietnam, Rafael Trujillo of the Dominican Republic, and Rene Schneider of Chile.[61] Some in the press hailed the committee for uncovering the intelligence community's dark past in the hopes of preventing future abuses. The *Los Angeles Times* acknowledged the costs of the exposure, but

---

[58] *CQ Almanac*, 1975, 397.

[59] *CQ Almanac*, 1975, 395.

[60] Nicholas Horrock, "Senate Unite Says Cable Companies Aided in Spying," *New York Times*, November 7, 1975, 10. The Senate Parliamentarian agreed; this ruling was the basis used by the committee to release its report on the secret operation to the public. Lawrence Knutson, "Panel Defiantly Reveals Cable Data," *Boston Globe*, November 7, 1975, 7.

[61] George Lardner, "Senators Issue Report on CIA's Death Plots," *Boston Globe*, November 21, 1975, 1; Jim Squires, "Senate CIA Report: They Didn't Fix the Blame," *Chicago Tribune*, November 23, 1975, A1.

maintained "such embarrassment is often the price paid for maintaining an open society, the cost exacted so that the American people can know of the activities of their government, and so that abuses of power, where they exist, can be exposed and corrected."[62] Similarly, the *Chicago Tribune* argued that one of the only bright aspects of the report was its very existence:

> The other [cheering aspect] is that the Senate report was made public, in spite of strenuous efforts to suppress it. And that, in our view, is a crucial victory for this country. One branch of our government has assessed a just penalty against another for having forgotten basic standards of decency; and as a result our government leaders will be much less likely to forget them in the future.[63]

Conservative commentator James Kilpatrick, however, charged that the committee's inconclusive report came at too dear a price:

> The committee report provides a rich meal for America's detractors to feed on. By reason of this publication, the CIA's vital task will be made more difficult; the intelligence services of friendly nations will think twice about cooperating in the future. The committee feels the assassination allegations should be told because democracy depends upon a well-informed electorate, but do the people have to know *everything?*[64]

Public opinion also seemed to reflect these divergent points of view. By the end of 1975, the American public was largely split in its evaluation of the Church Committee and its work. Just under 40% of Americans held a positive view of the committee; 40% held a negative assessment of it; and the remainder were unsure. However, the committee's revelations had undeniably tarnished the image of the CIA. In a December 1975 survey, less than a third of Americans held a positive view of the CIA, versus 49% who saw it in a negative light. When queried about specific abuses, public sentiment was even more one-sided. For example, 61% agreed that the CIA and FBI's spying on prominent Americans entailed a violation of basic rights. Finally, on the question of which party would do a better job at controlling the CIA, Democrats enjoyed an almost two-to-one advantage.[65]

---

[62] "Assassination and Foreign Policy," *Los Angeles Times*, November 23, 1975, 12.

[63] "Murder as a Foreign Policy," *Chicago Tribune*, November 24, 1975, A2.

[64] James Kilpatrick, "Reflections on the CIA Report," *Los Angeles Times*, November 28, 1975, A7.

[65] Just under a third, 32%, said Democrats; only 17% answered Republicans; 33% said it did not matter, while 18% were not sure. Survey conducted by Louis Harris & Associates, December 20–December 30, 1975 and based on 1,394 telephone interviews. Sample: National adult. [USHARRIS.012276.R02]. Storrs, CT: Roper Center for Public Opinion Research, iPOLL [distributor], accessed March 4, 2016.

By January 1976, the Church Committee had largely wrapped up its formal public hearings and had begun to focus on producing its final report and recommendations for legislative reforms. The committee was well aware that some measure of cooperation with the White House was essential; as Senator Miller reminded the group, "we've all got to keep the threat of a presidential veto in mind when we're spending all these long hours drafting reform legislation."[66] Despite efforts at accommodation, it was plain to all that many members of the Church Committee wished to see more far-reaching reform than the Ford administration would support. In his January 1976 State of the Union Address, President Ford levied a public blow against the committee, implicitly labeling its public airing of dirty laundry a "crippling of our foreign intelligence services [which] increases the danger of American involvement in direct armed conflict."[67] Such charges achieved even greater resonance following the December 23 murder of the CIA station chief in Athens, Greece, a tragedy that critics laid at the Church Committee's feet.[68] Rather than entrusting the task of reforming the intelligence agencies to a dangerous congressional committee, Ford announced his intention to do so unilaterally.

On February 17, 1976, in what the press accurately dubbed "a preemptive end-run on the Congress," President Ford announced Executive Order 11905 during a prime time press conference. The executive order reorganized the intelligence community along the lines suggested by the Rockefeller Commission in mid-1975. It also included new measures to prevent leaks, and banned any employee of the United States from engaging in or conspiring to engage in political assassination. Many Republicans hailed the measures, with Church Committee vice chair John Tower praising them as "positive and carefully planned." Most Democrats and many liberal pundits, such as Anthony Lewis, derided the reforms as little more than "a blueprint for more secrecy, greater executive power, and less congressional oversight."[69] The White House plainly hoped that making even these modest concessions would sap the political drive for more dramatic

[66] Johnson 1985, 164.

[67] Gerald R. Ford, "Address Before a Joint Session of the Congress Reporting on the State of the Union," January 19, 1976, in Gerhard Peters and John T. Woolley, The American Presidency Project, http://www.presidency.ucsb.edu/ws/?pid=5677, accessed February 28, 2016.

[68] For example, Washington Star columnist Charles Bartlett wrote, "the assassination of the CIA Station Chief, Richard Welch, in Athens is a direct consequence of the stagey hearings of the Church Committee . . . the Committee's prolonged focus on CIA activities in Greece left agents there exposed to random vengeance." Church flatly rejected the logic, and fired back at similar charges from the White House, "Utterly untrue. And unworthy of a spokesman of the president even to permit such an innuendo." Quoted in Johnson 1985, 161, 170.

[69] Johnson 1985, 193, 195.

changes. Church, however, remained undeterred, declaring, "I think the president reaches beyond his power. . . . You cannot change law by executive order." Committee Democrats continued their push for legislation that would strengthen congressional oversight and place greater restraints on the executive branch's monopolization of the intelligence community.

Most directly, the Church Committee led to the enactment of S. Res. 400 creating the Senate Select Intelligence Committee to bolster legislative oversight. More than twenty years after Mansfield's initial proposal for such a committee, Church and colleagues were able to harness the public uproar generated by the investigation to make Mansfield's vision a reality.[70] In addition to providing more vigorous oversight of intelligence activities, the select committee was specifically given sole jurisdiction over all intelligence authorization requests, and it required the administration to submit all major intelligence activities, including covert operations, to the committee for its review (though efforts to grant it veto power were defeated).[71] Because they were established by simple resolution, these requirements were not initially legally binding; however, they were later codified by the 1980 Oversight Act.

The Church Committee also set the stage for the passage two years later of another major piece of legislation during the Carter administration: the Foreign Intelligence and Surveillance Act of 1978 (FISA). Both contemporary journalistic sources and subsequent analysts make clear that FISA was a direct response to the Church Committee investigations and its revelations. For example, in 1978 the *Washington Post* reported, "The Senate intelligence reform bill, on which hearings have now begun, was an outgrowth of the detailed investigation into intelligence abuses by the Church Committee."[72] Similarly, a *Congressional Research Service* report prepared in the midst of a new intelligence-gathering scandal during the mid-2000s echoed this assessment: "The Foreign Intelligence Surveillance Act of 1978, P.L. 95–511, 92 Stat. 1783 (October 25, 1978), 50 U.S.C. §§ 1801 et seq. (hereinafter FISA), was enacted in response both to the Committee to Study Government Operations with Respect to Intelligence Activities (otherwise known as the Church Committee) revelations regarding past abuses of

---

[70] The House followed suit a year later and in 1977 created its own Permanent Select Committee on Intelligence.

[71] For an overview, see William Newby Raiford, "To Create a Senate Select Committee on Intelligence: A Legislative History of Senate Resolution 400," *CRS Report*, August 12, 1976. Since enactment of Hughes-Ryan in December 1974, the CIA had been required to submit briefings on covert operations to Congress; however, most such briefings were limited in scope. S. Res. 400 directed all intelligence agencies, not just CIA, to report on sensitive operations to the newly-created Select Intelligence Committee.

[72] David Wise, "Intelligence Reforms: Less than Half a Loaf," *Washington Post*, April 23, 1978, D3.

electronic surveillance for national security purposes and to the somewhat uncertain state of the law on the subject."[73]

FISA was an attempt to resolve the murkiness regarding the legality of electronic surveillance. In its final report, the Church Committee had reviewed the intelligence agencies' long history of wiretapping and bugging American citizens without a warrant. The report argued the dangers to privacy and abuse of power were even greater in the electronic age:

> The inherently intrusive nature of electronic surveillance, moreover, has enabled the Government to generate vast amounts of information— unrelated to any legitimate government interest—about the personal and political lives of American citizens. The collection of this type of information has, in turn, raised the danger of its use for partisan political and other improper ends by senior administration officials.[74]

FISA banned warrantless electronic eavesdropping on communications involving American citizens, and instead created the Foreign Intelligence Surveillance Court to review and approve executive branch requests for surveillance using different standards of evidence from those required in a civilian court. The law was hailed for restoring the balance between the exigencies of national security and cherished civil liberties, and it governed American intelligence-gathering policies for almost twenty-five years.[75] Following the terrorist attacks of September 11, 2001, Congress approved requests by the Bush administration to modify FISA, "modernizing" it to allow, for example, roving surveillance and to alter the standards for warrants so that foreign intelligence need only be a *significant* purpose of the surveillance, as opposed to the sole purpose.[76]

Despite securing these amendments, the Bush administration went even further unilaterally by secretly authorizing the National Security Agency to conduct electronic surveillance of the international communications of American citizens without a warrant from the Foreign Intelligence

[73] Elizabeth Bazan, "The Foreign Intelligence Surveillance Act: An Overview of Selected Issues," *CRS Report*, July 7, 2008, 1. Another report noted, "The legislative history of FISA reflects serious concerns about the past NSA abuses reflected in the Church Committee reports." Elizabeth Bazan and Jennifer Elsea, "Presidential Authority to Conduct Warrantless Electronic Surveillance to Gather Foreign Intelligence Information," *CRS Report*, January 5, 2006, 22.

[74] Quoted in Elizabeth Bazan and Jennifer Elsea, "Presidential Authority to Conduct Warrantless Electronic Surveillance to Gather Foreign Intelligence Information," *CRS Report*, January 5, 2006, 13.

[75] Ira Shapiro, "The Foreign Intelligence Surveillance Act: Legislative Balancing of National Security and the Fourth Amendment," *Harvard Journal on Legislation* 15 (1977–1978): 119–204.

[76] See Elizabeth Bazan, "The Foreign Intelligence Surveillance Act: An Overview of the Statutory Framework and Recent Judicial Decisions," *CRS Report*, March 31, 2003, RL 30465.

Surveillance Court. The disclosure of this program in 2005 caused political shockwaves precisely because it was in blatant contradiction to the legal strictures and procedures established by FISA. The president's violation of FISA earned costly rebukes from across the political spectrum, and it helped give rise to concerns among pundits and scholars alike about the emergence of a new imperial presidency.[77]

EPA INVESTIGATIONS AND ENVIRONMENTAL POLICY

In the late 1970s, stories of leaching toxic waste and widespread genetic mutations among the residents of the Love Canal subdivision of Niagara Falls, NY, shocked the nation and vividly dramatized the need to remediate vast areas contaminated with toxic industrial byproducts. After many fits and starts, Congress in 1980 passed the "Superfund" legislation (P.L. 96–510) creating a $1.6 billion emergency fund, most of which would be raised from fees on chemical companies themselves, to begin the clean-up of the most dangerous sites contaminated with toxic waste.[78] However, the election of Ronald Reagan, who had campaigned on the need to free businesses from overzealous regulations, sowed the seeds for interbranch conflict over the law's implementation.[79]

To head the Environmental Protection Agency, President Reagan selected Anne M. Gorsuch, a staunch conservative who was committed to changing the culture of the agency, particularly what she viewed as its antagonistic relationship with industry. Toward this end, Gorsuch picked many of her chief lieutenants at the agency from the ranks of corporate America, including from many of the very companies that the EPA was charged with regulating. To further cripple the EPA's enforcement capacity, the Reagan

---

[77] Savage 2007; Rudalevige 2005; Pfiffner 2008. A significant majority of the public also believed that Bush had gone too far. A 2006 *Newsweek* poll first told a representative sample of Americans, "As you may know, there are reports that the NSA (National Security Agency), a government intelligence agency, has been collecting the phone call records of Americans." It then asked them, "In light of this news and other executive actions by the Bush-Cheney administration, in general, do you think they have gone too far in expanding presidential power, or not?" Fifty-seven percent said that Bush had gone too far. Survey by Newsweek. Methodology: Conducted by Princeton Survey Research Associates International, May 11—May 12, 2006 and based on 1,007 telephone interviews. Sample: National adult. [USPS-RNEW.051306.R15].

[78] For an overview, see "Congress Clears 'Superfund' Legislation." *CQ Almanac* (1980), 584–593.

[79] Michael Kraft, "A New Environmental Policy Agenda: The 1980 Presidential Campaign and its Aftermath," in *Environmental Policy in the 1980s*, ed. Norma Vig and Michael Kraft (Washington, DC: Congressional Quarterly, 1984).

administration also proposed massive cuts in the agency's budget. In the assessment of former EPA assistant administrator William Drayton, "Unable to repeal the country's environmental laws because the public would never stand for it, Reagan is gutting them through the personnel and budgetary back doors."[80]

The president had plainly defied a decidedly more environmentalist Congress. It was a challenge that much political science research suggests the president was well-positioned to win. Exploiting his inherent institutional advantages in staffing the bureaucracy,[81] influencing the budgetary process,[82] and shaping policy unilaterally through the regulatory process,[83] Reagan should have had considerable leeway to significantly alter the implementation of environmental policy. Moreover, backed by a co-partisan majority in the Senate and the veto pen, there seemed to be little chance that Congress could enact new legislation compelling a more pro-environmental policy course.

Yet, Congress challenged the administration's environmental policies in the committee room, both through vigorous oversight and through a series of high-profile, sustained investigations of alleged abuses of power by top administration officials. The evidence suggests that these investigations did more than simply score political points for anti-Reagan forces; rather, they also materially affected the content of environmental policy.

The Superfund law required the EPA to create a list of the highest-priority toxic waste sites for remediation by July 1981. However, the administration did not produce its initial list until October, and even then it contained only 181 sites, a surprisingly low number contrasted with the thousands estimated to exist by EPA when Congress drafted the law. Congressional critics were also concerned by the Reagan EPA's slow progress in beginning the clean-up at the small number of sites it had identified. Both the House Public Works and Transportation Committee and the House Energy and Commerce Committee held hearings investigating alleged noncompliance with the law. Congressional investigators charged that the remediation fund had accumulated almost $384 million, while only $88 million had actually been spent on cleaning up toxic waste sites by the end of fiscal year 1982. More broadly, investigators on the House Energy and Commerce Committee were troubled by what they termed a "dramatic decline" in toxic waste

[80] "Environment," *CQ Almanac* 1981, 504. Even Gorsuch believed that the OMB had gone too far in paring down EPA. "Environmental Protection Agency Talking Points—FY 1984 Budget Passback Appeal," folder "EPAs Dingell Hearings: Fall 1983 (1)," Box 14, Counsel to the President, White House Office of Investigations; Records, Ronald Reagan Library.

[81] Lewis 2008.

[82] Berry, Burden and Howell 2011; Kriner and Reeves 2015.

[83] Howell 2003.

enforcement litigation and Department of Justice action against polluters since the Reagan administration gained power in 1981.[84]

As investigators continued to dig, the charges of administrative abuses became more politically explosive. For example, investigators procured evidence of "sweetheart deals" with polluters in which the administration failed to hold them liable for clean-up expenses as provided for in the law. The initial House Public Works and Transportation Committee report concluded: "Our preliminary finding suggests that many hazardous waste sites are not being fully cleaned up . . . [and] that chemical companies responsible for cleanup costs are not being held liable for their full share of the cleanup costs in every instance."[85]

The inquest came to a head in the winter of 1982 when investigators issued a subpoena to Administrator Gorsuch demanding virtually all EPA documents relating to 160 sites on its priority cleanup list. The EPA handed over many documents, but Gorsuch refused to turn over 74 documents, invoking executive privilege and citing instructions from President Reagan not to turn over any documents that "would impair my solemn responsibility to enforce the law."[86] First the House Public Works and Transportation Committee and then the full House voted to cite Gorsuch with contempt of Congress, prompting banner headlines such as the front page of the *Los Angeles Times* on December 17, 1982: "EPA Chief Cited for Contempt: Highest Official Ever Charged by Congress."[87] Still, Gorsuch refused.[88]

Unfazed, investigators continued to pound the administration. In February of 1983, John Dingell, the chair of the House Energy and Commerce

[84] "Buford Resigns From EPA Post Under Fire," *CQ Almanac* 1983, 332.

[85] "Gorusch Cited for Contempt of Congress," *CQAlmanac* 1982, 453.

[86] "Executive Privilege, Contempt of Congress," *CQ Almanac* 1982, 452.

[87] Paul Houston, "EPA Chief Cited for Contempt: Highest Official Ever Charged by Congress," *Los Angeles Times*, December 17, 1982, 1.

[88] Interestingly, Gorsuch supported turning over the documents. For example, on February 17, 1983, Gorsuch and John Daniels met with President Reagan, Meese, Fielding, and others. Daniels' notes indicate: "AMG made pitch to President that this is no longer a legal or Constitutional issue, but a political one and that his interests were not well served by the appearance that we had something to hide." Memo, Richard Hauser to Timothy Finn, September 27, 1983, folder "EPAs Dingell Hearings: Fall 1983 (1)," Box 14, Counsel to the President, White House Office of Investigations; Records, Ronald Reagan Library. Similarly in a discussion with Craig Fuller on February 24, 1983, Daniels recorded this exchange: "Gorsuch: I've never lied and I don't like it. I think we ought to turn these GD documents over or we're going to bring this President to his knees. Fuller: Personally, my heart goes out to you. And I don't like asking you to [lie]. Gorsuch: I don't like to lie and I love this President and he's being misadvised, it's not going to go away. Eroding confidence. He's being poorly served. Give the Democrats an issue and they'll ride forever."

Committee publicly charged a pattern of abuse that went far beyond failures to implement the law promptly. As House investigators probed further, they uncovered multiple allegations of cronyism, conflicts of interest, perjury, obstruction of justice, and abuses of power. Top EPA officials
were discovered overseeing cases in which they previously had worked for
the companies involved. Allegations surfaced that EPA officials, including
Gorsuch, were manipulating the targeting of clean-up grants for political purposes; one charge alleged that the EPA had postponed announcing
a grant for the Stringfellow Acid Pits in California for fear that it might
have aided the senatorial election prospects of Democratic governor Jerry
Brown.[89] A member of the Council of Environmental Quality remembers
Gorsuch explaining the reason for the delay at a meeting in August 1982:
"I'll be damned if I am going to let Brown take credit for that."[90] Investigators also heard evidence that the EPA and Reagan administration officials
maintained political "hit lists" that targeted EPA science advisers and other
civil servants who challenged the administration's deregulation policies.[91]
And investigators probed multiple alleged instances of perjury and agency
obstruction.[92]

On February 7, President Reagan fired Assistant EPA Administrator
Rita Lavelle, the former director of the Superfund program who had been
a major target of investigators.[93] Four days later, Stanley Brand, the general counsel to the Clerk of the House, charged that the EPA had begun
shredding documents in the wake of the December 16, 1982, contempt
citation. Although EPA largely denied the claims, it did confirm that
Lavelle's appointment calendars, which investigators had demanded, had

[89] John Hird, *Superfund: The Political Economy of Environmental Risk* (Baltimore: Johns
Hopkins University Press, 1994), 10.
[90] Memo, Richard Hauser to John Keeney, March 4, 1983, folder "EPAs Dingell Hearings:
Fall 1983 (1)," Box 14, Counsel to the President, White House Office of Investigations; Records, Ronald Reagan Library.
[91] Stuart Taylor, Jr., "Ex-EPA Official Tells of 'Pro and Con' Lists on Personnel," *New York
Times*, March 17, 1983, B14; "Buford Resigns From EPA Post Under Fire," *CQ Almanac*
1983, 332.
[92] "Documents Allegedly Shredded: White House Officials Seek Congress-EPA Compromise," *CQ Weekly*, February 23, 1983, 334.
[93] Among other charges levied against Lavelle were that she had extensive, improper contacts with the industries she was charged with regulating. For example, between February 1982
and January 1983, Lavelle had thirteen meetings with officials from Aerojet-General Corporation, her former employer and a target of the Superfund program. "Rita M. Lavelle Contacts
with officials of Aeroject-General Corporation and its subsidiary Aerojet Liquid Rocket Company," folder, "[110]20 EPA Inquiry—Hold [Miscellaneous Material Mostly re: "Rita Lavelle
Including Some of Her Work Product," Box 21, Counsel to the President, White House Office
of Investigations; Records, Ronald Reagan Library.

"disappeared."[94] On March 9, Administrator Gorsuch resigned; more than a dozen of her top aides also resigned or were fired amid the scandal's fallout.[95] By December of 1983, Lavelle would be convicted by a federal jury on multiple felony charges stemming from her tenure at EPA.

The high political drama unfolding daily on the front pages of national newspapers generated a swift and strong public backlash against Reagan's environmental policy. In this intense interbranch showdown, public opinion plainly sided with the congressional investigators. For example, a March 1983 poll asked the public, "Now let me read you some of the charges the Democrats are making about how the EPA has been operating during the Reagan administration. For each, tell me if you think the charge is justified or not." Almost twice as many Americans (55%) agreed with the charge that "many apparent violations of the Clean Air Act, the Clean Water Act, and hazardous waste laws were just ignored and not prosecuted" as believed this accusation was unjustified (30%). Similarly, a majority of Americans, 55%, agreed with the allegation that "hundreds of thousands of dollars of federal superfund money, meant to be used to clean up hazardous waste dumps, were wasted and not spent for the right purpose." By contrast, less than a third of Americans, only 32%, said that the charge was not justified. Finally, 46% of Americans agreed that by withholding documents from investigators until ordered to do so by a court, "Reagan officials tried to cover up wrongdoing in the EPA and were very close to obstructing justice." Only 39% sided, instead, with the administration.[96] On the question of the Reagan administration's handling of the Superfund program, an April 1983 poll showed that only 13% of Americans believed the program was being "administered correctly" by Reagan. A majority, 51%, said that the administration was misusing the fund.[97]

Undoubtedly, the investigations politically damaged the president and scored points for congressional Democrats. However, did the investigations materially affect policy outcomes, both within the Superfund program specifically and the EPA more generally? On both counts, the evidence strongly suggests that they did.

[94] "Documents Allegedly Shredded: White House Officials Seek Congress-EPA Compromise," *CQ Weekly*, February 12, 1983, 333.
[95] Administrator Gorsuch married the head of the Bureau of Land Management Robert Gorsuch in 1983 as the scandal unfolded. For the sake of clarity, we use the last name Gorsuch throughout.
[96] Survey conducted by Louis Harris & Associates, March 17–March 20, 1983, and based on 1,254 telephone interviews. Sample: National Adult. [USHARRIS.032483.R5]. Storrs, CT: Roper Center for Public Opinion Research, iPOLL [distributor], accessed Mar-4-2016.
[97] Survey Conducted by *Los Angeles Times*, April 4–April 10, 1983 and based on 1,233 telephone interviews. Sample: National Adults. [USLAT.67.R055] Storrs, CT: Roper Center for Public Opinion Research, iPOLL [distributor], accessed Mar-4-2016.

Even in the weeks leading up to Gorsuch's resignation, the White House had begun considering ways to reverse course and step up enforcement. In mid-February 1983, Assistant to the President for Cabinet Affairs Craig Fuller received a memorandum detailing how the Army Corps of Engineers could be used to accelerate the pace of enforcement.[98] In late February, Fuller announced the creation of a Commission on the Management and Administration of the Superfund Act to examine the allegations emanating from Capitol Hill and to recommend improvements in the site designation and evaluation process.[99]

To implement the necessary changes at EPA, President Reagan tapped William Ruckelshaus, the first head of the EPA in 1970, to return to his post and reform the agency. White House aides, sensitive to the political backlash resulting from the Gorsuch fiasco, privately hoped that nominating Ruckelshaus, whose record was widely acknowledged to be more pro-environment than Reagan's, would quell the political maelstrom.[100] And indeed, Ruckelshaus's appointment was greeted with cautious optimism by many in the environmental community.[101]

In his confirmation hearings, Ruckelshaus promised more transparency; the EPA would be operated "in a fishbowl" and would "attempt to communicate with everyone, from the environmentalists to those we regulate, and we will do so as early as possible."[102] In addition to committing to a change in *modus operandi*, Ruckelshaus also took concrete steps to bolster the EPA's enforcement capacity and activities. New personnel were hired, particularly on the scientific and technical side of Superfund enforcement. Career civil servants on the enforcement staff were again empowered to shape policy, and Administrator Ruckelshaus in January 1984 sought to reinforce the change in culture by hosting an EPA-wide "National Compliance and Enforcement Conference" in which the administrator personally made

[98] Information Paper, "EPA Superfund—Corps Assistance to EPA," February 16, 1983, folder "EPA Background, 02/09/1983–02/17/1983," Box 9, Craig Fuller Files, Ronald Reagan Library.

[99] Memorandum For the Record, Craig Fuller, "EPA Personnel/Management Actions," folder "EPA Background, 02/18/1983–02/24/1983," Box 9, Craig Fuller Files, Ronald Reagan Library. See also "Charter, Commission on the Management of the Superfund Act," February 23, 1983, folder "EPA Background, 02/18/1983–02/24/1983," Box 9, Craig Fuller Files, Ronald Reagan Library.

[100] Steven Weisman, "Overtures Made to Ruckelshaus to Head E.P.A.: Agency's Original Chief Asked to Help in Crisis," *New York Times*, March 20, 1983, 2.

[101] Steven Weisman, "President Names Ruckelshaus Head of Troubled E.P.A," *New York Times*, March 22, 1983, A1. Nonetheless, some environmentalists expressed skepticism about Ruckelshaus' environmental record as a vice president of Weyerhauser Company, a major timber producer. Seth King, "Return of First E.P.A. Chief: William Doyle Ruckelshaus," *New York Times*, March 22, 1983, A23.

[102] Joel Mintz, "Agencies, Congress and Regulatory Enforcement: A Review of EPA's Hazardous Waste Enforcement Effort, 1970–1987," *Environmental Law* 18 (1987): 683–778, 744.

the case for continued strengthened enforcement.[103] In the assessment of Thomas Church and Robert Nakamura, this represented a dramatic shift in course from his predecessor's conciliatory approach to corporate polluters "to a more aggressive, litigation-based strategy, including increased referrals to the Department of Justice for enforcement actions and more reliance on unilateral administrative orders. Polluters were identified as 'bad guys' and the EPA saw its role primarily in terms of enforcement."[104] The end result, was a significant reinvigoration of the EPA Superfund program.[105]

The empirical evidence also suggests that the investigations affected concrete environmental policy outcomes even outside of the narrow confines of the Superfund program. In a study of principal-agent relationships and bureaucratic control, B. Dan Wood obtained data on EPA Clean Air Act enforcement, including monthly counts of both monitoring and abatement actions. The former assure that polluters are complying with the law, while the latter involve enforcement actions to bring violators into compliance with legal standards. Consistent with conventional wisdom, Wood's data documents significant decreases in monitoring and abatement activity following both President Reagan's inauguration and the administration's sharp budget cuts for the EPA in the FY 1982 budget. However, immediately after the Gorsuch resignation triggered by congressional investigations, his data shows sharp and sustained increases in both Clean Air Act monitoring and enforcement actions. No major environmental legislation was passed in the spring and summer of 1983.[106] Rather, these significant changes in behavior can be directly traced to the investigations and the administration's response to them. Reagan's shift nicely illustrates our second posited mechanism in which presidents may adjust policy in an effort to preempt a more stringent congressional response.

Finally, one area where EPA continued to lag was in enforcement of the 1976 Resource Conservation Recovery Act (RCRA), which still suffered from funding shortages and a lack of top-level agency attention, given the

[103] Ibid., 745–46.

[104] Thomas Church and Robert Nakamura, *Cleaning Up the Mess: Implementation Strategies in Superfund* (Washington, DC: Brookings Institution Press, 1993), 10.

[105] Polling data suggests that a significant share of the public greeted the Ruckelshaus appointment favorably. In a November 1983 survey, 40% of respondents said it represented a big or slight improvement over Gorsuch, versus 21% saying no improvement, and only 5% believing it a step backward. Survey by Business Week. Methodology: Conducted by Louis Harris & Associates, November 4–November 7, 1983, and based on 1,250 telephone interviews. Sample: National Adult. [USHARRBW.121983.RE] Storrs, CT: Roper Center for Public Opinion Research, iPOLL [distributor], accessed March 4, 2016.

[106] B. Dan Wood, "Principals, Bureaucrats, and Responsiveness in Clean Air Enforcements," *American Political Science Review* 82 (1988): 213–234. See, specifically, Figure 2 (223) and Figure 3 (226).

emphasis on reforming Superfund.[107] Here, Congress in 1984 sprang into action by reauthorizing and strengthening the RCRA through the Hazardous and Solid Wastes Amendments, which the president reluctantly signed.[108] In the assessment of officials at the EPA, "almost every section of the RCRA Amendments might be read as expressing a sense of frustration over the pace and scope of EPA action."[109] Moreover, buoyed by the clear evidence of success in the Superfund investigations, Dingell's House Energy panel would launch new investigations in the winter of 1984 into the administration's failures to adequately enforce the new amendments. The intense and sustained battering by congressional investigators produced what some have termed "collective trauma" and "risk aversion" with respect to dealing with Capitol Hill that generated a high degree of policy responsiveness to congressional preferences.[110] Bowing to congressional pressure, EPA increased the priority accorded to RCRA enforcement and also channeled more resources into these programs. For example, in testimony before the Subcommittee on Oversight and Investigations of the House Energy and Commerce Committee, the EPA acknowledged:

> EPA realizes that just establishing a program infrastructure is not enough. There must also be enforcement results. This chart illustrates that EPA and States are aggressively pursuing enforcement at RCRA facilities. In the 18 months ending in December 1984, there was approximately a 200% increase in enforcement actions at these facilities. EPA fully expects this upward trend to continue as our additional resources are devoted to the problem.[111]

[107] Mintz, 1987, 749.

[108] The Reagan administration had long opposed RCRA's reauthorization. Notes from a meeting between Secretary of the Cabinet Craig Fuller and Anne Gorsuch and Rita Lavelle (which took place on September 9, 1982) make clear that the EPA leadership wanted to kill RCRA reauthorization in the Senate. Memo, Craig Fuller to Fred Fielding, March 22, 1983, folder "Lavelle, Rita (4)," Box 12, Counsel to the President, White House Office of Investigations; Records, Ronald Reagan Library. A White House memorandum from November 1982 suggests that tension over RCRA reauthorization fueled the conflict between EPA and House Democrats, which then intensified in the investigation over Superfund. Memorandum, Martin Smith to Edwin Harper, November 8, 1982, folder "Lavelle, Rita (2)," Counsel to the President, Legislative Records, Box 12, Ronald Reagan Library.

[109] Mintz, 1987, 749–750.

[110] Ibid., 750.

[111] For steps taken by EPA to comply with HSWA requirements, see "Statement by Jack W. McGraw, Acting Assistant Administrator for Solid Waste and Emergency Response, U.S. Environmental Protection Agency Before the Subcommittee on Oversight and Investigations, Committee on Energy and Commerce, U.S. House of Representatives." HRG-1985-HEC-0007, April 29, 1985, p. 118. See also "Statement of Dr. J. Winston Porter, Assistant Administrator for Sold Waste and Emergency Response Before the Subcommittee on Environmental Pollution

The data presented by EPA showed that whereas the agency had engaged in fewer than fifty enforcement actions in the last six months of 1982, the year in which the congressional investigation of the EPA began, it had conducted more than 350 enforcement actions in the last six months of 1984.

SOLYNDRA

We conclude our case studies by analyzing an investigation that failed to produce significant policy change: the Republican-led inquest into a massive federal loan guarantee to now-bankrupt solar panel manufacturer Solyndra. Title XVII of the Energy Policy Act of 2005 provided a new loan guarantee mechanism through which the federal government could support the development of advanced energy technologies that, because of the elevated risk involved, might struggle to secure sufficient private capital investment.[112] As part of the 2009 stimulus bill (the American Recovery and Reinvestment Act), the Obama administration created a new supplemental program, the Section 1603 grant program run by the Treasury Department, to foster renewable energy projects by paying a direct subsidy to the company to guarantee the loan. In so doing, the federal government assumed the risk of default.[113] Like most other provisions of the stimulus, the 1603 program was scheduled to expire at the end of 2010. However, the lame duck session of the 111th Congress granted it a one-year extension through 2011.

On August 31, 2011, the solar panel manufacturer Solyndra, which had received a $535 million federal loan guarantee under the stimulus act program in 2009, filed for bankruptcy and defaulted on its loan.[114] This was not the first time that a federally backed private energy project had failed, nor was it the largest. For example, in 1985 the nation's first coal-gasification plant defaulted after spending $1.5 billion of a total $2 billion federal loan

of the Committee on Environment and Public Works, United States Senate." S. Hrg. 99–549, February 24, 1986, 195–207.

[112] For an overview, see Mark Holt and Carol Glover, "Energy Policy Act of 2005: Summary and Analysis of Enacted Provisions," *CRS Report*, March 8, 2006, 120.

[113] Geof Koss, "Fueling Innovation Without Getting Burned," *CQ Weekly*, February 13, 2012, 285–286. See also Philip Brown and Molly Sherlock, "ARRA Section 1603 Grants in Lieu of Tax Credits for Renewable Energy: Overview, Analysis, and Policy Options," *CRS Report*, February 8, 2011.

[114] Solyndra was far from the only solar power company filing for bankruptcy in 2011. The industry fell on tough times that year, and two other companies, including Massachusetts' Evergreen Solar filed for bankruptcy in August 2011 alone. "U.S. Backed Solar Firm Files Bankruptcy," *Boston Globe*, September 1, 2011, B8.

guarantee.[115] However, the new Republican majority in the House quickly pounced on the default as a potential vantage point to attack President Obama and his green energy policy initiatives.

The House Energy and Commerce Committee's Subcommittee on Oversight and Investigations sent Secretary Chu an initial request for information on Solyndra in February 2011, long before the bankruptcy was announced; however, the investigation had failed to gain much traction in the press. A *Lexis Nexis* search from February 1, 2011, through August 30, 2011, identified only eleven articles across all news sources mentioning Solyndra. While several mentioned its failing health, none discussed the Republican investigation in detail. Seeking to capitalize on the opportunity to heighten the salience of their work, committee Republicans blasted the administration failures that left taxpayers footing the bill. Subcommittee chair Cliff Stearns (R-FL) argued that the administration wantonly overlooked many warning signs as "they were hell-bent on trying to get the solar industry up and running." Stearns argued that a thorough investigation was needed to identify and punish the officials responsible: "You can't lose this kind of money and have the FBI indicate there's criminal activity here and not have somebody fired."[116] Committee chair Fred Upton (R-MI) joined Stearns in declaring that he had "smelled a rat from the onset."[117]

Following the bankruptcy, the House investigation further intensified. The inquest was wide-ranging, but it largely focused on three main allegations. First, investigators charged that the Department of Energy (DOE) failed to respond to warning signs regarding Solyndra's financial health during the initial application process. The committee charged that DOE had recognized financial errors and faulty assumptions on Solyndra's application, but decided to proceed anyway. The committee also argued that the DOE blatantly ignored similar warning signs when it restructured the loan guarantee, including subordinating the government's stake to that of private investors, in a desperate attempt to keep the company afloat—a move that Republicans charged violated the Energy Policy Act of 2005.[118] Second, the committee charged political interference from the White House,

[115] Geof Koss, "Fueling Innovation Without Getting Burned," *CQ Weekly*, February 13, 2012, 285–286.
[116] Margaret Kriz Hobson, "Solyndra's Loan Guarantee Scrutinized," *CQ Weekly*, September 19, 2011, p. 1919.
[117] Ed Crooks. "Solyndra Bankruptcy Sparks Questions." *Financial Times*, September 2, 2011, 12.
[118] The Obama administration, by contrast, maintained that the prohibition on subordination applied only to an initial loan guarantee and not to a restructuring. Jim Snyder and Brian Wingfield, "Solyndra Funds Mostly Lost to Taxpayers, Chu Tells Lawmakers." *Bloomberg*, November 17, 2011, http://www.bloomberg.com/news/articles/2011-11-17/solyndra-loan-decisions-mine-chu-to-tell-republican-led-panel, accessed May 10, 2016.

which strongly desired a quick announcement of funds and hoped to make Solyndra a poster child for the administration's larger green energy policy. The committee noted that Office of Management and Budget (OMB) review of the Solyndra application was rushed by the premature scheduling of the grant announcement even before OMB review was complete. Whereas OMB averaged twenty-eight days of review time for such applications, it was forced to complete the Solyndra application in just nine days. Finally, Republican investigators alleged that major Obama donor George Kaiser, who was Solyndra's largest private shareholder, had improper contacts with Obama administration officials over Solynda's fate and exerted influence on policy decisions.[119]

Congressional Democrats almost uniformly rallied behind President Obama. California Democrat Henry Waxman argued that the Solyndra disaster was precipitated not by misconduct at the Department of Energy, but by Solyndra itself, which had lied to the government about its business plan and fiscal health.[120] Committee Democrats also noted that the Solyndra loan consideration began during the Bush administration.[121]

Despite an avalanche of Republican criticism of the Obama administration and the Solyndra escapade in the weeks following the bankruptcy, a September 27, 2011, Fox News Poll revealed an evenly split electorate: 46% of Americans judged the Solyndra loan to have been based on unethical behavior; 46% replied it was a simple story of a good faith loan that went bad; and 8% said they didn't know.[122] Republican investigators assiduously pursued the inquest through the remainder of 2011 and into 2012 as part of a strategy to make Obama's failure with Solyndra an issue in the 2012 presidential election. The majority report was not issued until August 2012, almost a full year after Solyndra filed for bankruptcy and more than seventeen months after the investigation formally began. However, despite these efforts, opinion polls again suggest that the Solyndra investigation failed to gain much traction with the American public. Two NBC News

[119] "The Solyndra Failure: Majority Staff Report," Committee on Energy and Commerce, Fred Upton, Chairman, Cliff Stearns, Chairman, Subcommittee on Oversight and Investigations, August 2, 2012.

[120] Margaret Kriz Hobson, "Solyndra's Loan Guarantee Scrutinized," *CQ Weekly*, September 19, 2011, 1919.

[121] However, in the waning days of the Bush administration in January 2009, the administration' review board declined to act on the loan guarantee request. "The Solar Orphan," *Wall Street Journal*, September 15, 2011, http://online.wsj.com/news/articles/SB10001424053 111903927204576570870957886068, accessed February 29, 2016.

[122] Survey by Fox News, Methodology: Conducted by Anderson Robbins Research/Shaw & Co., Research, September 25–September 27, 2011 and based on 925 telephone interviews. Sample: National registered voters. 718 respondents were interviewed on a landline telephone, and 207 were interviewed on a cell phone. [USASFOX.092911.R44]. Storrs, CT: Roper Center for Public Opinion Research, iPOLL [distributor], accessed March 4, 2016.

polls conducted in June and September of 2012 asked Americans about their attitudes toward Solyndra. In both polls, almost 60% of Americans replied that they had never even heard of Solyndra. Less than a quarter of all respondents replied that they had very or somewhat negative feelings toward Solyndra. As discussed in Chapter 7, this lack of voter attention is likely attributable to the absence of media coverage of the hearings, with the exception of the numerous stories on Fox News.

Given the investigation's failure to resonate with voters and bring significant political pressure to bear on Obama, it is unsurprising that legislative efforts to mandate changes in energy policy failed to become law. The first salvo was fired by the House in the fall of 2011 during the budget crisis. In their stopgap spending measure, House Republicans included a provision cutting $100 million from what remained of the stimulus program that funded Solyndra. The Senate, however, refused to comply, and the cut was removed from the final legislation.[123]

Only two weeks after the Solyndra bankruptcy, Representative Tom McClintock (R-CA) introduced H.R. 2915 to repeal borrowing authority granted to the Department of Energy under the 2009 stimulus law. The committee's final report on the bill summarized its purpose: "In conclusion, H.R. 2915 repeals a multi-billion dollar, federal government-knows-best program that explicitly envisions taxpayer bailouts. This bill allows projects to stand on their own merit in the private sector and protects American taxpayers from failed Solyndra-like investments."[124] While the measure was reported out of committee in April 2012, it never received a floor vote in the full House.[125]

While the stimulus provision expired at the conclusion of 2011, the larger loan guarantee program created by the Energy Policy Act of 2005 remained in force.[126] In an attempt to prevent the Obama administration from continuing to use loan guarantees to promote renewable energy, the House in August 2012 passed H.R. 6213, the "No More Solyndras Act." Republicans argued that the bill would phase out loan guarantees and clarify the 2005 statute to ban the subordination of taxpayer interests to those of private investors. Democrats wryly noted that the bill grandfathered almost $100

[123] Geof Koss, "Solar Forecast: Plenty of Sun, Dark Clouds Ahead," CQ Weekly, October 31, 2011, 2266–2267.

[124] "Report on the American Taxpayer and Western Area Power Administration Customer Protection Act of 2011," Report 112–431, Committee on Natural Resources, April 16, 2012, 3.

[125] Elham Khatami, "Bill to Trim Government Loan Authority Blasted as Attack on Renewable Power," CQ Weekly, October 10, 2011, 2106.

[126] Whether the Solyndra scandal defeated efforts to extend the 1603 grant program is debatable. Many other provisions of the stimulus act that were set to sunset were allowed to expire. If the Solyndra investigation played a role, it is notable that it only succeeded in effecting change in the unique circumstance where affirmative congressional action was required to extend the policy. To eliminate it, all Republicans had to do was block legislative action.

billion of loan considerations for nuclear and coal projects, while eliminating them for renewable energy. "You can see the crocodile tears," Ed Markey (D-MA) mocked, "how concerned they are about this loan guarantee program." Colorado Democrat Diana DeGette derided the bill as mere political posturing: "It's clear this legislation is a political exercise. It does nothing but attempt to keep the word Solyndra in the news and to give a platform to repeat these accusations, and it's a shame."[127]

Absent any political pressure to legislate in response to the Solyndra scandal, Majority Leader Harry Reid (D-NV) quietly killed the House measure in the Senate.

A Broader Assessment

The narrative case study approach allows us to trace precisely how each investigation succeeded or failed in triggering either the legislative or preemptive pathway for policy influence. The three investigations that succeeded in securing media coverage and generating public pressure for change each precipitated a significant change in public policy. The Solyndra investigation, which failed to resonate with the public, did not trigger either pathway. However, a concern with a case study approach is the generalizability of the patterns observed within the cases. Do investigations routinely spark new legislation or encourage presidents to make unilateral concessions, as observed in the Truman Committee, Church Committee, and EPA investigations cases? Or are these exceptions to the general rule in which most investigations fail to trigger either pathway of influence, as in the Solyndra case?

To address these concerns, we examined all thirty of the major investigations identified in Mayhew's seminal analysis from 1947 through 2002.[128] For each investigation, we conducted a thorough search of contemporary media coverage, *Congressional Quarterly* publications, and relevant secondary histories to identify whether prior journalism and scholarship has argued that the investigation either directly contributed to the passage of new legislation or precipitated a change in administration policy. The results of this analysis are summarized in Table 4.1.

[127] Matt Fuller, "Bill to Limit Loan Guarantee Program Passed on Largely Party-Line Vote," *CQ Weekly*, September 17, 2012, 1888.

[128] Because Mayhew's focus was on whether more investigations occurred under unified or divided government, the same investigation in the House and Senate (where partisan control could vary) or that spanned multiple congresses received separate entries in Mayhew's list. Because our focus here is on the policy impact of investigations, we combine multiple entries of the same investigation. Each instance in which we have combined items from Mayhew's list is indicated in footnotes to the relevant entry in Table 4.1.

Table 4.1: Policy Impact of Mayhew's Significant Investigations

Investigation	Legislative Response	Preemptive Action
Improper influence in airplane contracts (1947)		
Inside-info commodity speculation by government officials (1947–1948)	Amendment to Commodity Exchange Act to allow secretary of agriculture to publish names of commodity speculators.[1]	Assistant to secretary of the army, Edwin Pauley, who was accused of commodity speculation, compelled to resign.[2]
Disloyalty or espionage in or near government ranks (1948)	After several iterations, Congress passed the Internal Security Act of 1950.[3] In 1954, Congress passed the "Hiss Act" barring federal pensions for any governmental employee convicted of certain offenses.[4]	In April 1951, under the cumulative weight of numerous congressional investigations into alleged communist infiltration of the executive branch, Truman approved a lower threshold of evidence for removing officials for suspected disloyalty.[5]
Mismanagement and security problems at the Atomic Energy Commission (1949)	Rider to appropriations bill requiring FBI loyalty investigations for all recipients of AEC fellowships.[6] Additional rider to limit AEC spending authority, a focus of the investigation.[7]	President Truman accepted AEC chairman David Lilienthal's resignation, which was demanded by the committee.[8]
Influence peddling by and around the White House staff (1949)		
Disloyalty in the State Department (1950)	State Department given power to remove employees with dangerous associations under State, Justice, and Commerce Appropriations of 1950.[9]	Intensification of State Department background checks; purge of homosexuals from Department.[10]

(continued)

TABLE 4.1 (*continued*)

Investigation	Legislative Response	Preemptive Action
Maladministration and favoritism in the Reconstruction Finance Corporation (1951)	Within two years of investigation, RFC was eliminated by statute (RFC Liquidation Act of 1953).[11]	Truman reorganized RFC, replacing the five-man board with a single administrator, per Fulbright's recommendation.[12] RFC administrator Symington implemented most of the committee's suggested reforms and dramatically increased transparency of RFC operations.[13]
Truman Administration misconduct of the Korean War (1951)		
Disloyalty in making of China policy (1951–1952)		Many top targets of the investigation were forced from their positions.
Corruption in the Bureau of Internal Revenue (1951–1952)		Truman reorganizes Bureau to decrease political influence; nineteen employees are fired and dozens forced to resign.[14]
Maladministration in the Justice Department (1952)		Truman appoints special assistant to the attorney general to investigate corruption.[15] Truman signs Executive Order 10327 ordering all executive departments and agencies to cooperate with the new Special Assistant to root out misconduct and corruption. AG McGrath fires Special Assistant, and is then forced to resign. Others tied to scandal also fired.[16]

Investigation	Legislative Response	Preemptive Action
Soviet spy rings operating under Truman (1953)		
Subversion in the State Department and the army (1953–1954)	Even as senators began to turn on McCarthy, the red scare fueled by investigative fervor led to the passage of the Communist Control Act of 1954 and other antisubversive measures.[17]	
Improper influence in Dixon-Yates power contract (1955)		Eisenhower bows to congressional pressure and cancels the contract.[18]
Inadequate air-power planning (1956)	Final report issued in 1957 warning of waste and duplication helped provide impetus for Eisenhower's requests for DOD reorganization that became the Defense Reorganization Act of 1958.[19]	For FY1957, Eisenhower makes $547.1 million supplemental appropriation request, including $248.5 million to speed production of B-52 bombers, a major concern of investigators. Widely seen as an attempt to sap energy from investigation.[20]
Improper influence in the regulatory agencies (1958)	Revelations led to passage of Communications Act Amendments of 1960.[21] John F. Kennedy advocated during the 1960 campaign the need to clean up and reorganize the regulatory agencies, and Congress granted him the authority to submit reorganization plans to the legislature by reinstituting the Reorganization Act of 1949 for two years in April 1961.[22] From 1958 onward, Congress debated many legislative fixes to	White House Chief of Staff Sherman Adams forced to resign after revelations that he accepted gifts from a textile manufacturer being investigated by the Federal Trade Commission.[24] Shortly after his inauguration, President Kennedy proposed new legislation to reform governmental ethics rules and introduced a number of executive actions to institute new safeguards.[25]

(continued)

TABLE 4.1 (*continued*)

Investigation	Legislative Response	Preemptive Action
	conflict-of-interest laws; this process culminated in a comprehensive overhaul (H.R. 8140) in 1962.[23]	
Agriculture Department favoritism toward shady grain-storage dealer Billie Sol Estes (1962)	Senate passes House bill (H.R. 8140) overhauling conflict-of-interest regulations in the midst of Billie Sol Estes hearings.[26]	Three officials in the Department of Agriculture and an assistant secretary of labor were forced to resign.[27] Secretary Freeman created first nonmilitary inspector general within the U.S. Department of Agriculture.[28]
Favoritism in award of TFX fighter-plane contract to General Dynamics, rather than Boeing (1963)		Navy Secretary Fred Korth forced to resign for violating ethics rules, despite having been cleared of misconduct in TFX contract by the Justice Department.[29]
Fulbright hearings into Indochina policy (1966– 1970)[30]	The Fulbright hearings provided the impetus for a number of congressional actions to circumscribe the Vietnam War including a repeal of the Gulf of Tonkin Resolution; the Cooper-Church amendment cutting off funds for operations in Cambodia; and the Chase-Church amendment cutting off funds for all military actions in Vietnam, Cambodia, and Laos unless it received prior presidential approval. The hearings also provided the impetus for the War Powers Resolution of 1973.[31]	Pressure generated in large part by Fulbright's hearings encouraged Johnson to issue a bombing pause and intensify negotiations in late 1967.[32] Nixon withdrew American troops from Cambodia in the face of congressional pressure.[33]

Investigation	Legislative Response	Preemptive Action
Justice Department awarded ITT a favorable antitrust settlement in exchange for a $400,000 campaign donation (1972)	Directly led to passage of the Tunney Act in 1974, which provided for new procedures for settlement of antitrust claims.[34] The scandal (the ITT funds were to go to the 1972 Republican National Convention) also contributed to the impetus for the Federal Election Campaign Act of 1974.[35]	
Watergate break-in and cover up, Ervin and Rodino Committees, (1973–1974)	The legislative legacy of Watergate and its aftermath is wide-ranging. Two of the most direct products of the investigation were the Federal Election Campaign Act of 1974 and the 1978 Ethics in Government Act.[36]	President Nixon resigned in the face of almost certain impeachment.
Dubious covert operations by U.S. intelligence agencies, Church and Pike Committees (1975–1976)	S. Res. 400 creating Senate Select Intelligence Committee.[37] House creates its own Permanent Select Committee on Intelligence a year later. Provided impetus for passage of Foreign Intelligence Surveillance Act of 1978.[38]	Ford issues Executive Order 11905 reorganizing intelligence apparatus.[39]
Old shady bank dealings of Bert Lance, Director of the Office of Management and Budget (1977)	In 1978, Congress passed banking regulation reform targeting some of the questionable practices revealed during the Lance investigation.[40]	OMB Director Bert Lance resigns under pressure.
Dubious use of president's brother Billy Carter as an intermediary to Libyan government (1980)		

(continued)

TABLE 4.1 *(continued)*

Investigation	Legislative Response	Preemptive Action
Political favoritism, conflict of interest, and general laxness in toxic-waste cleanup by the EPA (1983)	Amendments to Resource Conservation Recovery Act.[41]	EPA administrator fired and replaced with pro-environment administrator.[42] Superfund program and environmental enforcement more generally accelerates.[43]
Arms for hostages deal with Iran (1987)	In 1989, Congress passed three bills to address legal loopholes uncovered during Iran-Contra. The first strengthened prohibitions on arms sales to countries alleged to sponsor terrorism. The second compelled the president to appoint an independent inspector general at the CIA. The third limited the administration's capacity to use foreign aid to compel another actor to do something that Congress had barred the administration from funding directly.[44]	Many officials, including Secretary of Defense Caspar Weinberger and National Security Adviser John Poindexter, resigned in the midst of the scandal or were dismissed.[45]
Corruption in Reagan's Department of Housing and Urban Development (1989–1990)	Congress enacted the Housing and Urban Development Reform Act to clean up the grants process and make the Department more transparent and accountable.[46]	
Improper White House behavior regarding Whitewater investments (1993–1996)	Congress reauthorizes the lapsed Watergate-era Independent Counsel statute.[47]	Deputy Treasury Secretary Roger Altman forced to resign.[48]

Investigation	Legislative Response	Preemptive Action
Clinton administration's shady campaign finance practices during 1996 (1997)	Supporters of campaign finance reform rallied behind the McCain-Feingold bill, which was filibustered in the Senate. The reform eventually passed in 2002.[49]	
Perjury and obstruction of justice by President Clinton in Monica Lewinsky coverup (1998)		

[1] William White, "Senate Sanctions Grain-Deal Listing," *New York Times*, December 19, 1947, 1. This course of action was recommended by the administration.

[2] Andrew Dunbar, *The Truman Scandals and the Politics of Morality* (Columbia: University of Missouri Press, 1984), 37–38. Also on the list of commodity speculators provided to congressional investigators by Truman and his secretary of agriculture was Brigadier General Wallace Graham, the president's personal physician. Despite intensive focus on Graham, he retained his post.

[3] As the Hiss investigation unfolded, Karl Mundt (R-SD) and Richard Nixon (R-CA) introduced H.R. 5852, the Subversive Activities Control Bill, which passed the House overwhelmingly but failed to reach a vote in the Senate. A second attempt to pass an amended version of the legislation also failed. In 1950, Pat McCarran (D-NV) introduced new legislation based heavily on the Mundt-Nixon bill that became the McCarran Act, or the Internal Security Act of 1950. "Senate Unit Backs Bill to Curb Reds," *New York Times*, July 23, 1949, 5.

[4] Lee McHughes, "The Hiss Act and its Application to the Military," *Military Law Review* 14 (1961): 67–108; "Pension Ban," *Congressional Quarterly Almanac, 1954,* 340.

[5] The immediate trigger appears to have been an investigation by moderate Republicans into William Remington, a Commerce Department official. Remington was dismissed by Secretary of Commerce Charles Sawyer, even though he had been cleared by the Loyalty Review Board. Alonzo Hamby, *Man of the People: A Life of Harry S. Truman* (New York: Oxford University Press, 1995), 568.

[6] "Atomic Energy," in *CQ Almanac 1949*, 752–757.

[7] John Morris, "New Curbs Urged on Atomic Program," *New York Times* July 8, 1949, 3; *CQ Almanac, 1949,* 206–207.

[8] Clayton Knowles, "Hickenlooper Asks Lilienthal Ouster," *New York Times* May 23, 1949, 1.

[9] "Internal Security Act of 1950," *CQ Almanac, 1950,* 398.

[10] *History of the Bureau of Diplomatic Security of the United States Department of State,* 121. http://www.state.gov/documents/organization/176702.pdf.

(*continued*)

TABLE 4.1 *(continued)*

[11] One of the instigators of this legislation, Homer Capehart (R-IN), was also a member of the Fulbright Committee that investigated the RFC. C. P. Trussell, "Action Demanded on R.F.C. Abolition," *New York Times*, January 25, 1952, 10. The RFC was replaced with the Small Business Administration. The first bill to abolish the RFC (S.1376) was introduced in 1950. *CQ Almanac, 1950,* p. 505.

[12] Joanna Grisinger, *The Unwieldy American State: Administrative Politics Since the New Deal* (New York: Cambridge University Press, 2012).

[13] Dunbar 1984, 94–95. Dunbar describes the case as a classic example of preemptive action: "By the time of the committee's report, the crusading impulse that had governed the most visible moments of the committee had been adopted by Symington."

[14] "Probe of Tax Collection Scandal," *Congressional Quarterly Almanac, 1951,* 517; Harold Gosnell, *Truman's Crises: A Political Biography of Harry S. Truman* (Westport, CT: Greenwood Press, 1980), 498.

[15] Grisinger 2012, 142.

[16] "Justice Department Investigations," *CQ Almanac, 1952,* 263–268.

[17] Robert Griffith, *The Politics of Fear: Joseph R. McCarthy and the Senate* (Amherst: University of Massachusetts Press, 1970), 292.

[18] Aaron Wildavsky, *Dixon-Yates: A Study in Power Politics* (New Haven: Yale University Press, 1962); "Dixon-Yates Contract," *CQ Almanac, 1955,* 535–538.

[19] Robert Frank Furtrell, *Ideas, Concepts, Doctrine: Basic Thinking in the United States Air Force, 1907–1960* (Maxwell Air Force Base, AL: Air University Press. 1989), 573.

[20] Warren Trest, *Air Force Roles and Missions: A History* (Washington, DC: Air Force History and Museums Program, Government Printing Office, 1998), 167–168.

[21] "Controls Sought for Regulatory Agencies," *CQ Almanac, 1960,* 728–733; "Congress Tightens Broadcasting Regulations." *CQ Almanac 1960,* 356–361.

[22] Woody Klein. *The Inside Stories of Modern Political Scandals: How Investigative Reporters Have Changed the Course of History* (Santa Barbara, CA: Praeger, 2010), 12–16.

[23] "Reorganization of Regulatory Agencies," *CQ Almanac 1961,* 352–356.

[24] "Congress Amends Conflict-of-Interest Laws," *CQ Almanac 1962,* 385–389.

[25] John F. Kennedy, "Special Message to the Congress on Conflict-of-Interest Legislation and on Problems of Ethics in Government.," April 27, 1961, in Gerhard Peters and John T. Woolley, The American Presidency Project. http://www.presidency.ucsb.edu/ws/?pid=8092, accessed, March 1, 2016. On May 5, 1961, Kennedy issued Executive Order 10939, "To Provide a Guide on Ethical Standards to Government Officials."

[26] "Congress Amends Conflict-of-Interest Laws," *CQ Almanac 1962,* 385–389.

[27] "Committees Air Billie Sol Estes Dealings," *CQ Almanac 1962,* 988–1002.

[28] "25th Anniversary of the IG Act of 1978." http://www.roigi.org/oig-25anniv.html, accessed March 1, 2016.

[29] "Senate Unit Probes TFX Contract Award," *CQ Almanac 1963,* 1089–1091.

[30] In this Table, we combine several of Mayhew's investigations that represent either the same investigation conducted by both the House and the Senate, or the same investigation that continues over multiple sessions. For example, Mayhew identifies three Fulbright investigations into Indochina policy; one in 1966; one in 1967–1968; and one in 1969–1970. For simplicity, we treat the Fulbright hearings as one investigation. Similarly, Mayhew treats the Church (Senate) and Pike (House) investigations into abuse by the intelligence agencies as separate investigations. Because it is all but impossible to disentangle the influence of the House and Senate investigations—both generated political pressure on the White House and on other members of Congress to act—we treat them as a single investigation.

[31] Randall Bennett Woods, *Fulbright: A Biography* (New York: Cambridge University Press, 1995).

[32] Ralph Carter and James Scott, *Choosing to Lead: Understanding Congressional Foreign Policy Entrepreneurs* (Durham, NC: Duke University Press, 2009), 110.

[33] Douglas Kriner, *After the Rubicon: Congress, Presidents, and the Politics of Waging War* (Chicago: University of Chicago Press, 2010), 40.

[34] "Antitrust Law Changes," *CQ Almanac 1974*, 291–292.

[35] R. Sam Garrett and Shawn Reese, "Funding of Presidential Nominating Conventions: An Overview," *CRS Report*, May 4, 2016; Ciara Torres-Spelliscy, "The I.T.T. Affair and Why Public Financing Matters for Political Conventions," *Brennan Center for Justice*, March 19, 2014, http://www.brennancenter.org/blog/itt-affair-why-public-financing-matters-political-conventions, accessed March 1, 2016.

[36] http://www.senate.gov/artandhistory/history/common/generic/Origins_WatergateLegislativeoutcome.htm, accessed March 1, 2016.

[37] William Newby Raiford, "To Create a Senate Select Committee on Intelligence: A Legislative History of Senate Resolution 400," *CRS Report*, August 12, 1976.

[38] David Wise, "Intelligence Reforms: Less than Half a Loaf," *Washington Post*, April 23, 1978, D3.

[39] Loch Johnson, *A Season of Inquiry: The Senate Intelligence Investigation* (Lexington: University of Kentucky Press, 1985), 193–195.

[40] "Banking Regulation," *CQ Almanac 1978*, 300–303.

[41] Joel Mintz, "Agencies, Congress and Regulatory Enforcement: A Review of EPA's Hazardous Waste Enforcement Effort, 1970–1987," *Environmental Law* 18 (1987): 683–778, 749–750.

[42] Steven Weisman, "Overtures Made to Ruckelshaus to Head E.P.A.: Agency's Original Chief Asked to Help in Crisis," *New York Times*, March 20, 1983, 2.

[43] Thomas Church and Robert Nakamura, *Cleaning Up the Mess: Implementation Strategies in Superfund* (Washington, DC: Brookings Institution Press, 1993) 10; B. Dan Wood, "Principals, Bureaucrats, and Responsiveness in Clean Air Enforcements," *American Political Science Review* 82 (1988): 213–234. See, specifically, Figure 2 (223) and Figure 3 (226).

[44] "Limited Legal Legacy Left by Iran-Contra," *CQ Almanac 1989*, 541–543.

(*continued*)

TABLE 4.1 *(continued)*

[45] Jack Nelson and Eleanor Clift, "Poindexter Resigns, North is Fired," *Los Angeles Times,* November 26, 1986, http://history.defense.gov/Multimedia/Biographies/ArticleView/tabid /8347/Article/571286/caspar-w-weinberger.aspx, accessed May 10, 2016.

[46] "Housing and Urban Development (HUD) Influence-Peddling Scandal Unfolds Before Hill Panels," *CQ Almanac 1989,* 639– 653. http://portal.hud.gov/hudportal/HUD?src=/program _offices/general_counsel/HUD_Reform_Act, accessed March 1, 2016.

[47] "Independent Counsel Law Renewed," *CQ Almanac 1994,* 295–297.

[48] Keith Bradsher, "Altman Resigns Post Amid Whitewater Clamor," *New York Times,* August 18, 1994, http://www.nytimes.com/1994/08/18/us/altman-resigns-his-post-amid-whitewater -clamor.html, accessed March 1, 2016.

[49] "Filibuster Halts Campaign Finance Bill," *CQ Almanac 1997,* 1-26–1-28; "Campaign Finance Comes Close," *CQ Almanac 2001,* 6-3–6-7; "Finance Battle Shifts to the Courts," *CQ Almanac 2002,* 14-7–14-9.

The overwhelming majority of the major investigations identified by Mayhew produced a tangible policy response through at least one of the two pathways. Nineteen of the thirty investigations triggered new legislation from Congress. Twenty investigations encouraged the administration to make unilateral concessions to congressional investigators. Finally, 80% of the major investigations—twenty-four of thirty—led to either new legislation or preemptive action by the administration. Of the six investigations that failed to produce any substantive policy response, four occurred during the Truman administration. Since 1953, only two of Mayhew's major investigations have failed to generate any policy response, and these two investigations—Billy Carter's relationships in Libya and President Clinton's actions in the Lewinsky scandal—were largely focused on alleged failures of personal conduct, not major issues of policy import. In such cases, it is unsurprising that an investigation failed to produce direct policy change. However, such investigations may nonetheless affect policymaking *indirectly* by changing the president's strategic calculations. We explore this dynamic in the next chapter.

CONCLUSION

Although they cannot themselves mandate changes in public policy, investigations have repeatedly precipitated important changes. In some cases, investigations spur the introduction and passage of legislation that never would have been enacted in the absence of the congressional probe. In many other cases, investigations have raised the political costs to the president of the status quo and have encouraged the incumbent administration to alter its preferred policy course to lessen these costs or to preempt more extreme legislation. Each of our first three case studies—the Truman Committee inquest into domestic production during World War II, the Church Committee investigation of abuse of power by the executive branch and the intelligence agencies, and the 1980s probes of maladministration at the EPA—produced significant changes in public policy through one or both pathways of influence. More broadly, when analyzing all thirty major investigations identified by Mayhew we found that 80% produced tangible policy change through at least one of the two pathways.

While the first three case studies involved very different investigations launched in disparate political climates against a diverse range of targets, one common thread linking these narratives of congressional influence is investigators' ability to attract sustained media attention to their efforts and to rally popular support for policy change. This is critical to overcoming the barriers to legislative action described at the outset, and to encouraging presidents to take independent action to minimize the political costs imposed by the investigation or preempt more robust congressional reform efforts.

The Solyndra investigation with which the chapter concludes shares many features with the other case studies. The investigation was energized by a highly public loss of more than half a billion dollars of taxpayer money. It probed allegations of major failures by the DOE, OMB, and the Obama administration itself to recognize the warning signs at Solyndra that resulted in the major policy blunder. It even included a potentially juicy charge of political interference from a high-profile campaign donor. However, opinion polling data shows that Republican investigators, who received virtually no cooperation from their colleagues across the aisle, were unable to generate much public interest in or even awareness of the scandal. Absent such political pressure, Republican-led legislative efforts were all but doomed to fail, and President Obama faced no pressure to make policy concessions. The Solyndra case highlights the importance of media attention in translating congressional hearings into a policy response; we take up this issue, both with respect to the Solyndra case and other investigations, in the concluding chapter.

The case studies in conjunction with the results of the preceding chapter speak to the critical importance of public opinion in shaping an investigation's capacity to have concrete influence on politics and policy. Investigations that capture the public's attention and bring its pressure to bear on other actors can generate significant influence. Investigations that fail to resonate with the public are unlikely to exert much sway beyond the hearing room.

CHAPTER 5

~ ~

The Indirect Influence of Congressional Investigations on Policy Outcomes

As THE CASE studies of the previous chapter showed, in certain political environments congressional investigations can produce concrete and significant changes in public policy, both by spurring new legislation that would not have passed in the absence of investigative pressures and by encouraging the White House to adjust its conduct of policy in an effort to preempt more extreme legislative action. These two pathways are the most direct means through which investigations tangibly affect policy outcomes; however, in many ways, they are also the narrowest. To be sure, Congress has held literally thousands of hearings investigating presidential actions across the gamut of issues over time. Yet the number of intensely investigated executive policies at any moment is limited. Indeed, it must be, as members' time and the media's and public's threshold for attentiveness are finite.

However, there is an additional, more indirect pathway through which investigations in one policy area may affect both congressional and presidential strategic calculations in a much wider range of policy areas. For example, while the Iran-Contra investigation ultimately produced three laws to address legislative loopholes exploited by the Reagan administration to pursue the Contra aid program, the end result fell fall short of investigators' initial lofty goals.[1] However, the wider impact of Iran-Contra stretched far beyond these narrow efforts to use legislation to circumscribe the president's freedom of action in foreign policy. The investigation significantly weakened Reagan's political position, and as the investigation unfolded the president lost two key veto battles over the Clean Water Act and a Highway reauthorization bill. Moreover, the Senate rejected Reagan's first Supreme Court nominee, and another was forced to withdraw.[2] Without the political damage caused by Iran-Contra, Reagan might well have prevailed in some

---

[1] "Limited Legal Legacy Left by Iran-Contra," CQ Almanac 1989, 541–543.
[2] "Special Report: The Iran-Contra Affair," CQ Almanac 1987, 61–76.

or even all of these cases, with considerable consequences for public policy. The intense media scrutiny of the scandal and erosion of public support for the president emboldened his critics and pressured fellow congressional Republicans to break with Reagan on issues where the president was on the wrong side of public opinion.

Congressional investigations may also affect presidential calculations more broadly. A costly investigation in one policy area reminds the president of the political costs he risks should he act too assertively and provoke new committee probes of his actions in another policy realm. Moreover, the volume and intensity of congressional investigative activity in the recent past provide presidents with important information about legislators' willingness to use this institutional tool to battle the executive should the White House push policy too far from congressional wishes or should presidential actions fail to unfold according to plan. In this way, investigations in one policy realm may also influence presidential behavior in other issue areas, limiting executive-branch aggressiveness. In this chapter, we focus intently on this dynamic.

The great difficulty for analysts, however, is concretely measuring the amount of influence that is exerted through such anticipatory mechanisms.[3] In the preceding chapter examining the direct effects of investigative activity on the issue at hand, demonstrating influence was relatively straightforward. For example, by following the development of the congressional probe into the EPA's maladministration of the Superfund program, we were able to trace the revelations of misconduct repeated in the media, observe the political backlash generated, and infer from the timing of the Reagan administration's hasty about-face that such a dramatic shift would not have occurred in the absence of the investigation. By contrast, it is considerably more difficult to demonstrate the indirect influence of congressional investigations on presidential policy making in policy spheres that are not directly related to the investigative activity. Not only are indirect effects always more difficult to demonstrate convincingly than direct effects, but the task here is also complicated by the inherently endogenous nature of interbranch politics.

Because presidents anticipate congressional reactions and respond accordingly, it is often all but impossible to assess the degree to which policy outcomes actually reflect the sincere preferences of the administration, rather than those that are revealed after presidents make this anticipatory calculation. For example, at first blush perhaps one of the best ways to measure the influence of congressional investigations on presidential power

---

[3] The increasing application of game theoretic approaches to the study of presidential-congressional relations (*inter alia* Cameron 2000; Howell 2003; Brandice Canes-Wrone, *Who Leads Whom? Presidents, Policy, and the Public* (Chicago: University of Chicago Press, 2006)) has emphasized the importance of anticipatory calculations to politics and policymaking.

and policy making is to look for a relationship between investigative activity and presidential legislative success. Toward this end, one could examine presidential box scores to compare legislative success rates in periods of high versus low investigative activity. In a similar vein, an analyst could compare presidential proposals with the final content of enacted legislation to see whether the degree of presidential influence over policy is in part a function of investigative activity in Congress. However, it is exceedingly difficult to draw firm conclusions from such data because the presidential agenda that is presented to Congress and the public is endogenous to domestic politics.[4] That is, presidents have considerable discretion as to which policy proposals they submit for congressional consideration and what form those proposals take.[5] Because presidents are forward-looking strategic actors, their proposals should reflect their anticipations of Congress's likely reactions. In many cases, presidents who anticipate a recalcitrant Congress may either significantly moderate or withdraw altogether a policy proposal that they fear has little chance of success. If a president is weakened by investigations, he may significantly alter his agenda in a conscious effort to avoid embarrassing political defeats. Thus, even presidents besieged by committee inquests may seemingly enjoy high success rates on their proposals. This would not mean that presidents are setting policy at their ideal point, but rather that they are anticipating congressional reactions well and making *ex ante* concessions.[6]

The logic is similar to the situation confronted by presidents whose parties suffer significant losses in a midterm election. Consider for instance President Clinton after the Republican Revolution of 1994 and President Obama after the strong GOP gains in the 2010 midterms. By most accounts, President Clinton significantly shifted course after 1994. Clinton identified priorities where he shared at least some common ground with congressional Republicans and engaged in a strategy of triangulation to build a record of success that buoyed his 1996 reelection bid. By contrast, President Obama largely resisted calls to reverse course after the 2010 midterms and as a result failed to secure meaningful legislative victories.[7] To be sure, a simple

[4] Paul Light, *The President's Agenda: Domestic Policy Choice from Kennedy to Carter* (Baltimore: Johns Hopkins University Press, 1982).

[5] It is for this reason that Canes-Wrone (2006) in her analysis of the legislative influence of presidential public appeals focuses exclusively on budget legislation, the rare type of legislation that presidents are compelled by law to submit every year.

[6] For an assessment of how presidential scandals, more narrowly defined, affect various aspects of presidential behavior, such as executive order issuance and public speechmaking, see Brandon Rottinghaus, *The Institutional Effects of Presidential Scandal* (New York: Cambridge University Press, 2015).

[7] Changes in the Republican Party—in which opposition to compromise has grown dramatically in recent decades—clearly contributed to the lack of legislative success as well.

comparison of box scores and success rates would reflect the greater leg-islative productivity of 1995–1996 versus 2011–2012; however, it would be wrong to conclude from this that Clinton faced little congressional con-straint in implementing his preferred policies. Rather, calculations of what could pass Congress shaped Clinton's agenda before it even arrived on Capitol Hill.

One strategy to estimate the influence of investigations on policy writ large is to identify policy issues that arise exogenously, or largely indepen-dent of the domestic political environment. Certain events unfold for rea-sons that are unrelated to domestic politics and then invite a presidential policy response. By comparing presidential responses to such outside forces in periods of high versus low investigative activity, we can assess whether the volume and intensity of Congress's activity in the committee room shapes the president's calculations when responding to such opportunities.

To examine the influence of investigations on policy outcomes through this indirect pathway, we focus on presidential conduct of the nation's for-eign affairs, particularly on decisions to dispatch American forces abroad. This focus on military policy decisions serves several goals simultaneously. First, foreign crises and the resulting opportunities to use force that they generate are as close to exogenous shocks that arise independently of do-mestic political circumstances as we regularly see in the American political system. Most potential international triggering events, such as coups, in-terstate armed clashes, or humanitarian emergencies, arise independently from the nature of the political landscape in Washington.[8] In this realm, presidents do not have the luxury of structuring the agenda to suit con-temporary domestic political realities. Rather, events unfold abroad largely outside of the president's control, and they demand a presidential response. Thus, examining the presidential response to such crises affords a unique opportunity to observe whether recent congressional investigative activity has a tangible impact on policy outcomes.

Second, a focus on military policy making also provides something akin to a "critical test" of our argument that investigations do indeed have broader

---

[8] This argument is a matter of some contention in the political science literature, as "strate-gic avoidance" theory suggests that foreign states may indeed consider the domestic politics of potentially intervening superpowers when making conflict decisions. However, the empirical evidence for strategic avoidance is modest at best. See, e.g., Benjamin Fordham, "Strategic Conflict Avoidance and the Diversionary Use of Force," *Journal of Conflict Resolution* 67 (2005): 132–153; David Clark, "Can Strategic Interaction Divert Diversionary Behavior? A Model of U.S. Conflict Propensity," *Journal of Politics* 65 (2003): 1013–1039; Brett Ash-ley Leeds and Donald Davis, "Domestic Political Vulnerability and International Disputes." *Journal of Conflict Resolution* 41 (1997): 814–834. Most important, Howell and Pevehouse (2007, 89–93 and 99–103) find little evidence of strategic avoidance behavior in their oppor-tunities data.

tangible impacts on public policy.[9] Scholars have long argued that presidents are preeminent in foreign affairs. Since Wildavsky's seminal article on the "two presidencies," a wealth of scholarship has documented the greater power that presidents wield in foreign affairs.[10] This is particularly true regarding decisions to use force. Amid the Vietnam quagmire, Schlesinger famously lamented the rise of an "imperial presidency" in which presidents have all but usurped the war-making power.[11] Fisher decried Congress's veritable "abdication" of its responsibilities in war-making to the president.[12] And after a brief period of congressional resurgence,[13] Rudalevige declared in 2005 that the imperial presidency once again characterizes the nation's foreign relations.[14] Even recent scholarship asserting that Congress retains some measure of influence over military affairs readily acknowledges that presidents are far and away the lead actors shaping the nation's foreign policy.[15] As a result, if congressional investigative activity can be shown to affect presidential policy decisions in the military arena—to make the president more likely to forgo a military response or, if chosen, to reduce its scope and scale in the hopes of avoiding costly congressional criticism and scrutiny—it is highly likely that investigations also shape policy in meaningful ways in other policy realms in which the president does not enjoy the same panoply of institutional advantages.

One caveat is in order before we proceed to the empirical analysis: our results indicate that presidents are less likely to use force following a period of intense investigative activity. This does not necessarily mean that presidents are acting in accordance with congressional preferences. At times, many

[9] Harry Eckstein, "Case Studies and Theory in Political Science," in *Handbook of Political Science,* vol. 7, ed., Fred Greenstein and Nelson Polsby, eds., (Reading, MA: Addison-Wesley, 1975); John Gerring, *Case Study Research: Principles and Practices* (New York: Cambridge University Press, 2007).

[10] Aaron Wildavsky, "The Two Presidencies," *Trans-Action* 4 (1966): 7–14. For a review and evidence of the proposition's continued relevance, see Brandice Canes-Wrone, William Howell, and David Lewis, "Toward a Broader Understanding of Presidential Power: A Reevaluation of the Two Presidencies Thesis," *Journal of Politics* 70 (2008): 1–16.

[11] Arthur Schlesinger Jr., *The Imperial Presidency* (Boston: Houghton Mifflin, 1973).

[12] Louis Fisher, *Presidential War Power* (Lawrence: University of Kansas Press, 1995); Fisher 2000.

[13] James Sundquist, *The Decline and Resurgence of Congress* (Washington, DC: Brookings Institution Press, 1981); Randall Ripley and James Lindsay, *Congress Resurgent: Foreign and Defense Policy on Capitol Hill* (Ann Arbor: University of Michigan Press, 1993).

[14] Rudalevige 2005.

[15] See Robert David Johnson, *Congress and the Cold War* (New York: Cambridge University Press, 2006); Howell and Pevehouse 2007; Ralph Carter and James Scott, *Choosing to Lead: Understanding Congressional Foreign Policy Entrepreneurship* (Durham, NC: Duke University Press, 2009); Kriner 2010.

members of Congress may favor intervention.[16] However, even in cases where many members supported intervention at the outset, as in Iraq and Somalia, congressional criticism emerged and intensified when the military mission ran into unanticipated trouble. As noted in Chapter 1, investigations are often a blunt instrument of congressional assertion: they limit the president's leeway to pursue policy initiatives, and in doing so, help maintain the legislative branch's relative influence. But the penalty imposed on a president by an investigative onslaught may have complicated ramifications, rather than simply bringing policy in line with congressional preferences.

FORGOING A MILITARY RESPONSE: THE RWANDAN GENOCIDE

While the distribution of war powers in the early Republic may have tilted toward Congress, in the contemporary era there is little doubt that it is skewed heavily toward the president. A new wave of legal scholarship has challenged the old consensus emphasizing Congress's Article I powers of the purse and to declare war, and instead has argued that presidents possess independent authority to order American military forces across the globe for almost any reason.[17] And once troops are in theater, proponents of the unitary executive theory have argued that decisions over how those troops are used and the scope of the mission are for the president alone to make.[18] Apart from the legal questions involved, political scientists have also emphasized the strong hand presidents possess as commander-in-chief. Congress rarely succeeds in using any of the formal legislative tools at its disposal, such as the power of the purse, to check the policies of a wartime president.[19] And even when Congress does act, Hinckley argues its influence is "less than meets the eye."[20]

Nevertheless, in some instances it seems clear that Congress can significantly affect decisions regarding the use of military force, without necessarily

[16] While individual members of Congress have often played a lead role in championing a military response to a foreign crisis (e.g., Nancy Kassebaum (R-KS) in Somalia; John McCain (R-AZ) in Kosovo), a strong majority in Congress has only rarely encouraged a reluctant president to use force.

[17] John Yoo, *The Powers of War and Peace: The Constitution and Foreign Affairs After 9/11* (Chicago: University of Chicago Press, 2005).

[18] John Yoo to Tim Flanigan, "The President's Constitutional Authority to Conduct Military Operations Against Terrorists and Nations Supporting them," United States Department of Justice, Office of Legal Counsel, September 25, 2001.

[19] For instance, James Meernik, "Congress, the President and the Commitment of the U.S. Military," *Legislative Studies Quarterly* 20 (1995): 377–392; Fisher 2000.

[20] Barbara Hinckley, *Less Than Meets the Eye: Foreign Policy Making and the Myth of the Assertive Congress* (Chicago: University of Chicago Press, 1994).

acting legislatively. Even though presidents have successfully claimed for themselves the power to use force unilaterally without congressional assent, their decisions often appear significantly influenced by concerns about Congress's likely reaction should they dispatch American forces abroad.

On April 6, 1994, a plane carrying the presidents of Rwanda and Burundi was shot out of the sky by Hutu security forces. The next day, the moderate Rwandan prime minister Agathe Uwilingiyimana was also assassinated. Ten Belgian soldiers who were protecting the prime minister as part of the UN Assistance Mission for Rwanda (UNAMIR) were also killed and their bodies savagely mutilated. By that evening, more than a thousand corpses littered Kigali Hospital. The general slaughter of Tutsis and moderate Hutus who supported a power-sharing agreement had begun.

As early as April 8, the commander of the UNAMIR force, General Romeo Dallaire, informed his superiors at the United Nations in New York that the intensifying killings appeared to be ethnically motivated; by April 10, Dallaire reported that Hutu radicals were ordering the systematic murder of all Tutsis in a massive genocidal campaign. Having personally witnessed militias killing fleeing Tutsi civilians at road blocks set up across the country, Dallaire concluded: "At that point you couldn't argue anymore that it was just politically motivated slaughter. . . . I saw that one side was eliminating civilians behind the line."[21] Dallaire implored UN headquarters to send reinforcements and help UNAMIR stop the slaughter. American officials in the State Department also received urgent calls for help from those in the field in Rwanda.

Ultimately, the Clinton administration did little to stop the genocide. Within a mere hundred days, an estimated 800,000 Rwandans were killed. The administration's main response to the humanitarian crisis was to safely evacuate Americans remaining in the country; with that goal accomplished, little American action was forthcoming. Rather than send American troops or even strongly back UN action, the administration ultimately supported the complete withdrawal of the UNAMIR force, since its safety could no longer be guaranteed.

The decision not to use force to respond to the humanitarian crisis in Rwanda is perhaps all the more surprising given the strong emphasis placed on human rights during the 1992 Clinton campaign. Indeed, on the campaign trail, Governor Clinton praised the Carter administration, which "challenged dictators of the left and the right when finally he put human rights on America's and the world's agenda."[22] Candidate Clinton had also criticized the Bush administration's failure to stop the violence in Bosnia,

---

[21] Quoted in Samantha Power, *A Problem From Hell: America and the Age of Genocide* (New York: Perennial, 2002), 350.

[22] Jack Germond and Jules Witcover, "Clinton Faces Early Test of Human Rights Ideals," *Baltimore Sun*, March 17, 1993.

its granting of most favored nation status to China in the wake of the Tiananmen Square massacre, and its insensitivity toward the plight of Haitians fleeing to the United States in boats.[23] Even the administration's staunchest critics, such as Samantha Power, acknowledge that "the Clinton administration had taken office better disposed toward peacekeeping than any other administration in U.S. history."[24] Why, then, did the administration opt against a direct military response to the Rwandan genocide?

Plainly, a myriad of factors combined to produce the failure to act in 1994. However, in the assessments of most analysts and in the recollections of the participants themselves, the anticipated response of Congress loomed large. Recent experience left little doubt concerning how most in Congress would have reacted to a new deployment in Africa, coming less than six months after the tragedy in Somalia. Following the Battle of Mogadishu in October of 1993, which resulted in the deaths of nineteen Americans, criticism of the White House and its policies, which had simmered under the surface for much of the summer, exploded.[25] The House and Senate Armed Services as well as the Senate Foreign Relations Committees launched formal inquests into the fiasco. In addition to leveling a broader critique of the administration's involvement in a region not vital to American interests, investigators also scored political points by hammering the decision by the Secretary of Defense Les Aspin to reject a September request from commanders on the ground for additional tanks and Bradley fighting vehicles. Aspin defended his actions as an effort to limit the scope of the American military mission in Somalia. He maintained that sending additional ground armor would have opened the door for an expanded American mission, one that included clearing roads and securing them. However, the blistering headlines went to committee members criticizing the administration's policies. Arizona senator and Armed Services Committee member John McCain, no stranger to the media spotlight, emphasized the "need to find out how many lives were lost because of the refusal of the civilian leadership in the Pentagon to listen to our military leadership."[26] Ultimately, Aspin would be forced to resign, in large part due to pressure generated by investigations pursued by the very committee that he used to chair.

The congressional furor provoked by Somalia left little doubt about the likely reaction on Capitol Hill should Clinton have opted for a military

[23] Clair Apodaca and Michael Stohl, "United States Human Rights Policy and Foreign Assistance," *International Studies Quarterly* 43 (1999): 185–198.

[24] Quoted in Power 2002, 341.

[25] Even before the deadly Battle of Mogadishu, Senator Robert Byrd (D-WV) had tried to move Somalia firmly onto the Senate's agenda by introducing an amendment to the defense authorization bill (S. 1298) to cut off funding for the mission.

[26] Bill Gertz, "Aspin Decision Probed," *Washington Times*, October 13, 1993, A1.

response to the crisis in Rwanda. If the administration needed further evidence of the mood on Capitol Hill, the continued congressional investigation into the Clintons' prepresidential investments in the Whitewater Development Corporation, coupled with contemporaneous congressional attacks on the administration's policies toward Bosnia and Haiti, only further clarified the steep political costs a new military deployment would entail. In his memoirs, President Clinton noted the almost certain opposition of Congress to any military response: "With the memory of Somalia just six months old, and with opposition in Congress to military deployments in faraway places not vital to our national interests . . . neither I nor anyone on my foreign policy team adequately focused on sending troops to stop the slaughter."[27] In retrospect, Clinton labeled the failure to act in Rwanda one of the greatest regrets of his presidency.

The investigations of American misadventures in Somalia, as well as Congress's use of its investigative powers to shine a spotlight on other alleged misdeeds by Clinton and his allies, helped create a political context in which the president believed that the risks of intervening in Rwanda were too great. These previous investigations served as an important signal to the Clinton White House that a combative Congress was all but certain to use all available means at its disposal to inflict political damage on the administration should it use force in Rwanda and the military action fail to deliver the expected results. Thus, past investigative activity informed the president's anticipatory calculus. Moreover, should Clinton have moved forward with a military response to the Rwandan genocide, the Somalia precedent served notice that investigations were a particularly potent tool through which Congress, though lacking the votes to compel policy changes legislatively, can capture media headlines, sway public opinion, and build considerable political pressure on the administration to shift course.[28]

RESPONDING TO "OPPORTUNITIES" TO USE FORCE

Is the Clinton administration's reluctance to use force in Rwanda in the face of almost certain congressional opposition the exception that proves the rule?

[27] Bill Clinton, *My Life* (New York: Alfred A. Knopf 2004), 593. In her memoirs, then ambassador to the United Nations Madeline Albright concurs; though she regrets not advocating more forcefully for United States intervention to stop the killing, Albright notes that such a response never would have won support in Congress. Madeline Albright, *Madam Secretary* (New York: Miramax Books, 2003), 155.

[28] Congress did pursue several legislative challenges to Clinton's Somalia policy after the Battle of Mogadishu. However, it failed to rally the requisite supermajorities to force Clinton to deviate from his announced plan to withdraw American forces by the end of March 1994. For an overview of these legislative responses, see Kriner 2010, 20–25.

Or is it indicative of a more generalizable pattern in which Congress constrains military policy making through indirect means? Recent research by
Howell and Pevehouse suggests that domestic politics, particularly congressional politics, regularly influences presidential decisions concerning the use
of force.[29] Howell and Pevehouse acknowledge that Congress rarely engages
questions of military policy when the use of force is under consideration, and
only in the rarest of circumstances has it legally constrained the president's
freedom of action at this stage.[30] Nevertheless, presidents anticipate Congress's likely reaction and adjust their policy choices accordingly. In making
this calculation, presidents look to the partisan composition of Congress.

When presidents dispatch American troops abroad, they transform the
political environment and put would-be opponents in Congress in a difficult
position. Some members, particularly those in the partisan opposition, may
sense the opportunity for political gain if they can challenge presidential
policies that fail to meet popular expectations for success. However, this
impulse is tempered by the fear of counter-charges of failing to support the
troops should they challenge the president's conduct of a war. Despite this
trade-off, members of Congress can and have historically employed a number of levers to make trouble for the commander-in-chief when his military
policies go awry; these range from introducing and voting on legislative
initiatives to curtail the use of force, to holding high-profile investigative
hearings, to speaking out against the war in the public sphere.[31] All of these
levers are more likely to be exercised by members of the partisan opposition
than by the president's co-partisans. Thus, presidents should logically anticipate greater risk from using force when the opposing party controls Congress. Consistent with this, Howell and Pevehouse find that presidents facing a strong partisan opposition on Capitol Hill are less likely, all else being
equal, to respond militarily to an opportunity than are presidents backed by
stronger ranks of co-partisans in Congress.

We build on this logic and argue that recent investigative activity should
also influence the nature of this anticipatory calculation. Indeed, we contend that the volume and intensity of recent investigative actions provide
an additional valuable signal to presidents concerning the likely response
on Capitol Hill should a military action fall short of expectations. The partisan composition of Congress affords a rough gauge of the baseline potential for members of Congress to challenge the president's wartime policies.
Recent investigative activity, however, yields even more information about

[29] Howell and Pevehouse 2005, 2007.

[30] For example, in the 1970s Congress legally prohibited the Ford administration from
aiding anticommunist rebels in Angola.

[31] Kriner 2010; Douglas Kriner and Francis Shen, "Responding to War on Capitol Hill: Battlefield Casualties, Congressional Response, and Public Support for the War in Iraq," *American
Journal of Political Science* 58 (2014): 157–174.

members' willingness to act on these incentives and to use the full resources of the legislative branch to challenge the president's policies should the actual costs exceed estimates. A Congress that has recently used the investigative machinery of its committees to challenge the president and his policies should be more likely, all else being equal, to confront a president through investigations and other means over military policy should a window of opportunity open than a Congress that has shown little penchant in the recent past for exercising its investigative capacity.

Consider again President Clinton's calculations in 1994. Nominally, he enjoyed a period of unified party control and strong Democratic majorities in both chambers. An assessment based solely on the partisan composition of Congress would suggest that Clinton had considerable leeway to respond to foreign crises as he saw fit with little threat of a hostile response in Congress. Yet, Clinton's recent experience with congressional investigations into the administration's missteps in Somalia surely reminded him of the likely response from Capitol Hill should another military venture in Africa lead to American casualties. These hearings, alongside the ongoing battle over Whitewater, offered a much clearer signal for Clinton's anticipatory calculations than an assessment based solely on the balance of partisan power on Capitol Hill. As a result, we hypothesize that presidents should be less likely to respond militarily to foreign crises in periods when congressional investigative activity is high than when it is low.

An alternative perspective suggests that presidents attacked in the hearing room might, paradoxically, be more rather than less eager to use force abroad. In this alternative account, presidents may attempt to "wag the dog" and use force in the hopes of distracting other politicians and the public alike from troubles at home. Might not embattled presidents seek to generate a rally around the flag by seizing on an opportunity to show the colors abroad?

While possible in some cases, we argue that on average such a dynamic is unlikely to prevail. First, while scholars have long posited that democratic leaders may engage in diversionary war,[32] the empirical evidence that leaders do so is strikingly limited and inconsistent.[33] Moreover, while many American uses of force generate rallies in public support for the president, many

[32] Jack Levy, "The Diversionary War Theory: A Critique," in *Handbook of War Studies*, ed. Manus Midlasky (Boston: Unwin Hyman, 1989); Amy Oakes, *Diversionary War: Domestic Unrest and International Conflict* (Stanford: Stanford University Press, 2012).

[33] James Meernik, "Presidential Decision Making and the Political Use of Force," *International Studies Quarterly* 38 (1994): 121–138; James Meernik and Peter Waterman, "The Myth of the Diversionary Use of Force by American Presidents," *Political Research Quarterly* 49 (1996): 573–590; Leeds and Davis 1997; Joanne Gowa, "Politics at the Water's Edge: Parties, Voters and the Use of Force Abroad," *International Organization* 52 (1998): 307–324; Alastair Smith, "International Crises and Domestic Politics," *American Political Science Review* 92 (1998): 623–638; Benjamin Fordham, "The Politics of Threat Perception and the Use of Force: A Political Economy Model of U.S. Uses of Force, 1949–1994," *International Studies Quarterly*

others do not.[34] Ironically, the strongest predictor of whether or not a use of force produces a rally in support for the president is Congress's reaction. If Congress backs the president, the public rallies. If members of Congress criticize the president, then the rally disappears or fails to materialize.[35]

As a result, military adventurism is unlikely to pay political dividends for a president with political problems on Capitol Hill. Instead, we argue that intense recent investigative activity provides presidents with a strong signal that Congress is unlikely to rally behind the commander-in-chief and instead is poised to pounce should a military venture fail to meet expectations for quick success. In such an environment, presidents have incentives to tread carefully, even in a policy arena where they enjoy significant institutional advantages.

To assess whether recent investigative activity enters into presidents' decision calculus when contemplating the use of force, we first must identify a set of foreign crises to which the president might reasonably have responded militarily. Accordingly, we use Howell and Pevehouse's opportunities database, which catalogs more than 10,000 "opportunities" to use force between 1945 and 2000. To construct the opportunities data, Howell and Pevehouse identified every front page *New York Times* article reporting on a category of international events—such as interstate armed clashes, coups, or attacks on American military or diplomatic personnel—that had the potential to trigger an American military reaction. Each front page story on such an event constitutes an "opportunity" in the resulting data set. The dependent variable is simply a binary indicator coded 1 if the United States used force in response to the given opportunity within thirty days of the story's appearance in the *Times,* and 0 if it did not.

To explore the factors influencing the president's willingness to use force in response to a foreign crisis, we construct a series of logistic regression models. These models allow us to examine the relationship between prior investigative activity and the president's response to a foreign crisis while controlling for a number of other factors—both in the domestic and in the larger geopolitical environment—that undoubtedly also influence presidential decisions either to use force or eschew a military response.

Our primary explanatory variable is the intensity of congressional investigative activity in the recent past. Because we know the exact date of each

42 (1998): 567–590; David Clark, "Can Strategic Interaction Divert Diversionary Behavior? A Model of U.S. Conflict Propensity," *Journal of Politics* 65 (2003): 1013–1039.

[34] See, e.g., Bradley Lian and John Oneal, "Presidents, the Use of Military Force, and Public Opinion," *Journal of Conflict Resolution* 37 (1993): 277–300.

[35] Brody 1991; Zaller 1992; William Baker and John Oneal, "Patriotism or Opinion Leadership? The Nature and Origin of the 'Rally 'Round the Flag' Effect," *Journal of Conflict Resolution* 45 (2001): 661–687; Cindy Kam and Jennifer Ramos, "Understanding the Surge and Decline in Presidential Approval Following 9/11," *Public Opinion Quarterly* 72 (2008): 619–650; Matthew Baum and Timothy Groeling, "New Media and the Polarization of American Political Discourse," *Political Communication* 25 (2008): 345–365.

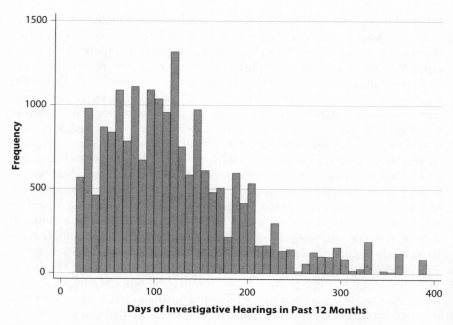

FIGURE 5.1.Variation in Levels of Investigative Activity Preceding Opportunities to Use Force.

opportunity in the data, we can construct precise measures of the number of days of investigative hearings held in Congress over the twelve months preceding each opportunity. As shown in Figure 5.1, there is considerable variation in the investigative climate presidents confronted prior to the opportunities in the Howell and Pevehouse data set. For the median opportunity, the president had confronted 106 days of investigative activity in the preceding year. However, for a quarter of the opportunities in the data set, Congress had been much more aggressive in its investigating of the administration over the preceding year, holding 156 days or more of investigative hearings. Indeed, many opportunities arose in periods of intense investigative activity during which Congress had held more than 200 days of investigative hearings in the preceding year. By contrast, in many other contexts presidents made the decision of whether or not to respond to an opportunity to use force in a more harmonious interbranch environment when Congress had been relatively quiescent on the investigative front. All else being equal, we hypothesize that presidents will be less likely to use force in periods of high investigative activity than in periods of low investigative activity.

Before estimating the relationship between investigative activity and decisions to use force, we had to grapple with a potential complication: how to assess the effects of recent investigative activity on new presidents in the first year of their administrations. In such cases, it is not clear how much influence the level of investigative activity in the past twelve months should have on the new president's anticipatory calculations, given that for some opportunities this measure might include investigations launched under the previous president. The cleanest solution to this conundrum is simply to exclude data from the first year of each new presidential administration. This is the approach that we follow in all of the models presented below in Table 5.1. However, as a robustness check, we estimate a number of alternative models relaxing this exclusion, including models that use data from all years from 1945 through 2000. The results are substantively identical to those presented in the text. Interested readers are referred to Appendix Table 5.1.

As an initial test of our hypothesis, the first column of Table 5.1 models the decision to respond to an opportunity with force solely as a function of prior investigative activity. The only other variables included in the model are a series of indicator variables for the different regions in which each opportunity arises as well as one for each president; this allows the base probability of a military response to vary across different regions and presidencies.

Consistent with our argument, the bare bones model in column 1 of Table 5.1 finds a negative and statistically significant relationship between the intensity of prior investigative activity and the probability of the president adopting a military solution to a foreign crisis.[36] The more aggressively Congress has investigated alleged misconduct in the executive branch in recent months, the more reluctant presidents are to use force in response to an opportunity, all else being equal.

It is important, however, to control for potential confounding variables. Perhaps most important, we must also account for the partisan composition of Congress.[37] As shown in Chapter 2, the partisan balance of power in Congress is strong and significant predictor of fluctuations in investigative activity. Investigative activity is significantly higher, on average, when the partisan opposition is in power on Capitol Hill than when the committees are controlled by the president's partisan allies. Moreover, Howell and Pevehouse have shown that the strength of the president's co-partisan ranks in

[36] The p-value for the relevant coefficient is .054 (two-tailed test).

[37] Howell and Pevehouse (2007) find a significant relationship between the partisan composition of Congress and the probability of a president responding to an opportunity with force, but not between divided government and use of force decisions. As a result, we include the partisan composition of Congress in our models. However, because divided government, which determines which party controls the committee gavels, is the most important predictor of investigative activity (and therefore the most important potential confounder), we also re-estimated our models with divided government. The results, presented in Appendix Table 5.2, are virtually identical to those presented in the text.

TABLE 5.1: Investigative Activity and the Probability of a Military Response

	(1)	(2)	(3)	(4)
Recent investigations	−0.005*	−0.006**	−0.006**	−0.008**
	(0.003)	(0.003)	(0.003)	(0.003)
% President's party		7.838*	7.863*	9.869*
		(4.186)	(4.396)	(5.308)
Presidential approval			−0.001	0.018
			(0.018)	(0.020)
Unemployment				0.452***
				(0.124)
Inflation				−0.007
				(0.033)
Election year				0.331
				(0.335)
Hegemony				−0.788
				(16.718)
World disputes				−0.059
				(0.061)
Major power				−0.363
				(0.797)
Democracy				0.209
				(0.342)
Alliances				−0.272
				(0.379)
Trade (billions)				0.006
				(0.023)
Soviet involvement				−0.281
				(0.385)
Capability ratio (log)				−0.280
				(0.173)
Previous opportunities				0.017**
				(0.008)
Contemporaneous opportunities				−0.396***
				(0.137)
Troops deployed (log)				−0.086
				(0.075)
Constant	−1.748**	−5.654**	−5.639***	−8.213
	(0.881)	(2.206)	(2.166)	(6.747)
Observations	12,327	12,327	12,327	10,918

Note: Models are logit regressions. All models also include unreported president and regional fixed effects. Robust standard errors clustered on country-president combinations are reported in parentheses. All significance tests are two-tailed.

* p < .10   ** p < .05   *** p < .01

Congress is also a strong predictor of conflict initiation.[38] We have argued that recent investigative activity sends an even clearer signal to presidents than the partisan composition of Congress about the likely reaction of Congress and the political costs it might impose on the administration should a war fail to achieve its objectives quickly.

Model 2 of Table 5.1 adds a control for the partisan composition of Congress to our baseline model. Consistent with Howell and Pevehouse, we find that a president becomes more likely to embrace a military response to an opportunity to use force as the strength of his party in Congress increases. The data plainly suggests that the partisan composition of Congress informs presidential anticipatory calculations. However, even after controlling for congressional partisanship, we continue to find a strong and statistically significant inverse relationship between investigative activity and the probability of a president responding to an opportunity with military action. Recent investigative activity provides additional information about possible future costs from Congress that presidents appear to incorporate into their strategic calculations, even in a policy realm where they enjoy considerable institutional advantages as commander-in-chief.[39]

In a similar vein, we must also control for another potential confounder: presidential approval. Chapter 3 showed evidence of a complex relationship between investigative activity and presidential approval. Presidents with lower approval ratings are more vulnerable to attack and therefore tend to be investigated more aggressively, all else being equal, than presidents who enjoy greater reserves of public support. At the same time, our instrumental variables models demonstrated that congressional investigations also have an independent downward impact on a president's standing with the public. Indeed, this is one of the most important mechanisms through which investigations have tangible impact on politics and policy: by eroding the president's base of support among the people. Because of this relationship and because a president's approval ratings may also influence his or her use-of-force decision making, model 3 adds this critical control variable to the model.[40]

---

[38] Interestingly, Howell and Pevehouse (2007, 96) found no relationship between unified/divided government and conflict initiation. As a result, we focus here on the strength of the presidential party's ranks in Congress, which if used instead of divided government in the models in Chapter 2 (e.g., Table 2.2) is a strong and statistically significant predictor of investigative activity.

[39] Since the volume of investigations is itself partially attributable to the partisan composition of Congress, it is possible that some of the total effect of partisan composition works through investigations. As a result, it would be incorrect to make inferences about the *relative* importance of investigative activity and Congress's partisan composition. The estimates suggest both matter, however.

[40] Controlling for approval does raise the possibility of post-treatment bias. Because investigative activity affects approval and approval may influence the president's decisions on whether

The results are very similar to those presented in model 2. Investigative activity appears to significantly decrease the likelihood that the president will opt to use force. While a strong co-partisan majority in Congress increases the probability that the president will use force, the coefficient on the presidential approval variable is substantively very small and not statistically significant. This null finding does not necessarily imply that presidents are unresponsive to concerns about their standing with the public when deciding to use force. However, presidents may be more concerned about their future approval rating, which will be shaped by how Congress reacts to a use of force. If members of Congress rally around the president or even simply hold their fire and refrain from criticizing his actions, then the public will likely rally behind the flag and the commander-in-chief. By contrast, if Congress openly criticizes a military action and the president's leadership of it, then even initially high approval ratings may prove fleeting as a military operation unfolds. Indeed, as Chapter 3 showed, investigations can be a particularly effective weapon through which Congress can erode public support for the president.[41] Thus, if presidents anticipate little opposition from Congress, a low approval rating would be unlikely to dissuade them from acting unilaterally; if anything, the use of force might bolster their standing among the public. If they anticipate pushback from Congress—a calculation informed by the intensity of recent investigative activity—then even popular presidents may forego the use of force to protect that popularity and the leverage it affords to pursue other aspects of their agenda.

Finally, model 4 of Table 5.1 includes the panoply of military, strategic, and domestic political control variables also employed by Howell and Pevehouse. Among others, this includes a military capabilities ratio, measure of alliance structures, the target state's democracy level, whether the Soviet Union was involved, and indicators of the health of the American domestic economy.

We continue to find a strong negative relationship between investigative activity and the likelihood of a president using force in a crisis scenario, even after including the full range of domestic and geopolitical controls. Presidents who had recently lived through periods of intense congressional investigative activity were significantly less likely to respond to a foreign

---

or not to use force, including approval in the model may cause us to underestimate the total influence of investigative activity on the initiation of military action. However, given the weak relationship observed between the level of presidential approval at the time of a crisis and the probability of conflict initiation (e.g., Howell and Pevehouse 2007, 97), we believe any such bias would be modest.

[41] See also Kriner (2009) for an analysis showing the negative effect of war-related hearings on support for the Iraq War.

crisis with force than were presidents who had a more tranquil recent history with congressional investigators, all else equal.[42]

Figure 5.2 illustrates the estimated substantive effect of recent investigative activity on the probability of a presidential military response to an overseas opportunity to use force. The solid line presents the effect of varying levels of investigative activity on the predicted probability of a military response to an opportunity holding all other variables constant at their means or medians.[43] Dotted lines indicate 95% confidence intervals around the point predictions. Increasing the level of recent investigative activity from approximately 45 to 200 days—that is from roughly one standard deviation below to one standard deviation above the mean—significantly decreases the predicted probability of a military response by two thirds, from .12 to .04. To be sure, a two standard deviation increase in recent investigative activity reduces an already low probability of a military response to an even lower figure. However, to understand the tangible impact of such a shift on military affairs, it is important to remember the sheer volume of opportunities in the Howell and Pevehouse database. Between 1945 and 2000, the median year witnessed more than 220 opportunities to use force.[44] Thus, for the median year, a two standard deviation increase in recent investigative activity decreases the predicted number of opportunities to which the president responds militarily from twenty-six to only nine.[45] Even a smaller shift in investigative activity, for example from 50

[42] As shown in Figure 5.1, recent investigative activity, the independent variable of interest, is roughly normally distributed, but with a right skew. To insure that outlying values in the right tail of the distribution (most of which occurred in the early 1950s and mid-1970s during the McCarthyism and Watergate eras, respectively) are not skewing our overall results, we conducted an additional robustness check. We replicated model 4 in Table 5.1 using the natural log of investigative activity in the last twelve months instead of the raw tally. Taking the natural log attenuates outlying values and produces a transformed independent variable that is normally distributed. The results of this analysis are virtually identical to those reported in the chapter; most important, the coefficient for logged recent investigative activity is negative and statistically significant.

[43] Because the uncertainty around these predicted values increases significantly at the tails of the distribution, Figure 1 plots predicted probabilities for values of recent investigative activity ranging from 28 to 294, the 5th to the 95th percentile of the distribution of the independent variable.

[44] Since the end of the Cold War, the median year has produced 105 opportunities to use force.

[45] Translating the estimated effect into a concrete number of foregone military actions is difficult because of the nature of the Howell and Pevehouse data. As discussed above, an "opportunity" is an event reported on the front page of the New York Times that met certain criteria. The dependent variable is coded 1 if the United States responded with force within thirty days of the article's publication. As a result, a single use of force could respond to multiple opportunities within the data set as each media report of a relevant event is treated as an "opportunity." Thus, the number of predicted military actions may not be reduced from twenty-six to nine;

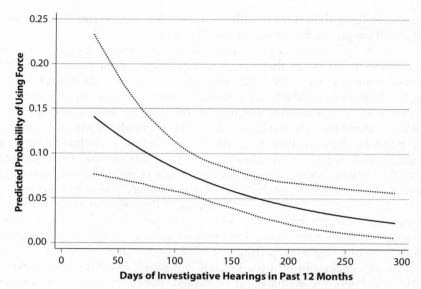

FIGURE 5.2. Effect of Investigative Activity on Probability of Using Force.
Note: The solid line plots the predicted probability of the president responding to an opportunity with the use of force at the given level of investigative
activity holding all other variables constant at their means or medians. Dotted
lines present 95% confidence intervals about the point estimates derived from
simulations. Estimates derived from model 4 of Table 5.1.

to 100 days, decreases the predicted probability of a military response to a
foreign crisis by roughly 33%.

To put the estimated effect size in comparative perspective, Howell and
Pevehouse show that an increase in the strength of the president's party
in Congress from one standard deviation below the mean to one standard deviation above the mean more than doubles the probability that
the United States will use force in response to a given opportunity.[46] Our
model suggests that—even after controlling for the partisan composition of
Congress—decreasing recent investigative activity from one standard deviation above the mean to one standard deviation below it triples the probability of a use of force. Presidents appear at least as responsive to the signal
sent by recent investigative activity as they are to the information about

rather the number of "opportunities" to which the president ultimately responds with force is
reduced from twenty-six to nine.
    [46] Howell and Pevehouse 2007, 95.

anticipatory congressional reactions conveyed by the legislature's partisan composition.

It is important to remember that these significant shifts in the probability of military action are observed even after controlling for the partisan composition of Congress, which also has a substantial independent influence on presidential war-making. Presidents backed by strong co-partisan ranks on Capitol Hill are more willing to respond militarily to foreign crises than are presidents who confront strong opposition parties in Congress. However, the level of recent investigative activity provides even more information to presidents about Congress's likely response to a risky military gambit.

Finally, most of the control variables also influenced presidential decision making as expected. The contextual setting of an opportunity affects the probability of an American military response. In the international arena, previous opportunities in the target state increase the probability of a military reaction. By contrast, the greater the number of competing opportunities arising in hot spots around the globe and the greater the pre-existing commitment of American troops in the target state, the less probable is a new American military response. On the home front, we find modest evidence that presidents are more willing to use force in periods of high unemployment, all else being equal.[47]

Investigations vs. Oversight

In Chapter 3, we showed that while investigations significantly erode public support for the president, more general congressional oversight—even oversight that is often openly critical of administration policies—does not. This suggests that trends in investigative activity provide presidents with an important signal about Congress's willingness to take action to impose tangible political costs on the administration, while trends in general oversight do not. As a result, only trends in investigative activity should affect presidential strategic calculations about decisions to use force.

Therefore, as a final robustness check on our results, we re-estimate all of the models from Table 5.1 with one additional independent variable: the

[47] See, e.g., Benjamin Fordham, "The Politics of Threat Perception and the Use of Force: A Political Economy Model of U.S. Uses of Force, 1949–1994," *International Studies Quarterly* 42 (1998): 567–590; Benjamin Fordham, "Another Look at 'Parties, Voters and the Use of Force Abroad,'" *Journal of Conflict Resolution* (2002) 46: 572–596; Patrick James and John Oneal, "The Influence of Domestic and International Politics on the President's Use of Force," *Journal of Conflict Resolution* 35 (2) (1991): 307–332. But see James Meernik and Peter Waterman, "The Myth of the Diversionary Use of Force by American Presidents," *Political Research Quarterly* 49 (1996): 573–590.

number of days of non-investigative oversight of the executive branch in the twelve months preceding each opportunity. Table 5.2 presents the results.

In each model specification, we continue to find a strong, negative, and statistically significant relationship between recent investigative activity and the probability of the president adopting a military response to a foreign crisis. By contrast, the new models find no evidence of any relationship between trends in noninvestigatve oversight and the president's decisions as commander-in-chief.[48] This suggests that our investigative activity variable is not simply tapping into some more general interbranch dynamic that is spuriously correlated with trends in military policy making. Rather, congressional investigations of concrete charges of abuse or misconduct affect presidential anticipatory calculations concerning the political costs of using force. Trends in congressional oversight more generally, which do not have the same capacity to shape public opinion, do not affect these calculations.

In sum, the results are strongly consistent with our larger argument that investigations of executive-branch misconduct or abuse, regardless of their content, can have wide-ranging effects in other policy areas by shaping presidents' anticipation of the future costs they may incur from Congress. Even in foreign policy and military policy making in particular—an arena long held to be dominated by the executive—members of Congress appear to significantly affect presidential decision making and resulting policy outcomes, despite Congress's repeated failures to mandate its preferred policy course legislatively. Presidents look to past experience with Congress to anticipate its future reaction should a military venture run into unexpected trouble. Presidents who have felt the sting of intense congressional investigative activity in the recent past appear to respond to anticipated future trouble from Congress when confronted with opportunities to use force abroad by being less willing to risk a military response than their counterparts who enjoyed more tranquil periods of interbranch relations. Moreover, this congressional influence persists despite Congress's repeated failure to enact legislation compelling presidents to abandon their preferred military policy course. The ability to cause political trouble through tools like investigations, rather than fears of concrete legislative action, appears more influential in shaping presidents' strategic calculus.

Yet forgoing a military response to a foreign crisis altogether is but one potential option for a president who anticipates considerable opposition

---

[48] Recent investigative activity and recent noninvestigative oversight are correlated in the opportunities data, but the two are far from collinear, $r = .51$. Nevertheless, as a robustness check we re-estimated all of the models in Table 5.2 with just the oversight variable. In each specification, the relevant coefficient is substantively trivial and not statistically significant. Investigations are significantly related to presidential decisions as commander-in-chief; our more general measure of noninvestigative oversight is not.

TABLE 5.2: Investigative Activity, Oversight, and the Probability of a Military Response

	(1)	(2)	(3)	(4)
Recent investigations	−0.005*	−0.006**	−0.006**	−0.008**
	(0.003)	(0.003)	(0.003)	(0.003)
Recent oversight	0.001	0.001	0.001	−0.000
	(0.001)	(0.001)	(0.001)	(0.001)
% President's party		7.705*	7.583*	9.989*
		(4.118)	(4.298)	(5.477)
Presidential approval			0.002	0.018
			(0.018)	(0.021)
Unemployment				0.451***
				(0.125)
Inflation				−0.007
				(0.033)
Election year				0.338
				(0.366)
Hegemony				−1.105
				(17.226)
World disputes				−0.060
				(0.061)
Major power				−0.364
				(0.799)
Democracy				0.212
				(0.333)
Alliances				−0.269
				(0.380)
Trade (billions)				0.006
				(0.023)
Soviet involvement				−0.279
				(0.383)
Capability ratio (log)				−0.280
				(0.173)
Previous opportunities				0.017**
				(0.008)
Contemporaneous opportunities				−0.397***
				(0.139)
Troops deployed (log)				−0.086
				(0.076)
Constant	−1.983**	−5.796**	−5.877***	−8.152
	(0.951)	(2.267)	(2.251)	(6.734)
Observations	12,327	12,327	12,327	10,918

Note: Models are logit regressions. All models also include unreported president and regional fixed effects. Robust standard errors clustered on country-president combinations are reported in parentheses. All significance tests are two-tailed.

* $p < .10$ ** $p < .05$ *** $p < .01$

from Congress. In some situations, presidents may judge that the precipitating crisis all but compels military action; however, they may moderate the scale and scope of that response, in part, to minimize the domestic costs of using force.

LIMITING THE SCOPE OF RESPONSE: INTERVENTION IN KOSOVO

While much of the world focused on the reunification of Germany and the disintegration of the Soviet Union in the early 1990s, further south in the Balkan peninsula the formerly communist state of Yugoslavia was also unraveling. Nationalist impulses and ethnic tensions that had long been suppressed under the iron hand of Marshal Tito were unleashed. First Slovenia declared its independence and then Croatia, which succeeded in securing its independence only after a seven-month war that left more than 10,000 dead. Tensions next erupted in the multiethnic former Yugoslav republic of Bosnia (which was 43% Muslim, 35% Serb, and 18% Croat), which voted to secede and appealed to the West for assistance in avoiding bloodshed.[49] How to deal with the Bosnian question and protect its Muslim population from ethnic cleansing by Bosnian Serb forces bedeviled American policymakers in the George H. W. Bush and Clinton administrations. Both presidents proclaimed the need to stop the violence in Bosnia; yet, for three and a half years the killing continued. Ultimately, an estimated 200,000 Bosnians died in the fighting.

Finally, in August of 1995 after Bosnian Serb forces overran the UN-declared safe area of Srebrenica, massacring almost 8,000 Bosnian Muslim men and boys who had taken refuge there, President Clinton authorized American warplanes to attack Bosnian Serb targets as part of NATO's first coordinated and sustained air campaign, Operation Deliberate Force.[50] During the two-and-a-half-week-long bombing campaign, NATO forces flew 3,515 sorties against Bosnian Serb Army targets. In the face of the onslaught, the Serb Army withdrew and Serbian president Slobodan Milosevic expressed a willingness to come to the bargaining table. By November, the administration had brokered the Dayton peace accords, which sought to forge a lasting peace among Croats, Serbs, and Bosnian Muslims. To enforce the agreement, President Clinton dispatched 20,000 American troops to Bosnia. The decision was politically risky, but ultimately successful in quelling the violence inside Bosnia.

---

[49] For an overview, see Power 2002, 247–251.

[50] While the Srebrenica massacre gave considerable impetus to overcome NATO's inertia, perhaps the most immediate trigger was the Serb bombing of a Sarajevo market on August 28, which killed thirty-eight civilians and injured eighty-five more.

Yet the problems in the Balkans were far from over. Kosovar Muslims had hoped that the NATO allies at Dayton would also force Serbia to restore the autonomy that their province had enjoyed under Tito; however, the issue was never seriously discussed at the conference. In March 1998, the Kosovo Liberation Army (KLA) killed several Serbian policemen, prompting a massive retaliation from the Milosevic government in Belgrade. Entire villages suspected of harboring KLA fighters or sympathizers were put to flames, scores of Kosovar Albanians were killed, and thousands were forced from their homes. As Serb forces pounded Kosovar towns with artillery, the civilian death toll continued to mount. In one such incident near the town of Racak, Serb paramilitary forces executed forty-five Albanians, including women and children, dumping their bodies into frozen mass graves. Upon viewing the mutilated corpses, William Walker, the American ambassador and head of the Kosovo Verification Mission, declared to the world that the Serbs were guilty of crimes against humanity.[51]

With a significant number of American forces already deployed to keep the peace in Bosnia, the president's own domestic problems in Washington, and a public not inclined to embrace an American role as global policeman, many advised President Clinton against intervening militarily in Kosovo. The public was almost evenly divided on whether the United States should join any NATO action to protect Kosovar Albanians; and on the eve of the bombing campaign a clear majority said bringing peace to Kosovo was not worth the loss of even some American soldiers' lives.[52] However, given American and NATO interests in and commitments to the region, as well as the desire of many key decision makers including the president and now Secretary of State Madeline Albright to atone for failing to stop the genocide in Rwanda, the Clinton administration ultimately decided to use force to stop Milosevic.

However, President Clinton did place significant limits on the scope of the military intervention: NATO would intervene, but only through the air. In an address to the nation, Clinton justified military intervention both in terms of the moral imperative to halt the crimes against humanity being perpetrated in Kosovo and in terms of vital American strategic interests in achieving stability in the Balkans. The president noted that while he would consider deploying additional American troops as peacekeepers once the war was concluded, he would not launch a ground war to stop Serbian forces: "I do not intend to put our troops in Kosovo to fight a war."[53]

[51] Power 2002, 444–445.

[52] ABC News Poll, March 23 1999. [USABC.032399.R07] Storrs, CT: Roper Center for Public Opinion Research, iPOLL [distributor], accessed March 4, 2016

[53] Bill Clinton, "Address to the Nation on Airstrikes Against Serbian Targets in the Federal Republic of Yugoslavia (Serbia and Montenegro)." *Public Papers of the President*, March 24, 1999.

The combination of high-altitude bombing runs that limited the prospects for casualties from Serb air defenses and bad weather blunted the initial force of the NATO strikes. Milosevic refused to cave and even intensified operations against civilians in Kosovo. Seeking to step up the pressure on Milosevic, NATO commander General Wesley Clark lobbied Washington aggressively both to plan for a ground invasion and to deploy low-flying Apache helicopters that could effectively target Serbian forces.[54] Yet neither ground troops nor the Apaches proved forthcoming. As the bombing campaign dragged on without forcing Milsoevic to capitulate, British prime minister Tony Blair also pressured Washington to consider a ground invasion. However, mindful of the political risks and casualties such escalations would entail, the White House resisted. Instead, NATO intensified its airborne assault, expanding the target list deep within Serbia to include dual-use targets such as the electric grid and transportation systems. Finally, on June 3, 1999, after seventy-eight days of NATO bombardment, Milsoevic surrendered. Serbian troops withdrew from Kosovo, and NATO peacekeepers, including Americans, entered.

The case of Kosovo makes clear that presidents do not necessarily eschew a military response to a foreign crisis, even when the potential domestic political costs are considerable. To be sure, some in Congress supported military action in Kosovo—even action bolder than that pursued by Clinton. However, many others vehemently opposed such humanitarian interventions. Moreover, the administration probably rightly feared that even those who nominally supported military action were likely to attack the administration should it result in American casualties. As Secretary of Defense William Cohen presciently warned, "The hearts that beat so loudly and enthusiastically to do something, to intervene in areas where there is not an immediate threat to our vital interests, when those hearts that had beaten so loudly see coffins, then they switch, and they say, 'What are we doing there?'"[55]

A spate of investigative activity under the Republican-controlled Congress, not the least of which involved investigations into the president's personal conduct culminating in impeachment proceedings, plainly testified to the strong possibility that Clinton's partisan opponents on Capitol Hill might exploit any policy failings in Kosovo to inflict political damage on the president.[56] Despite these concerns, Clinton chose to act militarily in Kosovo. However, perhaps in part to minimize the domestic political risks

---

[54] Wesley Clark, *Waging Modern War* (New York: Public Affairs, 2002).

[55] Quoted in Power 2002, 455.

[56] To be sure, other factors besides domestic politics certainly influenced this policy choice. For example, President Clinton argues that the time required to put ground troops in place with adequate support forces risked exacerbating the killing. He also argues that the civilian casualties that would have inevitably ensued from a ground campaign would have dwarfed those caused by the bombing. Thus, in his assessment, the heightened cost of a ground campaign in

of doing so, he narrowed the scale and scope of the mission to avoid the use of ground troops, and even of low-altitude air missions (such as Apache helicopter raids) that would have more readily targeted Serb ground forces killing Kosovars, but also exponentially increased the risk to NATO pilots.

DETERMINING THE SCALE AND SCOPE OF MILITARY ACTIONS

Previously we examined whether recent congressional activity—and the signals it sends presidents about the likelihood of future congressional investigations and public criticism should their military policies fail to produce the promised results—affected the probability of the president responding to a foreign crisis militarily. Now we shift focus to examine whether such calculations also affect the scale and scope of military action, given that the president has decided upon some sort of military response. To investigate the role that domestic political forces—and anticipations of congressional reactions in particular—play in such calculations, we examine the factors driving the scale of major American military actions since World War II.

Blechman and Kaplan (1978) pioneered much of the quantitative American use of force literature by identifying a list of "political" uses of force during the postwar era and coding them by intensity. Uses of force receiving a 1, 2, or 3 on the Blechman and Kaplan scale are commonly identified as "major." Using these criteria, subsequent scholarship has identified 122 major uses of force by the United States from 1945 through 2006.[57] However, even within this set of "major" uses of force, there is considerable variation in the scope of the military actions. For example, both the 1990–1991 Persian Gulf War and a brief series of joint exercises to signal improved relations with Morocco in 1982 are coded as major uses of force on the Blechman and Kaplan scale. Similarly, the 1965 American invasion of the Dominican Republic and the dispatch of American naval vessels to the Mediterranean following the killing of Colonel William Higgins in Lebanon are both coded as level 2, major uses of force on the Blechman and Kaplan scale. The former involved the deployment of more than 23,800 American marines and soldiers to a region torn by civil war (accompanied by 38 offshore naval vessels) to restore order and occupy the country. The latter involved

---

terms of American lives outweighed the minimal gains it would have produced in heightening the speed and prospects for victory. Clinton 2004, 851.

[57] Barry Blechman and Stephen Kaplan, *Force Without War: U.S. Armed Forces as a Political Instrument* (Washington, D.C., Brookings Institution, 1978). For a discussion of temporal updates to this list and amendments to the Blechman and Kaplan data (such as including the wars in Vietnam and Korea, which were excluded by Blechman and Kaplan as not being "political" uses of force, but full-scale wars), see Kriner 2010, 90–91.

a substantial redeployment of naval assets including aircraft carriers to the eastern Mediterranean; however, no shots were fired.

Reviewing the list of 122 "major" post–World War II uses of force, 3 categories of military engagements encompassing 20 cases stand out: deployments of ground troops to countries or regions where they were not already stationed; sustained uses of American firepower; and extended military operations involving American air or naval vessels in hostile zones. Kriner labels these "principal" uses of force to distinguish them as the subset of military actions with the greatest potential for significant economic, human, and political costs.[58]

Given that the president has decided upon a military response to a foreign crisis, does recent investigative activity encourage the administration to limit the military mission? To answer this question, we model the factors influencing the scale of the post–World War II major uses of force. Our dependent variable is coded 1 for large-scale, high-intensity uses of force involving ground troops, sustained firepower or the large-scale dispatch of air and/or naval units into hostile zones. The dependent variable is coded 0 for those smaller-scale missions that did not involve one of these features. As in the preceding analysis, we again drop observations from each president's first year in office.[59]

Our main explanatory variable of interest is the number of days of investigative hearings held by Congress in the preceding year. Investigative activity, we argue, sends particularly informative signals to the president about how Congress might respond should the president opt for a large-scale military response involving ground troops or firepower if that military venture proves more costly than anticipated. Given that they have decided upon a military response, presidents who have recently lived through intense congressional investigative activity should be more likely to moderate the scale of the use of force than presidents who have not experienced such difficulties with Congress.

The first model in Table 5.3 estimates the bivariate relationship between recent investigative activity and the scope of the use of force. With no other variables in the model, we see a strong and statistically significant negative relationship between investigative activity and the scale of military action. Presidents who choose to use force during periods in which Congress has investigated their administrations aggressively in the recent past are much less likely to choose large-scale military actions involving ground troops or firepower than are presidents who enjoy a better relationship with potential adversaries on Capitol Hill.

---

[58] For a complete list of these 20 military actions, see Kriner 2010, 143.

[59] However, as shown in Appendix Table 5.3 (and discussed below), our results are robust to the inclusion of these observations.

TABLE 5.3: Investigative Activity and the Scale of Major Military Actions

	(1)	(2)	(3)	(4)
Recent investigations	–0.014***	–0.014***	–0.014***	–0.017***
	(0.005)	(0.005)	(0.005)	(0.006)
% President's party		4.506	4.487	8.750*
		(3.310)	(3.420)	(4.643)
Public approval			–0.002	–0.016
			(0.023)	(0.043)
Military expenditures				–1.463**
				(0.714)
Military personnel				0.427
				(0.369)
Distance in miles				–0.000
				(0.000)
Similarity in alliances				–0.417
				(0.992)
Ongoing war				–1.077
				(1.172)
Election year				–0.022
				(0.896)
Unemployment				0.142
				(0.242)
Inflation				–0.071
				(0.137)
Constant	–0.249	–2.529	–2.416	–2.850
	(0.559)	(1.742)	(2.650)	(4.542)
Observations	101	101	101	101

Note: Models are logit regressions. Robust standard errors are reported in parentheses. All significance tests are two-tailed.

* $p < .10$ ** $p < .05$ *** $p < .01$

As in the conflict-initiation models above, models 2 and 3 of Table 5.3 again control for two important potential confounders: the partisan composition of Congress and presidential approval.[60] Previous research has shown that presidents who enjoy strong majorities on Capitol Hill are more likely to use ground troops or other intensive military operations than presidents confronted by strong opposition party ranks in Congress.[61] Because congressional partisanship is correlated with investigative activity, it is also included in the model to isolate the independent, additional influence of recent investigative activity on presidential decision making, above and beyond the influence exerted solely by congressional partisanship. Similarly, model 3 also includes presidential approval, which may be correlated with both investigative activity and the scale of the president's military response to a crisis.

Even after controlling for the partisan composition of Congress and presidential approval, we continue to find a strong negative relationship between recent investigative activity and the probability of the president pursuing a high-intensity military action involving ground troops or firepower to achieve his foreign policy goals. Consistent with prior research, both models show that presidents become more likely to employ large-scale military actions in pursuit of their foreign policy goals as the strength of their party in Congress increases. By contrast, model 3 finds little evidence that presidential approval at the outset of a use of force affects its scale and scope. Rather, presidents appear more responsive to calculations concerning future public support, calculations based in large part on Congress's anticipated reaction to a military venture.

Other factors in the geopolitical environment undoubtedly also influence American military interventions. To account for these factors, the final model in Table 5.3 includes a range of control variables drawn from past research.[62] This model includes measures of the target state's military expenditures and the size of its military, its distance from the United States, and the similarity of its alliance structure with that of the United States. To capture variation in the overarching strategic environment, the model also includes a variable indicating whether or not the United States was already involved in a major ongoing war (i.e., Korea or Vietnam) at the time the opportunity arose. Finally, to account further for the domestic political context, the model includes a variable indicating whether or not the military action began during an election year as well as measures of unemployment and inflation.

[60] We also estimated models controlling for divided government. These models, presented in Appendix Table 5.4, yield virtually identical results.
[61] Kriner 2010.
[62] Kriner 2010.

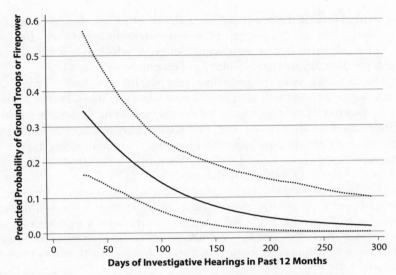

FIGURE 5.3. Effect of Investigative Activity on Scale of Use of Force.
Note: The dependent variable is coded 1 if the president uses ground troops,
sustained firepower, or a large-scale deployment of American naval or air assets
into a hostile zone to achieve his policy objectives. It is coded 0 otherwise. The
solid line plots the predicted probability of the president launching the most
intensive type of use of force at the given level of investigative activity holding
all other variables constant at their means or medians. Dotted lines present
95% confidence intervals about the point estimates derived from simulations.
Estimates derived from model 4 of Table 5.3.

Even after controlling for these additional factors, recent investigative
activity appears to significantly shape presidential decisions concerning the
scale of military actions.[63] Figure 5.3 illustrates the size of the estimated
effect of investigative activity on the probability of the president choosing
a large-scale use of force involving ground troops or firepower. Increasing the level of recent investigative activity from 70 to 150 days—that is
from roughly the 25th to the 75th percentile—significantly decreases the
predicted probability of the use of ground troops or sustained firepower,
from .23 to .08. It is important to remember that these significant shifts

---

[63] To insure that a handful of large outlying values of recent investigative activity are not
skewing our results, we again conducted a robustness check. We re-estimated model 4 in Table
5.3 with the natural log of recent investigative activity. We continue to find a negative and statistically significant relationship between recent investigative activity and the scale of military
action.

in the probability of the president using the most intense forms of military action—primarily ground troops or firepower—are observed even after controlling for the partisan composition of Congress, which also has a substantial independent influence on military policy outcomes.

A final concern, as in the preceding analysis, involves how to treat uses of force begun during the first year of a new administration. For such cases, some of the investigative activity in the preceding year likely occurred during the prior administration; as a result, this activity may or may not inform the new president's anticipatory calculations about the potential for aggressive congressional scrutiny should a military venture run into trouble. As in the preceding analyses in Table 5.1, the models in Table 5.3 exclude uses of force that began during the first year of a new administration. However, to ensure that our findings are robust to alternative strategies for dealing with this problem, Appendix Table 5.3 presents results from a number of alternative models, including one that includes all major uses of force during the period. In each instance, we observe substantively identical results to those presented in the text.

Investigations vs. Oversight

As a final robustness check, we re-estimate the preceding models with one additional variable: the volume of oversight over the year preceding the initiation of the use of force. Again, we argue that the intensity with which Congress has pursued allegations of executive-branch misconduct should influence presidents' anticipatory calculations, but trends in general oversight activity should not. Table 5.4 presents the results.

Across all specifications we continue to find a strong, negative, and statistically significant relationship between recent investigative activity and the scale of American military operations. By contrast, in each specification the coefficient for noninvestigative oversight is substantively trivial and not statistically significant.[64] Investigations influence presidential calculations as commander-in-chief; general noninvestigative oversight does not.

In sum, we find strong empirical evidence that investigative activity has significant effects on the conduct of American military policy. Investigative activity informs presidents' expectations regarding how Congress would respond to various policy options. Presidents who anticipate greater opposition from Congress are less likely to respond militarily to a foreign crisis; moreover, even if they do decide to use force, such presidents are likely to moderate the scale of their military response.

---

[64] Recent investigative activity and noninvestigative oversight activity correlated at $r = .45$ in the sample. Replicating all of the models in Table 5.4 with just the oversight variable yields null results across specifications.

TABLE 5.4: Investigative Activity, Oversight, and the Scale of Major Military Actions

	(1)	(2)	(3)	(4)
Recent investigations	−0.015***	−0.015**	−0.015**	−0.017***
	(0.006)	(0.006)	(0.006)	(0.006)
Recent oversight	0.001	0.001	0.001	0.001
	(0.001)	(0.001)	(0.001)	(0.002)
% President's party		4.466	4.538	8.496*
		(3.365)	(3.418)	(4.708)
Public approval			0.006	−0.010
			(0.028)	(0.048)
Military expenditures				−1.439**
				(0.684)
Military personnel				0.416
				(0.371)
Distance in miles				−0.000
				(0.000)
Similarity in alliances				−0.456
				(1.002)
Ongoing war				−0.898
				(1.323)
Election year				−0.068
				(0.928)
Unemployment				0.131
				(0.251)
Inflation				−0.086
				(0.145)
Constant	−0.401	−2.641	−3.077	−3.079
	(0.537)	(1.707)	(2.837)	(4.684)
Observations	101	101	101	101

Note: Models are logit regressions. Robust standard errors are reported in parentheses. All significance tests are two-tailed.

* $p < .10$ ** $p < .05$ *** $p < .01$

Conclusions

If investigations solely had the potential to impact presidential behavior in the policy area under scrutiny, then committee probes would offer, at best, a narrowly potent but ultimately limited tool for influence. Competing demands on legislators' time and resources ensure that the scope of executive-branch decisions subject to Congress's investigative eye is finite. When Congress leaps into action on an issue, investigations could precipitate concrete changes in policy through the direct pathways discussed in the previous chapter. However, presidents could nonetheless act with veritable impunity in a myriad of other policy areas that escape investigative scrutiny.

However, such a narrow view overlooks the broader influence investigations afford by shaping presidential anticipatory calculations. Through this additional mechanism, investigations in one policy area may encourage the president to expect similar scrutiny and political headaches should he stray too far from congressional preferences in another policy venue. By contrast, presidents who have enjoyed relatively harmonious relations with Congress, largely devoid of aggressive investigative activity, may judge themselves more at liberty to strike out in new directions, free from fear of congressional retaliation.

Assessing the influence of such anticipatory mechanisms is exceedingly difficult. However, by exploiting the exogenous nature of foreign crises, which arise mostly independently of domestic politics, we were able to isolate the wider policy influence investigations afford through anticipatory means. Perhaps most important in the anticipatory framework, recent investigative activity plays an informative role, providing a strong and readily interpretable signal concerning how much congressional meddling presidents risk incurring should they pursue costly military policies.

Moreover, as shown in the case study discussing the intertwined politics surrounding military intervention in Somalia and the corresponding lack of military intervention several months later in Rwanda, investigations provide a particularly attractive mechanism for legislators to inflict political damage on presidents. Past scholarship has uncovered multiple ways through which Congress can raise the costs of military action for the president, even when it cannot legislatively compel him to alter his preferred policy course.[65] Members can introduce, debate, and hold floor votes on various legislative vehicles to constrain the discretion of the commander-in-chief. Similarly, members can take to the airwaves and hit the Sunday morning talk show

[65] See, e.g., Mayhew 2000; Howell and Pevehouse 2007; Kriner 2010; Douglas Kriner, "Obama's Authorization Paradox: Syria and Congress's Continued Relevance in Military Affairs," *Presidential Studies Quarterly* 44 (2014): 309–327.

circuit to engage the policy debate in the public sphere and build public pressure on the president to change course. However, investigations also offer a particularly salient tool through which to challenge the actions of the commander-in-chief. From the very first congressional investigation—the inquiry into the disastrous defeat of St. Clair's army discussed in Chapter 1—through the flurry of Democratic investigations into the Bush administration's alleged misconduct of the war in Iraq, assertive legislators have repeatedly used committee investigations to cast public and media scrutiny on aspects of wartime policy that administrations would prefer to be kept out of the public eye. Our qualitative and quantitative data suggest that presidents anticipate Congress's reaction to their foreign policy choices and adjust their conduct of military affairs accordingly when they perceive a higher likelihood of incurring political costs from a quarrelsome Congress.

APPENDIX

APPENDIX TABLE 5.1: Robustness Checks on Use of Force Models

	(1)	(2)	(3)	(4)
Recent investigations	−0.008**	−0.006**	−0.006**	−0.005*
	(0.003)	(0.003)	(0.003)	(0.002)
% President's party	9.869*	11.186**	11.313**	8.982***
	(5.308)	(5.093)	(5.115)	(3.361)
Unemployment	0.452***	0.371***	0.404***	0.490***
	(0.124)	(0.109)	(0.109)	(0.108)
CPI	−0.007	−0.003	0.005	0.040*
	(0.033)	(0.032)	(0.029)	(0.022)
Public approval	0.018	0.003	0.004	−0.001
	(0.020)	(0.018)	(0.018)	(0.017)
Election year	0.331	0.175	0.171	0.168
	(0.335)	(0.325)	(0.326)	(0.319)
Hegemony	−0.788	−7.964	−7.095	−4.135
	(16.718)	(14.921)	(14.774)	(9.302)
World disputes	−0.059	−0.077	−0.071	−0.077
	(0.061)	(0.061)	(0.060)	(0.054)

(continued)

APPENDIX TABLE 5.1 (*continued*)

	(1)	(2)	(3)	(4)
Major power	−0.363	−0.472	−0.499	−0.642
	(0.797)	(0.764)	(0.762)	(0.707)
Democracy	0.209	0.186	0.198	0.195
	(0.342)	(0.313)	(0.313)	(0.309)
Alliances	−0.272	−0.287	−0.274	−0.246
	(0.379)	(0.397)	(0.393)	(0.421)
Trade (billions)	0.006	0.006	0.006	0.010
	(0.023)	(0.023)	(0.023)	(0.023)
Soviet involvement	−0.281	−0.167	−0.214	−0.209
	(0.385)	(0.359)	(0.352)	(0.336)
Capability ratio (log)	−0.280	−0.312*	−0.321*	−0.347**
	(0.173)	(0.166)	(0.168)	(0.150)
Previous opportunities	0.017**	0.013	0.013	0.014*
	(0.008)	(0.008)	(0.008)	(0.008)
Ongoing opportunities	−0.396***	−0.365***	−0.365***	−0.348**
	(0.137)	(0.130)	(0.131)	(0.138)
Troops deployed (log)	−0.086	−0.102	−0.105	−0.118*
	(0.075)	(0.069)	(0.069)	(0.067)
Constant	−8.213	−6.985	−8.770	−13.807***
	(6.747)	(6.406)	(5.917)	(4.563)
Observations	10,918	11,570	11,792	13,327

Note: Models are logit regressions. Model 1 is identical to that presented in the text and drops the first year of all presidential terms; model 2 drops the first year of all presidential terms, except for those presidents who gained office through succession (Truman; Johnson; Ford); model 3 drops the first year of presidential terms following a party switch; model 4 includes all observations. Investigations of Truman actions under Eisenhower are not included in misconduct counts. All models also include unreported president and regional fixed effects. Robust standard errors clustered on country-president combinations are reported in parentheses. All significance tests are two-tailed.

* $p < .10$ ** $p < .05$ *** $p < .01$

APPENDIX TABLE 5.2: Robustness Check on Use of Force Models—Divided
Government

	(1)	(2)	(3)	(4)
Recent investigations	−0.005*	−0.005*	−0.005*	−0.006**
	(0.003)	(0.003)	(0.003)	(0.003)
Divided government		0.148	0.138	0.606
		(0.640)	(0.635)	(0.677)
Presidential approval			0.005	0.026
			(0.018)	(0.020)
Unemployment				0.526***
				(0.131)
Inflation				−0.018
				(0.035)
Election year				0.170
				(0.323)
Hegemony				19.242
				(16.109)
World disputes				−0.042
				(0.057)
Major power				−0.502
				(0.766)
Democracy				0.202
				(0.345)
Alliances				−0.229
				(0.376)
Trade (billions)				0.009
				(0.021)
Soviet involvement				−0.230
				(0.386)
Capability ratio (log)				−0.279
				(0.174)
Previous opportunities				0.016*
				(0.009)
Contemporaneous opportunities				−0.381***
				(0.142)
Troops deployed (log)				−0.075
				(0.074)
Constant	−1.748**	−1.884*	−2.120	−5.858
	(0.881)	(1.049)	(1.410)	(7.280)
Observations	12,327	12,327	12,327	10,918

Note: Models are logit regressions. All models also include unreported president and regional
fixed effects. Robust standard errors clustered on country-president combinations are reported in parentheses. All significance tests are two-tailed.

* p < .10   ** p < .05   *** p < .01

APPENDIX TABLE 5.3: Robustness Checks on Scale of Force Models

	(1)	(2)	(3)	(4)
Recent investigations	−0.017***	−0.016***	−0.017***	−0.015***
	(0.006)	(0.006)	(0.006)	(0.005)
% President's party	8.750*	11.028**	10.115**	7.263*
	(4.643)	(4.813)	(4.503)	(3.753)
Public approval	−0.016	−0.005	0.006	−0.021
	(0.043)	(0.039)	(0.038)	(0.029)
Military expenditures	−1.463**	−1.544**	−1.558**	−1.578**
	(0.714)	(0.604)	(0.639)	(0.632)
Military personnel	0.427	0.400	0.411	0.365
	(0.369)	(0.277)	(0.288)	(0.266)
Distance in miles	−0.000	−0.000	−0.000	−0.000
	(0.000)	(0.000)	(0.000)	(0.000)
Similarity in alliances	−0.417	−0.616	−0.481	−0.154
	(0.992)	(0.915)	(0.904)	(0.828)
Ongoing war	−1.077	−2.154*	−2.144*	−1.950*
	(1.172)	(1.158)	(1.107)	(1.088)
Election year	−0.022	0.257	0.160	0.131
	(0.896)	(0.810)	(0.804)	(0.775)
Unemployment	0.142	0.047	0.061	−0.149
	(0.242)	(0.222)	(0.215)	(0.183)
Inflation	−0.071	−0.075	−0.041	−0.133
	(0.137)	(0.127)	(0.120)	(0.087)
Constant	−2.850	−3.847	−3.979	−0.188
	(4.542)	(4.179)	(4.044)	(2.982)
Observations	101	108	111	122

Note: Models are logit regressions. Model 1 is identical to that presented in the text and drops the first year of all presidential terms; model 2 drops the first year of all presidential terms, except for those presidents who gained office through succession (Truman; Johnson; Ford); model 3 drops the first year of presidential terms following a party switch; model 4 includes all observations. Investigations of Truman actions under Eisenhower are not included in misconduct counts. Robust standard errors are reported in parentheses. All significance tests are two-tailed.

* p < .10   ** p < .05   *** p < .01

APPENDIX TABLE 5.4: Robustness Checks on Scale of Force Models—Divided Government

	(1)	(2)	(3)	(4)
Recent investigations	−0.014***	−0.014***	−0.014***	−0.018***
	(0.005)	(0.005)	(0.005)	(0.006)
Divided government		−0.816	−0.820	−1.508*
		(0.587)	(0.633)	(0.772)
Public approval			0.001	−0.001
			(0.025)	(0.044)
Military expenditures				−1.409**
				(0.684)
Military personnel				0.397
				(0.365)
Distance in miles				−0.000
				(0.000)
Similarity in alliances				−0.377
				(0.983)
Ongoing war				−0.684
				(1.219)
Election year				0.038
				(0.939)
Unemployment				0.261
				(0.279)
Inflation				−0.019
				(0.131)
Constant	−0.249	0.241	0.182	0.790
	(0.559)	(0.669)	(1.341)	(3.724)
Observations	101	101	101	101

Note: Models are logit regressions. Robust standard errors are reported in parentheses. All significance tests are two-tailed.

* p < .10   ** p < .05   *** p < .01

CHAPTER 6

~ ~

Investigations in the Age of Obama

ALL OF OUR analyses to this point have examined investigative politics and their capacity to constrain presidential action across many decades of American history. Parts of the analysis have focused narrowly on the impact of specific investigations. For example, across a range of cases we have shown how important investigations have precipitated policy changes either by spurring legislation in Congress that would not have passed in the absence of the pressure generated by the investigation, or by encouraging preemptive presidential action. Other analyses have focused on the power of investigations—or the anticipation of them—to constrain presidential action more broadly. For example, by analyzing more than sixty years of public opinion data, we demonstrated that investigative fervor on Capitol Hill routinely erodes presidential support among the public. The anticipation of these and other political costs affects presidential strategic calculations. Presidents fear Congress's capacity to investigate alleged administration shortcomings should their policies fail to unfold according to plan. The result is that presidents, even when acting as commander-in-chief, often proceed more cautiously and labor under greater constraint than they would in the absence of Congress's investigative power.

However, as numerous politicians, pundits, and scholars alike have argued, today's intense polarization has transformed American politics. Concomitant with the rise of polarization, in the assessment of many Congress scholars, is a significant decline in the legislature's institutional capacity. For example, Mann and Ornstein document how partisan polarization has driven institutional dysfunction in Congress.[1] Increasing polarization, they warn, has also undermined a sense of institutional responsibility—always a tenuous and rare commodity—among members, decimating the ranks of legislative entrepreneurs willing to perform "institutional maintenance."[2]

---

[1] Mann and Ornstein 2006, 2013.

[2] Mayhew 1974; Gregory Wawro, *Legislative Entrepreneurship in the U.S. House of Representatives* (Ann Arbor: University of Michigan Press, 2000).

Has the contemporary Congress, often derided as the "broken branch," abdicated its investigative role? Can investigations continue to constrain presidents in the contemporary era of intense partisan polarization and diminished congressional capacity?

To answer these questions, we marshal a range of quantitative and qualitative evidence to conduct a more focused and comprehensive assessment of investigative politics from 2007 through 2014. In Chapter 4, we examined the 2011–2012 Solyndra investigation and noted how, in contrast to the other investigations examined, it failed to produce significant policy changes, either by encouraging the president to give ground in the hopes of preempting more extreme congressional action or by creating momentum behind new legislation from Congress to mandate a change in course. The limited impact of the Solyndra hearings raises questions about the capacity of investigations to bring about significant policy change in periods of extremely high partisan polarization and gridlock. The threat of legislative action from Congress may be less plausible in the current era. In such a political environment, might congressional investigators logically concentrate their energies on exerting influence through the more indirect pathway described in Chapter 5, by using investigations primarily to inflict political costs on the White House? Examining the role played by recent congressional investigations, with a special emphasis on the first six years of the Obama presidency, can shed important insight into these questions about the political ramifications of congressional investigations in a polarized polity.

RE-EXAMINING TRENDS IN INVESTIGATIVE ACTIVITY,
2007 TO 2014

As discussed briefly in Chapter 2, our initial dataset cataloguing more than a century of investigative activity extended from 1898 through 2006. We later updated the data through 2014 after the Congressional Information Service hearings data had migrated from Lexis Nexis to ProQuest.[3] Here, we focus more intently on the data from 2007 to 2014 to examine whether the dynamics governing variation in investigative activity are the same in today's intensely polarized polity as they were in earlier eras.

Figure 6.1 displays the number of days of investigative hearings held in both chambers by year for the 110th through 113th Congresses (2007–2014). The 110th Congress witnessed the return of divided government following the tremendous Democratic surge in the 2006 midterm elections. Following the victory of Barack Obama in 2008, the 111th Congress marked the first

---

[3] See Footnote 49 in Chapter 2 for details.

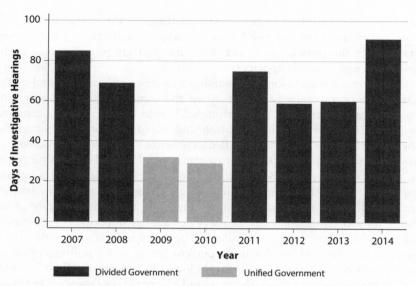

FIGURE 6.1. All Investigative Activity, 2007–2014.

time Democrats controlled both ends of Pennsylvania Avenue since 1994. Unified Democratic control, however, would prove short-lived as the Republicans, aided by the emergence of the Tea Party, recaptured the House in the 2010 midterms and continued to control the chamber for the remainder of the period. Consistent with the larger pattern observed in the aggregate data as a whole, the two years of unified government during the contemporary period produced significantly lower tallies of investigative activity than did years of divided government. Whereas Congress held only an average of 30.5 days of investigative hearings in the two years of unified government, it averaged almost two and a half times as many (73.2 days) in divided government.

Figure 6.2 disaggregates this data by chamber. Strongly consistent with the larger pattern described in Chapter 2, we again see that divided government significantly increases investigative activity in the House. The House averaged fewer than twenty days of investigations in the 111th Congress, during which Democrats controlled both chambers and the presidency.[4] By contrast, in divided government the House averaged almost sixty days of investigative hearings each year. In the Senate, however, investigative activity remained low and relatively constant over the entire period, with at most a modest increase

---

[4] Moreover, many of these investigative hearings were continuations of wartime investigations begun during the 110th Congress when President George W. Bush sat in the Oval Office.

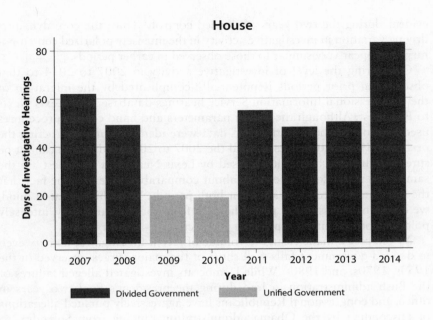

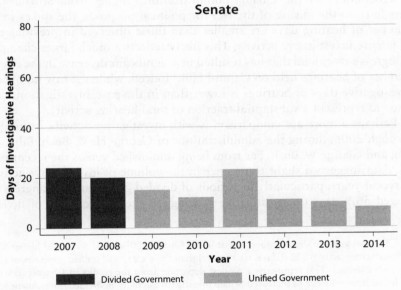

FIGURE 6.2. Investigative Activity by Chamber, 2007–2014.

evident during the two years of divided control.[5] Thus, the core dynamics driving variation in investigative activity in the intensely polarized contemporary era appear very similar to those observed in earlier periods.

Comparing the level of investigative activity in 2007 to 2014 to that observed in prior periods is potentially complicated by the migration of the Congressional Information Service hearings database from Lexis Nexis to ProQuest. Although the search parameters and hand coding procedures used to produce the investigations data were identical for constructing the original 1898 to 2006 data set and the 2007 to 2014 update, we cannot be sure that the search algorithms used by Lexis Nexis and ProQuest are the same. This raises some questions about comparability, despite the fact that the CIS data source is the same for both periods. With this caveat in mind, we can nonetheless try to place the data from the contemporary, intensely polarized period into comparative perspective.

As Chapter 2 made clear, the volume of recent investigative activity even in divided government falls well short of the major surges observed in the 1950s, 1970s, and 1980s. While Democrats investigated alleged failures of the Bush administration in Iraq during the president's final two years in office, and congressional Republicans have aggressively pursued allegations of misconduct by the Obama administration ranging from Solyndra, to Benghazi, to the misuse of the IRS for political purposes, the spikes in the number of hearing days are smaller than those observed in previous eras of intense investigative activity. This likely reflects a much larger change in Congress's workload that has resulted in a significant decrease in the overall number of hearings held on Capitol Hill.[6] Indeed, while the raw number of investigative days of hearings is lower than in the past, investigations continue to represent a substantial fraction of total hearing activity.[7]

Perhaps a more apt comparison is with investigative activity from 1989 through 2006, during the administrations of George H. W. Bush, Bill Clinton, and George W. Bush. Far from being diminished versus the recent past, the data suggests a slight resurgence in the volume of investigative activity in recent years, particularly in periods of divided government. Congress averaged 56.9 days of investigative hearings in the twelve years of divided

---

[5] The two years of divided government in the Senate (2007–2008) witnessed higher levels of investigative activity (22.0 days, on average) than the six years of unified government (13.2 days, on average). This represents a modest departure from the results in Chapter 2, where we found little evidence of increased Senate investigative activity in divided government when examining the entire time period from 1898 through 2014. However, this difference is only marginally significant (p = .07, two-tailed test) and modest in size compared to the differences in investigative activity observed in the contemporary House.

[6] See, e.g., Fowler 2015, 30.

[7] Indeed, between 2007 and 2012 (the 112th Congress is the last for which the Policy Agendas data provides complete data on total hearing activity), 3.6% of all hearings were investigative. Between 1946 and 2006, 3.7% of all hearings were investigative.

government from 1989 through 2006.[8] From 2007 through 2014, Congress averaged 73.2 days of investigations per year during divided government. Although the sample size is admittedly small, this represents roughly a 30% increase in the volume of investigative activity in recent years. By contrast, in unified government Congress averaged approximately thirty-one days of investigative activity per year in both periods.

This re-analysis of our aggregate data suggests that the very high level of partisan polarization in our contemporary polity has made divided government an even stronger motive force driving investigative activity than in the recent past. While the contemporary Congress has failed to do many things, such as pass appropriations bills in a timely fashion, it has continued to investigate alleged misconduct and abuse in the executive branch, at least during periods of divided government. Indeed, our data suggests that the volume of investigative activity in divided government since 2006 substantially exceeds the average level observed in the preceding sixteen years. While Congress may be institutionally broken in many ways, increasing partisan polarization appears not to have weakened Congress's use of its investigative function under divided government. By contrast, investigations remain rare in periods of unified government as polarization has only strengthened the incentives of the majority to clamp down on potentially damaging investigations of their party leader in the White House.

Identifying Major Investigations from the Obama Era

To this point, we have identified congressional investigative activity by directly examining the content of congressional hearings themselves. However, for investigations to have political bite, they almost certainly must attract media coverage to bring the allegations of wrongdoing into the public arena.

---

[8] One potential explanation for the perhaps surprisingly low level of investigative activity in the 1990s is the heavy reliance on independent counsels. While special prosecutors enjoy a long history dating back at least to the administration of Ulysses S. Grant, the Clinton era witnessed a proliferation of calls for special prosecutors. Ultimately, special prosecutors launched investigations into Cabinet officials Henry Cisneros, Mike Espy, Ron Brown, and Bruce Babbitt, as well as into Whitewater, the scope of which expanded so much over time that it eventually encompassed "Filegate," "Travelgate," the suicide of Vince Foster, the alleged sexual harassment of Paula Jones, the Lewinsky scandal, and the president's impeachment. As a result, the high-profile investigations launched by independent counsels often eliminated the need for Congress to conduct its own lengthy investigations. For example, during his five-year tenure as independent counsel, the *New York Times* mentioned Independent Counsel Kenneth Starr and his various inquests into the Clinton administration in a whopping 287 front-page stories. By the time the House Judiciary Committee opened its own investigation into the Lewinsky scandal, it held only four days of hearings before moving toward impeachment. The Judiciary Committee did not need to do more. Starr and his exhaustive report, which committee Republicans gleefully made public shortly after receiving it, did most of the digging and inflicted most of the political body blows for them.

To supplement the preceding analysis, we take a different tack and construct a list of major investigations based on media coverage. Rather than simply comparing the number of investigative hearings across periods of unified and divided government, this focus on high-profile investigations also allows us to examine more qualitative differences in investigative activity depending on the partisan control of Congress.

To gauge the level of significant investigative activity over the course of the Obama administration, we searched CQ Weekly for every reference to a congressional investigation from the president's inauguration in January 2009 through the midterm elections in 2014. The resulting list is not exhaustive; it does not include many relatively minor investigative hearings included in the tallies presented in Figure 6.1 that received little coverage in the mass media. However, relying on Congressional Quarterly allows us to construct a list of inquires that succeeded in generating enough notoriety that they merited some mention in a major publication on legislative politics. Table 6.1 presents the resulting list of investigations broken down by Congress.

Consistent with both the preceding analysis and the larger empirical patterns described in Chapter 2, a simple comparison across the two columns in Table 6.1 plainly shows that investigative activity increased significantly in the 112th and 113th Congresses when Republicans controlled the House of Representatives. Congress was remarkably quiescent on the investigative front during President Obama's first two years in office when the president was working with a Democratic Congress. Indeed, many mentions of investigative politics in Congressional Quarterly during this period discussed the debate in Congress over whether to continue investigations into alleged abuses during the Bush administration, including its employment of "enhanced interrogation techniques" with suspects detained in the war on terror and its allegedly politically motivated firing of a cadre of U.S. Attorneys.[9]

Leaving aside these backward-looking deliberations, Congressional Quarterly coverage mentioned only three investigations of executive-branch actions during the Obama administration in the 111th Congress. Strikingly, none of these investigations were primarily motivated by a desire to politically damage President Obama, and none focused on promoting policy or political goals opposed by the administration.

A bipartisan Senate panel led by Joseph Lieberman (I-CT) and Susan Collins (R-ME) probed the November 2009 Fort Hood shooting that killed thirteen soldiers and wounded dozens more. Specifically, investigators explored what the Departments of Defense and Justice knew about the shooter, U.S. Army major and psychiatrist Nidal Malik Hassan, and whether

---

[9] Bennett Roth, "Democrats Split on Interrogation Inquiry," CQ Weekly, April 27, 2009, 978; Bennet Roth, "House Adopts Package of Rule Changes," CQ Weekly, January 12, 2009, 75–76.

TABLE 6.1: Summary of Major Investigations of Obama Administration, 2009–2014

111th Congress	112th and 113th Congresses
BP oil spill	"Fast and Furious" ATF gun operation
NHTSA and Toyota recall	Solyndra bankruptcy
Fort Hood shooting	Benghazi consulate attack
	IRS scandal
	Libya and violations of WPR
	VA scandal
	Sebelius and Enroll America
	EPA investigations
	Rewriting drilling moratorium report
	AP phone records
	FDA and meningitis outbreak
	Fort Hood shooting

the massacre could have been prevented. Ultimately, the inquiry concluded that the DOD and FBI had ample evidence concerning the radicalization of Major Hassan. For example, while stationed at Walter Reed Army Medical Center, Hassan had openly stated that he believed suicide bombings were justified, American military operations in Iraq and Afghanistan were unjust, and that his duty to Islam superseded his oath of allegiance to the United States military. However, neither the Pentagon nor the FBI acted on this information.[10] While critical of the FBI and its Joint Terrorism Task Force, the committee report was careful to avoid political overtones and did not single out any high-ranking official in the Obama administration for blame.[11]

[10] See Brian Friel, "In GOP Congress, Gavels Gone Wild," CQ Weekly, October 18, 2010, 2374–76; "A Ticking Time Bomb: Counterterrorism Lessons From the U.S. Government's Failure to Prevent the Fort Hood Attack," United States Senate Committee on Homeland Security and Governmental Affairs, February 3, 2011.

[11] Indeed, during the investigation's early days President Obama irritated Lieberman and Collins by publicly warning investigators not to allow the inquiry to devolve into "political theater." While Lieberman and Collins insisted that their investigation was necessary and required executive-branch cooperation, they pledged to be fair and apolitical: "We totally agree with the president that this inquiry must not turn into 'political theater' and it will not." "Fort Hood Probes," The Hill, November 17, 2009, http://thehill.com/opinion/editorials/68013-fort-hood-probes, accessed May 10, 2016. See also "A Ticking Time Bomb: Counterterrorism Lessons from the U.S. Government's Failure to Prevent the Fort Hood Attack," A Special Report by Joseph I. Lieberman, Chairman, Susan M. Collins, Ranking Member, U.S. Senate Committee on Homeland Security and Governmental Affairs, February 3, 2011.

A second investigation assessed the National Highway Traffic Safety Administration's (NHTSA) response to the sudden acceleration problems experienced by Toyota that led to the recall of approximately 8 million cars in 2009–2010. A decade earlier, following the revelation that defective Firestone tires installed on Ford vehicles had led to the deaths of more than 100 people and injuries to hundreds more, Congress had passed legislation granting the NHTSA greater powers over automakers to prevent similar disasters from occurring. The similarities between the Toyota and Firestone scenarios led many in Congress to charge that the NHTSA had failed to act aggressively enough to prevent the Toyota problems from becoming a significant threat to public safety. Some lawmakers alleged that the agency may have grown too close to the industries it was charged with regulating. Secretary of Transportation Ray LaHood countered that NHTSA action had led to the widespread recall, and reiterated the Department's commitment to holding Toyota to account.[12] While both the Fort Hood and the NHTSA inquiries examined potential wrongdoing—primarily an alleged lack of action within the executive branch—neither of these investigations appear designed to inflict serious political damage on the administration.

The biggest and most intensive investigation during the 111th Congress was into the explosion of a BP-leased oil rig, Deepwater Horizon. The massive resulting oil leak became one of the greatest manmade ecological disasters in American history. While congressional investigators focused much scrutiny on the culpability of BP for the disaster, they also examined the role played by the Department of the Interior and whether mismanagement and negligence contributed to the disaster. We will discuss this case in more detail shortly with a particular emphasis on its policy influence, or lack thereof. However, in terms of characterizing investigative activity in the 111th Congress writ large, with Democrats in firm control of the committee gavels, the BP investigation was not primarily designed to inflict political damage on the White House. To be sure, there was some political sniping with Democrats pointing fingers at the Bush administration for its lax regulatory regime and Republicans emphasizing that the disaster unfolded on Obama's watch with final permits approved by the new administration. However, the main objective of the Democrats leading the investigation was to build political support for a stricter regulatory regime, a goal that was actually supported by the Obama administration.

In sum, consistent with the larger patterns observed in Chapter 2, unified government produced relatively little investigative activity during the first two years of the Obama administration. Moreover, the major investigations

[12] Kathyrn Wolfe, "What Did NHTSA Know, and When?" *CQ Weekly*, February 22, 201, 422–424.

that did occur were all responses to external events (i.e., the Toyota recall; BP oil spill; and Fort Hood shootings) and the investigations of NHTSA and the Department of the Interior focused on strengthening the federal regulatory regime, a goal that the Obama administration largely shared.

Sensing a Republican victory in the 2010 midterms, Congress-watchers anticipated a major increase in congressional scrutiny of the executive branch. In an October 2010 article provocatively titled "In GOP Congress, Gavels Gone Wild," *Congressional Quarterly* predicted that investigative activity would increase substantially if Republicans succeeded in capturing control of the House. "After two years of unified Democratic control of both the White House and the Capitol, there's plenty of pent-up demand among Republicans who have an interest in a robust congressional watch-dog role."[13]

As the second column of Table 6.1 makes clear, these predictions proved prescient. *Congressional Quarterly* coverage mentioned twelve investigations of the executive branch during the 112th and 113th Congresses.[14] Investigative activity after the Republican takeover of the House easily outpaced that observed in the Democratically controlled 111th Congress. Qualitatively, the investigations launched in the 112th and 113th Congresses also differed dramatically from those begun under unified government in 2009 and 2010. Whereas all three major investigations under unified government were begun in response to actions that took place outside of the administration and examined whether the government could have been more proactive in preventing unfortunate events, virtually all of the divided government inquiries, which were spearheaded by the Republican-led House, focused squarely on alleged abuses by the Obama administration itself.

Four of the investigations in Table 6.1 stand out as the most intensive: the Bureau of Alcohol, Tobacco, Firearms and Explosives' (ATF) failed gun-tracking program, "Operation Fast and Furious"; the Solyndra bankruptcy; the IRS scandal; and the attack on the American consulate in Benghazi. Each investigation spanned many months if not years, and each represented a sustained effort by the administration's adversaries on Capitol Hill to inflict political damage on the White House.

"Fast and Furious" became the first major investigation of the Obama administration after the Republicans gained control of the House in the 112th Congress. What made the investigation unusual is that Republican criticism of ATF normally centered on allegations by the National Rifle Association that the agency was being too aggressive and infringing on the

[13] Brian Friel, "In GOP Congress, Gavels Gone Wild," CQ *Weekly*, October 18, 2010, 2374–2376.

[14] The investigation into the Fort Hood shooting continued into the 112th Congress, and its final report was issued in 2011. As a result, it is included in both columns of Table 6.1.

rights of gun owners. In this case, however, investigators charged that the ATF had failed to be vigilant enough in the conduct of its duties. Congressional investigators led by House Oversight and Government Reform chair Darrell Issa (R-CA) took aim at a bungled ATF program to track down Mexican cartels illegally acquiring assault rifles in the United States. In 2009, ATF directed gun retailers in Phoenix, Arizona, to sell guns to "straw purchasers," whom ATF believed were buying the guns for Mexican cartels. ATF then planned to track these guns to identify the cartels and the web of individuals that made up its supply chain. ATF commenced the operation over the strenuous objections of many senior agents who warned of the risks of assault rifles ending up in the hands of the ultraviolent cartels. ATF lost track of many of the guns, and several were recovered at crime scenes in both the United States and Mexico. Most notoriously, two of the guns were found at the crime scene where a U.S. Border Patrol Agent was shot in Arizona in December 2010.[15] In addition to accusing the ATF of extreme misconduct, Republicans focused their attacks on Attorney General Eric Holder, blaming him both for allowing the dangerous operation to take place and for withholding information about an internal Department of Justice probe into the bungled operation.[16] The House investigation spanned sixteen full months.[17]

Republican investigators proved more interested in exploiting "Fast and Furious" for political gain, however, than in using it to tighten federal laws against "straw purchasing." Only a single Senate Judiciary Committee Republican, Charles Grassley of Iowa, voted in favor of a measure to tighten gun-trafficking laws that arose in response to the Democratically controlled Senate panel's more limited "Fast and Furious" investigation.[18] In the House, Chairman Issa also broke from Grassley and argued that "Fast and Furious" was a result of the Obama administration's failure to enforce and abide by existing law; new statutes were not required. Inflicting political pain, not effecting policy change, was the primary goal of investigators.

The next major scandal to attract significant congressional scrutiny was the Solyndra bankruptcy. As discussed in Chapter 4, the Solyndra investigation

[15] Seth Stern, "Under the Gun, ATF's Weakness Exposed," CQ Weekly, July 4, 2011, 1425–1427.

[16] John Gramlich, "'Fast and Furious' Report Doesn't End Wrangling," CQ Weekly, September 24, 2012, 1940–1941.

[17] Holder first testified before Issa's committee on May 4, 2011. On September 20, 2012, Issa's committee held a final hearing to review the Inspector General's report on the bungled operation.

[18] "When I conducted my oversight of the Justice Department's failed Operation 'Fast and Furious,' I was told by whistleblowers that there were gaps in federal laws concerning straw purchases which should be addressed, and this is our opportunity to do it." Cristina Marcos, "Still Furious but Not So Fast," CQ Weekly, March 18, 2013, 480.

involved a series of congressional hearings into the propriety of the Obama administration awarding more than a half billion dollars in loan guarantees to the start-up solar panel manufacturer under a program created by the 2009 stimulus bill. The House Committee on Energy and Commerce held one of its first investigative hearings into the Solyndra loan in June of 2011. That hearing focused on the role played by the Office of Management and Budget in reviewing the loan and approving its restructuring, despite considerable evidence of financial problems at Solyndra; investigators also attacked OMB for failing to provide requested documentation specifying its role in the process.[19] The pace of the investigation accelerated significantly with a flurry of hearings following Solyndra's bankruptcy filing in September of 2011. In an effort to keep Solyndra in the public eye into the upcoming presidential election year, the House continued to a hold a number of hearings throughout 2012 repeating allegations of wrongdoing by Obama administration officials.[20]

The roots of the IRS scandal reach back to March 2012 when Douglas Shulman, who was then the Internal Revenue Service (IRS) commissioner, testified before the House Ways and Means Committee that the IRS was not targeting Tea Party and other conservative groups for additional scrutiny in determining whether they met the criteria for tax-exempt status.[21] A year later in May 2013 it was revealed that the IRS, in direct contradiction of Shulman's testimony, had improperly targeted conservative groups for additional scrutiny since 2011.[22] The revelations renewed the Ways and Means inquiry into IRS targeting, and prompted a new investigation by Issa's House Committee on Oversight and Government Reform. In addition to hammering the IRS, investigators probed for evidence that the White House knew of and colluded in the targeting program. The new IRS commissioner (Shulman had resigned in fall 2012), Lois Lerner, publicly asserted her Fifth Amendment right against self-incrimination during her testimony, and eventually resigned in September 2013 after an internal review board recommended her removal for "neglect of duties."[23] Lerner's resignation did not end the matter. Indeed, almost a full year later the House Committee on

---

[19] "OMB's Role in the DOE Loan Guarantee Process," June 24, 2011. Committee on Energy and Commerce Serial No. 112–68.

[20] Some of these hearings focused on legislative initiatives, such as the No More Solyndras Act, discussed in Chapter 4, which rehashed the main themes of the investigation.

[21] "Internal Revenue Service Operations and the 2012 Tax Return Filing Season," March 22, 2012, Committee on Ways and Means Serial No. 112-OS10, p. 93.

[22] John McKinnon and Siobhan Hughes, "Wider Problems Found at IRS: Probe Says Tax Agency Used Sweeping Criteria to Scrutinize Conservative Groups," Wall Street Journal, May 12, 2013, http://www.wsj.com/news/articles/SB10001424127887324715704578478851998004528, accessed May 10, 2016.

[23] Josh Hicks, "Central IRS Figure in Tea Party Scandal Resigns," Washington Post, September 24, 2013, A15.

Oversight and Government Reform was still holding hearings on Lerner's missing emails and the targeting scandal.[24]

Perhaps the most high-profile probe, the investigation into alleged administration misconduct concerning the September 11, 2012, attacks on the American consulate in Benghazi, Libya, began almost immediately after the deadly assault. It resumed and even intensified following President Obama's reelection as the focus of investigators shifted to Secretary of State Hillary Clinton. And a new House select committee was created in spring 2014 to continue the inquest, presumably as far into the 2016 presidential election cycle as possible. We discuss this case in greater detail, both later in this chapter and in the concluding chapter.

Finally, it bears repeating that these four investigations, while the most highly salient, were far from the sum total of the investigative actions that attracted media scrutiny in the 112th and 113th Congresses. *Congressional Quarterly* identified eight other investigations during this period. Two of these investigations directly targeted high-profile members of President Obama's cabinet, including Department of Health and Human Services Secretary Kathleen Sebelius and Secretary of Veterans Affairs Eric Shinseki, who eventually was forced to resign.[25] President Obama himself came under fire for intervening militarily in Libya without congressional authorization.[26] Investigators also challenged Obama's efforts to change domestic policy unilaterally particularly concerning the environment.[27]

The contrast between Congress's relative quiescence on the investigative front in the 111th Congress and the aggressiveness with which it investigated

---

[24] "IRS Targeting Scandal: Changing Stories of Missing Emails," September 17, 2014, H60–20140917–02.

[25] On Sebelius, see Eliza Newlin Carney, "Sebelius' Sales Job Leads to Hot Seat," *CQ Weekly*, June 3, 2013, 922–923. On Shinseki, see Shawn Zeller, "Hands-Off Presidency Bottoms Out," *CQ Weekly*, August 4, 2014, 1094–1097.

[26] Jonathan Broder and Seth Stern, "Obama Faces Criticism Over War Powers Resolution Interpretation," *CQ Weekly*, June 27, 2011, 1368–1369; "War Powers, United States Operations in Libya, and Related Legislation," House Committee on Foreign Affairs, May 25, 2011, Serial No. 112–38; "Libya and War Powers," Senate Foreign Relations Committee, June 28, 2011, S. Hrg. 112–819.

[27] "Is EPA Leadership Obstructing Its Own Inspector General?" May 7, 2014, Committee on Oversight and Government Reform Serial No. 113–124. Shawn Zeller, "GOP Claims EPA Gave TMI Under FOIA," *CQ Weekly*, April 15, 2013, 656; "Committee Oversight of Department of the Interior: Questioning of Key Department of the Interior Officials," September 13, 2012, Committee on Natural Resources Serial No. 112–129; Margaret Hobson, "White House Adviser Out of Energy," *CQ Weekly*, January 31, 2011, 244–245. For *CQ* mentions of the FDA inquiry and the investigation into the Department of Justice's role in securing the phone records of AP reporters, see Emily Ethridge, "FDA Under the Microscope," *CQ Weekly*, October 22, 2012, 2082–2084; Frank Oliveri and Kerry Young, "Stuck on Sequester," *CQ Weekly*, June 3, 2013, 926–931.

the Obama administration in the 112th and 113th Congresses underscores the paramount importance of partisan incentives in driving investigative activity during polarized political periods. However, while Republicans controlled the House from 2011 through 2014, Democrats retained control of the Senate. Given the historical responsiveness of House investigative activity to party control, we expect that the lower chamber likely played a disproportionate role in driving investigative activity in the 112th and 113th Congresses.[28]

To examine this possibility, we identified the number of hearings held by both the House and Senate for each investigation receiving coverage in *Congressional Quarterly* from 2009 to 2014.[29] Table 6.2 summarizes the data.

During the Democratically controlled 111th Congress, the House and Senate both pursued each of the three major investigations with roughly equal levels of intensity. In each case, the House held more hearings than the Senate; however, in no case was the difference across chambers large. On the whole, the Senate held thirty-one hearings (44% of the total) as part of these investigations, as compared to forty in the House.

By contrast, the Republican-led House pursued investigations much more aggressively than did the Democratically controlled Senate in the 112th and 113th Congresses. Indeed, several of these investigations—Solyndra, the IRS scandal, Secretary Sebelius's ties with Enroll America, and investigations into various issues at the EPA—were almost exclusively House affairs. Other investigations, such as the probe into the Benghazi attacks, were actively pursued by both the House and Senate. The security lapses that permitted the shocking assassination of the American ambassador to Libya all but demanded an inquest by both chambers. Indeed, the Democratically

---

[28] The data through 2014 do not allow us to assess whether partisanship continues to matter less in the Senate than in the House (since there is no variation in Senate party control from 2009–2014), but the data for this period do allow us to assess whether partisanship matters in the House, with the Democratic Senate offering a useful baseline for comparison.

[29] To identify these hearings, we conducted a series of key word searches using ProQuest's database of congressional hearings. We included in our tallies any hearing that contained the search terms: "Deepwater Horizon"; "Toyota AND NHTSA"; "Fort Hood"; "Solyndra"; "Fast and Furious"; "Benghazi"; "IRS AND conservative"; "Libya AND war powers"; "VA AND wait AND manipulation (the latter term anywhere including in full text)"; "FDA AND meningitis"; "Enroll America"; "drilling moratorium"; "AP AND telephone"; "Fort Hood" in all fields except full text during the relevant time periods. Because the EPA investigations were multifaceted, including charges of obstructing OIG (Office of Inspector General) investigations, improper regulatory activities, and failures of transparency and accountability, to construct a tally we searched for all hearings including "EPA" and then went through the returned hits one by one to identify those dealing with a charge of abuse or wrongdoing. Employing more restrictive searches for several of the investigations (for example, requiring a hearing to mention White House Energy Czar Carol Browner in the summary) also yields similar results, confirming the lead role played by the GOP House in the 112th and 113th Congresses.

TABLE 6.2: Relative Investigative Activity in House and Senate

	House	Senate
111th Congress		
BP oil spill	31	26
NHTSA and Toyota recall	4	2
Fort Hood shooting	5	3
Cumulative Percentage	*56%*	*44%*
112th and 113th Congresses		
Fast and Furious	7	2
Solyndra	11	0
Benghazi	15	9
IRS scandal	27	2
Libya and violations of WPR	2	2
VA scandal	6	0
Sebelius and Enroll America	12	1
EPA investigations	12	2
Rewriting drilling moratorium report	7	1
AP phone records	1	0
FDA and meningitis outbreak	4	1
Fort Hood shooting	3	1
Cumulative Percentage	*84%*	*16%*

Note: In the 111th Congress, Democrats controlled both chambers. In the 112th and 113th Congresses, Republicans controlled the House while Democrats controlled the Senate.

controlled Senate held nine hearings on the administration's handling of Benghazi. However, the House has already held fifteen hearings into Benghazi with more promised in the future under the aegis of the House's new select committee to continue investigating the attack. Across the twelve investigations from the 112th and 113th Congresses, the Democratic Senate held just 21 hearings (16% of the total), as compared to 107 hearings in the GOP-controlled House. The contrast between the dramatic change in the House and the relative stability in the Senate gives greater confidence in attributing the increase in investigations to partisan forces, rather than to changes in the Obama administration's behavior.

The intense partisan polarization of the contemporary era has not undermined Congress's capacity to use the investigative arm of its committees to cause political headaches for the executive branch. Rather, in periods of divided government recent Congresses have aggressively used this power to launch a number of high-profile investigations of alleged wrongdoing by the Obama administration. The twelve major investigations conducted between the return of a GOP-led House in the 112th Congress and the 2014 midterms represent a vigorous campaign of sustained investigative oversight.

The aggressive investigation of multiple instances of alleged abuse and misconduct during the Obama years stands in stark contrast to the relative lull in investigative activity observed in the late 1980s and early 1990s.[30] This flare-up of investigative activity in the first four years of divided government under President Obama shows unequivocally that investigations remain an important tool through which legislators seek to impose political costs on the president.

INVESTIGATIVE INFLUENCE IN A POLARIZED POLITY

A vast literature in political science has explored how increasing partisan polarization has fostered gridlock, stalling efforts to secure major legislative change. There are strong reasons to expect that these developments have also altered Congress's capacity to effect policy change through investigations, and consequently how members approach investigations in the contemporary era.

In Chapter 4, we explored two pathways through which investigations could directly bring about significant changes in policy. First, by raising the salience of an issue and generating public demand for action, investigations may help would-be reformers in Congress overcome collective action dilemmas and build the large coalitions across chambers necessary to pass new legislation. Second, presidents may seek to preempt looming congressional action by unilaterally making policy concessions. In a diverse range of cases, from the Truman Committee in the 1940s through the EPA investigations of the early 1980s, we saw congressional investigations producing significant policy change through both the legislative and preemptive pathways.

Increasing levels of partisan polarization, however, make it less likely that an investigation will be able to spur significant policy change through either of these direct pathways. Only investigations that generate very strong public demands for action will be able to encourage lawmakers to bridge the

---

[30] We suspect that if many of these Obama-era scandals had occurred in the 1990s, congressional opponents of the administration would have demanded the appointment of a special prosecutor to investigate alleged administration misconduct. Without the option to request a special prosecutor to do most of the legwork and publicizing of the scandal for them, House Republicans in the 112th and 113th Congresses led the investigative charge themselves.

ideological chasm between the parties. Instead, most investigations will fail to generate sufficient pressure for a legislative response to make it to the president's desk, let alone survive a presidential veto. Moreover, because polarization exacerbates these barriers to legislative action on Capitol Hill, presidents have weaker incentives to change policy unilaterally to preempt congressional action—action that they know is unlikely to be forthcoming.

This does not, however, mean that investigations are of little political consequence in the contemporary era. Rather, particularly in divided government, it suggests that opposition legislators should logically seek to influence politics and policy more indirectly by crafting investigations designed to inflict political costs on the incumbent administration. A primary objective of such a strategy is to secure electoral benefits. By eroding the president's base of popular support, the congressional opposition may bolster its own electoral fortunes in midterm elections as well as the prospects for securing election of their party's standard bearer in the next presidential contest. Yet, investigations crafted to pursue a negative objective (as opposed to a positive one of building support for legislative change) may still yield policy benefits in certain conditions. Besieged by congressional investigations, presidents may in some cases change their policy course in the hopes of minimizing the political costs they will incur from continued or future investigations, even if they know Congress will be unable to assemble the supermajorities needed to compel a legislative change. More broadly, as discussed in Chapter 5, the political costs investigations generate can also inform presidential anticipations about future congressional reactions should they push policy far from congressional preferences. As a result, even if investigations are less likely to spur legislation in an intensely polarized era, they can continue to have major political and policy ramifications.

To examine these arguments, we consider a pair of investigations from Table 6.1 in greater detail. The investigation into the Deepwater Horizon disaster was the most important investigation begun during a period of unified government in the 111th Congress, and it spurred a number of legislative efforts to tighten the regulatory regime on offshore drilling. Because Democrats controlled the gavels, its main purpose was not to inflict partisan political damage on the Obama administration. Rather, investigators clearly tried to rally public opinion to build pressure for environmental regulatory reforms that would not have passed in the absence of the accident. Exploring how this investigation unfolded and why the legislative efforts that stemmed from the investigation failed, even when they were backed by the administration, provides important insight into limitations on the capacity of an investigation to effect change directly in the contemporary era, even in a favorable political climate.

The second case examines the still ongoing investigation into the administration's role in the attacks on the American consulate in Benghazi. This investigation, pursued most aggressively by the Republican House, has not endeavored to spur policy changes directly through the pathways described in Chapter 4. Rather, its main objective has been to generate political advantage for congressional Republicans and impose political costs on the Obama administration through indirect means in a manner similar to that described in Chapter 5. The Benghazi investigation failed to pay political dividends at the polls in 2012 as President Obama secured reelection. However, by shifting the focus of the investigation to Secretary of State Hillary Clinton, Republican investigators appear to be seeking to weaken the presumptive Democratic front-runner for 2016.

Deepwater Horizon

On April 20, 2010, an explosion shook the Deepwater Horizon oil rig operating about forty miles off the coast of Louisiana. Eleven crewmembers were killed in the blast, and an additional fifteen were wounded. Two days later, the rig sank, and shortly thereafter a large oil slick appeared as oil gushed from the ruptured riser pipe. The leak continued for eighty-seven days until the well was finally capped on July 15, 2010. In all, 4.1 million barrels of oil leaked into the Gulf, making the Deepwater Horizon disaster by far the largest oil spill in American history.

As images of the ecological devastation filled the airwaves, President Obama issued an executive order on May 21 to create a bipartisan commission chaired by former Democratic senator Bob Graham and former EPA director William Reilly (1989–1993) to investigate the disaster and develop policy recommendations to prevent such spills in the future. Congress also responded aggressively to the disaster, with no fewer than six committees, four in the House and two in the Senate, holding hearings.[31]

Congressional investigators reserved most of their animus for the oil industry, including Transocean, Ltd., which built the rig; British Petroleum, which operated it in the Macondo Prospect; and Vice President Cheney's former employer, Haliburton, which only twenty-four hours before the disaster had completed some cement casings that were supposed to have sealed the well temporarily until BP returned to commercially develop the deposit in the future. Repeatedly, top industry executives were hauled before committee members for a public grilling. Investigators landed a number of damaging blows against BP in particular. For example, Henry Waxman's (D-CA) House Energy and Commerce Committee learned that BP possessed underwater robotic cameras on the site. Waxman successfully demanded that BP make public the images of oil plumes shooting forth into the waters

---

[31] See Light 2014, 247.

of the Gulf, which only further rallied public opinion against BP. By analyzing more than 170,000 documents obtained from BP and its contractors, the
Waxman Committee identified a number of key mistakes made by BP both
leading up to the disaster and in its aftermath.[32]

Even as they kept the pressure on the oil industry, congressional investigators also examined the role of the executive branch in allowing the disaster to occur. The main targets of the investigation were the Department of
the Interior and the Minerals Management Service (MMS). The lede for a
Christian Science Monitor article on the congressional inquiry emphasized
the provocative questions motivating the hearings: "Was the government
adequately monitoring the drilling by the Deepwater Horizon? Is the government too cozy with the industry it is regulating?" The initial focus of
congressional investigators was on the failures of the MMS. Massachusetts
Democrat Ed Markey was scathing in his critique of the agency: "MMS used
to stand for Minerals Management Service. Now it stands for misconduct,
mismanagement and spills." Critical members also highlighted the contents
of an Inspector General investigation into the MMS, which revealed ethical
lapses involving MMS officials receiving gifts, lavish dinners, and sporting
event tickets from industry contacts.[33]

Senate investigators were equally harsh in their allegations that misconduct at MMS helped create the climate that made Deepwater Horizon possible. In a Senate Appropriations Committee hearing, California Democrat
Diane Feinstein charged, "Ultimately, at virtually every juncture leading up
to the Deepwater Horizon explosion and fire, the MMS failed in its duty."[34]

Investigators uncovered evidence that on at least four separate occasions,
MMS had received warnings about problems with blowout preventers,
which were designed to shut off a well in the event of a major accident.[35]
One of the most shocking revelations uncovered at a House Committee
on Natural Resources Hearing involved unseemly collusion between MMS
and the industries it was supposed to regulate. As the committee's chair
Nick Rahall (D-WV) lamented, "To now learn that certain agency personnel allowed industry to fill out their inspection reports in pencil with MMS
inspectors then writing on top of the pencil in ink prior to turning in their
reports is truly reprehensible."[36]

[32] Alan Ota, "Black Gold for a Veteran Inquisitor," *CQ Weekly*, June 7, 2010, 1392–1393.
[33] Ron Scherer, "BP Gulf Oil Spill: Congress Zeroes in on Federal Oversight," *Christian Science Monitor*, May 27, 2010.
[34] "Minerals Management Service Reorganization," Hearing before a Subcommittee of the Committee on Appropriations, United States Senate, May 26, 2010, S. Hrg. 111–1035.
[35] Mark Clayton, "Studies Suggest MMS Knew Blowout Preventers Had 'Critical' Flaws," *Christian Science Monitor*, June 17, 2010.
[36] "Outer Continental Shelf Oil and Gas Strategy and Implications of the Deepwater Hori-zon Rig Explosion: Parts 1 and 2," Committee on Natural Resources, U.S. House of Represen-tatives, May 26–27, 2010. Serial No. 111–54, p. 2.

As the investigations progressed, the largely bipartisan criticism of MMS disappeared and stark partisan splits emerged over the role played by the Department of the Interior in contributing to the ecological disaster. While congressional Democrats blamed both the Obama and Bush administrations for lapses, unsurprisingly they placed considerable emphasis on the loosening of environmental regulations on oil drilling during the Bush years. In a House Energy and Commerce Committee hearing into the Interior Department's role in the tragedy, Ed Markey charged that the disaster was a direct product of reckless deregulation under Bush. Markey hearkened back to Vice President Cheney's secret energy task force, which set the stage for a deregulatory flurry in the years to follow. He recounted how the Bush administration issued sweetheart royalty deals to companies to increase offshore oil production, and when these proved insufficient, slashed the environmental planning and impact requirements from drilling applications and plans. "On April 20, 2010," Markey charged, "the regulatory house of cards erected over an eight year period by the Bush/Cheney administration collapsed with the explosion of the BP Deepwater Horizon rig."[37] Other Democrats echoed Markey's sentiment, but acknowledged that both Bush and Obama shared responsibility for the disaster. For example, Henry Waxman leveled criticism at both presidents: "Today we are going to examine the role of the regulators. We will learn that the DOI under both President Bush and President Obama made serious mistakes. The cop on the beat was off duty for nearly a decade, and this gave rise to a dangerous culture of permissiveness."[38] While Waxman agreed that the initial failures began under Bush, he also acknowledged that Secretary Salazar "oversaw the deeply flawed assessment of potential environmental impacts associated with this lease sale, an assessment that did not anticipate the possibility or impacts of a catastrophic sub-sea blowout."[39] The remedy was clear: congressional action to redress these regulatory failures by stiffening statutory requirements.

Committee Republicans, by contrast, wasted little time in attempting to absolve the Bush administration from all responsibility for the disaster and instead to place the blame for it squarely at the feet of Obama. Moreover, Republicans vociferously rejected Democratic diagnoses that the disaster was a clarion call for more regulation. Rather, they argued that the problem

[37] "The Role of the Interior Department in The Deepwater Horizon Disaster," Joint Hearing Before the Subcommittee on Oversight and Investigations and the Subcommittee on Energy and Environment of the Committee on Energy and Commerce, House of Representatives, July 20, 2010, Serial No. 111-145, pp. 15–16.

[38] Ibid., 18.

[39] Ibid. Subcommittee on Oversight and Investigations chairman Bart Stupak (D-MI) similarly acknowledged that blame was shared by officials in both administrations. For example, after recounting failures at Interior in the Bush administration, Stupak described some helpful changes implemented by Salazar and Obama. However, these changes were "more cosmetic than substantive." Ibid., 2–3.

could be fixed solely by properly enforcing regulations already on the books. The ranking minority member, Michael Burgess of Texas, claimed that the Democratic charges were a sham: "The majority tries to trace the Deepwater Horizon back to the Bush administration, and has technical regulatory issues in his hearing memo to imply that the blowup protector and cementing problems can be traced to that administration. But the majority knows all available evidence suggests the disaster resulted from the failure to follow existing regulations and best industry practices, not that George W. Bush prevented a second set of shear arms." After citing two widows of the disaster who said that better compliance with existing regulations, not the enactment of new ones would have prevented the accident, Burgess reminded the committee that the Obama administration had approved the latest BP plan. "The fact remains it was under Secretary Salazar that BP's initial exploration plan was reviewed and approved by the Minerals Management Service. It was under this administration that BP's permit to drill the well was granted, and all the inspections of the operation and procedures were approved leading up to the explosion."[40]

Republicans also blamed Obama for failing to approve a number of steps that might have mitigated the environmental costs of the spill. Joe Barton (R-TX) used his time to detail a litany of alleged Obama administration missteps:

> It was the Obama Administration, not the Bush Administration, that didn't waive the Jones Act so that some of our foreign friends could bring in their oil spill equipment. It was the Obama Administration, not the Bush Administration, that wouldn't waive certain environmental impact studies so that our friends in LA and MA and AL could put up some berms that could have prevented the oil from reaching their beaches. It was the Obama Administration, not the Bush Administration, that made the decision not to transfer pre-position equipment in other parts of the country for oil spills to the Gulf of Mexico to help in this spill.[41]

At the investigation's outset, the prospects for significant legislation to tighten restrictions on drilling looked bright amidst the public outcry in the wake of the spill. In May 2009, BP chairman Carl-Henric Svanberg warned "it will be, in many ways, a game-change in the way that Three Mile Island was."[42] Public concern seemed to all but demand legislative action; indeed, a pair of public opinion polls taken two months after the explosion showed roughly two-thirds of Americans supporting greater federal regulation of

[40] Ibid., 7.
[41] Ibid., 222.
[42] John Cranford, "Oil, Water, Profit, and Peril," *CQ Weekly*, June 7, 2010, 1388.

offshore drilling.[43] A significant impediment to legislative efforts, however, was timing. With the 2010 midterm elections approaching and Republicans' prospects for picking up seats and even taking back control of the House appearing bright, the GOP showed little interest in compromising on legislation to address the crisis. Equally important, a handful of Democrats from oil-producing states also balked at new regulations that might damage the local economy. As the investigation itself turned increasingly partisan, the prospects for major legislative action dimmed even further.

Ultimately, Congress introduced more than 150 legislative proposals related to the oil spill. Only three relatively minor initiatives, two of which were exceedingly short term, were enacted into law.[44] House Speaker Nancy Pelosi did succeed in rallying her troops to pass a comprehensive overhaul. The House bill mandated the restructuring of MMS; eliminated the $75 million cap on corporate liability for economic damages produced by a spill; and imposed additional safety requirements on the oil industry. Despite laborious negotiations with House Republicans, only two crossed party lines and voted for the bill.[45] The measure gained no traction in the Senate. Instead, Majority Leader Harry Reid tried on several occasions to move a weaker bill to the floor for a vote; however, he repeatedly failed to secure the sixty votes needed to break a Republican filibuster. Republican unity and Democrats' divisions doomed comprehensive reform to defeat. A series of other bills that were more limited in scope—including measures to increase criminal penalties for violations of the Clean Water Act; to lift the liability cap; to impose new safety requirements on offshore drilling; and to amend an ultra-deep-water drilling research program to focus primarily on safety concerns—also failed to reach the Senate floor for a vote.[46]

---

[43] Survey by Cable News Network. Methodology: Conducted by Opinion Research Corporation on June 16, 2010 and based on 534 telephone interviews. Sample: National adult. [USORC.061810A.R25D]; Survey by NBC News, *Wall Street Journal*. Methodology: Conducted by Hart and McInturff Research Companies, June 17–June 21, 2010 and based on 1,000 telephone interviews. Sample: National adult. The sample included 200 respondents who use a cell phone only. [USNBCWSJ.10JUN.R27A]

[44] Jonathan L. Ramseur and Curry L. Hagerty, "Deepwater Horizon Oil Spill: Recent Activities and Ongoing Developments," *CRS Report*, May 12, 2014, R42942. The only modestly important changes were included in the Coast Guard Authorization Act for Fiscal Years 2010 and 2011.

[45] Margaret Kriz Hobson, "2010 Legislative Summary: Oil Spill Response," *CQ Weekly*, December 27, 2010, 2923.

[46] The comprehensive overhaul passed by the House was H.R. 3534. Reid's weaker alternative, which failed to survive a filibuster, was S. 3663. More limited Senate bills related to the BP scandal included S. 3446, S. 3472, S. 3516, and S.3509. See Geof Koss, "Legislative Response to Spill Takes Shape," *CQ Weekly*, July 5, 2010, 1364; Geof Koss and Jennifer Scholtes, "Oil Legislation Spills Over Into Fall," *CQ Weekly*, August 2, 2010, 1868; Geof Koss, "Fall 2009 Outlook: Oil Spill Response," *CQ Weekly*, September 13, 2010, 2098.

The Republican-controlled 112th Congress followed up with additional modest legislation relating to oil spills. The RESTORE Act of 2012 mandated that 80% of Clean Water Act penalties be put into a fund for economic and environmental restoration in Gulf Coast states. In 2012, Congress also passed and President Obama signed a bill relating to pipeline safety. However, these modest successes paled in comparison to the major changes envisioned in 2010, and they did little to change the laws governing offshore drilling.[47]

While the investigations had limited influence in terms of promoting legislative remedies, they did help generate pressure on the White House that produced two administrative shifts. The first, focusing on the immediate response to the spill itself, had a significant, but ultimately short-term influence on policy. Congressional Democrats held multiple hearings on the use of highly toxic chemical dispersants by BP to break up the spill. Although BP maintained that the dispersants were safe, Democrats pushed aggressively to limit their use. In the face of considerable congressional pressure, the EPA on May 26, 2010, told BP to stop using surface dispersants except in "rare cases," and they significantly scaled back the maximum allowance for usage by 75%. When investigators learned that the Coast Guard was approving the usage of dispersants on an almost daily basis, not in rare circumstances, they pushed back and demanded greater enforcement of the EPA order restricting the use of dispersants.[48]

Second, scathing congressional investigations of misconduct and mismanagement at MMS encouraged Secretary of the Interior Ken Salazar to break up the agency and reorganize it into three separate entities: the Bureau of Safety and Environmental Enforcement, the Bureau of Ocean Energy Management, and the Office of Natural Resources Revenue. Finally, the disaster's aftermath prompted more expeditious and aggressive action by the Department of the Interior to tighten regulations over offshore drilling.[49]

The investigation may thus have had some policy impact by helping to prompt unilateral action within the executive branch. However, this occurred primarily because many in the Obama administration were already sympathetic toward moving regulatory policy in a more pro-environment direction. If Deepwater Horizon had occurred under the Bush administration,

---

[47] Jonathan L. Ramseur and Curry L. Hagerty, "Deepwater Horizon Oil Spill: Recent Activities and Ongoing Developments," *CRS Report*, May 12, 2014.

[48] "Final Staff Report for the 111th Congress," Submitted by Mr. Markey, Chairman, Select Committee on Energy Independence and Global Warming, January 3, 2011, Report 111–709, 53–54.

[49] "Interior Department Completes Reorganization of MMS," Interior Department Press Release, October 1, 2011, http://www.doi.gov/news/pressreleases/Interior-Department-Completes-Reorganization-of-the-Former-MMS.cfm, accessed March 1, 2016.

which was decidedly less receptive to such calls for tightened environmental regulations on energy production, such administrative action might not have been forthcoming given the long odds any legislative action to mandate a change in course would have faced.

The Attack on the American Consulate in Benghazi, Libya

On September 11, 2012, protesters enraged by the media firestorm surrounding an amateur video insulting the Prophet Muhammad, scaled the walls of the American Embassy in Cairo, tore down the Stars and Stripes, and replaced it with the black banner of militant Islam.[50] That same evening, heavily armed militants stormed the American consulate in Benghazi, Libya. An extended firefight reduced the compound to a smoldering ruin and left four Americans dead, including the ambassador to Libya, Christopher Stevens.[51] On September 12, President Obama addressed the nation from the Rose Garden to memorialize the Americans who had given their lives both for their country and to build a new, democratic Libya following the NATO-assisted ouster of Libyan dictator Moammar Gaddhafi. The president's speech, given in a climate of considerable uncertainty about the precise nature of the events that had transpired, was short on details. Instead, the president spoke more generally about American resilience in the face of tragedy: "No acts of terror will ever shake the resolve of this great Nation, alter that character, or eclipse the light of the values that we stand for."[52]

Republican presidential candidate Mitt Romney wasted little time criticizing the administration for its handling of the crisis. Governor Romney initially focused his criticism on a statement issued by the American Embassy in Cairo denouncing the video for inciting religious intolerance. Governor Romney attacked the administration for sending "mixed messages" and "sympathizing with those who waged the attacks." While a number of prominent Republicans initially were reluctant to attack the administration in the immediate aftermath of the tragedy, a growing number of Republican

---

[50] "Mysterious Anti-Muslim Movie Prompts Protest in Egypt," *Associated Press*, September 11, 2012, http://www.nytimes.com/2012/09/12/world/middleeast/movie-stirs-protest-at-us-embassy-in-cairo.html?_r=0, accessed March 1, 2016. Some experts argue that while the attacks were planned in advance, the video was used by its organizers to incite violence and rally supporters. Sara Lynch, Oren Dorell, and David Jackson, "We Hate America," *USA Today*, September 13, 2012, 1A.

[51] David Kirkpatrick and Steven Lee Myers, "Libya Attack Brings Challenges to the U.S.," September 13, 2012, *New York Times*, A1.

[52] Barack Obama, "Remarks on the Attack on the U.S. Mission in Benghazi, Libya," September 12, 2012, in Gerhard Peters and John T. Woolley, The American Presidency Project, http://www.presidency.ucsb.edu/ws/?pid=102024, accessed March 1, 2016.

leaders soon condemned the administration and its "feckless foreign policy" of "appeasement and apology" that allowed the attacks to occur. [53]

To rebut critics' charges, the administration dispatched UN Ambassador Susan Rice to the Sunday morning talk show circuit on September 16 to answer growing questions about what precipitated the attack and about the government's response. Rice asserted that the best intelligence suggested that the assault on the consulate was an unplanned attack arising from the same sense of popular anger that precipitated the nonfatal storming of the American embassy in Egypt. "Our current best assessment," Rice said, "based on the information that we have at present, is that, in fact, what this began as, it was a spontaneous—not a premeditated—response to what had transpired in Cairo."[54]

As discussed in Chapter 3, conservative media wasted little time in vociferously rejecting the Obama administration's assessment of what precipitated the Benghazi attack and in laying blame for the tragedy squarely at the feet of the president. Indeed, many were quick to allege an administration cover-up to prevent public scrutiny of their negligence and failed policies.[55]

With only four weeks to go before Election Day, the House Oversight and Government Reform Committee led by chair Darrell Issa (R-CA) launched the first investigative hearing into the Benghazi attack. The October 10 session set the stage for an investigation that more than three years later is still ongoing. Unlike the Deepwater Horizon investigation in the Democratically controlled 111th Congress, the primary objective of the Benghazi investigation was not building pressure for legislative action. Rather, it was to shine a light on alleged misconduct and negligence by the Obama administration.

Issa and committee Republicans launched a two-pronged assault on the administration. The first focus of the investigation was on the White House's public response to the tragedy, particularly the assertions made by Susan Rice that the attack was a spontaneous reaction to the controversial internet video offensive to Islam that had also triggered the Cairo protests. Republicans charged that the intelligence community had informed the administration within twenty-four hours that Benghazi was a planned terrorist attack. The administration consciously chose to deceive the American people,

[53] Peter Baker and Ashley Parker, "A Challenger's Criticism is Furiously Returned," *New York Times*, September 13, 2012, 1. See also Jonathan Broder, "Old Policies for an Angry Era in the Middle East," *CQ Weekly*, September 24, 2012, 1928–1933.

[54] Jake Tapper, "Ambassador Susan Rice: Libya Attack Not Premeditated," *ABC News*, September 16, 2012, http://abcnews.go.com/blogs/politics/2012/09/ambassador-susan-rice-libya-attack-not-premeditated/, accessed March 1, 2016.

[55] Emily Arrowood and Chelsea Rudman, "Fox Conspiracy Theory: Obama Administration Is Engaged in 'Cover-Up' of Libya Consulate Attacks," September 21, 2012, *Media Matters*, http://mediamatters.org/research/2012/09/21/fox-conspiracy-theory-obama-admin-is-engaged-in/190058, accessed March 1, 2016.

Republicans alleged, in a desperate effort to obscure the larger failure of its Middle East policies and the resurgence of Al Qaeda. On *CBS News' Face the Nation*, Senator Lindsey Graham (R-SC) charged:

> They're trying to sell a narrative, quite frankly, that the Mid East, the wars are receding and al Qaeda has been dismantled, and to admit that our embassy was attacked by al Qaeda operatives and Libya [. . .] leading from behind didn't work I think undercuts that narrative. They never believed that media would investigate. Congress was out of session, and this caught up with them. I think they've been misleading us, but it finally caught up with them.[56]

A second prong of the investigation focused on alleged failures by the State Department to provide adequate security for its diplomatic mission. Worse than mere negligence, Issa's committee heard testimony alleging that the State Department had explicitly rejected requests for additional security at the consulate. State Department security official Eric Nordstrom recounted how, when he asked for twelve additional security agents, he was told that he was asking "for the sun, moon, and stars." In a damning indictment of the State Department, Nordstrom responded, "you know what [is] most frustrating about this assignment? It is not the hardships, not the gunfire, not the threats; it is dealing and fighting against the people, programs and personnel who are supposed to be supporting me."[57]

Committee Democrats rallied behind the administration and pushed back against the charges of wrongdoing. Ranking Minority Member Elijah Cummings noted inconsistencies in Nordstrom's testimony. For example, while Nordstrom opined to the committee that there should have been five diplomatic security agents in Benghazi, the committee learned that there were indeed five agents in the city on the day of the attack. More generally, Cummings launched what would be a common refrain that the committee's work had been transformed into a partisan witch hunt. Issa's claim that the committee was operating on a bipartisan basis "was simply not the case," Cummings argued, and he accused the chair of abusing his power by withholding documents and access to witnesses from Democrats to further his partisan political purposes.[58] The Democrats also pointed to the testimony of other State Department officials asserting that even if a larger security unit had been present in Benghazi that night, it could not have prevented the deadly attack.

[56] Transcript. "Face the Nation." October 14, 2012. http://www.cbsnews.com/news/face-the-nation-transcripts-october-14-2012-sen-graham-rep-issa-rep-cummings/, accessed May 10, 2016.

[57] "The Security Failures of Benghazi," Hearing before the Committee on Oversight and Government Reform, House of Representatives, October 10, 2012, 112–193, 106.

[58] Ibid., 4–5.

The investigation was temporarily put on hold as Congress recessed for the general elections. By the late evening of November 6, it was clear that Republican efforts to use Benghazi to weaken the president had failed; President Obama coasted to a comfortable reelection victory, winning by almost five million votes in the country as a whole and by 126 in the Electoral College.

Undeterred, congressional investigators aggressively resumed their inquest into Benghazi. Between November 13 and 15, three different committees held hearings on the Benghazi attacks with a primary focus on the first prong of Issa's initial inquiry: the truthfulness of White House statements about what led to the attack. The star witness in this second round of hearings was General David Petraeus, who was then director of the Central Intelligence Agency and a hero of the Iraq War. Petraeus informed lawmakers that the CIA had quickly determined that the gunmen who attacked the consulate were extremists linked to Al Qaeda. However, to bolster efforts to identify and apprehend those responsible, the CIA wanted to avoid tipping off the terrorists by making the information public. As a result, the talking points provided to the administration suggested that the attack appeared to be an outgrowth of the spontaneous riots protesting the anti-Islam video that had also triggered the embassy attack in Cairo.[59] Democrats seized on Petraeus's testimony to exculpate the president and Rice. Adam Schiff (D-CA) emphasized that "the general was adamant there was no politicization of the process, no White House interference or political agenda."[60]

Republicans, however, remained unconvinced. For example, Dana Rohrabacher (R-CA) stood by earlier charges of administration deceit: "The president himself has intentionally misinformed—read that, lied—to the American people in the aftermath of this tragedy."[61] Conservative media also continued to press the attack. An editorial in *Investor's Business Daily* went so far as to accuse the Obama administration of blackmailing General Petraeus to give the White House political cover. The paper charged that the White House may have threatened Petraeus with its knowledge of his affair with Paula Broadwell to coerce the general into saying that the CIA had altered the report, thereby absolving Rice.[62]

Although the Petraeus testimony did not end all charges that the administration had misled the public, the main focus of the ongoing investigations

[59] Jonathan Landay, "Petraeus: CIA Secrets Cut from Public Account After US Consulate Attack," November 16, 2012, *McClatchy Tribune News Service*.

[60] Eric Schmitt, "Petraeus Says U.S. Tried to Avoid Tipping Off Terrorists After Libya Attack," *New York Times*, November 17, 2012, 10.

[61] Anne Gearan and William Branigin, "Clinton to Testify Before Congress About Benghazi Attack," November 16, 2012, *Washington Post*, A7.

[62] "Was Petraeus Blackmailed into Echoing Benghazi Lie?" *Investor's Business Daily*, November 19, 2012, A17.

did shift more squarely onto the State Department and who was responsible for the security failures in Benghazi. With President Obama re-elected, this shift had the added bonus of allowing congressional investigators to focus their energies and attacks on a new target: the prospective front-runner for the Democratic presidential nomination in 2016, Secretary of State Hillary Clinton.

Three factors complicated the Republican investigators' efforts to blame the State Department and inflict political damage on Secretary Clinton. First, during recent budget showdowns, Republicans had led the charge for budget cuts—including substantial cuts to the diplomatic security budget. The 2012 fiscal year budget included only $2.1 billion to secure more than 275 diplomatic posts.[63] Indeed, Vice President Biden used this counterattack to considerable effect in his vice-presidential debate with Congressman Paul Ryan, arguing that blaming the administration for security lapses was hypocritical: "This lecture on embassy security—the congressman here cut embassy security in his budget by $300 million below what we asked for, number one. So much for the embassy security piece."[64]

Second, before investigators could ramp up their attacks on security lapses, the blue ribbon commission created by the administration to analyze the security failure and produce recommendations for reforms released its report in December 2012. While critical of inadequate security, the Pickering and Mullen Accountability Review Board concluded that the intelligence community had no advance warning of the attacks and that, despite "a lack of proactive leadership" by some at State, no "individual U.S. government employee breached his or her duty."[65] The Board put forward twenty-nine specific recommendations to beef up diplomatic security, all of which were immediately endorsed by Secretary Clinton. This allowed State Department officials to turn the emphasis back to the steps the Department was already taking to prevent the recurrence of similar attacks.

Finally, and most problematically, November 2012 media reports—based on executive-branch leaks—revealed that the American consulate in Libya was more than a diplomatic post. It was also a screen for a clandestine CIA presence in Benghazi. A front-page *Wall Street Journal* article boldly began, "The U.S. effort in Benghazi was at its heart a CIA operation." Within the diplomatic compound was an annex that housed the CIA mission. Indeed, of the thirty Americans evacuated from Benghazi, only seven worked for

[63] Jonathan Broder, "Getting the Diplomatic Security You Pay For," *CQ Weekly*, October 15, 2012, 2050–2051.

[64] http://www.debates.org/index.php?page=october-11-2012-the-biden-romney-vice-presidential-debate.

[65] Accountability Review Board Report, 7, http://www.state.gov/documents/organization/202446.pdf, accessed March 1, 2016.

State; almost all of the others were clandestine CIA personnel. Two of the four Americans who died in the attack were also former Navy SEALS who were then in the employ of the Agency. The *Journal* continued:

> The CIA's secret role helps explain why security appeared inadequate at the U.S. diplomatic facility. State Department officials believed that responsibility was set to be shouldered in part by CIA personnel in the city through a series of secret agreements that even some officials in Washington didn't know about. It also explains why the consulate was abandoned to looters for weeks afterward while U.S. efforts focused on securing the more important CIA quarters.[66]

Many at the State Department thus believed that the CIA was in charge of providing security for the consulate. Moreover, as *Congressional Quarterly* noted, the hefty CIA presence in Benghazi helped explain the State Department's "cagey" responses to requests for increased security: "If security personnel had flooded into Benghazi, it would almost certainly have raised the visibility of American operations and drawn more scrutiny from locals."[67]

Revelations about the CIA's secret mission and role in providing security for the diplomatic mission could have easily tempered the investigative furor on Capitol Hill. Probing further into security arrangements almost certainly risked revelations of sensitive intelligence activities in Libya. However, congressional Republicans pushed on largely undeterred. Senator Lindsay Graham accused the State Department of hiding behind the CIA and endeavoring to pass the buck: "Obviously somebody in the State Department [is] trying to say, when it comes to security, it was their job, not ours." "Well here's what somebody needs to ask," Graham continued. "If that were so, why did the people on the ground not know that?" Idaho Republican senator Jim Risch was more measured, but equally insistent that the investigation must be continued.

> Everyone knows that both the State Department and the intelligence community work very closely together and have to work closely together, not just on the immediate security of American personnel at the embassies and in country, but on all kinds of other issues that affect the relationship between two countries. So it's absolutely critical that you have no daylight between the two agencies. My experience is that

[66] Adam Entous, Siobhan Gorman, and Margaret Coker, "CIA Takes Heat for Role in Libya," *Wall Street Journal*, November 2, 2012, A1. See also Max Fisher, "WSJ: State Dept. and CIA had Secret, Botched Deal for Benghazi Security," *Washington Post*, November 2, 2012, https://www.washingtonpost.com/news/worldviews/wp/2012/11/02/wsj-state-dept-and-cia-had-secret-botched-deal-for-benghazi-security/, accessed May 10, 2016.

[67] Emily Cadei and Tim Starks, "Looking at the Real Legacy of Benghazi," *CQ Weekly*, November 19, 2012, 2326–2328.

there's a lot of that that goes on, [but] as with all other operations, improvements always can be made.[68]

On January 23, 2013, investigators finally took aim directly at Secretary Clinton when she appeared before both the Senate Foreign Relations and House Foreign Affairs Committees. Clinton praised the State Department's response to the attacks, noting that the Accountability Review Board had also commended the Department for "timely and exceptional coordination" and speedy decision making. Clinton also emphasized the progress already made in implementing the board's twenty-nine recommendations. Committee Republicans strained mightily to focus the hearing on the State Department's refusal to grant requests for additional security in the summer of 2012 and to tie Secretary Clinton personally to those decisions.[69] Secretary Clinton denied that she ever saw the requests, let alone personally considered them, and she referred her inquisitors to the Accountability Review Board, which noted that such requests do not ordinarily reach the secretary of state.[70] Clinton's response did little to placate Senator Rand Paul (R-KY) who used his time to blast a potential 2016 presidential rival:

I am glad that you are accepting responsibility. I think that ultimately with your leaving, you accept the culpability for the worst tragedy since 9/11, and I really mean that. Had I been president at the time and I found that you did not read the cables from Benghazi, that you did not read the cables from Ambassador Stevens, I would have relieved you of your post. I think it is inexcusable.[71]

Perhaps surprisingly, amidst the charges and Clinton parries, any discussion or even acknowledgment of the CIA role in providing security at the compound was all but absent. The Agency was the two-ton elephant in the room whose name could not be spoken. Indeed, the only oblique reference to the CIA at all occurred when Senator Paul asked Secretary Clinton whether the administration was facilitating the transfer of arms from Libya

[68] Ibid.
[69] The hearings did briefly rehash old arguments over the administration's initial characterization of the attack as a response to the anti-Islam video. In response to a question by Senator Ron Johnson (R-WI) contending that the administration had misled Americans, Clinton erupted: "Was it because of a protest or was it because of guys out for a walk one night who decided they would go kill some Americans? What difference, at this point, does it make? It is our job to figure out what happened and do everything we can to prevent it from happening again, Senator." "Benghazi: The Attacks and the Lessons Learned," Hearing before the Committee on Foreign Relations United States Senate, January 23, 2013, S. Hrg. 113–184, 28.
[70] Ibid., 15.
[71] Ibid., 42.

to Turkey via the annex. Following protocol. Clinton replied curtly, "You will have to direct that question to the agency that ran the annex," never mentioning the CIA by name.[72]

Democrats in both chambers largely rallied to Clinton's defense. In the House Foreign Affairs Committee, Elliot Engel (D-NY) sought to put the attacks in historical perspective and to argue that the Obama administration, like its predecessors, was not responsible for every act of violence against Americans around the world:

> Clearly mistakes were made. But let's be absolutely clear. Barack Obama was not responsible for the Benghazi attacks any more than George W. Bush was responsible for the 9/11 attacks, or Ronald Reagan was responsible for the attacks on our Marine barracks in Beirut, which killed over 200 Marines.[73]

Similarly, Senator Diane Feinstein publicly argued that instead of conducting a serious investigation into security failures and how best to correct them, Republicans had hijacked the hearings, turning them into a politically motivated sideshow. "My concern is when Hillary Clinton's name is mentioned 32 times in a hearing, then the point of the hearing is to discredit the Secretary of State, who has very high popularity and may well be a candidate for president." Feinstein specifically alluded to Senator Rand Paul's aggressive questioning of Clinton—in a speech in Iowa, the first presidential caucus state, Paul went even further arguing that Benghazi should "preclude her [Clinton] from holding higher office"—and said "I think it's nonsense, and I think the American people will think that's nonsense."[74]

Yet, Clinton's testimony did not conclude the investigation into Benghazi. In April 2013, Issa's House committee, which began the investigative spate, issued its preliminary report on the attacks, including a strong indictment of Secretary Clinton. The report maintained that reductions in security at the consulate were approved at the highest level, even by Secretary Clinton herself. The report minced few words, claiming that this "contradicts her testimony before the House Foreign Affairs Committee on January 23, 2013."[75] Chairman Issa reiterated the claims on Fox News: "The Secretary of State was just wrong. She said she did not participate in this, and yet only a few

[72] Ibid., 42–43.

[73] Hearing Before the Committee on Oversight and Government Reform, House of Representatives, May 8, 2013, 113–30, 3.

[74] "On Benghazi Probe, GOP's Issa Says 'Hillary Clinton's Not a Target,'" May 12, 2013, *NBC News*, http://firstread.nbcnews.com/_news/2013/05/12/18209616-on-benghazi-probe-gops-issa-says-hillary-clintons-not-a-target?lite, accessed March 1, 2016.

[75] Interim Progress Report for the Members of the House Republican Conference on the Events Surrounding the September 11, 2012, Terrorist Attacks in Benghazi, Libya, April 23, 2013, http://thehill.com/images/stories/blogs/globalaffairs/benghazi.pdf.

months before the attack, she outright denied security in her signature in a cable in April, 2012."[76] Congressional investigators were buoyed by strong public support for continued investigations. A May 2013 poll revealed 69% of Americans agreeing that the Benghazi attack involved serious questions that needed to be investigated further; a majority, 52%, strongly agreed with this statement, versus only 21% who disagreed.[77]

House Republicans held additional hearings on Benghazi in September of 2013 and in April 2014. These hearings charged the administration with stacking the Accountability Review Board with allies and of limiting the Board's independence. Furthermore, the discovery of an email sent by White House Deputy Strategic Communications Adviser Ben Rhodes about the talking points for Susan Rice prompted a new slate of allegations that the administration had lied to the public about the events precipitating the attack.[78]

Almost twenty full months after the attack, on May 8, 2014, the House passed H. Res. 567 to create a new Select Committee on the Events Surrounding the 2012 Terrorist Attack in Benghazi, charged with continuing the investigation into all administration policies, decisions, and activities that contributed to the attack. In the assessment of *Congressional Quarterly*, the prospects for the committee to have any tangible impact on policy were minimal at best. The committee's efforts "will be shadowed by the shortcomings of previous investigations by California Republican Darrell Issa and hamstrung by Democrats' determination to undermine its credibility. Whatever recommendations the panel makes on how to protect overseas diplomats in the future are likely to be lost in a political firestorm of blame."[79]

The decision to continue the investigation can only be explained as a political calculation that keeping Benghazi in the public eye could redound to the Republicans' electoral advantage by weakening Hillary Clinton's

[76] Kevin Cirilli, "Darrell Issa: Hillary Clinton 'Wrong' on Benghazi," April 24, 2013, *Politico*, http://www.politico.com/story/2013/04/darrell-issa-hillary-clinton-benghazi-90560.html#, accessed March 1, 2016.

[77] Survey Conducted by Gallup Organization, May 14–May 15, 2013 and based on 1,022 telephone interviews. Sample: National adult. Interviews were conducted with respondents on landline telephones and cellular phones. [USGALLUP.13MAY14.R03] One year later, support for continued investigations was just as strong, if not stronger: Conducted by Gallup Organization, June 9–June 10, 2014 and based on 1,012 telephone interviews. Sample: National adult. Interviews were conducted with respondents on landline telephones and cellular phones. The sample includes 50% landline and 50% cell phone respondents. [USGALLUP.061314.R01C]

[78] The Rhodes email was labeled a "smoking gun" by Lindsay Graham. The administration, however, continued to insist (as Petraeus had testified) that the CIA had drafted the talking points. Stephanie Condon, "Emails Illustrate How White House Shaped Benghazi Talking Points," *CBS News*, April 30, 2014, http://www.cbsnews.com/news/emails-illustrate-how-white-house-shaped-benghazi-talking-points/, accessed March 1, 2016.

[79] Shawn Zeller, "Probe to Nowhere: Partisanship Hobbles Benghazi Panel," *CQ Weekly*, May 19, 2014, 704–711.

presidential candidacy. Public opinion polls suggest that Republicans may well have succeeded in turning Benghazi into a political liability. A May 2014 CNN poll showed that only 43% of Americans were satisfied with Clinton's handling of the Benghazi attack, versus 55% who were dissatisfied. The public was split largely along partisan lines with Democrats predictably backing Clinton and Republicans opposing her. However, among the key independent demographic, only 38% were satisfied with Clinton's job performance versus 60% who were dissatisfied.[80] Moreover, the email scandal that has most directly cast a pall over Clinton's campaign for the Democratic nomination was itself an indirect product of the Benghazi investigation; Clinton's use of a private email server during her tenure as secretary of state was first discovered pursuant to a request for records by the Benghazi Committee. We return to Benghazi and discuss the potential for public backlash against investigators in the concluding chapter.

CONCLUSION

Investigative activity since 2007 fits neatly into the larger pattern observed in Chapter 2 describing variation in investigations from 1898 through 2006. The newly empowered Democratic majority in the 110th Congress aggressively investigated the Bush administration during its final two years in office. However, the Democratically controlled 111th Congress was loath to continue the investigative fervor after President Obama took office. *Congressional Quarterly* coverage mentioned only three investigations during this period, all of which were prompted by major external events. By contrast, the Republican victories in the 2010 midterms unleashed a flurry of investigations into alleged misconduct by various parts of the Obama administration in the 112th and 113th Congresses. All of these major investigations were spearheaded and pursued most vigorously by Republican committee chairmen in the House of Representatives. The Democratic Senate continued its earlier stance of undertaking only limited investigations of the Obama administration.

In addition to the raw number of investigations increasing dramatically with the return of divided government, the nature of the investigations also changed significantly from the 111th to the 112th Congress. As expected, the divided government investigations were much bolder in their attacks on

[80] Survey by Cable News Network. Methodology: Conducted by ORC International, May 29–June 1, 2014 and based on 1,003 telephone interviews. Sample: National adult. The sample included 702 interviews among landline respondents and 301 interviews among cell phone respondents. [USORC.061614B.R17]

the administration, and they were much more consciously designed to inflict political damage on President Obama and his fellow Democrats.

While the partisan dynamic to investigative activity in the Obama era is similar to that observed in earlier periods, our analysis suggests that the intense polarization of the contemporary Congress may be changing the way in which members of Congress approach investigations. Polarization complicates efforts to effect policy change through the direct pathways described in Chapter 4. Indeed, the Deepwater Horizon case study shows that even the investigation into the largest oil spill in American history was unable to generate enough political pressure to prompt passage of comprehensive legislation to address the federal regulatory lapses that made the accident possible.

Rather, particularly in divided government, investigators may reap the most influence by designing an investigation to maximize the political costs it inflicts on the administration. Such a strategy may yield dividends at the ballot box. Although the nascent Benghazi inquiry did not damage President Obama in the 2012 election, the flurry of Republican-led probes exposing the administration's alleged failures may well have been an important factor contributing to the precipitous fall in President Obama's approval rating after November of 2012, which in turn hurt Democrats' prospects in the 2014 midterms. Moreover, by politically weakening the president, the investigations may well have increased the political leverage of the new Republican majority in its legislative battles with Obama. Investigations in a polarized era may be less likely to increase the prospects for legislative action to rein in wayward executive-branch policies than investigations in earlier eras. However, contemporary investigations are well designed to influence politics and policy making indirectly by imposing substantial political costs on the president, weakening his base of political support among the public, and altering the cost-benefit calculations underlying major policy decisions.

CHAPTER 7

~ ~

Conclusion

WHEN DESCRIBING CONGRESSIONAL powers and duties, Woodrow Wilson argued that "quite as important as legislation is vigilant oversight of administration." By shining a bright light on the activities of the executive branch, congressional investigators provide the public "the instruction and guidance in political affairs" that can only occur by keeping "all national concerns suffused in a broad daylight of discussion." However, Wilson lamented that Congress had largely failed to fulfill this key function of democratic accountability. Unlike parliaments, the United States Congress "in a way superintends administration by the exercise of semi-judicial powers of investigation, whose limitations and insufficiency are manifest."[1] Our comprehensive analysis of more than a century of investigative activity from 1898—just thirteen years after Wilson wrote—through 2014 suggests that Congress makes more effective use of its investigative authority than Wilson acknowledged.

To be sure, there is considerable variation in Congress's willingness to investigate alleged wrongdoing in the executive branch. Legislators are much more eager to investigate the executive branch in some political environments than they are in others. However, investigations are not rare phenomena. Rather, they have been a hallmark of our separation of powers system since the earliest days of the Republic, and they continue to be a prominent feature of interbranch politics today. Indeed, while the 112th and 113th Congresses have been routinely derided as "do-nothing" Congresses because of their historically low levels of legislative productivity, similar charges cannot be lodged against their performance in the hearing room.[2] As shown in the previous chapter, Congress has aggressively

---

[1] Wilson 1885, 297.

[2] For example, Susan Milligan, "The Do-Nothing Congress: Neither the Public Nor Lawmakers Believe Anything Will Be Done to Address Pressing Crises," *U.S. News and World Report*, September 8, 2014, http://www.usnews.com/news/articles/2014/09/08/the-do-nothing -congress, accessed March 1, 2016; Philip Bump, "The 113th Congress Is Historically Good at Not Passing Bills," *Washington Post, The Fix Blog*, July 9, 2014, http://www.washingtonpost

investigated a wide range of alleged abuses and missteps in the executive branch in recent years, especially in the Republican-controlled House of Representatives.

Even more important, our analyses show that when Congress investigates it packs a significant political punch. A crucial mechanism through which investigations can produce tangible impacts on politics and policy making is by eroding the president's standing among the public. The president's public approval rating is among the most important and most visible metrics of a president's political capital. Presidents with high approval ratings are more successful in Congress and at the ballot box. Presidents with low approval ratings struggle to enact their legislative priorities on Capitol Hill, and they frequently become an electoral burden to their partisan allies in Congress, as demonstrated so convincingly in the 2014 midterm elections. Investigations critically influence this key measure of presidential clout. In both an analysis of more than sixty years of presidential approval data and in a series of survey experiments, we showed that congressional investigations significantly diminish the president's standing among the public. By aggressively investigating alleged administrative misconduct, members of Congress can impose steep political costs on the president. Moreover, a president who anticipates such costly investigations has strong incentives to tread softly and adjust his actions to avoid interbranch battles before the cameras in committee hearing rooms.

Indeed, the case studies of Chapter 4 and broader analysis of all thirty of Mayhew's significant committee probes clearly show that a wide range of investigations have generated popular pressure for policy change. In some cases, this political pressure provided the impetus for Congress to enact new legislation that would have been unlikely to pass in the absence of the investigation. In others, presidents preempted congressional action by making policy concessions, either in the hopes of sapping support for more dramatic policy shifts or to avoid the political costs of clinging to their preferences in the face of public disapproval.

Beyond these direct policy effects, Chapter 5 illustrates the broader, indirect influence of congressional investigations. Focusing on a policy domain in which the president is thought to have major advantages, we show that presidents are more likely to use military force when they have faced little investigative pressure than when they have confronted intense hearing activity. Thus, our analysis shows that investigations can have significant policy consequences, both in the specific policy realm at hand, and across policy areas more widely by shaping presidential anticipatory calculations.

.com/blogs/the-fix/wp/2014/07/09/the-113th-congress-is-historically-good-at-not-passing-bills/, March 1, 2016.

To accurately capture the balance of power between the branches, separation of powers scholarship must do more than simply consider Congress's ability to write its preferences into law over those of the president. It must also consider Congress's capacity to influence policy through more informal means, such as by using its power of investigation to raise the political costs presidents risk incurring by pursuing their preferred policies. By giving short shrift to congressional investigations, existing scholarship has underestimated Congress's political and policy influence. Nevertheless, we conclude with four important, inter-related caveats that may limit the influence that the contemporary Congress wields through the investigative arm of its committees.

Polarization and Unified Government

For more than a century of American political history, investigative activity in the U.S. House of Representatives has been more intense in periods of divided government than when the same political party controls both Congress and the White House. However, this dynamic is particularly acute in the intensely polarized contemporary era. Indeed, as the data in both Chapters 2 and 6 show, investigations in the contemporary period have become almost exclusively a feature of divided government, particularly in the House. In unified government, recent Congresses have routinely failed to investigate allegations of executive wrongdoing and abuse of power. And as a result, in these conditions the pendulum of power in Washington swings firmly toward the executive branch.

For the last twenty-five years, scholars have vigorously debated the consequences of divided government for democratic governance.[3] Much of this debate has focused on whether divided government hamstrings legislative productivity. While the bulk of the evidence suggests that divided partisan control does indeed reduce legislative output, our analysis suggests that, particularly in the contemporary era of intense polarization, it may also significantly *increase* democratic accountability through investigative action.

Consider for example what are now regarded by many as the most important abuses of power during the presidency of George W. Bush: the indefinite detention of enemy combatants at Guantanamo Bay; the unilateral

[3] Among others, see James Sundquist, "Needed: A Political Theory for the New Era of Coalition Government in the United States," *Political Science Quarterly* 103 (1988): 613–635; Mayhew 1991; Gary Cox and Samuel Kernell, *The Politics of Divided Government* (Boulder, CO: Westview Press, 1991); George Edwards, Andrew Barrett, and Jeffrey Peake, "The Legislative Impact of Divided Government," *American Journal of Political Science* 41 (1997): 545–563; Coleman 1999; Cameron 2000; Sarah Binder, *Stalemate: Causes and Consequences of Legislative Gridlock* (Washington, DC: Brookings Institution Press, 2003).

establishment of military tribunals; the manipulation of prewar intelligence concerning the threat posed by Saddam Hussein and Iraq's alleged weapons of mass destruction; prisoner abuse at Abu Ghraib; the systematic use of torture and "enhanced interrogation techniques"; expanded domestic surveillance and infringement on civil liberties. In the aftermath of the 9/11 terrorist attacks, it was all but certain that presidential power would grow considerably. However, some of the most flagrant abuses of power might have been mitigated had President Bush confronted a Congress willing to scrutinize his actions. Instead, as plainly shown at the end of the time series presented in Chapter 2, investigative activity all but disappeared during the first six years of the Bush presidency. It was not until Democrats gained control of the committee gavels in the 110th Congress that legislators began to hold a slew of hearings aggressively shining light on alleged administration wrongdoing.

The end result is that presidents holding office during periods of unified government face far less congressional scrutiny when they take questionable administrative actions. Freed from such constraints, presidents are empowered to move aggressively on their priorities. This, in turn, can lead to the concentration of power in the executive branch, with all of the attendant consequences that the Framers' separation of powers system was consciously designed to prevent.

Investigations do offer an important tool through which members of Congress can exercise a check on presidential assertions of power and retain a measure of influence over policy, even when institutional barriers prevent it from writing its preferences into law. However, in a polarized era investigations are increasingly likely to safeguard the interbranch balance of power between the branches only during periods of divided government.

The Changing Nature of Investigations in a Polarized Era

Throughout American history, congressional investigations have repeatedly been crafted to serve political purposes. Even the very first investigation into the disaster that befell the St. Clair expedition was exploited by some members to land political blows against leading Federalists, particularly Secretary of War Henry Knox. Federalist congressmen rallied behind Knox and Treasury Secretary Alexander Hamilton, blocking publication of the report. Few if any major investigations have been conducted completely divorced from partisan politics. However, it seems likely that investigations in our contemporary highly polarized era are more partisan and explicitly political in their orientation than many inquiries launched in less polarized environments. Rather than seek to effect change primarily by spurring new legislation or policy concessions from the White House, contemporary investigators have increasingly sought to exert influence indirectly by inflicting political damage on the White House.

In a gridlocked political environment, legislative change is unlikely following even a major investigation. Consider, for example, the investigation into the Deepwater Horizon oil spill discussed in the previous chapter. Despite public outcry and a strong popular demand for action, the ideological divide between most Democrats and Republicans (joined by a handful of Democrats from oil-producing states) frustrated all efforts to reach a legislative compromise to address the regulatory lapses that allowed the spill to occur. The likelihood of gridlock, in turn, may also make presidents less likely to make preemptive concessions on policy (as President Reagan did during the EPA investigations of the early 1980s) as they have less to fear from legislative action.

Given this political reality, congressional investigators might rationally focus on inflicting political damage on the president and his allies in the hopes of securing longer-term gains. Indeed, many of the high-profile investigations from 2011 to 2014 reviewed in the preceding chapter, such as the Solyndra and Benghazi inquiries, appear to have been designed with this as their primary aim, not building support for concrete legislative changes. Similarly, Democrats in the 110th Congress happily held hearings featuring charges that President Bush had violated the law and abused his constitutional authority by unilaterally authorizing warrantless wiretapping. But rather than using these hearings to build political momentum behind efforts to re-invigorate FISA and other laws on surveillance, the 110th Congress ultimately caved and passed a measure backed by the administration that weakened FISA, expanded presidential surveillance powers, and put Bush's actions on a sounder legal footing. In the same way, most of the high-profile investigations of the Clinton years focused not on policy abuses, but on alleged personal failings and misconduct. The emphasis on scoring political points was captured in Clinton's phrase dismissing such efforts as "the politics of personal destruction."[4]

While such investigations largely fail to meet the normative objectives articulated by Wilson and others, they nonetheless may continue to have important, if blunt, policy ramifications. A president besieged by criticism from investigators on one front, may decide not to risk provoking institutional challenges on another and instead to alter his actions and policy decisions accordingly. We saw strong evidence of this indirect pathway of policy influence within the realm of military affairs in Chapter 5. Indeed, this indirect pathway may be even more important in an intensely polarized era than it was in prior decades.

---

[4] Bill Clinton. "Interview with Larry King," *Public Papers of the President*, January 20, 1994.

The Potential for Overreach

As legislators have increasingly crafted investigations with the express purpose of inflicting political damage on their partisan foes, the dangers of overreach have expanded considerably. As our survey experiment in Chapter 3 showed, an overwhelming majority of Americans support congressional investigations of alleged misconduct by the executive branch. Even a large share of presidential co-partisans are supportive of congressional efforts to investigate alleged abuse by their party leader in the White House. However, as Republicans' prolonged investigation into former secretary of state Hillary Clinton's responsibility for the Benghazi terror attacks demonstrates, investigators risk provoking a backlash against hearings that are perceived to be simply political.

The newly created House Select Committee on Benghazi held its first hearing in September 2014, shortly after the two-year anniversary of the terrorist attack. The committee held two more hearings in the months that followed. However, in January 2015 the committee receded from the spotlight as it continued its work in private and delayed further hearings until closer to the 2016 presidential election cycle. This relative calm was broken on September 29, 2015, when House Majority Leader Keven McCarthy (R-CA)—the leading candidate to succeed John Boehner as the Speaker of the House—bragged that his leadership in creating the Benghazi Committee had seriously damaged Hillary Clinton's prospects of winning the presidency in 2016.

> Everybody thought Hillary Clinton was unbeatable, right? But we put together a Benghazi special committee. A select committee. What are her numbers today? Her numbers are dropping. Why? Because she's untrustable. But no one would have known that any of that had happened had we not fought to make that happen.[5]

Rather than help McCarthy's cause by illustrating how he would be a conservative speaker capable of implementing a "strategy to win," McCarthy's quip generated a significant backlash. Congressional Democrats, long critical of the investigation, seized on the comments as proof that Republicans were more interested in playing politics than uncovering some hidden truth about what happened in Benghazi. Indeed, McCarthy's gaffe breathed new life into old calls to disband the Benghazi Select Committee.[6] In announcing an

---

[5] Transcript, *Hannity*, September 29, 2015, http://www.foxnews.com/transcript/2015/09/29/rubio-cruz-talk-foreign-policy-govt-shutdown-mccarthy-on-how-differs-from/, accessed March 1, 2016.

[6] For example, Democratic committee member Adam Schiff denounced the committee in September as "little more than a partisan tool to influence the presidential race, a dangerous precedent that will haunt Congress for decades." Adam Schiff, "Disband the Benghazi Committee," *New York Times*, September 4, 2015, A23.

amendment to dissolve the committee, Louise Slaughter (D-NY) inveighed: "Speaker-in-Waiting Kevin McCarthy accidentally told the truth last week and admitted that the Benghazi Select Committee had one mission alone: to influence a presidential election."[7] Florida Democrat Alan Grayson even filed an ethics complaint against both Majority Leader McCarthy and committee chair Trey Gowdy (R-SC), alleging that the investigation improperly used funds for political expenses. McCarthy's statement, Grayson charged, was tantamount to "a confession that this is totally for political purposes."[8]

Many media outlets echoed Democrats' call for an end to the investigation. A *New York Times* editorial denounced the "inquisition of Hillary Rodham Clinton" as a "laughable crusade," and called on House Republicans to "shut down the Benghazi Committee."[9] Moreover, the Democratic charges of extreme politicization were only bolstered when a former investigator for the Benghazi Committee charged that the focus on Secretary Clinton's use of a private email server had transformed the investigation into a purely partisan enterprise focused on damaging Clinton, not uncovering the facts of what happened in Benghazi.[10]

Amidst this controversy, Chairman Gowdy gaveled to order his committee's fourth hearing on October 22, 2015. The star witness: Hillary Clinton. In almost eleven hours of televised hearings, Republican investigators largely failed to land any new blows. The media overwhelmingly declared Clinton the victor. For example, CNN led with the title: "Marathon Benghazi Hearing Leaves Hillary Clinton Largely Unscathed."[11] A *Washington Post* editorial judged that the committee "further discredited itself on Thursday as its Republican members attempted to fuel largely insubstantial suspicions about Hillary Clinton's role in the 2012 Benghazi attacks." Despite hours of questioning, the committee "elicited little new information and offered little hope that their inquiry would find anything significant that seven previous

---

[7] Press Release, "Slaughter Forces Committee Vote on Amendment to Dissolve Benghazi Committee," October 6, 2015, https://louise.house.gov/media-center/press-releases/slaughter-forces-committee-vote-amendment-dissolve-benghazi-committee, accessed March 1, 2016.

[8] Hannah Hess, "Grayson Files Ethics Complaint Against McCarthy, Gowdy," *The Hill*, October 7, 2015, http://blogs.rollcall.com/218/grayson-file-benghazi-ethics-complaint-mccarthy-gowdy/, accessed March 1, 2016.

[9] "Shut Down the Benghazi Committee," *New York Times*, October 7, 2015, A26.

[10] Jake Tapper and Jeremy Diamond, "Ex-Staffer: Benghazi Committee Pursuing 'Partisan Investigation' Targeting Hillary Clinton," *CNN.com*, October 11, 2015, http://www.cnn.com/2015/10/10/politics/benghazi-committee-investigation-political-hillary-clinton-brad-podliska-lawsuit/index.html, accessed March 1, 2016.

[11] Stephen Collinson, "Marathon Benghazi Hearing Leaves Hillary Clinton Largely Unscathed," *CNN.com*, October 23, 2015, http://www.cnn.com/2015/10/22/politics/hillary-clinton-benghazi-hearing-updates/, March 1, 2016. Even many conservative outlets declared the day a victory for Clinton.

investigations didn't."[12] Even an analysis of conservative media outlets concluded that "many on the right begrudgingly say the former Secretary of State avoided missteps and bested her interrogators in Thursday's House committee marathon."[13]

Public opinion polls taken immediately before the October hearing painted a mixed picture for the investigation's future. On the one hand, 72% of Americans said that the investigation was designed "to gain political advantage," versus only 23% who believed it was "an objective investigation of what happened in the Benghazi attack." However, only 40% of Americans replied that the investigators had gone too far, versus 51% believing they had acted appropriately. Moreover, a majority of Americans continued to express dissatisfaction with Secretary Clinton's handling of the attack, a testament to the lasting power of the committee's allegations.[14] Committee Republicans pledged in November 2015 to press onward with the investigation.[15] It remains to be seen whether the ongoing investigation will ultimately impose an enduring political cost on Secretary Clinton or instead will be dismissed by most voters as merely a political sideshow. The email scandal, which was born from a request for documentation by the Benghazi Committee, continues to capture headlines, even as Clinton marches toward securing the Democratic nomination in 2016. But regardless of how Clinton ultimately fares, the Benghazi case highlights the concern that investigations may lose their credibility if they are seen as simply "partisan politics by other means" in a highly polarized environment.[16]

An Increasingly Partisan Media Environment

Finally, throughout this book we have emphasized the critical role played by public opinion. We have argued that one of the most important mechanisms through which investigations can affect presidential politics and policy making is by lowering the president's standing among the public.

---

[12] "Benghazi Business as Usual," *Washington Post*, October 23, 2015, A22.

[13] David Graham, "What Conservative Media Say About the Benghazi Hearing," *The Atlantic*, October 23, 2015, http://www.theatlantic.com/politics/archive/2015/10/conservative-media-hillary-clinton-benghazi-committee/412117/, accessed March 1, 2016.

[14] CNN/ORC poll, October 14–17, 2015, http://i2.cdn.turner.com/cnn/2015/images/10/21/rel11e.-.benghazi.pdf, accessed March 1, 2016.

[15] Elise Viebeck and Karoun Demerjian, "Republicans Moving Full Steam Ahead with Benghazi Investigation," *Washington Post*, October 23, 2015, https://www.washingtonpost.com/news/powerpost/wp/2015/10/23/democrats-to-stay-with-benghazi-investigation/, accessed March 1, 2016.

[16] This phrase is adapted from Benjamin Ginsberg and Martin Shefter, *Politics by Other Means: Politics, Prosecutors, and the Press from Watergate to Whitewater* (New York: W.W. Norton, 2003).

Similarly, all three of the pathways discussed in Chapters 4 and 5 rely, either directly or indirectly, on public opinion. Investigations can make legislation more likely by raising an issue's public salience and mobilizing popular pressure for action. Moreover, mobilizing public opinion against the White House is the primary means through which investigations can impose political costs on the president. These costs—be they actual or anticipated—can lead presidents to make policy concessions or forgo other actions altogether.

A necessary precursor for investigations to influence the public is for them to attract sustained and widespread attention in the media. Increasingly, congressional investigators wishing to capture the public eye must overcome two major challenges. First, changing coverage norms mean that most major media outlets devote less attention to goings on in Congress than they did in the recent past. Instead, the center of gravity has shifted to the White House.[17] For example, Fowler and Law show that *New York Times* coverage of Congress and its members has dwindled from an average of almost 800 stories per year in 1947 to only 450 by 2006.[18] Simply attracting and keeping reporters' attention may be more difficult for contemporary congressmen than for their forebearers.

Moreover, efforts to generate sustained media attention are further complicated by the well documented rise of an increasingly fragmented and partisan mass media. Traditional large media outlets, such as the major network news programs and newspapers of record, have long been and continue to be mostly centrist, if with a modest liberal bias, in their coverage and orientation.[19] However, as these traditional media giants have lost market share and as more Americans get their news from an explosion of alternative media sources both on cable and online, the media environment has become significantly more partisan.[20] Indeed, there is growing evidence

[17] Timothy Cook, *Governing with the News: The News Media as a Political Institution* (Chicago: University of Chicago Press, 1998); Stephen Hess, "The Decline and Fall of Congressional News," in *Congress, the Press, and the Public*, ed. Thomas E. Mann and Norman J. Ornstein (Washington, DC: Brookings Institution, 1994).

[18] Linda Fowler and Brian Law, "Seen but Not Heard: Committee Visibility and Institutional Change in the Senate National Security Committees, 1947–2006," *Legislative Studies Quarterly* 33 (2008): 363–364. See also Fowler 2015, 53.

[19] Tim Groseclose and Jeffrey Milyo, "A Measure of Media Bias," *Quarterly Journal of Economics* 120 (2005): 1191–1237; Matthew Gentzkow and Jesse Shapiro, "What Drives Media Slant? Evidence from U.S. Daily Newspapers," *Econometrica* 78 (2010): 35–71; John Gasper, "Shifting Ideologies? Re-examining Media Bias," *International Quarterly Journal of Political Science* 6 (2011): 85–102; Markus Prior, "Media and Political Polarization," *Annual Review of Political Science* 16 (2013): 101–127.

[20] Tim Groeling, "Who's the Fairest of Them All? An Empirical Test for Partisan Bias on ABC, CBS, NBC, and Fox News," *Presidential Studies Quarterly* 38 (2008): 631–657; Baum and Groeling 2009; Lada Adamic and Natalie Glance, "The Political Blogosphere and the 2004

that Americans are self-selecting media outlets that share their pre-existing ideological orientations,[21] particularly with respect to television news.[22]

For an investigation to affect public opinion and impose political costs on the president, it must receive enough coverage in an increasingly partisan media environment to reach a wide swath of voters. In this transformed context, virtually all investigations should find a sympathetic ear and attract considerable coverage in at least some corners of the mass media. For example, Democratic-leaning publications should gleefully highlight investigations into Bush-era abuses, while Republican-leaning outlets should trumpet even the flimsiest charges of misconduct by the Obama administration. However, for an investigation to have a tangible impact on politics and policy, it will need to break through such narrow coverage patterns and attract sustained attention from a wider range of media outlets that can reach a large cross-section of Americans. Given structural changes in the media environment, this may be more difficult today than in previous decades.

In Chapter 4, we presented polling evidence showing that the Solyndra investigation largely failed to resonate with most voters. Indeed, despite a sustained effort by congressional investigators to inflict political damage on President Obama for the half billion dollar bust, public opinion polls showed that even a year after the scandal began a solid majority of Americans had never even heard of Solyndra. This inability to capture the public's attention and mobilize public opinion against the administration is at least partially responsible for the failure of GOP-sponsored legislation undermining the president's green energy agenda, and for the Republicans' inability to capitalize on the scandal at the ballot box.

Why did the Solyndra hearings fail to rally the public against the president? Perhaps the most persuasive explanation is that it largely failed to attract sustained coverage apart from on Fox News. To examine the variation in attention to Solyndra across media outlets, we conducted a series of searches for any broadcast news story mentioning Solyndra across the flagship evening news programs of the big three networks (*ABC World News*;

U.S. Election: Divided They Blog," *Proceedings of the 3rd International Workshop on Link Discovery*, ACM, 2005.

[21] Shanto Iyengar and Kyu S. Hahn, "Red Media, Blue Media: Evidence of Ideological Selectivity in Media Use," *Journal of Communication* 59 (2009): 19–39; Solomon Messing and Sean Westwood, "Selective Exposure in the Age of Social Media: Endorsements Trump Partisan Source Affiliation When Selecting News Online," *Communication Research* 41 (2014): 1042–1063; Matthew Gentzkow and Jesse Shapiro, "Ideological Segregation Online and Offline," *Quarterly Journal of Economics* 126 (2011): 1799–839.

[22] Kathleen Jamieson and Joseph Cappella, *Echo Chamber: Rush Limbaugh and the Conservative Media Establishment* (New York: Oxford University Press, 2008); Natalie Stroud, *Niche News: The Politics of News Choice* (New York: Oxford University Press, 2011). But see Prior 2013 for concerns about measurement error.

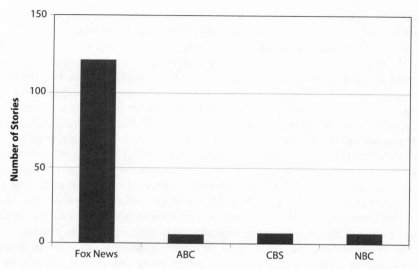

FIGURE 7.1. News Coverage of Solyndra Scandal Across Flagship Evening News Programs.

CBS Evening News; NBC Nightly News) and Fox News' flagship evening news program, Special Report. [23] It is important to note that Special Report, in contrast to its broadcast network peers, is an hour-long program, rather than a half-hour show. As a result, we might expect the counts to be somewhat higher for Special Report than for its competitors. However, the disparities presented in Figure 7.1 are startling.

All three of the major network evening news broadcasts ran stories on the Solyndra episode. However, the story failed to attract sustained coverage on these programs, despite Republican investigators' holding months of hearings on the alleged abuses by Obama. By contrast, Fox News' Special Report hammered the Obama administration over Solydra again and again, airing more than 120 stories mentioning the scandal. Indeed, Special Report aired more than six times as many stories mentioning Solyndra as did the other three major networks' evening news broadcasts combined.

A similar pattern emerges when we broaden the scope of the analysis to examine coverage of Solyndra on all broadcasts by Fox News, its liberal counterpart MSNBC, CNN, and the three major networks. The data is presented in Figure 7.2. The Republican-leaning audience that routinely tunes into the Fox News Channel received a steady diet of stories and allegations

[23] All searches described in this chapter were conducted using *Lexis Nexis*.

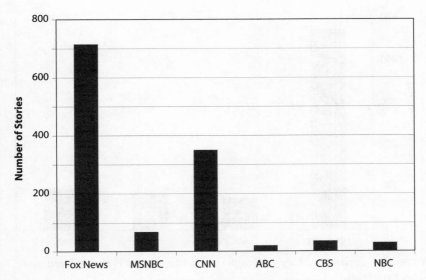

FIGURE 7.2. News Coverage of Solyndra Scandal Across Networks.

concerning the House Republican investigation of the Solyndra case. By contrast, the primarily Democratic-leaning audience that watches MSNBC was exposed to many fewer stories on Solyndra. Whereas Fox News aired more than 700 stories mentioning Solyndra, MSNBC aired only 70. Adding the networks' weekend news programs to the mix slightly boosted the total mentions of Solyndra on ABC, CBS, and NBC; however, even these expanded tallies are quite small. Finally, the more ideologically neutral twenty-four hour news network, CNN, did air a significant number of stories mentioning Solyndra; however, the total paled in comparison to the deluge of coverage bombarding the airwaves from Fox News. Given these patterns in coverage, it is perhaps little wonder that so many Americans answered that they had never heard of Solyndra despite Republican investigators' year-long effort to make it a costly political scandal for the president.

Yet, not all investigations will fail to receive widespread coverage across media outlets in the contemporary era. In Chapter 6, we discussed the Republican House's extraordinary efforts to keep the investigation into the attack on the American consulate in Benghazi in the public eye even years after the assault. Similar searches of broadcast news transcripts show that these efforts bore considerable fruit. Figure 7.3 presents the number of stories mentioning Benghazi from the day of the attack itself through December 3, 2014. While Fox News' *Special Report* again aired a wildly disproportionate number of stories on Benghazi, the scandal also received substantial coverage in the major evening news programs of the big three

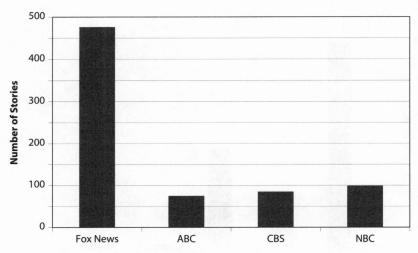

FIGURE 7.3. News Coverage of Benghazi Scandal Across Flagship Evening News Programs.

broadcast networks. Whereas ABC, CBS, and NBC ran a cumulative total of 20 stories mentioning Solyndra, together they aired more than 250 stories mentioning Benghazi during this period. The diffusion of this story across the major networks suggests that a wider range of Americans were exposed to information about the attack and the alleged Obama administration missteps that Republican investigators charged contributed to the disaster.

Casting a wider net and examining patterns in coverage across all programming on a range of cable and broadcast networks reveals a similar story. Figure 7.4 presents the results. Most important, in stark contrast to Solyndra, which received significant coverage only on Fox News and, to a lesser extent, on CNN, Benghazi was mentioned in a large number of stories across all of the networks surveyed. Indeed, CNN aired more stories mentioning Benghazi than did Fox News. Even liberal-leaning MSNBC, whose coverage of Solyndra was less than 10% of Fox News' total, aired more than 750 stories mentioning Benghazi. Of course, the editorial slant of these stories almost certainly differed from that on Fox News programs. However, the large tallies across networks—even the big three broadcast networks each aired hundreds of stories mentioning Benghazi—demonstrates the wide diffusion of the scandal and the intensity with which the media brought the issue before the public eye. The media salience of the Benghazi debacle and congressional efforts to tie both President Obama and, even more important, former secretary of state Hillary Clinton to it, helps explain why the public opinion data from Chapter 6 suggest that

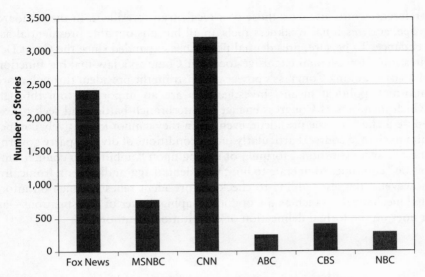

FIGURE 7.4. News Coverage of Benghazi Scandal Across Networks.

these allegations have resonated with the public, whereas those made by Solyndra investigators did not. The Solyndra-Benghazi comparison suggests that a key question for further research is under what conditions will highly partisan investigations nonetheless gain the attention of a wide variety of media outlets?

The Future of Investigative Politics

Although often overlooked, investigations have long been an important tool through which members of Congress have sought to constrain the executive branch and exert tangible influence on policy outcomes. With the return of levels of polarization not seen since the early twentieth century and major changes in the mass media environment, investigative politics, like legislative politics more generally, are constantly evolving. In key respects, many contemporary investigations may unfold quite differently from their counterparts conducted forty or fifty years ago. However, the weight of the evidence suggests that investigations remain a potent tool through which Congress can, in certain conditions, materially affect interbranch politics and policy outcomes.

For too long, separation of powers scholarship has focused on Congress's capacity to enact legislation as virtually the only mechanism through which it can constrain the rampant growth of presidential power. Fundamental institutional barriers, exacerbated in the contemporary era of intense polarization, all but guarantee that Congress will rarely be able to write its preferences into law over those of a recalcitrant president. In the standard trope, congressional weakness fuels an all but unstoppable presidential ascendance. To be sure, presidential power has expanded since the Great Depression. However, an exclusive focus on Congress's law-making function risks overlooking Congress's power to constrain the president through more informal, political means. Investigations are an important tool through which members of Congress engage in interbranch battles and seek to exercise a check on the president, even when they cannot legislatively compel him to change course. Particularly under conditions of divided party government, the constitutional formula of relying upon "ambition to counter ambition" continues to operate to limit presidential aggrandizement. Ironically, however, Congress's ability to check the president relies as much on informal mechanisms—such as the opinion-shaping power of investigations—as it does on the formal delineation of constitutional authority.

References

~ ~

Aberbach, Joel. 1990. *Keeping a Watchful Eye: The Politics of Congressional Oversight.* Washington, DC: Brookings Institution Press.

Aberbach, Joel. 2002. "What's Happened to the Watchful Eye?" *Congress and the Presidency* 29: 3–23.

Ackerman, Bruce, and Oona Hathaway. 2011. "Limited War and the Constitution: Iraq and the Crisis of Presidential Legality." *Michigan Law Review* 109: 447–517.

Adamic, Lada, and Natalie Glance. 2005. "The Political Blogosphere and the 2004 U.S. Election: Divided They Blog." *Proceedings of the 3rd International Workshop on Link Discovery.* ACM, 2005.

Aldrich, John. 1995. *Why Parties? The Origin and Transformation of Political Parties in America.* Chicago: University of Chicago Press.

Aldrich, John, and David Rohde. 1995. "Theories of the Party in Legislature and the Transition to Republican Rule in the House." Paper Presented at annual meeting of the American Science Association, Chicago.

Althaus, Scott, Jill Edy, Robert Entman, and Patricia Phalen. 1996. "Revising the Indexing Hypothesis: Officials, Media, and the Libya Crisis." *Political Communication* 13: 407–421.

Ansolabehere, Stephen, James Snyder Jr, and Charles Stewart III. 2001. "Candidate Positioning in U.S. House Elections." *American Journal of Political Science* 45: 136–159.

Apodaca, Clair, and Michael Stohl. 1999. "United States Human Rights Policy and Foreign Assistance." *International Studies Quarterly* 43: 185–198.

Baker, William, and John Oneal. 2001. "Patriotism or Opinion Leadership? The Nature and Origin of the 'Rally 'Round the Flag' Effect." *Journal of Conflict Resolution* 45: 661–687.

Barrett, Andrew, and Matthew Eshbaugh-Soha. 2007. "Presidential Success on the Substance of Legislation." *Political Research Quarterly* 60: 100–112.

Baum, Matthew, and Timothy Groeling. 2008. "New Media and the Polarization of American Political Discourse." *Political Communication* 25: 345–365.

Baum, Matthew, and Timothy Groeling. 2009. "Shot by the Messenger: Partisan Cues and Public Opinion Regarding National Security and War." *Political Behavior* 31: 157–186.

Beckmann, Matthew. 2010. *Pushing the Agenda: Presidential Leadership in US Lawmaking, 1953–2004.* New York: Cambridge University Press.

Bennett, W. Lance. 1990. "Toward a Theory of Press-State Relations in the United States." *Journal of Communication* 40: 103–125.

Bennett, W. Lance, Regina Lawrence, and Steven Livingstone. 2007. *When the Press Fails: Political Power and the News Media from Iraq to Katrina*. Chicago: University of Chicago Press.

Berinsky, Adam. 2009. *In Time of War: Understanding American Public Opinion from World War II to Iraq*. Chicago: University of Chicago Press.

Berinsky, Adam. 2012. "Rumors, Truths, and Reality: A Study of Political Misinformation." Typescript, MIT.

Berinsky, Adam, Greg Huber, and Gabriel Lenz. 2012. "Evaluating Online Labor Markets for Experimental Research: Amazon.com's Mechanical Turk." *Political Analysis* 20: 351–368.

Berry, Christopher, Barry Burden, and William Howell. 2010. "The President and the Distribution of Federal Spending." *American Political Science Review*, 104(4): 783–799.

Binder, Sarah. 2003. *Stalemate: Causes and Consequences of Legislative Gridlock*. Washington, DC: Brookings Institution Press.

Binder, Sarah, Eric Lawrence, and Forrest Maltzman. 1999. "Uncovering the Hidden Effect of Party." *Journal of Politics* 61: 815–831.

Blechman, Barry, and Stephen Kaplan. 1978. *Force Without War: U.S. Armed Forces as a Political Instrument*. Washington, DC: Brookings Institution.

Bolingbroke, Henry St. John. 1997 [1738]. "The Idea of a Patriot King." In *Bolingbroke: Political Writings*, edited by David Armitage, 217–294. New York: Cambridge University Press.

Box-Steffensmeier, Janet, and Renee Smith. 1998. "Investigating Political Dynamics Using Fractional Integration Methods." *American Journal of Political Science* 42: 661–689.

Brace, Paul, and Barbara Hinckley. 1992. *Follow the Leader*. New York: Basic Books.

Brady, David, and Craig Volden. 1998. *Revolving Gridlock: Politics and Policy from Carter to Clinton*. Boulder, CO: Westview Press.

Brandt, Patrick, and John Williams. 2001. "A Linear Poisson Autoregressive Model: The Poisson AR(p)." *Political Analysis* 9: 164–184.

Brody, Richard. 1991. *Assessing the President: The Media, Elite Opinion, and Public Support*. Stanford: Stanford University Press.

Burden, Barry, and Anthony Mughan. 2003. "International Economy and Presidential Approval." *Public Opinion Quarterly* 67: 555–578.

Burns, James MacGregor. 1956. *Roosevelt: The Lion and the Fox, 1882–1940*. New York: Harcourt Brace Jovanovich, 1956.

Calabresi, Steven. 1994. "Political Parties as Mediating Institutions." *University of Chicago Law Review* 61: 1479–1533.

Calvert, Randall. 1985. "The Value of Biased Information: A Rational Choice Model of Political Advice." *Journal of Politics* 47: 530–555.

Cameron, Charles. 2000. *Veto Bargaining: Presidents and the Politics of Negative Power*. New York: Cambridge University Press.

Campbell, Andrea, Gary Cox, and Mathew McCubbins. 2002. "Agenda Power in the US Senate, 1877–1986." In *Party, Process and Political Change in Congress*, edited by David Brady and Mathew McCubbins, 146–165. Stanford: Stanford University Press.

Campbell, James. 1991. "The Presidential Surge and Its Midterm Decline, 1868–1988." *Journal of Politics* 53: 477–487.

Canes-Wrone, Brandice. 2006. *Who Leads Whom? Presidents, Policy, and the Public.* Chicago: University of Chicago Press.

Canes-Wrone, Brandice, and Scott De Marchi. 2002. "Presidential Approval and Legislative Success." *Journal of Politics* 64: 491–509.

Canes-Wrone, Brandice, William Howell, and David Lewis. 2008. "Toward a Broader Understanding of Presidential Power: A Reevaluation of the Two Presidencies Thesis." *Journal of Politics* 70: 1–16.

Carter, Ralph, and James Scott. 2009. *Choosing to Lead: Understanding Congressional Foreign Policy Entrepreneurship.* Durham, NC: Duke University Press.

Caughey, Devin, and Eric Schickler. 2016. "Substance and Change in Congressional Ideology: NOMINATE and Its Alternatives." *Studies in American Political Development* 30.

Chalou, George. 1975. "St. Clair's Defeat, 1792." In *Congress Investigates: A Documented History, 1792–1974,* edited by Arthur Schlesinger Jr. and Roger Burns, 3–101. New York: Chelsea House Publishers.

Church, Thomas, and Robert Nakamura. 1993. *Cleaning Up the Mess: Implementation Strategies in Superfund.* Washington, DC: Brookings Institution Press.

Clark, David. 2003. "Can Strategic Interaction Divert Diversionary Behavior? A Model of U.S. Conflict Propensity. *Journal of Politics* 65: 1013–1039.

Clark, Wesley. 2002. *Waging Modern War.* New York: Public Affairs.

Clarke, Harold and Matthew Lebo. 2003. "Fractional (Co) Integration and Governing Party Support in Britain," *British Journal of Political Science* 33: 283–301.

Clarke, Harold, and Marianne Stewart. 1994. "Prospections, Restrospections, and Rationality: The "Bankers" Model of Presidential Approval Reconsidered." *American Journal of Political Science* 38: 1104–1123.

Clinton, Bill. 2004. *My Life.* New York: Alfred A. Knopf.

Coleman, James. 1999. "Unified Government, Divided Government, and Party Responsiveness." *American Political Science Review* 93: 821–35.

Cook, Timothy. 1998. *Governing with the News: The News Media as a Political Institution.* Chicago: University of Chicago Press.

Cooper, Phillip. 2002. *By Order of the President: The Use and Abuse of Executive Direct Action.* Lawrence: University of Kansas Press.

Corwin, Edward. 1940. *The President: Office and Powers.* London: H. Milford, Oxford University Press.

Cox, Gary, and Samuel Kernell. 1991. *The Politics of Divided Government.* Boulder, CO: Westview Press.

Cox, Gary, and Mathew McCubbins. 1993. *Legislative Leviathan: Party Government in the House.* Berkeley: University of California Press.

Cox, Gary, and Mathew McCubbins. 2005. *Setting the Agenda: Responsible Party Government in the U.S. House of Representatives.* New York: Cambridge University Press.

Delli Carpini, Michael, and Scott Keeter. 1997. *What Americans Know about Politics and Why It Matters.* New Haven: Yale University Press.

Den Hartog, Chris, and Nathan Monroe. 2006. "Home Field Advantage: An Asymmetric-Costs Theory of Legislative Agenda Influence in the U.S. Senate." Paper presented at the Conference on Party Effects in the United States Senate, Duke University.

Den Hartog, Chris, and Nathan Monroe. 2011. *Agenda Setting in the United States Senate: Costly Consideration and Majority Party Advantage*. New York: Cambridge University Press.

Devins, Neal. 1996. "Congressional-Executive Information Access Disputes: A Modest Proposal—Do Nothing." *Administrative Law Review* 48: 109–137.

Druckman, James. 2001. "On the Limits of Framing Effects: Who Can Frame?" *Journal of Politics* 63: 1041–1066.

Dunbar, Andrew 1984. *The Truman Scandals and the Politics of Morality*. Columbia: University of Missouri Press.

Eckstein, Harry. 1975. "Case Studies and Theory in Political Science." In *Handbook of Political Science.*, Vol. 7, edited by Fred Greenstein and Nelson Polsby, 79–138. Reading, MA: Addison-Wesley.

Edwards, George. 2006. *On Deaf Ears: The Limits of the Bully Pulpit*. New Haven: Yale University Press.

Edwards, George, Andrew Barrett, and Jeffrey Peake. 1997. "The Legislative Impact of Divided Government." *American Journal of Political Science* 41: 545–563.

Eichenberg, Richard, and Richard Stoll, and Matthew Lebo. 2006. "War President: The Approval Ratings of George W. Bush." *Journal of Conflict Resolution* 50: 783–808.

Entman, Robert. 2012. *Scandal and Silence: Media Response to Presidential Misconduct*. Cambridge, MA: Polity Press.

Epstein, David, and Sharyn O'Halloran. 1999. *Delegating Powers: A Transaction Cost Politics Approach to Policy Making under Separate Powers*. New York: Cambridge University Press.

Erikson, Robert, Michael MacKuen, and James Stimson. 2000. "Bankers or Peasants Revisited: Economic Expectations and Presidential Approval." *Electoral Studies* 19: 295–312.

Evans, C. Lawrence, and Daniel Lipinski. 2005. "Obstruction and Leadership in the U.S. Senate." In *Congress Reconsidered*, 8th ed., edited by Lawrence C. Dodd and Bruce I. Oppenheimer, 227–248. Washington, DC: CQ Press.

Farrier, Jasmine. 2010. *Congressional Ambivalence: The Political Burdens of Constitutional Authority*. Lexington: University of Kentucky Press.

Fisher, Louis. 1995. *Presidential War Power*. Lawrence: University of Kansas Press.

Fisher, Louis. 2000. *Congressional Abdication on War and Spending*. College Station, TX: Texas A&M University Press.

Flemming, Gregory. 1995. "Presidential Coattails in Open-Seat Elections." *Legislative Studies Quarterly* 20: 197–211.

Fordham, Benjamin. 1998. "The Politics of Threat Perception and the Use of Force: A Political Economy Model of U.S. Uses of Force, 1949–1994." *International Studies Quarterly* 42: 567–590.

Fordham, Benjamin. 2002. "Another Look at 'Parties, Voters and the Use of Force Abroad.'" *Journal of Conflict Resolution* 46: 572–596.

Fordham, Benjamin. 2005. "Strategic Conflict Avoidance and the Diversionary Use of Force." *Journal of Conflict Resolution* 67: 132–153.

Fowler, Linda. 2015. *Watchdogs on the Hill: The Decline of Congressional Oversight of U.S. Foreign Relations*. Princeton: Princeton University Press.

Fowler, Linda, and Brian Law. 2008. "Seen but Not Heard: Committee Visibility and Institutional Change in the Senate National Security Committees, 1947–2006." *Legislative Studies Quarterly* 33: 357–385.

Furtrell, Robert Frank. 1989. *Ideas, Concepts, Doctrine: Basic Thinking in the United States Air Force, 1907–1960*. Maxwell Air Force Base, AL: Air University Press.

Gailmard, Sean, and Jeffery Jenkins. 2007. "Negative Agenda Control in the Senate and House: Fingerprints of Majority Power." *Journal of Politics* 69: 689–700.

Gartner, Scott. 2008. "The Multiple Effects of Casualties on Popular Support for War: An Experimental Approach." *American Political Science Review* 102: 95–106.

Gartner, Scott, and Gary Segura. 1998. "War, Casualties and Public Opinion." *Journal of Conflict Resolution* 42: 278–300

Gasper, John. 2011. "Shifting Ideologies? Re-examining Media Bias." *International Quarterly Journal of Political Science* 6: 85–102.

Gelpi, Christopher, Peter Feaver, and Jason Reifler. 2005/2006. "Success Matters: Casualty Sensitivity and the War in Iraq." *International Security* 30: 7–46.

Gentzkow, Matthew, and Jesse Shapiro. 2010. "What Drives Media Slant? Evidence from U.S. Daily Newspapers." *Econometrica* 78: 35–71.

Gentzkow, Matthew, and Jesse Shapiro. 2011. "Ideological Segregation Online and Offline." *Quarterly Journal of Economics* 126: 1799–1839

Gerring, John. 2007. *Case Study Research: Principles and Practices*. New York: Cambridge University Press.

Gerring, John. 2008. "Case Selection for Case-Study Analysis: Qualitative and Quantitative Techniques." In *The Oxford Handbook of Political Methodology*, edited by Janet Box-Steffensmeier, Henry Brady, and David Collier, 645–684. New York: Oxford University Press.

Ginsberg, Benjamin, and Martin Shefter. 2003. *Politics by Other Means: Politics, Prosecutors, and the Press from Watergate to Whitewater*. New York: W.W. Norton.

Gosnell, Harold. 1980. *Truman's Crises: A Political Biography of Harry S. Truman*. Westport, CT: Greenwood Press.

Gowa, Joanne. 1998. "Politics at the Water's Edge: Parties, Voters and the Use of Force Abroad." *International Organization* 52: 307–324.

Graber, Doris. 1997. *Mass Media and American Politics*. Washington, DC: CQ Press.

Grabow, John. 1988. *Congressional Investigations: Law and Practice*. Clifton, NJ: Prentiss Hall Law and Business.

Griffith, Robert. 1970. *The Politics of Fear: Joseph R. McCarthy and the Senate*. Amherst: University of Massachusetts Press.

Grisinger, Joanna. 2012. *The Unwieldy American State: Administrative Politics Since the New Deal*. New York: Cambridge University Press.

Groeling, Tim. 2008. "Who's the Fairest of Them All? An Empirical Test for Partisan Bias on ABC, CBS, NBC, and Fox News." *Presidential Studies Quarterly* 38: 631–657.

Groeling, Timothy. 2010. *When Politicians Attack: Party Cohesion in the Media.* New York: Cambridge University Press.

Groeling, Timothy, and Matthew Baum. 2008. "Crossing the Water's Edge: Elite Rhetoric, Media Coverage, and the Rally-Round-the-Flag Phenomenon." *Journal of Politics* 70: 1065–1085.

Gronke, Paul, and John Brehm. 2002. "History, Heterogeneity, and Presidential Approval: A Modified ARCH Approach." *Electoral Studies* 21: 425–452.

Groseclose, Tim, and Jeffrey Milyo. 2005. "A Measure of Media Bias." *Quarterly Journal of Economics* 120: 1191–1237.

Hamby, Alonzo. 1995. *Man of the People: A Life of Harry S. Truman.* New York: Oxford University Press.

Hamilton, James. 1976. *The Power to Probe: A Study of Congressional Investigations.* New York: Vintage Books.

Hess, Stephen. 1994. "The Decline and Fall of Congressional News." In *Congress, the Press, and the Public,* edited by Thomas E. Mann and Norman J. Ornstein, 141–156. Washington, DC: Brookings Institution.

Hibbs, Douglas. 2000. "Bread and Peace Voting in U.S. Presidential Elections." *Public Choice* 104: 149–180.

Hinckley, Barbara. 1994. *Less Than Meets the Eye: Foreign Policy Making and the Myth of the Assertive Congress.* Chicago: University of Chicago Press.

Hird, John. 1994. *Superfund: The Political Economy of Environmental Risk.* Baltimore: Johns Hopkins University Press.

Hofstadter, Richard. 1969. *The Idea of a Party System: The Rise of Legitimate Opposition in the United States, 1780–1840.* Berkeley: University of California Press.

Howell, William. 2003. *Power without Persuasion: The Politics of Direct Presidential Action.* Princeton: Princeton University Press.

Howell, William, E. Scott Adler, Charles Cameron, and Charles Riemann. 2000. "Divided Government and the Legislative Productivity of Congress, 1945–94." *Legislative Studies Quarterly* 25: 285–312.

Howell, William, and David Brent. 2013. *Thinking About the Presidency: The Primacy of Power.* Princeton: Princeton University Press.

Howell, William, and Douglas Kriner. 2007. "Bending so as Not to Break: What the Bush Presidency Reveals about Unilateral Action." In *The Polarized Presidency of George W. Bush,* edited by George Edwards and Desmond King, 96–141. Oxford: Oxford University Press.

Howell, William, and Douglas Kriner. 2009. "Congress, the President, and the Iraq War's Domestic Political Front." In *Congress Reconsidered.* 9th ed., edited by Lawrence Dodd and Bruce Oppenheimer, 311–336. Washington, DC: CQ Press.

Howell, William, and Jon Pevehouse. 2005. "Presidents, Congress and the Use of Force." *International Organization* 59: 209–232.

Howell, William, and Jon Pevehouse. 2007. *While Dangers Gather: Congressional Checks on Presidential War Powers.* Princeton: Princeton University Press.

Howell, William, Saul Jackman, and Jon Rogowski. 2013. *The Wartime President: Executive Influence and the Nationalizing Politics of Threat.* Chicago: University of Chicago Press.

Iyengar, Shanto, and Kyu S. Hahn. 2009. "Red Media, Blue Media: Evidence of Ideological Selectivity in Media Use." *Journal of Communication* 59: 19–39.

Jacobson, Gary. 2004. *The Politics of Congressional Elections*. New York: Pearson Longman.

James, Patrick, and John Oneal. 1991. "The Influence of Domestic and International Politics on the President's Use of Force." *Journal of Conflict Resolution* 35 (2): 307–332.

Jamieson, Kathleen, and Joseph Cappella. 2008. *Echo Chamber: Rush Limbaugh and the Conservative Media Establishment*. New York: Oxford University Press.

Jenkins, Jeffery. 2000. "Examining the Robustness of Ideological Voting: Evidence from the Confederate House of Representatives." *American Journal of Political Science* 44: 811–822.

Johnson, Loch. 1985. *A Season of Inquiry: The Senate Intelligence Investigation*. Lexington: University of Kentucky Press.

Johnson, Robert David. 2006. *Congress and the Cold War*. New York: Cambridge University Press.

Kam, Cindy, and Jennifer Ramos. 2008. "Understanding the Surge and Decline in Presidential Approval Following 9/11." *Public Opinion Quarterly* 72: 619–50.

Keele, Luke. 2007. "Social Capital and the Dynamics of Trust in Government." *American Journal of Political Science* 51: 241–254.

Keele, Luke, and Nathan Kelly. 1996. "Dynamic Models for Dynamic Theories: The Ins and Outs of Lagged Dependent Variables." *Political Analysis* 14: 186–205.

Kernell, Samuel. 1997. *Going Public: New Strategies of Presidential Leadership*. Washington, DC: CQ Press.

Kiewiet, D. Roderick, and Mathew McCubbins. 1991. *The Logic of Delegation: Congressional Parties and the Appropriations Process*. Chicago: University of Chicago Press.

Koger, Gregory. 2010. *Filibustering: A Political History of Obstruction in the House and Senate*. Chicago: University of Chicago Press.

Krehbiel, Keith. 1993. "Where's the Party?" *British Journal of Political Science* 23: 235–266.

Krehbiel, Keith. 1998. *Pivotal Politics: A Theory of U.S. Lawmaking*. Chicago: University of Chicago Press.

Kriner, Douglas. 2009. "Can Enhanced Oversight Repair the 'Broken Branch'?" *Boston University Law Review* 89: 765–793.

Kriner, Douglas. 2010. *After the Rubicon: Congress, Presidents, and the Politics of Waging War*. Chicago: University of Chicago Press.

Kriner, Douglas. 2014. "Obama's Authorization Paradox: Syria and Congress's Continued Relevance in Military Affairs." *Presidential Studies Quarterly* 44: 309–327.

Kriner, Douglas, and Andrew Reeves. 2015. "Presidential Particularism and Divide-the-Dollar Politics." *American Political Science Review* 109: 155–171.

Kriner, Douglas, and Eric Schickler. 2014. "Investigating the President: Committee Probes and Presidential Approval, 1953–2006." *Journal of Politics* 76: 521–534.

Kriner, Douglas, and Liam Schwartz. 2008. "Divided Government and Congressional Investigations." *Legislative Studies Quarterly* 33: 295–321.

Kriner, Douglas, and Liam Schwartz. 2009. "Partisan Dynamics and the Volatility of Presidential Approval." *British Journal of Political Science.* 39: 609–631.

Kriner, Douglas, and Francis Shen. 2014. "Responding to War on Capitol Hill: Battlefield Casualties, Congressional Response, and Public Support for the War in Iraq." *American Journal of Political Science* 58: 157–174.

Kuklinski, James, and Norman Hurley. 1994. "On Hearing and Interpreting Political Messages: A Cautionary Tale of Citizen Cue-Taking." *Journal of Politics* 56: 729–751.

Lai, Brian, and Dan Reiter. 2005. "Rally 'Round the Union Jack? Public Opinion and the Use of Force in the United Kingdom, 1948–2001." *International Studies Quarterly* 49 (2005): 255–272.

Larson, Eric. 1996. *Casualties and Consensus: The Historical Role of Casualties in Domestic Support for U.S. Military Operations.* Santa Monica, CA: RAND.

Lebo, Matthew, and Daniel Cassino. 2007. "The Aggregated Consequences of Motivated Reasoning and the Dynamics of Presidential Approval." *Political Psychology* 28: 719–746.

Lebo, Matthew, Robert Walker, and Harold Clarke. 2000. "You Must Remember This: Dealing with Long Memory in Political Analyses." *Electoral Studies* 19: 31–48.

Lee, Frances. 2009. *Beyond Ideology: Politics, Principle and Partisanship in the U.S. Senate.* Chicago: University of Chicago Press.

Lee, Frances. 2013. "Presidents and Party Teams: The Politics of Debt Limits and Executive Oversight, 2001–2013," *Presidential Studies Quarterly* 43: 775–791.

Leeds, Brett Ashley, and Donald Davis. 1997. "Domestic Political Vulnerability and International Disputes." *Journal of Conflict Resolution* 41: 814–834.

Levy, Jack. 1989. "The Diversionary War Theory: A Critique." In *Handbook of War Studies,* edited by Manus Midlasky, 259–288. Boston: Unwin Hyman.

Lewis, David. 2008. *The Politics of Presidential Appointments: Political Control and Bureaucratic Appointments.* Princeton: Princeton University Press.

Lian, Bradley, and John Oneal. 1993. "Presidents, the Use of Military Force, and Public Opinion." *Journal of Conflict Resolution* 37: 277–300.

Light, Paul. 1982. *The President's Agenda: Domestic Policy Choice from Kennedy to Carter.* Baltimore, MD: Johns Hopkins University Press.

Light, Paul. 2014. *Government by Investigation: Congress, Presidents, and the Search for Answers, 1945–2012.* Washington, DC: Brookings Institution Press.

Lippmann, Walter. 2007 [1922]. *Public Opinion.* Minneapolis: Filiquarian Publishing.

Lupia, Arthur. 1994. "Shortcuts Versus Encyclopedias: Information and Voting Behavior in California Insurance Reform Elections." *American Political Science Review* 88: 63–76.

Lupia, Arthur, and Mathew McCubbins. 1998. *The Democratic Dilemma: Can Citizens Learn What They Need to Know?* Cambridge: Cambridge University Press.

MacKuen, Michael, Robert Erikson, and James Stimson. 1992. "Peasants or Bankers? The American Electorate and the U.S. Economy." *American Political Science Review* 86: 597–611.

Macoll, John. 1975. "The Second Bank of the United States, 1832." In *Congress Investigates: A Documented History, 1792–1974,* edited by Arthur Schlesinger Jr. and Roger Burns, 591–685. New York: Chelsea House Publishers.

Madison, James. 1906 [1793]. *The Writings of James Madison*. Vol. 6, *1790–1802*, edited by Gaillard Hunt, New York: G.P. Putnam's Sons.

Mann, Thomas, and Norman Ornstein. 2006. *The Broken Branch: How Congress Is Failing America and How to Get It Back on Track*. New York: Oxford University Press.

Mann, Thomas, and Norman Ornstein. 2013. *It's Even Worse than it Looks: How the American Constitutional System Collided with the New Politics of Extremism*. New York: Basic Books.

Marshall, Bryan, and Brandon Prins. 2007. "Strategic Position Taking and Presidential Influence in Congress." *Legislative Studies Quarterly* 32: 257–284.

Mayer, Kenneth. 2002. *With the Stroke of a Pen: Executive Orders and Presidential Power*. Princeton: Princeton University Press.

Mayhew, David. 1974. *Congress: The Electoral Connection*. New Haven: Yale University Press.

Mayhew, David. 1991. *Divided We Govern: Party Control, Lawmaking, and Investigations, 1946–1990*. New Haven: Yale University Press.

Mayhew, David. 2000. *America's Congress: Actions in the Public Sphere, James Madison through Newt Gingrich*. New Haven: Yale University Press.

Mayhew, David. 2005. *Divided We Govern: Party Control, Lawmaking, and Investigations, 1946–2002*. 2nd ed. New Haven: Yale University Press.

McCartney, Laton. 2008. *The Teapot Dome Scandal: How Big Oil Bought the Harding White House and Tried to Steal the Country*. New York: Random House.

McCarty, Nolan, Keith Poole and Howard Rosenthal. 2006. *Polarized America: The Dance of Political Ideology and Unequal Riches*. Cambridge: MIT Press.

McCubbins, Mathew, Roger Noll, and Barry Weingast. 1987. "Administrative Procedures as Instruments of Political Control." *Journal of Law, Economics, and Organization* 3: 243–277.

McCubbins, Mathew, Roger Noll, and Barry Weingast. 1989. "Structure and Process, Politics and Policy: Administrative Arrangements and the Political Control of Agencies." *Virginia Law Review* 75: 431–482.

McCubbins, Mathew, and Thomas Schwartz. 1984. "Congressional Oversight Overlooked: Police Patrols Versus Fire Alarms." *American Journal of Political Science* 28: 165–179.

McCullough, David. 1992. *Truman*. New York: Simon and Schuster.

McGeary, Nelson. 1940. *The Developments of Congressional Investigative Power*. New York: Columbia University Press.

McGrath, Robert. 2013. "Congressional Oversight Hearings and Policy Control." *Legislative Studies Quarterly* 38: 349–376.

McHughes, Lee. 1961. "The Hiss Act and its Application to the Military." *Military Law Review* 14: 67–108

Meernik, James. 1994. "Presidential Decision Making and the Political Use of Military Force." *International Studies Quarterly* 38: 121–138.

Meernik, James. 1995. "Congress, the President and the Commitment of the U.S. Military." *Legislative Studies Quarterly* 20: 377–392.

Meernik, James, and Peter Waterman. 1996. "The Myth of the Diversionary Use of Force by American Presidents." *Political Research Quarterly* 49: 573–590.

Mermin, Jonathan. 1999. *Debating War and Peace: Media Coverage of U.S. Intervention in the Post-Vietnam Era*. Princeton: Princeton University Press.

Messing, Solomon, and Sean Westwood. "Selective Exposure in the Age of Social Media: Endorsements Trump Partisan Source Affiliation When Selecting News Online." *Communication Research* 41 (2014): 1042–1063.

Mintz, Joel. 1987. "Agencies, Congress and Regulatory Enforcement: A Review of EPA's Hazardous Waste Enforcement Effort, 1970–1987." *Environmental Law* 18: 683–778.

Miscamble, Wilson. 2011. *The Most Controversial Decision: Truman, the Atomic Bombs, and the Defeat of Japan*. New York: Cambridge University Press.

Moe, Terry. 1985. "The Politicized Presidency." In *New Directions in American Politics*, edited by John Chubb and Paul Peterson, 235–271. Washington, DC: Brookings Institution Press.

Moe, Terry. 1994. "The Presidency and the Bureaucracy: The Presidential Advantage." In *The Presidency and the Political System*, edited by Michael Nelson, 443–474. Washington, DC: Congressional Quarterly Press.

Moe, Terry. 2012. "Delegation, Control, and the Study of Public Bureaucracy." *The Forum* 10: Article 4.

Moe, Terry, and William Howell. 1999. "The Presidential Power of Unilateral Action." *Journal of Law, Economics, and Organization* 15: 132–179.

Mondak, Jeffrey. 1993. "Source Cues and Policy Approval." *American Journal of Political Science* 37: 186–212.

Mondak, Jeffery, and Carl McCurley. 1994. "Cognitive Efficiency and the Congressional Vote: The Psychology of Coattail Voting." *Political Research Quarterly* 47: 151–175.

Mueller, John. 1973. *War, Presidents, and Public Opinion*. New York: Wiley.

Neustadt, Richard. 1990 [1960]. *Presidential Power and the Modern Presidents*. New York: The Free Press.

Nyhan, Brendan. 2014. "Governors and the Politics of Scandal: How Contextual Factors Affect Coverage of Alleged Wrongdoing." Paper Presented at the Annual Meeting of the American Political Science Association, Washington, DC, August 28–31, 2014.

Nyhan, Brendan. 2015. "Scandal Potential: How Political Context and News Congestion Affect the President's Vulnerability to Media Scandal." *British Journal of Political Science* 45: 435–466.

Nyhan, Brendan, and Jason Reifler. 2010. "When Corrections Fail: The Persistence of Political Misperceptions." *Political Behavior* 32: 303–330.

Oakes, Amy. 2012. *Diversionary War: Domestic Unrest and International Conflict*. Stanford: Stanford University Press.

Ogden, August Raymond. 1945. *The Dies Committee: A Study of the Special House Committee for the Investigation of Un-American Activities, 1938–1944*. Washington, DC: Catholic University of America Press.

Olson, Keith. 2003. *Watergate: The Presidential Scandal that Rocked America*. Lawrence: University of Kansas Press.

Parker, David, and Matthew Dull. 2009. "Divided We Quarrel: The Politics of Congressional Investigations, 1947–2004." *Legislative Studies Quarterly* 34: 319–345.

Parker, David, and Matthew Dull. 2013. "Rooting Out Waste, Fraud, and Abuse: The Politics of Congressional Investigations, 1947–2004." *Political Research Quarterly* 66: 630–44.

Pearson, James. 1975. "Oversight: A Vital Yet Neglected Congressional Function." *Kansas Law Review* 23: 277–288.

Pfiffner, James. 2008. *Power Play: The Bush Presidency and the Constitution.* Washington, DC: Brookings Institution Press.

Popkin, Samuel. 1991. *The Reasoning Voter: Communication and Persuasion in Presidential Campaigns.* Chicago: University of Chicago Press.

Potts, C. S. 1926. "Power of Legislative Bodies to Punish for Contempt." *University of Pennsylvania Law Review* 74: 691–725.

Power, Samantha. 2002. *A Problem From Hell: America and the Age of Genocide.* New York: Perennial.

Prior, Markus. 2013. "Media and Political Polarization." *Annual Review of Political Science* 16: 101–127.

Riddle, Donald. 1964. *The Truman Committee: A Study in Congressional Responsibility.* New Brunswick, NJ: Rutgers University Press.

Ripley, Randall. 1978. *Congress: Process and Policy.* New York: Norton.

Ripley, Randall, and James Lindsay. 1993. *Congress Resurgent: Foreign and Defense Policy on Capitol Hill.* Ann Arbor: University of Michigan Press.

Rivers, Douglas, and Nancy Rose. 1984. "Passing the President's Program: Public Opinion and Presidential Influence in Congress." *American Journal of Political Science* 29: 183–196.

Rohde, David. 1991. *Parties and Leaders in the Postreform House.* Chicago: University of Chicago Press.

Rosenberg, Morton. 1995. "Investigative Oversight: An Introduction to the Law, Practice, and Procedure of Congressional Inquiry." *CRS Report:* 95–464.

Rottinghaus, Brandon. 2015. *The Institutional Effects of Presidential Scandal.* New York: Cambridge University Press.

Rudalevige, Andrew. 2005. *The New Imperial Presidency: Renewing Presidential Power After Watergate.* Ann Arbor: University of Michigan Press.

Schickler, Eric. 2000. "Institutional Change in the House of Representatives, 1867–1998: A Test of Partisan and Ideological Power Balance Models." *American Political Science Review* 94: 269–288.

Schickler, Eric. 2001. *Disjointed Pluralism: Institutional Innovation and the Development of the U.S. Congress.* Princeton: Princeton University Press.

Schickler, Eric. 2007. "Entrepreneurial Defenses of Congressional Power." In *Formative Acts: Reckoning with Agency in American Politics*, edited by Stephen Skowronek and Matthew Glassman, 293–314. Philadelphia: University of Pennsylvania Press.

Schickler, Eric, and Katherine Pearson. 2009. "Agenda Control, Majority Party Power, and the House Committee on Rules, 1937–52." *Legislative Studies Quarterly* 34: 455–491.

Schlesinger Jr., Arthur. 1973. *The Imperial Presidency.* Boston: Houghton Mifflin.

Schlesinger Jr., Arthur, and Roger Burns. 1975. *Congress Investigates: A Documented History, 1792–1974.* New York: Chelsea House Publishers.

270 ~ References

Schneider, Judy. 2005. "Minority Rights and Senate Procedure." *CRS Report, August 22, 2005,* RL30850.

Schouler, James. 1885. *History of the United States Under the Constitution.* Vol. 3, *1817–1831.* New York: Dodd, Mead and Company.

Shane, Peter. 1987. "Legal Disagreement and Negotiation in a Government of Laws: The Case of Executive Privilege Claims Against Congress." *Minnesota Law Review* 71: 461–542.

Sinclair, Barbara. 2000. *Unorthodox Lawmaking: New Legislative Processes in the United States Congress.* 2nd ed. Washington, DC: Congressional Quarterly Press.

Sinclair, Barbara. 2006. *Party Wars: Polarization and the Politics of National Policy Making.* Norman: University of Oklahoma Press.

Smith, Alastair. 1998. "International Crises and Domestic Politics." *American Political Science Review* 92: 623–638.

Smith, Steven. 2007. *Party Influence in Congress.* New York: Cambridge University Press.

Snyder Jr, James, and Tim Groseclose. 2000. "Estimating Party Influence in Congressional Roll-Call Voting." *American Journal of Political Science* 44: 193–211.

Stroud, Natalie. 2011. *Niche News: The Politics of News Choice.* New York: Oxford University Press.

Sundquist, James. 1981. *The Decline and Resurgence of Congress.* Washington, DC: Brookings Institution Press.

Sundquist, James. 1988. "Needed: A Political Theory for the New Era of Coalition Government in the United States." *Political Science Quarterly* 103: 613–635.

Taylor, Andrew. 2001. "Congress as Principal: Exploring Bicameral Differences in Agent Oversight." *Congress & the Presidency* 28: 141–159.

Taylor, Andrew. 2012. "When Congress Asserts Itself: Examining Legislative Challenges to Executive Power." *The Forum* 10: Article 2.

Taylor, Telford. 1955. *Grand Inquest: The Story of Congressional Investigations.* New York: Simon and Schuster.

Theriault, Sean. 2008. *Party Polarization in Congress.* New York: Cambridge University Press.

Thompson, Wayne. 1975. "The Pearl Harbor Inquiry, 1945." In *Congress Investigates: A Documented History, 1792–1974,* edited by Arthur Schlesinger Jr. and Roger Burns, 3265–3435. New York: Chelsea House Publishers..

Trest, Warren. 1998. *Air Force Roles and Missions: A History.* Washington, DC: Air Force History and Museums Program, Government Printing Office.

Voeten, Erik, and Paul Brewer. 2006. "Public Opinion, the War in Iraq, and Presidential Accountability." *Journal of Conflict Resolution* 50: 809–830.

Walsh, Thomas. 1924. "The True History of Teapot Dome." *The Forum* 72(1): 1–12

Wawro, Gregory. 2000. *Legislative Entrepreneurship in the U.S. House of Representatives.* Ann Arbor: University of Michigan Press.

Wawro, Gregory, and Eric Schickler. 2006. *Filibuster: Obstruction and Lawmaking in the United States Senate.* Princeton: Princeton University Press.

Wildavsky, Aaron. 1962. *Dixon-Yates: A Study in Power Politics.* New Haven: Yale University Press.

Wildavsky, Aaron. 1966. "The Two Presidencies." *Trans-Action* 4: 7–14.

Wilson, James Q. 1986. "Political Parties and the Separation of Powers." In *Separation of Powers—Does it Still Work?* edited by Robert Goldwin and Art Kaufman, 18–37. Washington, DC: American Enterprise Institute.

Wilson, Theodore. 1975. "The Truman Committee, 1941." In *Congress Investigates: A Documented History, 1792–1974,* edited by Arthur Schlesinger Jr. and Roger Burns, 3115–3262. New York: Chelsea House Publishers.

Wilson, Woodrow. 1885. *Congressional Government: A Study in American Politics.* Boston: Houghton Mifflin.

Wood, B. Dan. 1988. "Principals, Bureaucrats, and Responsiveness in Clean Air Enforcements." *American Political Science Review* 82: 213–234.

Woods, Randall Bennett. 1995. *Fulbright: A Biography.* New York: Cambridge University Press.

Yoo, John. 2005. *The Powers of War and Peace: The Constitution and Foreign Affairs After 9/11.* Chicago: University of Chicago Press.

Zaller, John. 1992. *The Nature and Origins of Mass Opinion.* New York: Cambridge University Press.

Zaller, John. 1998. "Monica Lewinsky's Contribution to Political Science." *PS: Political Science & Politics* 31: 182–189.

Zeisberg, Mariah. 2013. *War Powers: The Politics of Constitutional Authority.* Princeton: Princeton University Press.

Index

~ ~

Ford, Gerald, 57, 141
Foreign Intelligence and Surveillance Act
(FISA [1978]), 146–148, 147n73, 248
Foreign Intelligence Surveillance Court, 147
Fort Hood shootings, investigation of,
216–217, 217n11
Fort Jefferson, 9
Foster, Vince, 36, 58, 215n8; investigation of
his death, 59, 59n89
Fowler, Linda, 89–90n38, 252
Fox News, 113, 159, 253; *Special Report*
segment of, 254–255; stories of mention-
ing the Solyndra investigation, 255–256
Foy, David, lack of an investigation into the
death of, 78
Freedom of Information Act (1974), 128n5
Fuller, Craig, 153

Gadhafi, Moammar, 106, 108, 233
General Land Office. *See* Ballinger-Pinchot
Affair
generalizability, 99, 127, 128, 160
Giles, William, 10
Goldwater, Barry, 142
Gorsuch, Anne M., 148, 150n88, 151–152,
152n95; citing of for contempt of Con-
gress, 150; resignation of, 153
Gorsuch, Robert, 152n95
Gonzalez, Henry, 57, 58, 59
Gowdy, Trey, 250
Graham, Bob, 227
Graham, Lindsay, 238
Grant, Ulysses S., 215n8
Grassley, Charles, 220
Grayson, Alan, 250
Great Depression, 46
Groeling, Timothy, 77
gun-trafficking, legislation concerning, 220

Haditha massacre, 62
Hagel, Chuck, 92
Hamilton, Alexander, 11, 12, 247
Hannity, Sean, 79–80
Hanson, Jean, 60
Harding, Warren G., 13
Harken Energy, 33
Harrington, Michael, 139

Hassan, Nidal Malik, 216–217
Higgins, William, 197
Hodgdon, Samuel, 12
Hersh, Seymour, 139–140
Hinckley, Barbara, 177
Howell, William, 126, 181, 183, 185, 185n37,
187, 187n38, 190
Huber, Greg, 99
Hull, Cordell, 14
Hussein, Saddam, 65, 247; toppling of statue
of in Firdos Square, 62

"In GOP Congress, Gavels Gone Wild," 219
Independent Counsel statute (1978), 56n75
Independents, 92–93, 102, 103
Index of Consumer Sentiment (ICS), 85
inflation, 54
Internal Revenue Service (IRS) scandal,
investigation of, 221–222
investigations. *See* U.S. congressional investigations; *specifically listed individual
investigations*
Iran-Contra scandal/hearings/investigation,
2, 7, 21, 38, 57, 172
Iraq/Iraq War, 104–105; alleged mishandling
of the war, 92; deteriorating conditions in
Iraq after the U.S. victory, 62. *See also* Iraq
War investigations
Iraq War investigations, 62–65, 62n93,
64n95, 65n100, 86; increase in House
investigative activity after the Democrats
gained control of Congress (2006), 63–64;
Republicans' stymying of investigations
through all of 2003, 62; strength of negative agenda control during the investigative period, 62–63
Issa, Darrell, 28, 220, 221, 234, 241

Jackson, Andrew, investigation of by the U.S.
Congress, 12n28
Jefferson, Thomas, 10
Johnson, Andrew, 7, 12n29
Johnson, Lyndon, 41n55, 140n50
Joint Committee on Atomic Energy, 139
Joint Committee on Intelligence, 139
Jones, Jesse, 137
Jones, Paula, 215n8

LIPTAK 2016
FARRELL 2017
TURNER 2018